JEWISH AND CHRISTIAN TEXTS IN CONTEXTS AND RELATED STUDIES

Series
Executive Editor
James H. Charlesworth

Editorial Board of Advisors
Motti Aviam, Michael Davis, Casey Elledge, Loren Johns, Amy-Jill Levine, Lee McDonald, Lidia Novakovic, Gerbern Oegema, Henry Rietz, Brent Strawn

An Ecology of Scriptures

Experiences of Dwelling behind Early Jewish and Christian Texts

By
Jolyon G. R. Pruszinski

t&tclark
LONDON • NEW YORK • OXFORD • NEW DELHI • SYDNEY

T&T CLARK
Bloomsbury Publishing Plc
50 Bedford Square, London, WC1B 3DP, UK
1385 Broadway, New York, NY 10018, USA
29 Earlsfort Terrace, Dublin 2, Ireland

BLOOMSBURY, T&T CLARK and the T&T Clark logo are trademarks of Bloomsbury Publishing Plc

First published in Great Britain 2021
This paperback edition published 2023

Copyright © Jolyon G. R. Pruszinski, 2021

Jolyon G. R. Pruszinski has asserted his right under the Copyright, Designs and Patents Act, 1988, to be identified as Author of this work.

For legal purposes the Acknowledgments on p. 171 constitute an extension of this copyright page.

Cover design: Charlotte James

All rights reserved. No part of this publication may be reproduced or transmitted in any form or by any means, electronic or mechanical, including photocopying, recording, or any information storage or retrieval system, without prior permission in writing from the publishers.

Bloomsbury Publishing Plc does not have any control over, or responsibility for, any third-party websites referred to or in this book. All internet addresses given in this book were correct at the time of going to press. The author and publisher regret any inconvenience caused if addresses have changed or sites have ceased to exist, but can accept no responsibility for any such changes.

A catalogue record for this book is available from the British Library.

Library of Congress Cataloging-in-Publication Data
Names: Pruszinski, Jolyon G. R., author.
Title: An ecology of scriptures : experiences of dwelling behind early Jewish and Christian texts / by Jolyon G.R. Pruszinski.
Description: London ; New York : T&T Clark, 2021. | Series: Jewish and Christian texts in contexts and related studies ; 33 | Includes bibliographical references and index. | Summary: "Jolyon G.R. Pruszinski examines the experiences of domestic and quotidian space that contributed to the extant form of many foundational early Jewish and Christian scriptures"– Provided by publisher.
Identifiers: LCCN 2020051510 (print) | LCCN 2020051511 (ebook) | ISBN 9780567694942 (hb) | ISBN 9780567694959 (epdf) | ISBN 9780567694973 (epub)
Subjects: LCSH: Dwellings in the Bible. | Place (Philosophy) in the Bible. | Bible. New Testament–Criticism, interpretation, etc.
Classification: LCC BS2545.H627 P78 2021 (print) | LCC BS2545.H627 (ebook) | DDC 225.8/64–dc23
LC record available at https://lccn.loc.gov/2020051510
LC ebook record available at https://lccn.loc.gov/2020051511

ISBN:	HB:	978-0-5676-9494-2
	PB:	978-0-5676-9995-4
	ePDF:	978-0-5676-9495-9
	ePUB:	978-0-5676-9497-3

Typeset by Integra, Pondicherry

To find out more about our authors and books visit www.bloomsbury.com and sign up for our newsletters.

To Emily Pruszinski,
to Kyra, Teddy, Joseph, and Balian Pruszinski,
and to Ellen Rivoir and Glenn Pruszinski;
Εὐχαριστῶ τῷ θεῷ μου πάντοτε περὶ ὑμῶν.

Contents

List of Figures	viii
List of Abbreviations	ix
Foreword	xv
Preface	xvii
Introduction	1
1 The Ecology of the Fourth Gospel: Bachelard's Hermeneutics of Home and Martyn's "Two-Level Drama"	9
2 Space Matters for Scripture and Ecology Matters for Space: Critical Observations from John 4	39
3 The Undisputed Pauline Corpus and Gentile Believers as the Dwelling of God	59
4 Identification with a Marginal Home: Waters of Judgment as the Oppressed in the *Parables of Enoch*	77
5 Prison and Pit, Doors and Dwelling: Phenomenologies of the Familiar in the Book of Revelation	97
6 "Real" Visions of the Ideal Home: From Ascetic Dwellings to the Isle of the Blessed Ones in the *History of the Rechabites*	121
7 Augustine's Christological Emphasis in *De Trinitate*: An Affirmation of the Human Ecology	145
8 Conclusions and Prospect: The Core Function of "Ecology" in Scriptural Production and Interpretation	161
Acknowledgments	171
Bibliography	175
Ancient Sources Index	187
Modern Author Index	200
Topical Index	203

Figures

2.1	The Lower Jordan Valley from the Western Highlands.	42
2.2	Topography of the Jordan Valley and Samaria.	44
4.1	Map of the Huleh Valley and the Kinnereth/Sea of Galilee.	80
4.2	Huleh Valley Wet Lands Prior to Reclamation.	84
5.1	Schematic of the Radvansky et al. Doorway Experiment.	111
6.1	Line of Sight without Atmospheric Refraction, Marseille to Canigou.	127
6.2	Canigou Effect.	128
6.3	Calendrical Conditions for Sunset Alignment, Marseille to Canigou.	128
6.4	Line of Sight without Atmospheric Refraction, Zaphon to Olympus.	130
6.5	Calendrical Conditions for Sunset Alignment, Zaphon to Olympus.	131
6.6	Orographic Lift, Santa Lucia Mountains, California.	131
6.7	Dust Storm with Orographic Clouds over Cypriot Mt. Olympus.	132
6.8	View South to Jebel Aqra/Zaphon/Kasios from Turkey.	133
6.9	The Baal Stele.	135

Abbreviations

Hebrew Bible/Old Testament

Gen	Genesis
Exod	Exodus
Num	Numbers
Deut	Deuteronomy
Josh	Joshua
Judg	Judges
Ruth	Ruth
1–2 Sam	1–2 Samuel
1–2 Kgs	1–2 Kings
1–2 Chr	1–2 Chronicles
Ezra	Ezra
Neh	Nehemiah
Job	Job
Ps	Psalms
Prov	Proverbs
Eccl	Ecclesiastes
Song	Song of Songs
Isa	Isaiah
Jer	Jeremiah
Lam	Lamentations
Ezek	Ezekiel
Dan	Daniel
Hos	Hosea
Joel	Joel
Amos	Amos
Obad	Obadiah
Jonah	Jonah
Mic	Micah
Nah	Nahum
Hab	Habakkuk
Zeph	Zephaniah
Hag	Haggai
Zech	Zechariah
Mal	Malachi

New Testament

Matt	Matthew
Mark	Mark
Luke	Luke
John	John
Acts	Acts
Rom	Romans
1–2 Cor	1–2 Corinthians
Gal	Galatians
Eph	Ephesians
Phil	Philippians
Col	Colossians
1–2 Thess	1–2 Thessalonians
1–2 Tim	1–2 Timothy
Titus	Titus
Phlm	Philemon
Heb	Hebrews
Jas	James
1–2 Pet	1–2 Peter
1-2-3 John	1-2-3 John
Jude	Jude
Rev	Revelation

Deuterocanon and Old Testament Pseudepigrapha

1-2-3 En.	1-2-3 Enoch
1 Esd	1 Esdras
1-2-3-4 Macc	1-2-3-4 Maccabees
2-3-4 Bar	2-3-4 Baruch
Bar	Baruch
Sir	Sirach
Tob	Tobit
Wis	Wisdom of Solomon
Hist. Rech.	*History of the Rechabites*
T. Ab.	*Testament of Abraham*
T. Levi	*Testament of Levi*

Dead Sea Scrolls

1QS	*Rule of the Community*, Qumran Cave One
4QS	*Rule of the Community*, Qumran Cave Four
5Q11	*Possible Fragment of the Rule of the Community*, Qumran Cave Five
CD	*Damascus Document*

Rabbinic Texts

b. Šabb.	Babylonian Talmud, tractate Šabbat
b. Soṭ.	Babylonian Talmud, tractate Sotah
b. Yoma	Babylonian Talmud, tractate Yoma

Greek and Latin Works

2 Apol.	*Apologia ii*	Justin Martyr
Abr.	*De Abrahamo*	Philo of Alexandria
Aet.	*De aeternitate mundi*	Philo
Ag.	*Agamemnon*	Aeschylus
Agr.	*De agricultura*	Philo
Ant.	*Antiquitates Judaicae*	Josephus
Cher.	*De cherubim*	Philo
Comm. Jo.	*Commentarii in evangelium Joannis*	Origen
Conf.	*De confusione linguarum*	Philo
Deipn.	*Deipnosophistae*	Athenaeus
Ebr.	*De ebrietate*	Philo
Flacc.	*In Flaccum*	Philo
Fug.	*De fuga et inventione*	Philo
Geogr.	*Geographica*	Ptolemy
Geogr.	*Geographica*	Strabo
Gig.	*De gigantibus*	Philo
Gorg.	*Gorgias*	Plato
Haer.	*Refutatio omnium haeresium*	Hippolytus of Rome
Hel.	*Helena*	Euripedes
Her.	*Quis rerum divinarum heres sit*	Philo
Hist.	*Historiae*	Herodotus
Hom. Gen.	*Homiliae in Genesim*	Origen

Il.	*Ilias*	Homer
Leg. 1, 2, 3	*Legum allegoriae* I, II, III	Philo
Legat.	*Legatio ad Gaium*	Philo
Med.	*Medea*	Seneca (the Younger)
Menex.	*Menexenus*	Plato
Metam.	*Metamorphōseōn synagōge*	Antoninus Liberalis
Mos. 1, 2	*De vita Mosis* I, II	Philo
Off.	*De officiis*	Cicero
Ol.	*Olympionikai*	Pindar
Op.	*Opera et dies*	Hesiod
Opif.	*De opificio mundi*	Philo
Plant.	*De plantatione*	Philo
Post.	*De posteritate Caini*	Philo
Praem.	*De praemiis et poenis*	Philo
Princ.	*De principiis*	Origen
Resp.	*Respublica*	Plato
Sacr.	*De sacrificiis Abelis et Caini*	Philo
Sert.	*Sertorius*	Plutarch
Somn. 1, 2	*De somniis* I, II	Philo
Spec.	*De specialibus legibus*	Philo
Spir.	*De Spiritu Sancto*	Ambrose
Symp.	*Symposium*	Plato
Tim.	*Timaeus*	Plato
Tract. Ev. Jo.	*In Evangelium Johannis tractatus*	Augustine
Trin.	*De Trinitate*	Augustine
Val.	*Adversus Valentinianos*	Tertulian
Vigil.	*Adversus Vigilantium*	Jerome
Virt.	*De virtutibus*	Philo
Vita. Apoll.	*Vita Apollonii*	Philostratus

Modern Publications and General Abbreviations

ABSA	*Annual of the British School at Athens*
Add.	Additional
ANF	Ante-Nicene Fathers
ASV	American Standard Version
ATR	*Anglican Theological Review*
ATRSup	*Anglican Theological Review, Supplement*
BDAG	Bauer, Danker, Arndt, and Gingrich, *Greek Lexicon* (3rd ed., 2000)

BibInt	*Biblical Interpretation*
BnF	Bibliotèque Nationale de France
BTB	*Biblical Theology Bulletin*
CBQ	*Catholic Biblical Quarterly*
CCSL	Corpus Christianorum Series Latina
CINMS	Channel Islands National Marine Sanctuary
Cod. Par. Gr.	Codex Parisinus Graece
CSCO	Corpus Scriptorum Christianorum Orientalium
FC	The Fathers of the Church Series
gk.	Greek
JAAR	*Journal of the American Academy of Religion*
JBL	*Journal for Biblical Literature*
JSHRZ	Jüdische Schriften aus hellenistisch-römischer Zeit
JSNT	*Journal for the Study of the New Testament*
JSNTSup	Journal for the Study of the New Testament Supplement Series
JSOTSS	Journal for the Study of the Old Testament Supplement Series
LCL	Loeb Classical Library
LHBOTS	Library of Hebrew Bible/Old Testament Studies
LNTS	The Library of New Testament Studies
LSJ	Liddell, Scott, and Jones, *Greek-English Lexicon* (9th ed., 1940)
LXX	Septuagint
MS(S)	manuscript(s)
n(n).	note(s)
NOAA	National Oceanic and Atmospheric Administration
NOS	National Ocean Service
NPNF	Nicene and Post-Nicene Fathers
NRSV	New Revised Standard Version
NT	New Testament
NTS	*New Testament Studies*
OT	Old Testament
OTP	Charlesworth, *Old Testament Pseudepigrapha* (2 Vols., 1982–5)
RSV	Revised Standard Version
SBLMS	Society for Biblical Literature Monograph Series
SNT	Supplements to Novum Testamentum
SNTS	Studiorum Novi Testamenti Societas
syr.	Syriac
WBC	Word Biblical Commentary
WMANT	Wissenschaftliche Monographien zum Alten und Neuen Testament
WUNT	Wissenschaftliche Untersuchungen zum Neuen Testament
ZNW	*Zeitschrift fur die Neutestsamentliche Wissenschaft*

Foreword

Improving Perception through an Ecology of Ancient Compositions

Scholars who strive to shift biblical studies in a new direction are abundant but few succeed. Dr. Jolyon G. R. Pruszinski's *An Ecology of Scriptures* seems to me to be an exploration that may succeed. Scholars of early Judaism and early Christianity have long toyed with the importance of space in interpretation, with several important twentieth-century studies advancing the state of the field. R. H. Lightfoot's *Locality and Doctrine in the Gospels*, W. D. Davies' *The Gospel and the Land*, and J. Z. Smith's *To Take Place* come to mind. However, it was not until the 1990s that scholars began to think beyond the standard historical-critical and nascent anthropological approaches of the guild and began to borrow ideas directly from spatial theorists. Among those who embraced this approach was Halvor Moxnes, whose attention to the importance of space for understanding the historical Jesus has been unparalleled. Some biblical experts have borrowed from the geographer Edward Soja, who is best known for popularizing the concept of "Thirdspace," though this concept is better known than understood or applied. Having studied geography at Dartmouth College and brought spatial theory to bear on his dissertation at Princeton Seminary, Pruszinski has the cross-disciplinary training in critical geography necessary to enrich biblical methodology responsibly.

In *An Ecology of Scriptures*, Pruszinski draws on seminal ideas from Henri Lefebvre and Gaston Bachelard to ask of ancient religious texts: "What can we learn if we attend to humanity's most important spatial influences: the domestic and quotidian?" Lefebvre's idea of "spatial practice" critically informs Pruszinski's work. Humans reproduce spaces in an unending iterative process. They receive meanings and then reimagine them. They conceive new meanings based on their experiences. They shape spaces and spaces shape them. That this reproduction of space is a constant function of human social and intellectual life also suggests that the participants in this process may, at times, be unwitting participants, unaware of the depth of their influences or the effect of their reproductions.

Thus, to understand the spatial practice of a text one should read deeper than what the author says about space. One should notice what authors are doing with space and how they do it. Should we any longer claim that physical space is spiritualized or irrelevant in the Fourth Evangelist's story of the woman at the well if the author's spatial practice depends on embodied "indwelling," local spatial traditions, and material experiences within the Johannine community? How is our understanding of the new heaven and the new earth, according to the author of Revelation, improved if we notice that they were the likely product of a challenging experience of imprisoned life? These analyses of spatial practice lead inexorably to a consideration of the most commonplace formative spatial experiences that lie behind a text; that dimension of a composition is what Pruszinski calls "textual ecology."

The theory Pruszinski draws on most heavily is derived from Gaston Bachelard and his classic work on the psychologies of dwelling in *The Poetics of Space*. Attending to ancient religious texts like the Gospel of John, the *Parables of Enoch*, and the *History of the Rechabites*, Pruszinski looks to the ecology of the text, that is, its author's experiences of dwelling—or what M. Merleau-Ponty at times referred to as "indwelling." This phenomenon can range anywhere from a protected, restful ideal to an austere, or even life-threatening environment. Most of the texts considered in Pruszinski's work were shaped by both types of places. As such, attention to the likely spatial experiences of the authors and their communities as formative influences on literary production is the responsible and necessary perspective of "textual ecology."

It is likely that scholars have been hesitant to apply Bachelard's observations about the influence of domestic space after they were briefly described as anachronistic by J. Z. Smith in *To Take Place*. Pruszinski's work suggests that Smith's dismissal was premature and that the hermeneutical utility of Bachelard's observations can transcend concerns over nostalgia and anachronism. There is much to be gained for biblical scholars from a judicious application of Bachelard's work and further attention to the experiences of dwelling which gave rise to a vast amount of early Jewish and Christian literature. Pruszinski's penetrating analysis and cogent explanations succeed in this bold endeavor, but his conclusions go far beyond scholarly debates about theory, bringing exciting new insights to long-cherished scriptures.

Who hasn't walked through a door and forgotten what they had intended to do beyond the door? Pruszinski's interpretation of Revelation suggests that this phenomenon matters deeply for how we understand Revelation. What reader of Paul's letters hasn't struggled to understand the logic of Jesus-as-sacrifice? Pruszinski's spatial reading has the potential to alter long-held theories of Paul's teachings on not only sacrifice but the holy spirit and salvation as well. His observations on the *History of the Rechabites*, presented at the Larnaca conference on Cyprus and the Bible, astounded the experts there. His suggestion that the legend of the *Isle of the Blessed Ones* may have been incorporated into the Jewish story of the Rechabites by a Christian ascetic is not shocking. That a literal vision of Cyprus from a cave on the upper slopes of Mt. Kasios (Zaphon) may have provoked this appropriation is surprising and exciting. He claims that a local manifestation of the Novaya Zemlya effect could have produced exactly the kind of sight described in Hist. Rech., not to mention other religious texts linked to Zaphon traditions and even the Atlantis legends.

Biblical experts will be challenged by Pruszinski's methodology and arguments. The task of scholars is to allow themselves to be challenged by the texts in view, methods chosen, and reflections that may be disturbingly new. I have learned from Pruszinski, perhaps most when he stimulated me to think with new perspectives.

James H. Charlesworth
George L. Collord Professor of New Testament
Language and Literature, Emeritus
President, Foundation on Judaism and Christian Origins
Princeton, NJ

Preface

The most intimate, beautiful, and cherished spaces are those most given to appropriation. Homes and homelands perhaps most of all. Images of these places sustain and drive, even when the places themselves are lost or traumatized. Oppressors seek to appropriate them for their own coercive ends. The oppressed imagine and reimagine them as part of their emancipation. There is no special place, no beautiful place, no place of intimacy, no place touched by human thoughts and experience that is not caught up in this dynamic of oppression and freedom. The scriptures are not immune from these phenomena. They are perhaps most subject to them and bear throughout their pages the evidence of imagination, appropriation, and re-appropriation of spaces of intimacy, dwelling, and rest. May this work of analysis begin to lay bare the often-obscure operations of the human imagination of space evident in the Jewish and Christian scriptures. And from that work of elucidation of the experiences and imaginations of their authors, may we be prepared to discern whether we ourselves, as we imagine and appropriate, are choosing oppression or emancipation.

I write as an American author. As such I write as one who sees that the cancer of the Confederacy, nourished so long on whispered lies of imagined home and homeland, is still alive and well throughout America. I would have us cut out that cancer irreversibly and forever. But it is only in truth, clear thinking, and resolute action that such a thing may be cut out. Such thinking must include thinking about scripture, as it has been so often twisted to suit evil ends. Such thinking must include thinking about homes, and homelands, as evil too often lives and breathes about and through these most precious places. And this is not an idle inquiry. The increasing isolation of Americans from each other, and from communities of care, a phenomenon described by many modern sociologists and political observers, is bearing violent reactionary fruit. Such psychological dynamics of traumatized and marginalized dwelling, described by Gaston Bachelard and highlighted in this book, are not in their operation confined to modernity, but appear in the early Jewish and Christian scriptures. Only by carefully examining such dynamics as they appear in scripture can communities of faith avoid their uncritical reception as examples, rather than taking them for what they should be: *warnings*.

Meanwhile, beyond this comparatively older evil, we have of late been confronted by a pandemic that has reshaped our experiences of home in unexpected ways. Some have relished their time of protected retreat during lockdown. Many others have been trapped at home alone or in homes rife with abuse, with little recourse to alternate spaces of protection and relationship that had previously been available. Moreover, we live on the edge of a new and massive domestic homelessness crisis, to say nothing of the spate of homelessness induced internationally by American foreign adventurism. Will we choose to make a society where the perils of homelessness remain a deadly specter, haunting tens of millions of people? Or will we choose to make shelter a protected right that we might collectively ensure shelter not only for the bodies but for the dreams of a generation? This crisis shows that our most deeply held beliefs about home and shelter require reassessment.

As you read, consider well the spaces of intimacy in these texts, but consider also those from your own experience and which live most fervently in your imagination. Every day we reimagine and reproduce space, for good or ill. Know that as you reproduce the spaces of your experience and imagination you must always choose between life and death, between oppression and emancipation. It has always been thus, but the way is not always easy, or obvious. Nevertheless, I challenge you, dear reader, to ensure that the places you yourself make are places of deep solidarity with all people yet yearning for life and emancipation.

Jolyon G. R. Pruszinski
Princeton, NJ
Juneteenth 2020

Introduction

This book is a book about space and specifically about the necessity of attention to space in the interpretation of ancient religious texts. To some readers, this concern may seem eccentric. That is the reason for this book: to show that responsible interpretation of ancient religious texts and practice requires responsible spatial analysis. As geographer Edward Soja has shown, "Space can be made to hide consequences from us, [particularly] how relations of power ... are inscribed into the apparently innocent spatiality of social life."[1]

For decades scholars of early Judaism and Christianity have haltingly acknowledged the importance of space in interpreting religious history. Perhaps the boldest claim in this direction comes from those who suggest the necessity of attention to the "fifth gospel"—that is, "the land"—in order to understand the historical Jesus and his movement.[2] However, scholars of these religions and their extant texts have, in general, been loath to adopt methods and perspectives derived from scholarship pertaining particularly to space. This tendency is indicative of what Soja refers to as a "critical silence" among historians with respect to spatial analysis.[3] There have been exceptions of course, indicated in part by the recent work of the Society of Biblical Literature "Space, Place, and Lived Experience in Antiquity" group.[4] However, the broader

---

[1] Edward W. Soja, *Postmodern Geographies: The Reassertion of Space in Critical Social Theory* (London and New York: Verso, 1989), 2.

[2] Thus, for example, the title of B. Pixner's *With Jesus through Galilee According to the Fifth Gospel* (Collegeville, MN: Liturgical Press, 1996).

[3] Soja, *Postmodern Geographies*, 15: "Historicism [is] an overdeveloped historical contextualization of social life and social theory that actively submerges and peripheralizes the geographical or spatial imagination. This definition does not deny the extraordinary power and importance of historiography as a mode of emancipatory insight, but identifies historicism with the creation of a critical silence, an implicit subordination of space to time that obscures geographical interpretations of the changeability of the social world and intrudes upon every level of theoretical discourse, from the most abstract ontological concepts of being to the most detailed explanations of empirical events."

[4] See, for example, the following studies which largely focus on Hebrew Bible texts: Jon L. Berquist and Claudia V. Camp, eds., *Constructions of Space I: Theory, Geography, and Narrative*, LHBOTS 481 (New York: T&T Clark, 2007); Jon L. Berquist and Claudia V. Camp, eds., *Constructions of Space II: The Biblical City and Other Imagined Spaces*, LHBOTS 490 (New York: T&T Clark, 2008); Jorunn Økland, J. Cornelis de Vos, and Karen J. Wenell, eds., *Constructions of Space III: Biblical Spatiality and the Sacred*, LHBOTS 540 (New York: T&T Clark, 2016); M. George, ed., *Constructions*

adoption of spatial theory for biblical studies and for the study of early Judaism and Christianity has been limited and, to a significant degree, siloed. Increasing attention to material culture in religious studies and, to a lesser extent, in biblical studies perhaps heralds an opportunity to open the interpretive frame wider, and more fruitfully, to

of Space IV: Further Developments in Examining Ancient Israel's Social Space, LHBOTS 569 (New York: T&T Clark, 2013); Gert T. M. Prinsloo and Christl M. Maier, eds., *Constructions of Space V: Place, Space and Identity in the Ancient Mediterranean World*, LHBOTS 576 (New York: T&T Clark, 2013). See also Jon L. Berquist, "Critical Spatiality and the Construction of the Ancient World," in *"Imagining" Biblical Worlds: Studies in Spatial, Social and Historical Constructs in Honor of James W. Flanagan*, eds. David M. Gunn and Paula M. McNutt, JSOTSS 359 (Sheffield, UK: Sheffield Academic Press, 2002), 14–29; James W. Flanagan, "Ancient Perceptions of Space/Perceptions of Ancient Space," in *The Social World of the Hebrew Bible: Twenty-Five Years of the Social Sciences in the Academy*, eds. R. A. Simkins and S. L. Cook, Semeia 87 (Atlanta, GA: Society of Biblical Literature, 1999) 15–43; M. George, *Israel's Tabernacle as Social Space* (Atlanta, GA: Society of Biblical Literature, 2009); V. H. Matthews, "Physical Space, Imagined Space, and 'Lived Space' in Ancient Israel," *BTB* 33 (2003): 12–23. Some works have incorporated elements of critical theories of space into their analysis of New Testament texts: J. Økland, *Women in Their Place: Paul and the Corinthian Discourse of Gender and Sanctuary Space*, JSNTSup 269 (London: T&T Clark, 2004); J. Neyrey, "'Teaching You in Public and from House to House' (Acts 20:20): Unpacking a Cultural Stereotype," *JSNT* 26 (2003): 69–102; Elisabeth S. Malbon, *Narrative Space and Mythic Meaning in Mark*, Biblical Seminar 13 (Sheffield: JSOT Press, 1986); Carolyn Osiek and David L. Balch, *Families in the New Testament World: Households and House Churches* (Louisville, KY: Westminster John Knox, 1997); H. Moxnes, "Placing Jesus of Nazareth: Toward a Theory of Place in the Study of the Historical Jesus," in *Text and Artifact in the Religions of Mediterranean Antiquity: Essays in Honour of Peter Richardson*, eds. S. G. Wilson and M. Desjardins (Waterloo, ON: Wilfred Laurier, 2000), 158–75; H. Moxnes, "Kingdom Takes Places: Transformations of Place and Power in the Kingdom of God in the Gospel of Luke," in *Social Scientific Models for Interpreting the Bible: Essays by the Context Group in Honor of Bruce J. Malina*, ed. J. J. Pilch (Leiden: Brill, 2001), 176–209; H. Moxnes, "The Construction of Galilee as a Place for the Historical Jesus—Part 1," *BTB* 31 (2001): 26–37; H. Moxnes, "The Construction of Galilee as a Place for the Historical Jesus—Part 2," *BTB* 31 (2001): 66–77; H. Moxnes, *Putting Jesus in His Place: A Radical Vision of Household and Kingdom* (Louisville, KY: Westminster John Knox, 2003); H. Moxnes, "Body, Gender and Social Space: Dilemmas in Constructing Early Christian Identities," in *Identity Formation in the New Testament*, eds. B. Holmberg and M. Winninge (Tübingen: Mohr Siebeck, 2008), 163–81; H. Moxnes, "A Man's Place in Matthew 19:3–15: Creation and Kingdom as Transformative Space of Identity," in *Finding a Woman's Place: Essays in Honor of Carolyn Osiek*, eds. D. L. Balch and J. T. Lamoreaux (Eugene, OR: Pickwick Publications, 2010), 103–23; H. Moxnes, "Identity in Jesus' Galilee: From Ethnicity to Locative Intersectionality," *BibInt* 18 (2010): 390–416; H. Moxnes, "Landscape and Spatiality: Placing Jesus," in *Understanding the Social World of the New Testament*, eds. D. Neufeld and R. DeMaris (New York: Routledge, 2010), 90–106; P. Schreiner, *The Body of Jesus: A Spatial Analysis of the Kingdom in Matthew*, LNTS 555 (London: T&T Clark, 2016); M. Sleeman, *Geography and the Ascension Narrative in Acts* (Cambridge: Cambridge University Press, 2009); M. Clark and M. Sleeman, "Writing the Earth, Righting the Earth: Committed Presuppositions and the Geographical Imagination," in *New Words, New Worlds: Reconceptualising Social and Cultural Geography*, ed. C. Philo (Aberystwyth, Wales: Cambrian, 1991), 49–59; E. Stewart, "The City in Mark," in *In Other Words: Essays on Social Science Methods and the New Testament in Honor of Jerome H. Neyrey*, eds. A. C. Hagedorn, Z. A. Crook, and E. Stewart (Sheffield: Sheffield Phoenix, 2007); E. Stewart, *Gathered around Jesus: An Alternative Spatial Practice in the Gospel of Mark* (Eugene, OR: Cascade, 2009); E. Stewart, "New Testament Space/Spatiality," *BTB* 29.3 (2012): 139–49; K. Wenell, "Contested Claims: Roman Imperial Theology and Matthew's Gospel," *BTB* 29.2 (1999): 56–67; K. Wenell, "Contested Temple Space and Visionary Kingdom Space in Mark 11–12," *BibInt* 15.3 (2007): 323–37; K. Wenell, *Jesus and Land: Sacred and Social Space in Second Temple Judaism*, LNTS 334 (London: T&T Clark, 2007); Peter Claver Ajer, *The Death of Jesus and the Politics of Place in the Gospel of John* (Eugene, OR: Pickwick, 2016).

include spatial analysis,⁵ but it cannot be said that this work has yet passed beyond a beginning.

Rather, we are perhaps at a similar inflection point in the adoption of insights and methods from critical geography among scholars of religion as that at which the field stood regarding sociology when Wayne Meeks published his masterful *The First Urban Christians*. Though no doubt since then the way has been made somewhat straighter for scholars of ancient Judaism and Christianity to adopt methods that did not originate within their field, nevertheless Meeks' book dealt directly in its introduction with the issues most at stake in adopting new methods from a different field. And while it is too much to expect that the effect of the current work will be nearly as significant as that of *The First Urban Christians*, some of Meeks' observations are certainly germane to the approach and purpose of this book.

At the outset Meeks noted the reticence of scholars of early Christianity to trust conclusions based in "theory"—specifically, the concern that the modern theories cannot help but return anachronistic results in the interpretation of ancient texts and phenomena. According to this logic:

> The ... interpreter is tempted to infer what *must* have happened and the conditions that *must* have obtained on the basis of certain assumed regularities in human behavior. To the extent that he yields to this temptation, he modernizes. He recreates the people of the past in his own image, for the supposed laws of behavior are based on observations in our own or other contemporary cultures that may differ in fundamental ways from those of antiquity. To avoid these dangers, the exegetical critic insists that the task of the historian is only to report the facts: what the texts say, what the monuments show .... [T]hese are important warnings. There are good reasons to be chary of grand theory and unproven "laws." We ought to keep as closely as possible to the observed facts. The difficulty is that without interpretation there are no facts ... To collect facts without any theory too often means to substitute for theory our putative common sense. Making that substitution modernizes no less than does the scientist who follows his theory, for our common sense, too, is a cultural artifact. The advantage of an explicitly stated theory is that it can be falsified.⁶

Here we see stated eloquently both the just concern that anachronistic theory not be shoehorned into interpretation of the past and the equally just concern that complete eschewal of any theory often results in anachronistic conclusions based upon modern instincts of equivalent inaccuracy. The path charted by Meeks was to attend to historical and literary data as far as they were available and to consider "theory" inasmuch as

---

⁵ Recent works such as John M. Vonder Bruegge, *Mapping Galilee in Josephus, Luke, and John: Critical Geography and the Construction of an Ancient Space*, Ancient Judaism and Early Christianity 93 (Leiden and Boston: Brill, 2017), and M. Ahuvia and A. Kocar, eds., *Placing Ancient Texts: The Ritual and Rhetorical Use of Space*, Texts and Studies in Ancient Judaism 174 (Tübingen: Mohr Siebeck, 2018), are heartening. For an excellent summary of the modern scholarship on space in John, see Vonder Bruegge, *Mapping Galilee*, 195–212. See also Patrick Schreiner, "Space, Place and Biblical Studies: A Survey of Recent Research in Light of Developing Trends," *CBR* 14.3 (2016): 340–71.

⁶ Wayne A. Meeks, *The First Urban Christians: The Social World of the Apostle Paul*, 2nd ed. (New Haven, CT: Yale University Press, 2003), 5, emphasis original.

it offered useful explanatory power. It is the aim of the current work to do this as well, and in so doing, work to end the critical silence highlighted by Soja and fostered through the kinds of "historicism" that neglect spatial concerns.

Meeks described his employment of sociological theory as "eclectic," that is, "piecemeal, as needed, [and] where it fits."[7] Citing the anthropologist Victor Turner, he quotes, "Although we take theories into the field with us, these become relevant only if and when they illuminate social reality."[8] So the spatial theories employed in the following chapters are also intended: not to impose upon the ancients modern experiences or philosophies of space nor to serve in lieu of rigorous attention to the texts at hand. Rather, the ancient texts and data from those texts are the starting point for spatial analysis, and "theory" is only considered secondarily for its potential explanatory power.[9] But indeed it has explanatory power. As in Meeks, the theory is "ad hoc" and may similarly be found "distasteful to the purist"[10] but the findings speak for themselves. Coherence, as Meeks warned, may be too bold an expectation. In 1983 he wrote:

> To what degree of overall coherence can we reasonably aspire, without endangering our appreciation of our objects' stubborn particularity? There is no comprehensive theory ... so commanding that we would be prudent to commit our method to its care. Even if there were, we should be suspicious of it. Christianity, even at the earliest moment we can get any clear picture of it, was already a complex movement taking form within several complex societies. What ... theory is adequate to grasp the whole?[11]

If anything, the scholarship of intervening years has only further confirmed the truth of this statement. However, if there is any coherence to be found in the current project it will be found in two ideas: namely, "spatial practice" and "textual ecology."

Spatial Practice

"Spatial practice," a concept derived from the French philosopher Henri Lefebvre,[12] simply means than any human activity imbues spaces with meaning and that those

---

[7] Meeks, *The First Urban Christians*, 6. To quote in full: "In short, the application of social science in the following chapters is eclectic. I take my theory piecemeal, as needed, where it fits. This pragmatic approach will be distasteful to the purist; its effect will be many rough edges and some inconsistencies. Nevertheless, given the present state of social theory and the primitive state of its use by students of early Christianity, eclecticism seems the only honest and cautious way to proceed."

[8] Meeks, *The First Urban Christians*, 6, citing Victor Turner, *Dramas, Fields, and Metaphors: Symbolic Action in Human Society* (Ithaca, NY: Cornell University Press, 1974), 23.

[9] For an example of this approach, see Mark Smith, *Where the Gods Are: Spatial Dimensions of Anthropomorphism in the Biblical World*, Anchor Yale Bible Reference Library (New Haven: Yale University Press, 2016).

[10] Meeks, *The First Urban Christians*, 6.

[11] Meeks, *The First Urban Christians*, 5.

[12] Henri Lefebvre, *The Production of Space*, trans. Donald Nicholson-Smith (Malden, MA: Blackwell, 1991).

meanings in turn shape human activity, whether or not humans acknowledge it. Not only then do spaces have meanings, often layers of them, but humans often have neither a full awareness of those meanings nor an awareness of how spaces shape us in subtle, hidden, or imperceptible ways.[13] We tend either to view space as simply physical, essentially opaque, and resistant to analysis, or conversely, to assume it is entirely transparent and open to the penetrating gaze of the theorist.[14] The first misunderstanding limits appreciation for the importance of space, and the latter presumes too facile a process of understanding it. Lefebvre famously wrote that "spatial practice consists in a projection onto a [spatial] field of all aspects, elements, and moments of social practice."[15] In saying this, he claims that our social life shapes the spaces we inhabit, and that the inscribing of social experience onto space is not limited to physical places. It extends to the social practice of thinking and writing about places as well. Just as physical spaces accumulate meanings with every additional experience of life related to them, so literary representations of space exhibit those accumulated meanings. Spaces are palimpsests upon which social practice is inscribed, and the texts that describe and reimagine space are no less reflective of these complex layers of social meaning.

A clear implication of this idea for the study of scripture is that the spaces, "real" and "imagined," that appear in religious texts both represent the complex layers of accumulated meaning associated with the physical spaces they describe, and *reproduce those spaces in new forms with additional layers of meaning*. Literal geographic spaces are neither entirely "opaque" and "resistant" to analysis nor entirely "transparent" to the theorist. In the same way, the literary productions of space that appear in religious texts contain a trove of social data while still resisting easy and generic theory. Physical spaces and literary spaces are not identical, but co-informing because social life shapes the meaning of spaces, and spaces shape social life. Thus, analysis of spatial practice in scripture can begin to penetrate the apparent opacity of physical space by interrogating accumulated meaning from social practice. But responsible analysis will also complicate the "transparency" of ostensibly straightforward theologies of space that appear in scripture, recognizing that teaching and practice do not always entirely agree.

To put this in terms more familiar to scholars of religion, Meeks states, "The comprehensive question concerning the texts that are our primary sources is not

---

[13] Geographer Yi Fu Tuan, *Space and Place: The Perspective of Experience* (Minneapolis and London: University of Minnesota Press, 1977), 130, has written, "Every activity generates a particular spatio-temporal structure, but this structure seldom thrusts to the front of awareness."

[14] Soja, *Postmodern Geographies*, 7: "The 'illusion of opaqueness' reifies space, inducing a myopia that sees only a superficial materiality, concretized forms susceptible to little else but measurement and phenomenal description: fixed, dead, and undialectical: the Cartesian cartography of spatial science. Alternatively, the 'illusion of transparency' dematerializes space into pure ideation and representation, an intuitive way of thinking that equally prevents us from seeing the social construction of affective geographies, the concretization of social relations embedded in spatiality, an interpretation of space as a 'concrete abstraction' .... Philosophers and geographers have tended to bounce back and forth between these two distorting illusions for centuries, dualistically obscuring from view the power-filled and problematic making of geographies, the enveloping and instrumental spatialization of society."

[15] Lefebvre, *The Production of Space*, 8.

merely what each one says, but what it does."¹⁶ That is, an author may allege a certain philosophy, or theology, of space but may in fact produce space in her text in a way that is at odds with her purported theology. Thus, in any given text the spatial practice of the author may be different from her ostensible spatial statements. In this sense our task is not unlike that of many historians, for "the questions that the social historian addresses to religious texts, … seek to extract from them something contrary to or at least different from their manifest content, or 'intention.'"¹⁷ Clearly the general outlines of this concept are not new to the fields of religious or biblical studies, but in this study I attend to a specifically *spatial* aspect.

Textual Ecology

"Textual ecology" is the idea that the spaces that are most important to us shape us the most and, as such, have an outsized effect on literary production. This idea is based, in part, on the "gravity model," a social-science tool that is employed to analyze the relative importance of various things to each other.¹⁸ For example, two high-population cities, located very near each other, will generate comparatively more traffic between them than will two smaller cities the same distance apart or two equally high-population cities that are further apart, just as the gravitational force between two more massive objects is greater than that between two less massive objects or greater between closer objects than more distant ones. The implication for literary spatial analysis is that interpretation of any particular spatial theme or language in the text must occur according to the hierarchy of importance of spaces for the author. A person, generally, will be more shaped by their daily experience of home, or dwelling, than by their experience of a single, non-repeated trip to a park that occurred many years ago. But the meaning of that single, perhaps unusual, experience of the park will inevitably be filtered through their experiences of space that are more regular and which loom larger in their lived experience. It will be interpreted in comparison and contrast to the familiar or even in reaction to the familiar. The same dynamic holds for authors and the literary spaces they produce. As a result, the most fundamentally shaping human experiences of space, specifically those of "dwelling," but of the quotidian more generally, must be considered paramount for spatial-critical hermeneutics. This can also be called textual ecology.

For our purposes this idea of the ecology, literally the *oiko-logos* (home logic), or "eco-genesis" of a text is more directly derived from the work of Gaston Bachelard, whose treatment of the *literary* products of psychologies of domestic space in *The Poetics of Space*¹⁹ is unmatched. It is also, to this point, a work almost entirely neglected

---

[16] Meeks, *The First Urban Christians*, 7.
[17] Meeks, *The First Urban Christians*, 2.
[18] It is employed across many disciplines but was first popularly posited by William J. Reilly, *The Law of Retail Gravitation* (New York: Knickerbocker Press, 1931).
[19] Gaston Bachelard, *The Poetics of Space*, trans. Maria Jolas (Boston: Beacon Press, 1994).

in the scholarly productions related to ancient Judaism and Christianity and their early textual artifacts. Bachelard's observations will play a central hermeneutical role in the subsequent chapters of this project. Close attention to the psychological dynamics at play in quotidian spaces of dwelling (like homes, doorways, and even caves or prison) will then better enable interpretation of special, distant, or unusual spatial language (like that used for the heavens or the Isle of the Blessed Ones). Here I aim to heed the relevant warning of Paul Valéry: "N'oublie pas que tout esprit est façonné par les expériences les plus banales."[20]

What follows then is a series of eclectic analytical forays into some of the extant texts of early Judaism and Christianity (the Gospel of John, the undisputed Pauline Letters, the *Parables of Enoch*, the book of Revelation, the *History of the Rechabites*, and Augustine's *De Trinitate*),[21] attending specifically to the role of spatial practice and textual ecology in the hermeneutic endeavor. Each examination will give primary attention to the interpretation of spatial practice according to a concern for textual ecology, or rather, according to the most important generative spaces of human experience: the domestic and quotidian. Chapter 1 on the Gospel of John will give primary consideration to the conflationary function of the reimagination of the home. Chapter 2 will consider John 4, a text commonly considered to suggest the irrelevancy of physical space, as a test case for the importance of spatial practice and textual ecology in hermeneutics. Chapter 3, on the Pauline Epistles, will consider how a gentile-focused theological ecology might inform interpretation of Pauline soteriology. With respect to the *Parables of Enoch* (Chapter 4), we will consider the function of identification with and auto-valorization of a marginal locus of dwelling after having been expelled from ancestral lands. As regards Revelation (Chapter 5), we will consider the phenomenology of the quotidian space of doorways with regard to the Apocalypse's generative background in a carceral geography of dwelling. For Chapter 6, on the *History of the Rechabites*, we will consider the possibility of an unusual natural vision from a marginal dwelling as the possible spark that fostered the novel appropriation of the Greco-Roman legend of the Blessed Isle. Finally, regarding Augustine's *De Trinitate*, a reconsideration of the structure of the text will elucidate Augustine's affirmation of the *scientia* and space of material human experience. It is my intent to show that the explanatory utility of insights from critical geography, carefully employed, will be fully evident.

---

[20] Paul Valéry, *Oeuvres*, Vol. II, ed. J. Hytier (Paris: Gallimard, 1960), 785. "Don't forget that every mind (all life?) is fashioned by the most mundane experiences."

[21] The engagement across a spectrum of largely contemporaneous antique texts employing perspectives gleaned from a number of modern theorists is precedented in the work of Rush Rehm, *The Play of Space: Spatial Transformation in Greek Tragedy* (Princeton: Princeton University Press, 2002); Irene F. de Jong, *Space in Ancient Greek Literature: Studies in Ancient Greek Narrative*, Vol. 3, Mnemosyne Supplements 339 (Leiden: Brill, 2012); and Nicole L. Telford, *Sensing World, Sensing Wisdom: The Cognitive Foundation of Biblical Metaphors*, Ancient Israel and Its Literature 31 (Atlanta: SBL Press, 2017). Of course, *History of the Rechabites* and *De Trinitate* are rather later than these other texts but will be considered alongside them because of their particularly relevant characteristics.

1

The Ecology of the Fourth Gospel: Bachelard's Hermeneutics of Home and Martyn's "Two-Level Drama"

Introduction

J. L. Martyn, in his landmark work *History and Theology in the Fourth Gospel*, famously suggested the "two-level drama" as a possible explanatory model for some of the seemingly anachronistic data present in the Gospel of John. He wrote, "The past—[that is,] specific events and teachings of the past—lived on with power and *somehow* mingled with events of the present."[1] The experiences of earlier communities that ultimately flowed into the Johannine community (specifically, stories of the *einmalig*, or "unique" events of Jesus' life) not only shaped it but were viewed in continuity with it and were conflated with the situation of the Johannine community at the time of the composition of the Gospel. The "somehow" of this phenomenon is often attributed, theologically, to the view of the active work of the Holy Spirit as a mode of continuity within the community of disciples, reaching back to the earliest disciples. Or, at its most pedestrian, it is attributed to the normal work of history, according to which the past is remembered inasmuch as it is relevant to the concerns of the present. However, neither of these ideas adequately explain the singularly powerful manifestation of this anachronistic conflationary phenomenon as it appears in the Gospel of John.[2] This chapter contends that the prominent use of language related to home and dwelling in John, when considered in light of Gaston Bachelard's psychology of home, allows for an "ecological"[3] reading of John that both explains Martyn's "somehow" and allows for reconsideration and novel reframing of the history versus theology issue.

It is no innovation to say that language of home and dwelling appear prominently in the Fourth Gospel. From the *logos* dwelling with (or in) us (1:14), to the "many

---

[1] J. Louis Martyn, *History and Theology in the Fourth Gospel*, 2nd ed. (Nashville, TN: Abingdon, 1979), 18; emphasis added.

[2] Jörg Frey, *Theology and History in the Fourth Gospel: Tradition and Narration* (Waco, TX: Baylor University Press, 2018), 143, emphasizes the "uniqueness of this gospel" in this respect.

[3] Ecological meaning here "home-logical."

rooms" of the Father's house (14:2), to the language of "remaining," "abiding," and mutual indwelling it is clear that the image of home and dwelling is important. For this reason alone, Bachelard's treatment of intimate spaces of dwelling in *The Poetics of Space* merits consideration in the interpretive process. However, in his treatment of the phenomenology of home, Bachelard insists that a hermeneutic localized "in the spaces of our intimacy" is transcendent of both biography and history. Bachelard claims that any particular understanding of home is an amalgam of previous experiences of rest and belonging. In any new incarnation of home, he writes: "An entire past comes to dwell in [the] new house ... [in a] synthesis."[4] Thus, Bachelard's theory helps explain not only the presence of amalgamated "home" and "dwelling" data in the Gospel but also the historically conflated perspective of the Gospel as a whole based in the experience of the Johannine community.

The Johannine community, in spite of its difficulties,[5] was a home for those who composed and received the Gospel. The Gospel's imagery preserves evidence of the role that cherished experiences of dwelling played in the community. According to Bachelard's paradigm, these experiences of home were naturally conflated with, or provided fodder for reaction against, previous experiences of home and belonging (or rejection), dating back to the ministry of Jesus, to produce the anachronistic composition we have in the Gospel of John. Bachelard's "ecology," including his description of the "psychological elasticity" of home, provides a more complete explanation for the puzzling data in the Gospel and a solution to the quizzical "somehow" of Martyn's two-level drama.

To my knowledge, no one has ever endeavored to consider together all of the Johannine data that pertains to the images of home, dwelling, and inhabiting.[6] This is a curious characteristic of the scholarly treatment of a text that so clearly shows evidence of interest in compelling "universal" images, especially when ideas of house, home, dwelling, and inhabiting are not only present but clearly comingle. In this chapter I will not analyze all instances of these exhaustively, as that is not my purpose. Rather, I intend to note this panoply of related images of intimate space not only because these ideas are central to the human experience but also because so many of these themes that are often addressed separately impinge directly upon each other and exhibit a meaningful imaginative solidarity in the Fourth Gospel. It is the *presence* of this vivid

---

[4] Gaston Bachelard, *The Poetics of Space*, trans. Maria Jolas (Boston: Beacon Press, 1994), 5.
[5] Such as those familial rifts perhaps indicated by the synagogue expulsion scene (e.g., John 9:20-23) or the community rifts indicated in the Johannine epistles (e.g., 1 John 2:18-19; 3 John 9-10).
[6] Various scholars obviously have treated the indwelling or Temple imagery, but no one has considered the full spectrum of all home and dwelling-related imagery. Neither studies by Mary L. Coloe (*God Dwells with Us: Temple Symbolism in the Fourth Gospel* [Collegeville, MN: The Liturgical Press, 2001] and *Dwelling in the Household of God: Johannine Ecclesiology and Spirituality* [Collegeville, MN: The Liturgical Press, 2007]), Craig Keener ("The Function of Johannine Pneumatology in the Context of Late First-Century Judaism," [PhD diss., Duke University, 1991]), nor Michael Daise ("Ritual Transference and Johannine Identity," *Annali di storia dell'esegesi* 27 [2010]: 45–51) capture the full scope of this dwelling language and imagery. Michael F. Trainor (*The Quest for Home: The Household in Mark's Community* [Collegeville, MN: The Liturgical Press, 2001]) and John H. Elliot (*A Home for the Homeless: A Sociological Exegesis of 1 Peter, Its Situation and Strategy* [Philadelphia: Fortress, 1981]) pursue studies of the metaphorical household in other early Christian texts.

constellation of dwelling images that I wish to highlight. Further conclusions will be suggested based upon an establishment of their presence and importance.

Home Themes in John

J. L. Martyn's great achievement in *History and Theology in the Fourth Gospel* was to identify the layers of historical events, the "two-level drama" as he called it, which were conflated in the writing of the Gospel. He showed convincingly that the *einmalig* events of Jesus' life had become interwoven in their narrative retelling with events from the life of the Johannine community to create a composition rife with anachronism and historical conflation. Martyn introduces the issue of anachronism asking, "Why should the Johannine Jesus, himself a Jew, engage in such an intensely hostile exchange with 'the Jews'" in chapter eight?[7] The question suggests that the Gospel was composed so much later than the life of Jesus that Jesus has come to be viewed as differentiated from "the Jews," which is certainly an anachronism. The synagogue expulsion scene of chapter nine is another significant example. Martyn quotes John 9:22, "For the Jews had already agreed that if anyone should confess [Jesus] to be the Messiah, he would become an excommunicate from the synagogue."[8] Why would the narrator claim this at a point chronologically prior to Jesus having been shown to be the Messiah and before synagogue excommunication under these terms had yet become a formally decreed practice?[9]

In their broad outlines the ideas Martyn put forward about the two-level drama have largely been upheld by subsequent scholarship.[10] However, in his treatment he consistently attended to historical, that is, temporal, concerns in the formative

---

[7] Martyn, *History and Theology*, 16.
[8] As quoted in Martyn, *History and Theology*, 38.
[9] There are, of course, many more anachronisms than these including the previously mentioned inauguration of the age of the Spirit (John 4:23-24). Some critics attribute these to the Gospel's "post-resurrection perspective," and anachronism is by no means unique to the Gospel of John, but the density of appearance of anachronism in the Gospel *is* highly distinctive.
[10] His specific assertions about Jamnia have received the most skepticism but by no means universally. Joel Marcus ("*Birkat Ha-Minim* Revisited," *NTS* 55 [2009]: 523–51) for one has ably defended Martyn in this area and no one has responded meaningfully to him. Nevertheless, the general ideas suggested by Martyn have endured. Even scholarship that has emphasized evidence of synagogue excommunication prior to the experience of the Johannine community (see J. Bernier, *Aposynagōgos and the Historical Jesus in John: Rethinking the Historicity of the Johannine Expulsion Passages*, Biblical Interpretation Series 122 [Leiden: Brill, 2013]; see also James H. Charlesworth, *Jesus as Mirrored in John: The Genius in the New Testament* [London: T&T Clark, 2018], 13 n. 10, 45) does not undermine the well-established anachronism present in the synagogue expulsion language of the Gospel. Rather, such studies have simply established plausible *einmalig* events which may have formed the basis of the ostensible narrative of the Gospel. The "two-level drama" thesis is actually buttressed by identification of *einmalig* events. See Frey, *Theology and History*, 26: "There is no need to ascribe such a rejection to a decision of the rabbis in Palestine, as J. Louis Martyn and others have suggested, but it is quite plausible that diaspora synagogues after 70 CE were in the position to reject such a deviant group from their assemblies." Frey also extends the temporal conflation phenomenon to three historic layers (*Theology and History*, 119–20), even as he admits that parsing these layers can only be done "roughly." Frey's third layer is that of the "theological" insight of the author, which he locates later than the period of events in the Johannine community. Again, the broad outlines of Martyn's thesis hold.

background to the Gospel and gave short shrift to spatial issues.[11] He does suggest that the Paraclete, through the indwelling, "resolves" many of the spatial "conundrums" of the Gospel, but in his attention to historical concerns he neglects the possibilities latent in his initial spatial observations. He does not seem to realize that all the imagery of dwelling present in the Gospel, not simply the "solution" of the Paraclete, may in fact together suggest a larger and more broadly explanatory account of the historical *and* spatial data present in the Gospel.

Interestingly, the observations of Martyn and Meeks[12] regarding the social location of the Johannine community as the proper locus of attention for interpretation of the Gospel have paralleled observations made by Henri Lefebvre on the nature of "spatial practice." As previously mentioned, Lefebvre wrote that "spatial practice consists in a projection onto a [spatial] field of all aspects, elements and moments of social practice."[13] The most natural supposition to make from such an idea for the interpretation of the Gospel is that the author has inevitably inscribed the experience of the Johannine community upon the text. The spatial data in John necessarily reflect this social location. Thus, the basic structure of Martyn's thesis accords well with an analytical approach based in "spatial practice."

Further, as also previously mentioned, spatial-analytical methods for this approach to the Gospel, by way of a partial corrective to Martyn, will draw from the work of twentieth-century French philosopher Gaston Bachelard, especially from his penetrating treatment of the psychology of intimate spaces in *The Poetics of Space*. Though more spatial work in the field of biblical studies has drawn on the writings of such theorists as Lefebvre and Soja, no other theorist of space has produced a more complete or essential work on the psychology of intimate spaces and their literary representation than Bachelard. To our purpose, Bachelard is engaged in an analysis of the *literary* productions of space, which he views as largely a function of the imagination. In this sense, for him, all σχολή[14] is a function of an environment of rest or protected dwelling, and the phenomenology of space is relevant to any creative literary endeavor because an environment of protected dwelling and rest is its normative generative environment (ecogenic). As a result, his observations are germane for analysis of the germ of "dwelling" in any literature, but especially those which take up the image of dwelling as particularly important. Our further analysis will show that the Gospel of John is just such a literary production.[15] But, analysis of

---

[11] He does not entirely ignore spatial issues (Martyn, *History and Theology*, 135–51), but his intensive focus is historical, not spatial.

[12] Martyn in *History and Theology in the Fourth Gospel* and Wayne A. Meeks in "The Man from Heaven in Johannine Sectarianism," *JBL* 91.1 (1972): 44–72.

[13] Henri Lefebvre, *The Production of Space*, trans. Donald Nicholson-Smith (Malden, MA: Blackwell, 1991), 8.

[14] Here I envision the full semantic range of σχολή, including not only the ideas of scholarship, writing, and study (e.g., Acts 19:9) but the leisure and comfort necessary to engage in them (e.g., Plato, *Resp.* 370b).

[15] Thus, because the author of John must be writing from a place where he (or she) has some degree of protected rest and, as we will see, is imagining imagery of dwelling in the Gospel, all previous environments of dwelling and rest for the author and his (or her) community come to bear on the imaginative literary process of producing dwelling imagery in the Gospel. Clearly this dynamic must be understood to be implicated for nearly every author, but the imagery in John is particularly vivid and apropos.

dwelling themes in any literature is not a simple thing because of some of the basic phenomenological features of the image of home.

Bachelard suggests that "all really inhabited space bears the essence of the notion of home"[16] and that "the imagination functions in this direction whenever the human being has found the slightest shelter."[17] The phenomenology of dwelling is thus marked by a particular "psychological elasticity"[18] and, as such, in the process of "topoanalysis,"[19] as he calls it, the analyst must be careful "not to break up the solidarity"[20] of the diverse and overlapping images it produces. The following analysis will proceed accordingly, showing some of the manifold ways in which the image of home appears in the Fourth Gospel.

The Heavenly Dwellings

At its most straightforward, we may say at this point that the Gospel of John displays at least a passing interest in the heavenly dwellings of the righteous, which appear in many contemporaneous texts.[21] In the Farewell Discourse Jesus states: "In my Father's house (οἰκίᾳ) there are many dwelling places (μοναί) … I go to prepare a place (τόπον) for you" (14:2). These dwellings have an entirely positive valence in John, while the other Gospels are mostly silent.[22] This would suggest that the idea is perhaps more important in John than in the other Gospels, but perhaps not as crucial as it appears to be in a text seemingly obsessed with the idea like the *Parables of Enoch*. Interestingly, this "home" theme appears rather reversed later in the Farewell Discourse. In 14:23 Jesus states that "those who love me will keep my word, and my Father will love them, and *we will come to them* and make our home (μονήν) *with them*."[23] This teaching seems to suggest not a heavenly home to which the faithful will ultimately repair or ascend but a home in which the faithful dwell with the Father and Jesus, and which, in contradistinction, appears to involve their divine condescension. Not that the one image (indwelling) negates the other (heavenly dwellings), but the emphasis in terms of the primary interest of the author and the author's community is clearly on

---

[16] Bachelard, *The Poetics of Space*, 5.
[17] Bachelard, *The Poetics of Space*, 5.
[18] That is to say, variously manifested depending on the individual or even for a single individual depending on context. See Bachelard, *The Poetics of Space*, 6.
[19] Bachelard, *The Poetics of Space*, 8.
[20] Bachelard, *The Poetics of Space*, 6.
[21] Of special note in this regard are the *Parables of Enoch*.
[22] In the transfiguration scene (Mark 9:2-8; Matt 17:1-8; Luke 9:28-36) the heavenly dwellings may be what is, somewhat indirectly, alluded to when Peter awkwardly suggests setting up three tents. Jesus clearly has a different priority in all three Gospels that employ this scene. This may not be a negative portrayal, but the emphasis is certainly away from those dwellings and toward the current action of Jesus in those Gospels. Luke dilutes this ambiguous treatment with a positive statement in 16:9, but the idea appears to be otherwise untreated in the Synoptic Gospels. Of course, other authors deal with the idea more explicitly, like Paul in 2 Cor 5, or the author of Hebrews in 11:16 and 12:22, or various places in Ephesians, where the references are entirely positive. On the other hand, there are references to the perishability of the current heaven and its replacement with a new heaven in 2 Peter (3:7-13) and Revelation (21:1), suggesting a possibly less "perfect" view of the heavenly dwellings.
[23] Emphasis added.

the image of imminent dwelling available through the divine condescension in the indwelling.

Abiding and Dwelling (μένω)

The Farewell Discourse is also, of course, the primary locus in the Gospel of John for the language of "abiding." This language is by no means unique to the Farewell Discourse nor to the Fourth Gospel, but the relative frequency of appearance of this language, specifically of the verb μένω, indicates the importance of this image in John. There are twenty-three instances of μένω in John while only five between the other three Gospels combined. There are twenty-five instances in the Johannine Epistles, which exhibit far and away the greatest density of use in the New Testament. Certainly μένω does not always exclusively imply dwelling.[24] It can carry a temporal valence,[25] but the primary and most common usage, both generally and in John, does imply dwelling, as is the archetypal usage in the Farewell Discourse.[26] The first clearly archetypal usage that appears to agree with the general sense of its usage in the Farewell Discourse occurs with "the one who eats my flesh and drinks my blood abides in me, and I in him" (ὁ τρώγων μου τὴν σάρκα καὶ πίνων μου τὸ αἷμα ἐν ἐμοὶ μένει κἀγὼ ἐν αὐτῷ [6:56]). This is of course similar in sense to 14:10 in which Jesus states "but the Father who dwells in me (ὁ δὲ πατὴρ ἐν ἐμοὶ μένων) does these things." This kind of usage pervades the Farewell Discourse and clearly establishes a vivid image of "inhabiting" as central to the understanding of the relations between Father, Son, Spirit, and believers. At this stage it is enough to establish employment of the image,[27] the most relevant details of its usage will be considered later.

Temple/Tabernacle as House of God

The language of home is vividly on display in language used for the Jerusalem Temple as "God's house." This is a well-established image in the Hebrew Bible as shown, most relevantly for this study, by the Fourth Gospel's appropriation of the Hebrew Scriptures. In the Temple cleansing scene of chapter 2 Jesus is quoted as saying "stop making my Father's house (οἶκον) a marketplace" (2:16) and then the Gospel writer, by way of explanation, cites Psalm 68:10 (LXX): "Zeal for your house (οἴκου) will consume me" (2:17). All language related to the physical Jerusalem Temple in the Gospel of John must then be understood to implicate some understanding of this language of divine domestic habitation and reverberate, back at least as far as 2 Sam 7:5, with the long history of its use. Of course, the abode of God on earth before that time was considered

---

[24] Such as the first instance of its use in the Gospel in 1:32 where it appears only to have the sense of "remained."
[25] As in John 15:16 where it appears to mean "endure."
[26] See Charlesworth, *Jesus as Mirrored in John*, 49. He sees the use of this verb as "paradigmatic" in John.
[27] As seen most vividly in John 14:10, 14:17, 15:4, 15:5, 15:6, 15:10.

to be the tent (or tabernacle).²⁸ That image is certainly relevant for John for interpreting the data in the Gospel regarding the "Jewish Festival of Booths" (ἡ ἑορτὴ τῶν Ἰουδαίων ἡ σκηνοπηγία, 7:2). It is perhaps most relevant, though, for the importance of the concept in the Prologue where it appears prominently in 1:14, "And the Word became flesh and lived (ἐσκήνωσεν) among us," that is to say, literally, "tented." The language of the human body as a tent, or temporary dwelling, though not necessarily present in John,²⁹ was prevalent enough at the time that it can be considered relevant for interpreting this theme as well.³⁰

Household Language and the Home

Another category of language that requires consideration is that related to relationships of the household. Of course, parsing the distinctions between the place that is the locus of the relationships and the relationships themselves is difficult. But even aside from the consideration that familial relationships inherently implicate home themes, a couple of examples from the Gospel suggest that passages ostensibly related only to relationships actually require consideration of the spatial valence to accurately identify home and dwelling imagery.

The first example comes from the cleansing of the Temple pericope (2:13-22). Here, of course, the familial language Jesus uses for God relates directly to the image of the Temple as the House of God. The Temple is, by extension, Jesus' house, and he, because of his household relation to God, cares deeply about the place of God's dwelling as well.

Another example appears in John 8:35. Here Jesus is quoted as saying, "The slave does not have a permanent place in the household; the son has a place there forever" (8:35). On its face, the NRSV translation does not appear to implicate home themes directly, however, the spatial nuance appears more obvious in the Greek text. Lost in English translation is the fact that there is no explicit separation of association with the family from association with the home: ὁ δὲ δοῦλος οὐ μένει ἐν τῇ οἰκίᾳ εἰς τὸν αἰῶνα, ὁ υἱὸς μένει εἰς τὸν αἰῶνα. The NRSV rendering is so figurative as to obscure the plain meaning of the saying. Perhaps rather we should read "the slave does not dwell in the house forever, the son does dwell [there] forever." The familial implications are not lost but to choose to downplay the possible spatial valence of the text in translation seems irresponsible.

Of course, οἰκία can imply merely the relationships of the household, as is likely in John 4:53 where it is written that "he himself believed, along with his whole household" (ἐπίστευσεν αὐτὸς καὶ ἡ οἰκία αὐτοῦ ὅλη). However, even in cases so apparently straightforward as this, it is critical to consider and understand the implications of household relational language for conjuring images of dwelling.³¹ Relational and

---

²⁸ See especially Exod 25–40; Num 3–4; 9.
²⁹ Unless you include 1:14, which I do.
³⁰ For example, Wis 9:15; 2 Cor 5:1-4.
³¹ For one treatment, see Daise, "Ritual Transference and Johannine Identity," 45–51.

spatial language are deeply intertwined, as seen vividly in the language describing Jesus in 1:18, ὁ ὢν εἰς τὸν κόλπον τοῦ πατρός (the one abiding in the bosom of the father).[32]

Implied Home: τὰ ἴδια

Other texts in the Fourth Gospel, implicitly but truly, suggest the importance of imagery for home and dwelling. Though in 16:32 Jesus does not explicitly state that he retains a home even when rejected, the implication is clear. He states, "The hour is coming, indeed it has come, when you will be scattered, each one to his home, and you will leave me alone. Yet I am not alone because the Father is with me" (16:32, NRSV).[33] The implication here is that when his followers abandon him, returning to their own homes, leaving Jesus ostensibly "homeless," he is not in fact homeless because he is "at home" with the Father. This is clearly suggested by the robust language of dwelling that surrounds this passage in the Farewell Discourse. However, a further implication for the subtle usage of dwelling language in the Gospel must be drawn from this passage. If τὰ ἴδια is to be translated here to the effect of "own home," then surely it could be similarly translated in the Prologue (1:11).[34] The sense in John 19:27, in which the beloved disciple takes Jesus' mother εἰς τὰ ἴδια, again is clearly that of domestic space rather than "possessions" or "private affairs."[35] Not that τὰ ἴδια must be translated consistently but in light of the precedents[36] and context of other usages in the Gospel, combined with the immediate context of use in the Prologue, it seems likely we should render εἰς τὰ ἴδια ἦλθεν, καὶ οἱ ἴδιοι αὐτὸν οὐ παρέλαβον (1:11) not "he came to what was his own, and his own people did not accept him" (NRSV) but rather "he came to his own home."[37] Further, the Prologue of John is clearly drawing on wisdom traditions

---

[32] Even just the rich image of "father" or "mother" may carry with it associations of dwelling, rest, and safety. Bachelard quotes Henri Bachelin to this effect when he writes of his father: "Comfortably seated in my chair, I basked in the sensation of your strength" (*The Poetics of Space*, 31). Here we see that the parental relationship can take up into itself much of the image of dwelling. The parental language throughout John must carry some of this sense with it whenever it appears. Jerome Neyrey ("Spaces and Places, Whence and Whither, Homes and Rooms," in *The Gospel of John in Cultural and Rhetorical Perspective* [Grand Rapids, MI: Eerdmans, 2009], 72) recognizes the importance of this relational aspect of "Jesus' 'territoriality,' [in] the bosom of the father," and, with Sverre Aalen ("'Reign' and 'House' in the Kingdom of God in the Gospels," *NTS* 8 [1962]: 223), extends the idea of "household" to mean the "kingdom of God" (Neyrey, "Spaces and Places," 74–6).

[33] ἰδοὺ ἔρχεται ὥρα καὶ ἐλήλυθεν ἵνα σκορπισθῆτε ἕκαστος εἰς τὰ ἴδια κἀμὲ μόνον ἀφῆτε· καὶ οὐκ εἰμὶ μόνος, ὅτι ὁ πατὴρ μετ' ἐμοῦ ἐστιν.

[34] While the sense of ἴδιος is basically "private" (*BDAG*, 467), as opposed to δημόσιος or "public" (*LSJ*, 387), the usage in the neuter plural (τὰ ἴδια) carries the sense of "home" as the primary valence. Interestingly, both Goodspeed and Field advocate for just such a translation (contra Bultmann) in John 1:11 (*BDAG*, 467). One might imagine that Bultmann would balk at this translation due to his commitment to gnostic symbolism in John, according to which the physical earth could not really be understood as the redeemer's "home."

[35] There can be an alternate sense of "one's own belongings" or "private affairs" for τὰ ἴδια (e.g., 1 Thess 4:11) but that is a less common sense (*LSJ*, 818).

[36] The predominance of uses without a clear antecedent or modified noun in the New Testament and Septuagint suggests "home." See, for instance, Esth 5:10; 6:12; 3 Macc 6:27; 6:37; 7:8; Luke 18:28.

[37] The bare fact that τὰ ἴδια and οἱ ἴδιοι appear in the same sentence would suggest the importance of translating them with slightly different nuance. In Sir 24, which uses many of the same themes and language, there is clear reference to both place of dwelling and the people associated with that place being (somewhat) distinguished.

such as that evident in Sir 24 in which wisdom is depicted as searching the earth *for a home*. This suggests that the imagery of home and dwelling is more present in and relevant to the Prologue than many English translations indicate.[38]

Derivation and Home

The importance of language in the Gospel related to derivation, so-called "ἐκ-ness," has been well established by Leander Keck.[39] To a significant degree, though of course not entirely, this language is indicative of an understanding of home. One's locus of derivation is, at its most basic, one's original home. This concept is the subject of ambiguity in the Gospel, in light especially of its deployment in the service of misunderstanding through double entendre in John 7:40-44.[40] One's derivation is related to one's destiny, but as shown from the very outset of the Gospel, to some degree one's derivation can be chosen by believing "in his name" and becoming "children of God" (1:12), that is, those born "from the Spirit" (3:6), "from above" (3:3), and attached to the household of God, who will ultimately return to their "Father's house" (14:2). Clearly ideas of dwelling and home are implicated in this pervasive interest in "derivation."

Dwelling and Being

One of the difficulties in identifying all of the "home" or "dwelling" related data in any text is that the act of dwelling is so utterly central to human existence that many of the commonest words may, or may not, take on the valence of dwelling depending on the context. In John, we see this particularly sticky issue with respect to the verb εἰμί. While it is undoubtedly true that this verb can be used without any necessary sense of "home" or "dwelling," it is nevertheless also the case that it does regularly connote these ideas. For instance, in John 7:42, in the debate over messianic derivation and David's hometown, the verb used here is ἦν but the sense is clearly that David dwelt there, as given by the NRSV "the village where David lived." Later, in John 14:17, "he abides with you, and he will be in you" (παρ' ὑμῖν μένει καὶ ἐν ὑμῖν ἔσται), there appears an equation between "abiding" and "being."[41] And the rest of the Farewell Discourses bear this out, where statements such as "the Father ... dwells in me" (14:10) are used synonymously with statements such as "the Father is in me" (vv. 14:10, 11).

---

[38] The only standard one that renders it explicitly so is the RSV (and the alternate suggestion in the NRSV). A few others give the sense of "own world" or "own country" but the vast majority, rather inexplicably, do not.

[39] Leander Keck, "Derivation as Destiny: 'Of-ness' in Johannine Christology, Anthropology, and Soteriology," in *Exploring the Gospel of John*, eds. R. Alan Culpepper and C. Clifton Black (Louisville, KY: Westminster/John Knox, 1996), 274–88.

[40] John 7:40-44 (NRSV): "When they heard these words, some in the crowd said, 'This is really the prophet.' Others said, 'This is the Messiah.' But some asked, 'Surely the Messiah does not come from Galilee, does he? Has not the scripture said that the Messiah is descended from David and comes from Bethlehem, the village where David lived?' So there was a division in the crowd because of him. Some of them wanted to arrest him, but no one laid hands on him."

[41] This equation exists for Bachelard as well, but his account of it is less relevant for our understanding of the Gospel of John. Bachelard, *The Poetics of Space*, 7.

Dwelling and Becoming: *Timaeus*, γένεσις, and χώρα

The difficulty noted with εἰμί in John is also present, and possibly further complicated, with γίνομαι due to the possible Platonic resonances present. The differences between being and becoming, especially in the Prologue, but also throughout the rest of the text, may have suggested to some readers or hearers the then-popular understanding of distinctions made in *Timaeus*.[42]

For anyone familiar with Plato's *Timaeus*, which admittedly may be too much to assume for our author or the Johannine community, the idea of "becoming" necessarily carries with it an inherent property of inhabiting space (χώρα) as its cosmic dwelling. At its most elemental, the importance of this distinction is that "being" (οὐσία), or its semi-synonymous λόγος, only "becomes" when it inhabits space (χώρα). Thus, due to the resonances possibly present in John with the terms of Platonic cosmology, if not the exact valences as Plato understood them, the use of γίνομαι, particularly in a context suggesting creation, or new creation, must be considered possibly to carry some degree of the idea of dwelling or inhabiting. For instance, the idea may be implicated in the creation accounts of the Prologue including ὁ κόσμος δι' αὐτοῦ ἐγένετο ("the cosmos became through him," 1:10), which parallels Plato's cosmological structure quite well. The focal statement of the Prologue, ὁ λόγος σὰρξ ἐγένετο ("the word became flesh"), may also evince this idea, not only for the reasons previously mentioned but in light of the specific contextual usage in creation.[43] The same valence is possibly present in John 4:14 when Jesus says "the water that I will give will become (γενήσεται) in them a spring of water gushing up to eternal life." Here "becoming" certainly carries with it the sense of "inhabiting" due to the relationship of these "new creation" concepts (living water in the believer) to the indwelling of the Holy Spirit (see 7:39).

---

[42] The implication is not necessarily that the author of the Gospel was reading Plato but that ideas which appear in Plato certainly came to influence the Gospel, at the very least, by refraction through other traditions. For observations on such indirect influence of Plato on the Gospel, see G. H. Cohen Stuart, *The Struggle in Man between Good and Evil* (Kampen: Kok, 1984). Evidence of such refractive practice can be seen, as early as the second century CE, in Justin Martyr's interpretation of the Christian λόγος (somewhat) according to the categories of Hellenistic philosophy (*2 Apol.* 8). In Plato's speculative account of the order of the universe he demarcates three primary facets of the cosmos: being (οὐσία, from εἰμί), becoming (γένεσις, from γίνομαι), and space (χώρα, from χωρέω). Being is permanent, enduring, and preexistent: the forms from which all material is copied. Becoming is that which is impermanent, temporary, and contingent: the fleeting shadows or copies of the true forms that we know as everything material. Space (χώρα) is more challenging to parse. Plato himself refers to it as "baffling and obscure" (*Tim.* 49a [Bury, LCL]) and requests patience from the reader for the difficulties that will inevitably arise (29c-d). In a sense, χώρα is the receptacle for all of the γένεσις that is generated by the οὐσία (through the λόγος). Like the οὐσία it is preexistent and enduring, and γένεσις is utterly dependent on it: "What essential property, then, are we to conceive it (χώρα) to possess? This is particular, that it should be the receptacle, and as it were the nurse, of all Becoming" (49a [Bury, LCL]). And χώρα becomes this "nurse" of "becoming" first by being its mother. Plato writes, "it is proper to liken the Recipient to the Mother, the Source to the Father, and what is engendered between these two to the Offspring" (50d [Bury, LCL]). χώρα, then, "provides room for all things that have birth" (52b [Bury, LCL]), namely γένεσις. It is the womb, nest, and home of all "becoming."

[43] We further see usage which suggests this valence of "dwelling" in 1:17 in which grace and truth "become" through Jesus Christ (ἡ χάρις καὶ ἡ ἀλήθεια διὰ Ἰησοῦ Χριστοῦ ἐγένετο), suggesting the means by which they come to dwell in the believer.

The Synagogue

While it is clear that the synagogue is important to the Johannine community,[44] it should also be clear that the synagogue constitutes an important part of the constellation of ideas contributing to the images of home and dwelling in the Gospel. If it can be safely said, with Bachelard,[45] that status as a locus of "rest" constitutes a significant aspect of the understanding of home,[46] then the synagogue clearly must be included in our topo-analysis of dwelling. From a conceptual standpoint this should be clear from the association of the synagogue with the Sabbath. In early Judaism the only two places that can be said to have been focal to the regular celebration of the Sabbath are the home and the synagogue. As such, both would have accumulated rich associations not only with "rest" but also with each other as the two normative loci of "rest." The significance of this association for the Fourth Gospel will no doubt begin to be clear in light of Martyn's interest in the synagogue expulsion episode, but we will return to a fuller analysis of this space later on, specifically in relation to Martyn's hypothesis.[47] Further observations regarding the importance of the synagogue for understanding dwelling themes are certainly possible,[48] but the above must suffice for now.

The Preposition ἐν

Perhaps most obviously, and as hinted at in a few of the previous sections, the preposition ἐν is often employed to suggest inhabitation or dwelling. This is certainly the case when the associated verb implies dwelling ("abide in," "dwell in," "remain in," etc.) but also may involve its use with verbs that do not necessarily imply dwelling (e.g., εἰμί in 14:17). It must be considered carefully in every instance of usage, including those which are not typically rendered in English to suggest this sense. For instance, in the aforementioned verse 1:14, which is typically rendered figuratively as "lived among us" or "dwelt with us," it should at least be considered possible that the most common rendering of ἐν ἡμῖν should be used, that is to say, "in us." This option should be considered of particular importance in light of the emphasis, by this stage in the redaction of John, on the indwelling. Other prepositions could have been used to

---

[44] As can be seen in the centrality of the issue of excommunication from the synagogue to the passages surrounding John 9:22, 12:42, and 16:2.
[45] Bachelard, *The Poetics of Space*, 226.
[46] And such an understanding appears to be on display, for instance, in Sir 24:7 in which wisdom seeks a home on the earth saying, "Among all these I sought a resting place; in whose territory should I abide?" (NRSV).
[47] Many others have also noted the rift that likely shaped the Johannine community, including R. Brown, *The Community of the Beloved Disciple* (New York: Paulist Press, 1979) and R. Alan Culpepper, *Anatomy of the Fourth Gospel: A Study in Literary Design* (Philadelphia: Fortress, 1983).
[48] Such as the relationship between (and partial conflation of the function of) the synagogue and the Temple. The Temple clearly implicates home themes as previously mentioned. Evidence from excavations at Migdal suggests a close connection between the function of the synagogue for worshippers there and the function of the Temple. For a discussion of relevant imagery on recovered artifacts, see M. Aviam, "The Decorated Stone from the Synagogue at Migdal, a Holistic Interpretation and a Glimpse into the Life of Galilean Jews at the Time of Jesus," *Novum Testamentum* 55 (2013): 205–20.

emphasize the meaning of "among" or "with." According to this reading the meaning of the verse would be "the word became flesh and tented in us." This would emphasize the two-stage ministry of Jesus that the Fourth Gospel depicts: first the incarnation, then the indwelling, both of which involve very significant dwelling-related imagery.

Negative Images of Home and Dwelling

No serious interpreters of the Fourth Gospel have dismissed the importance of the κόσμος to the author of John and the Johannine community. One might be inclined to view this regularly appearing theme to be irrelevant for our consideration of images of home and dwelling; however, this is unwise for a few reasons. Firstly, the employment of the language of the κόσμος on display in the Gospel is not one that seems preoccupied with the operations of the heavenly realms or "nature" as we understand it.[49] The use of κόσμος is much more synonymous with the idea of the inhabited world (οἰκουμένη) or appears at times to act as a metonym[50] for the people who dwell in the κόσμος but who reject the gospel as understood by the Johannine community. In that sense, κόσμος seems to operate as a foil for the community of the indwelling, or for the believer as the locus of the indwelling, and attention to its deployment in the Gospel can flesh out, by way of negative image, the community's understanding of their positive home imagery.

Further Concepts Related to Home and Dwelling

Due to the universal function of dwelling and its relevance to much of human experience, there are many further possible avenues of inquiry to determine the outer edges of the full constellation of dwelling imagery present in the Fourth Gospel. Among these certainly would be uses of the language of light,[51] and

---

[49] Such an interest pervades 1 Enoch for instance.
[50] As is a very common occurrence with spatial language.
[51] While light does not necessarily at first appear to suggest the idea of home, in fact in many contexts it likely would have. During the day, obviously, outdoor places are lit by the sun. However, at night, or in a context of normative or dominant darkness, the primary spatial association with light would have been the home. Outside of this association, any use of light at night would not necessarily have had a strong spatial association because light would have only been present when carried by the individual in transit between, typically, dwellings that were lit. As a result of this association, deployment of light imagery in the Gospel can carry with it a significant association with home and dwelling. No doubt most will assume when attending to the "light" imagery in the Gospel that association of Jesus with light relies primarily on an association with the sun. This may be appropriate in some instances, such as in the Prologue. However, imagery that employs the idea of a lamp (e.g., λύχνος) is much more suggestive of a valence of habitation. For instance, the reference to the ministry of John the Baptist in 5:35 or, somewhat less directly, the language in the dialogue with Nicodemus describing those who do, or do not, "come to the light" (3:19-21). The sense of this language is clearly that of coming to a lamp rather than the sun, and the scene itself occurs at night, presumably within a home, lit by a lamp. (The setting of the story appears to be private and in Jerusalem. It is hard to believe that the setting for this interchange would be outdoors or, in some way, public.) And while the association with protected habitation is perhaps faint, it certainly colors the understanding and the overall positive valence of the deployment of light imagery here. Much of the language of light in the Gospel emphasizes the identity of Jesus as "the light," but at times, light imagery is used to refer to the idea of having the light in oneself (1:4; 11:10). Due to the prominence

filling,[52] or making room. For now, however, the briefly treated areas of concern highlighted above will need to suffice.

Bachelard and the Phenomenology of Dwelling

This brief survey has shown that, at the least, the image of home and dwelling seems very important in the Gospel of John. It is likely that the significance of this imagery has not yet been fully adduced. Attention to some of the observations of Gaston Bachelard regarding the phenomenology of dwelling will prove illustrative.

Psychological Complexity of the Image of Dwelling

As previously mentioned, according to Bachelard the idea of the house is psychologically complex. It "furnishes us with dispersed images and a body of images at the same

---

of indwelling language in the Gospel, and the clear sense that the believer becomes a dwelling-place for God, the ideas of Jesus as light and light in oneself would not only carry the image of protected habitation but would also serve to intensify the image of dwelling otherwise present in the Gospel. See Bachelard on light imagery and dwelling, *The Poetics of Space*, 33–5, 171. On this subject of the relation of light imagery to habitation, clearly many of the same phenomena appear operative in the Qumran documents (to say nothing of the similarity of other dwelling themes), and these certainly bear on the relationship between the Johannine literature and Qumran. See, for example, 1QS 3.18-19 "a habitation of light" and similar.

[52] At the outer edge of relevance to our inquiry we have idea of "filling" as it relates to the semantics of "inhabiting." Though this may appear an ancillary idea, it merits inclusion due to the aforementioned "psychological elasticity" of the images of home and dwelling. Bachelard insists that this category of thought is relevant for understanding intimate space. See Bachelard, *The Poetics of Space*, 105–35. John 8:37: "there is no place in you for my word" (ὁ λόγος ὁ ἐμὸς οὐ χωρεῖ ἐν ὑμῖν) is an example of this idea. The typical English rendering does not adequately explicate the underlying idea. A translation more to the effect of "my word does not have (or 'make') room in you" might better preserve the sense, suggesting the idea of the λόγος (not) "inhabiting" someone, parallel to the synonymous idea expressed in 5:38 ("you do not have his word abiding in you, because you do not believe him whom he has sent") and in contrast to those in whom it does dwell (e.g., "If you abide in me, and my words abide in you, ask for whatever you wish, and it will be done for you" [15:7]). This is not unlike the idea from the *Parables of Enoch* of wisdom finding nowhere on earth to dwell (1 En. 42:1) or that from Philo's exegesis in *Leg.* 3.1 according to which wisdom provides a home, is a home, and for which the wise themselves are a home. Somewhat at odds with this idea, but still relevant to our overall concern, is the idea from the Prologue of the λόγος-become-σάρξ as "full (πλήρης) of grace and truth" (1:14). This language is suggestive, not of the λόγος needing a vessel or dwelling as in 8:37 and 5:38 but of the λόγος itself as a vessel or dwelling-place, for grace and truth. This dwelling/vessel overflows with grace (1:16), and the dwelling/welling metaphors mix, but synergistically, just as they continue to do as pertaining to "life" and "the Spirit" throughout the Gospel. Other less relevant usages of χωρέω also appear, including the description of the jars at the wedding at Cana, "each holding (χωροῦσαι) twenty or thirty gallons" (2:6). Here the sense is "making space for." In the conclusion of the Gospel as we have it now, we see another instance of χωρέω: "I suppose that the world itself could not contain the books that would be written (οὐδ' αὐτὸν οἶμαι τὸν κόσμον χωρήσειν τὰ γραφόμενα βιβλία)" (21:25). The sense here is "hold" or "make space for," and the portrayal of the "world" is really a rather cozy one compared with the immensity of potential testimony about Jesus. See Bachelard, *The Poetics of Space*, 183–210, on the idea of "intimate immensity."

time."⁵³ These images of the house "give mankind proofs or illusions of stability" and, due to their importance and polyvalence, "we are constantly re-imagining [their] reality."⁵⁴ Even the barest hint of refuge can powerfully conjure these images since "all really inhabited space bears the essence of the notion of home" and "the imagination functions in this direction whenever the human being has found the slightest shelter."⁵⁵ Indeed, "every corner in a house, every angle in a room, every inch of secluded space in which we like to hide, or withdraw into ourselves, is a symbol of solitude for the imagination; that is to say, it is the germ of a room, or of a house."⁵⁶ As such, when it comes to the home, the imagination flies from even the humblest of perches, and the relations between spaces, experienced and imagined, become irreducibly complex. So, not only is "an immense cosmic house ... a potential of every dream of houses,"⁵⁷ but the dialectics of inside and outside, small and large, are no longer mathematical.⁵⁸ "Here, geometry is transcended."⁵⁹ Here, "the coalescence of images ... refuse an absolute anatomy."⁶⁰ But complexity does not prevent some useful observations.

"Rest" as Native to Dwelling Imagery

At its most basic, the image of the home is deeply linked with the idea of rest. Their overlapping semantic ranges require no explanation, but a reminder of the association is necessary to our purpose. Bachelard writes: "Every retreat on the part of the soul possesses ... figures of havens."⁶¹ In describing this essential association Bachelard is, perhaps, at his most vague. But that is only because he cannot help but wax poetic and indeed oneiric.⁶² In describing this essential relation between home and rest, he drifts into language often used for the Sabbath.⁶³

---

[53] Bachelard, *The Poetics of Space*, 3.
[54] Bachelard, *The Poetics of Space*, 17.
[55] Bachelard, *The Poetics of Space*, 5.
[56] Bachelard, *The Poetics of Space*, 136.
[57] Bachelard, *The Poetics of Space*, 51.
[58] Bachelard, *The Poetics of Space*, 201: "The two kinds of space, intimate space and exterior space, keep encouraging each other, as it were, in their growth."
[59] Bachelard, *The Poetics of Space*, 51.
[60] Bachelard, *The Poetics of Space*, 29.
[61] Which fall under the aegis of images of habitation and home. Bachelard, *The Poetics of Space*, 137.
[62] Bachelard, *The Poetics of Space*, 15: "Each one if its nooks and corners was a resting-place for daydreaming. And often the resting-place particularized the daydream. Our habits of a particular daydream were acquired there. The house, the bedroom, the garret in which we were alone, furnished the framework for an interminable dream, one that poetry alone, through the creation of a poetic work, could succeed in achieving completely. If we give their function of shelter for dreams to all of these places of retreat, we may say, as I pointed out in an earlier work, that there exists for each one of us an oneiric house of dream-memory, that is lost in the shadow of a beyond of the real past."
[63] Bachelard, *The Poetics of Space*, 201: "From being imagined, calm becomes an emergence of being. It is like a value that dominates, in spite of minor states of being, in spite of a disturbed world." And further (*The Poetics of Space*, 7): "Being is already a value. Life begins well, it begins enclosed, protected, all warm in the bosom of the house. From my viewpoint, from the phenomenologist's viewpoint, the conscious metaphysics that starts from the moment when being is 'cast into the world' is a secondary metaphysics. It passes over the preliminaries, when being is being-well, in

But, essentially, he establishes the co-magnifying imaginative effect that home and repose have upon each other:

> In order to derive benefit from the oneirism of such an image, one must no doubt first place oneself "in the palm of repose," that is, withdraw into oneself, and condense oneself in the being of a repose, which is the asset one has most easily "at hand." Then the great stream of simple humility of the room becomes our intimacy. And correlatively, intimate space has become so quiet, so simple, that all the quietude of the room is localized and centralized in it. The room is very deeply our room, it is in us. We no longer *see* it. It no longer *limits* us, because we are in the very ultimate depth of its repose, in the repose that it has conferred upon us. And all our former rooms come and fit into this one. How simple everything is![64]

Spatial Conflation Native to Dwelling Imagery

An additional characteristic of the phenomenology of dwelling is the pervasive imaginative tendency to conflate spatially the various locations of habitation. Bachelard writes that "through dreams, the various dwelling-places in our lives co-penetrate and retain the treasures of former days. And after we are in the new house ... memories of other places we have lived come back to us."[65] And not merely houses or homes are subject to this conflation but "centers of daydream group together to constitute the oneiric house which is more lasting than the scattered memories of our birthplace."[66] This conflation occurs when "the places in which we have experienced daydreaming reconstitute themselves in a new daydream, and it is because our memories of former dwelling-places are relived as daydreams that these dwelling-places of the past remain in us for all time."[67] In this way, similar language of repose, dwelling, and protection is attributed to a diverse set of places, not to mention attribution of "house" or "home" status to them, by a normative process of imaginative conflation. It allows a particular location to become "both cell and world."[68] "And all our former rooms come and fit into this one,"[69] that is, the current one. That this conflationary phenomenon occurs in

---

the well-being originally associated with being. To illustrate the metaphysics of consciousness we should have to wait for the experiences during which being is cast out, that is to say, thrown out, outside the being of the house, a circumstance in which the hostility of men and of the universe accumulates. But a complete metaphysics, englobing both the conscious and the unconscious, would leave the privilege of its values within. Within the being, in the being of within, an enveloping warmth welcomes being. Being reigns in a sort of earthly paradise of matter, dissolved in the comforts of an adequate matter. It is as though, in this material paradise, the human being were bathed in nourishment, as though he were gratified with all the essential benefits. When we dream of the house we were born in, in the utmost depths of revery, we participate in this original warmth, in this well-tempered matter of the material paradise."

[64] Bachelard, *The Poetics of Space*, 226, emphasis original.
[65] Bachelard, *The Poetics of Space*, 5.
[66] Bachelard, *The Poetics of Space*, 17.
[67] Bachelard, *The Poetics of Space*, 6.
[68] Bachelard, *The Poetics of Space*, 51.
[69] Bachelard, *The Poetics of Space*, 226.

the powerful instance of homes and home-related imagery is perhaps less surprising when one considers that similar phenomena have been documented to occur even in the case of such differing spaces as the deep undersea ocean and the desert.[70] In many ways Bachelard anticipated recent findings in the field of cognitive science.[71]

Temporal Conflation Native to Dwelling Imagery

It is perhaps, then, not surprising upon noting the commonness of spatial conflation in the imagination of places of habitation that this tendency is matched by an equally pervasive tendency to conflate habitation-related memories temporally or *historically*. Aspects of this phenomenon were, no doubt, already clear from the previous discussion of conflation of spaces, which occurs across successive inhabited spaces or, more simply, across time. The idea that "an entire past comes to dwell in a new house"[72] means that the current experience of home is inextricably conflated with previous experiences of it. "Thus the house is not experienced from day to day only, on the thread of a narrative, or in the telling of our own story"[73] because all of our current experience of it is understood through our previous experiences of it, and vice versa. As such, when it comes to stories or literary depictions of such places, "we are never real historians, but always near poets" due to the "solidarity of memory and imagination."[74] On this subject Bachelard deserves to be quoted in full:

> Memory—what a strange thing it is!—does not record concrete duration …. We are unable to relive duration that has been destroyed. We can only think of it, in the line of an abstract time that is deprived of all thickness. The finest specimens of

---

[70] Bachelard relates a fascinating episode told by Philippe Diolé, quoted on page 207 of *The Poetics of Space*, which illustrates this point vividly: "I once wrote that a man who was familiar with the deep sea could never be like other men again. Such moments as this (in the midst of the desert) prove my statement. Because I realize that, as I walked along, my mind filled the desert landscape with water! In my imagination I flooded the space around me while walking through it. I lived in a sort of invented immersion in which I moved about in the heart of a fluid, luminous, beneficent, dense matter, which was sea water, or rather the memory of sea water. This artifice sufficed to humanize for me a world that was dishearteningly dry, reconciling me with its rocks, its silence, its solitude, its sheet of sun gold hanging from the sky. Even my weariness was lessened by it. I dreamed that my bodily weight reposed on this imaginary water. I realize that this is not the first time that unconsciously, I have had recourse to this psychological defense. The silence and the slow progress I made in the Sahara awakened my memories of diving. My inner images were bathed then in a sort of gentleness, and in the passage thus reflected by dream, water appeared quite naturally. As I walked along, I bore within me gleaming reflections, and a translucent density, which were none other than memories of the deep sea."

[71] For early speculation on this normative spatial conflationary function in the imagination, see Arthur Koestler, *The Act of Creation* (London: Hutchinson & Co. Ltd, 1964). For more recent discussion of "conceptual blending," see Gilles Fauconnier and Mark Turner, *The Way We Think: Conceptual Blending and the Mind's Hidden Complexities* (New York: Basic Books, 2002), 6, 37. These ideas have been taken up in the field of biblical studies by, among others, Timothy Hogue, "An Image on the Stele or a Ghost in the Shell? A Cognitive Scientific Approach to Katumuwa's *nbš*" (paper presented at the Annual Meeting of the SBL, Denver, CO, November 17, 2018).

[72] Bachelard, *The Poetics of Space*, 5.

[73] Bachelard, *The Poetics of Space*, 5.

[74] Bachelard, *The Poetics of Space*, 6.

fossilized duration concretized as a result of long sojourn, are to be found in and through space. The unconscious abides. Memories are motionless, and the more securely they are fixed in space, the sounder they are. To localize a memory in time is merely a matter for the biographer and only corresponds to a sort of external history, for external use, to be communicated to others. But hermeneutics, which is more profound than biography, must determine the centers of fate by ridding history of its conjunctive temporal tissue, which has no action on our fates. For a knowledge of intimacy, localization in the spaces of our intimacy is more urgent than determination of dates.[75]

Bachelard insists that the idea of home is so imaginatively powerful for humans that its status and operation as an image displaces any real objectivity in its operation. As a result, it is more important, even for the writing of history, to attend to "home" and "dwelling" as *images* rather than as distinct memories:

Great images have both a history and a prehistory; they are always a blend of memory and legend, with the result that we never experience an image directly. Indeed, every great image has an unfathomable oneiric depth to which the personal past adds special color. Consequently, it is not until late in life that we really revere an image, when we discover that its roots plunge well beyond the history that is fixed in our memories.[76]

It is a challenging reality for the topo-analyst that "the moment we love an image, it cannot remain the copy of a fact"[77] but one that must nevertheless be considered carefully. With an image so auto-valorizing[78] as "home" one cannot help but love the image, but this phenomenon defies traditional historicism. "In human daydreams, everything remote intermingles."[79]

Imagination of Home as Responsive to Trauma

Bachelard highlights a final characteristic of the psychology of home that is germane to this study—that is, the responsiveness of the imagination of home to experiences of trauma. At its most elemental, this is due to the fact that positive imagery of home, dwelling, and rest is naturally oppositional to negative experiences of alienation and suffering. The one implies the other. But beyond this simple mirror-image relation,[80]

---

[75] Bachelard, *The Poetics of Space*, 9.
[76] Bachelard, *The Poetics of Space*, 33.
[77] Bachelard, *The Poetics of Space*, 100.
[78] Bachelard, *The Poetics of Space*, 12: "I shall therefore put my trust in the power of attraction of all the domains of intimacy. There does not exist a real intimacy that is repellent. All the spaces of intimacy are designated by an attraction. Their being is well-being. In these conditions, topoanalysis bears the stamp of a topophilia, and shelters and rooms will be studied in the sense of this valorization."
[79] Bachelard, *The Poetics of Space*, 120.
[80] Bachelard, *The Poetics of Space*, 40: "outside the occupied house, the … cosmos is a simplified cosmos. It is a non-house in the same way that metaphysicians speak of a non-I, and between the house and the non-house it is easy to establish all sorts of contradictions."

Bachelard identifies and emphasizes the responsiveness of the human imagination of home to experiences of trauma. This reaction to being "cast into the world," as he calls it, implies only a "secondary metaphysics" to that of the primary and original experience of being (at home) but a powerful one nevertheless.[81]

Certainly, in the experience of everyday difficulty, the home is a sustaining image. In it, "we live ... fixations of happiness. We comfort ourselves by reliving memories of protection."[82] On the most basic level, "In the life of a [hu]man, the house thrusts aside contingencies, its councils of continuity are unceasing. Without it, [the hu]man would be a dispersed being. It maintains him [or her] through the storms of the heavens and through those of life."[83] Places of rest allow rejuvenation in spite of a "disturbed world."[84]

But Bachelard asserts that the full depth of the image of home is not accessible to the imagination without serious loss. He says that "the houses that were lost forever continue to live on in us,"[85] and that "we must lose our earthly Paradise in order actually to live in it, to experience it in the reality of its images, in the absolute sublimation that transcends all passion."[86] This experience of loss[87] or trauma fosters an even deeper and more vital imagination of home.

Even the "meager" experience[88] of being "cornered" is highly generative of the imagination of dwelling. When humans have been forced out of the comfort or shelter of their dwelling or repose, the corner, both literal and figurative, to which they retreat becomes a new and powerful locus for dreaming new dreams of dwelling and repose. And this experience of distressed retreat to a marginal, though imaginatively generative,[89] experience of dwelling almost inevitably carries with it a generation of a

---

[81] Bachelard, *The Poetics of Space*, 7: "Being is already a value. Life begins well, it begins enclosed, protected, all warm in the bosom of the house. From my viewpoint, from the phenomenologist's viewpoint, the conscious metaphysics that starts from the moment when being is 'cast into the world' is a secondary metaphysics. It passes over the preliminaries, when being is being-well, in the well-being originally associated with being. To illustrate the metaphysics of consciousness we should have to wait for the experiences during which being is cast out, that is to say, thrown out, outside the being of the house, a circumstance in which the hostility of men and of the universe accumulates. But a complete metaphysics, englobing both the conscious and the unconscious, would leave the privilege of its values within. Within the being, in the being of within, an enveloping warmth welcomes being."

[82] Bachelard, *The Poetics of Space*, 6.

[83] Bachelard, *The Poetics of Space*, 7.

[84] Bachelard, *The Poetics of Space*, 210: "From being imagined, calm becomes an emergence of being. It is like a value that dominates, in spite of minor states of being, in spite of a disturbed world."

[85] Bachelard, *The Poetics of Space*, 56.

[86] Bachelard, *The Poetics of Space*, 33.

[87] Bachelard, *The Poetics of Space*, 100: "the home of other days has become a great image of lost intimacy."

[88] Bachelard, *The Poetics of Space*, 137: "Every retreat on the part of the soul possesses, in my opinion, figures of havens. That most sordid of all havens, the corner, deserves to be examined. To withdraw into one's corner is undoubtedly a meager expression. But despite its meagerness, it has numerous images, some, perhaps, of great antiquity, images that are psychologically primitive. At times, the simpler the image the vaster the dream."

[89] Bachelard, *The Poetics of Space*, 142: "From the depths of his [or her] corner, the dreamer sees an older house, a house in another land, thus making a synthesis of the childhood home and the dream home."

sense of reaction against the world[90] outside of the "corner." Cohabiting in this corner, then, with new and creative dreams of home, are world-negating[91] emotions formed in the crucible of trauma.

Each of these categories of observations from Bachelard on the psychology of dwelling—concerning loci of rest, temporal conflation, spatial conflation, and responsiveness to trauma—have direct bearing upon interpretation of the Fourth Gospel.

Martyn and the "Somehow" of the Two-Level Drama

In *History and Theology in the Fourth Gospel*, J. Louis Martyn identified the outlines of a "two-level drama" present in the Fourth Gospel. That is, into what is ostensibly a narrative of important episodes in the life of Jesus are deftly woven many elements that speak much more relevantly to the experience of the author's own community and time. As previously mentioned, Martyn writes, "The past—specific events and teachings of the past—lived on with power and *somehow* mingled with the events of the present."[92] This observation, and the support he marshals for his case, earned justifiable praise for its identification of the *crux interpretum*[93] in the Gospel. Yet while he deftly identifies the anachronism present in the Gospel and posits a plausible generative background for this anachronism, nevertheless the "somehow" of Martyn's primary contention has neither been adequately argued nor widely agreed upon. In essence, his contention relies most heavily upon the Johannine community's "present" experience of the Holy Spirit as the generative background behind the anachronistic impulse. This observation, while certainly correct, is held in reserve until the final few pages of his book and the full picture of this generative impulse is not highly developed. Martyn accurately sensed that the felt operation of the Holy Spirit in the experience of the community represented a crucial aspect of the formative background lying behind the "two-level drama," that is, the heavy anachronism in the Gospel. However, the action of the Paraclete represents only one part of that constellation of related phenomena,

---

[90] Bachelard, *The Poetics of Space*, 46: "Such a [space] invites mankind to heroism of cosmic proportions. It is an instrument with which to confront the cosmos." See also ibid., 143: "The dreamer in his [or her] corner wrote off the world in a detailed daydream that destroyed, one by one, all the objects of the world."

[91] Bachelard, *The Poetics of Space*, 136: "Every corner in a house, every angle in a room, every inch of secluded space in which we like to hide, or withdraw into ourselves, is a symbol of solitude for the imagination; that is to say, it is the germ of a room, or of a house .... Also, in many respects, a corner that is 'lived in' tends to reject and restrain, even to hide, life. The corner becomes a negation of the Universe."

[92] Martyn, *History and Theology*, 18. Emphasis added.

[93] That is, the heavy anachronism, on display most prominently in John 9: "The most specific problem or process behind the composition of the Gospel is then identified [by Martyn] in the miracle story of the man born blind in John 9, in which it is even said that members of the synagogue community do not openly confess Jesus because the Jews had decided to expel those who would confess him (John 9:22)." Frey, *Theology and History*, 4; see also R. Alan Culpepper, *The Gospel and Letters of John* (Nashville, TN: Abingdon, 1998), 43–4, 176–7; John Ashton, *Understanding the Fourth Gospel*, 2nd ed. (Oxford: Oxford University Press, 2007), 6, 31, 196.

the rest of which he did not appear to consider. More fully, it is the whole panoply of imagery related to dwelling[94] and the operative phenomenology that accompanies this imagery which more robustly and accurately explain the data present in the Gospel of John and which help flesh out the coy and quizzical "somehow"[95] suggested by Martyn in his text.

Excommunication from the Synagogue

Martyn's starting point for his discussion of the two-level drama is John 9, that is, the story of the healing of the blind man and his subsequent excommunication from the synagogue. As such, we must note at the very outset that the narrative necessarily employs an imagery of home and dwelling. This connotation of the synagogue is not immediately obvious for many Christian readers of the Gospel but must be viewed as inherent.

In the context of the writing of the Gospel, the synagogue would have been one of only two Sabbath-associated loci for Jews. The synagogue was the public one, and the home as a (relatively) private place of rest would be the other. And, as already mentioned in the discussion of Bachelard's observations on the imagery of rest,[96] this imagery is inextricably intertwined with the concepts of shelter, protection, home, and dwelling. Thus, anyone who had belonged to the synagogue would understand it with imagery, language, and imagination very similar to that with which they understood the home. The synagogue would be felt to be a place for rest and communal religious dwelling.[97] To be excommunicated from the synagogue, as is contemplated in John 9, would necessarily implicate a sense of homelessness.[98]

The narrative of John 9 further emphasizes this stress on the ties of home by noting the strains that appear in familial relations in the passage. The excommunication implicates a significant degree of family separation, not just from the corporate family of Israel but from the immediate family. The healed blind man is kept at arm's length by his parents due to their fear of being excommunicated.[99] And as was mentioned previously, family relationships necessarily bear a significant imagery of home and dwelling. In addition to the corporate-religious home of the synagogue, the familial home itself is also imperiled by the excommunication.[100]

A further aspect of the dwelling imagery found in John 9 relates to the specific language of excommunication employed when the narrator states that "anyone

---

[94] Of which the "present" experience of the Holy Spirit in the Johannine community is part.
[95] Which he reduces to the work of the Paraclete.
[96] Which includes dwelling imagery, places of rest, and imagination of rest.
[97] And Martyn (*History and Theology*, 65) writes that "it is important to note that this group [the Johannine community] did not consider itself [originally] to be an entity socially distinct from the synagogue fellowship."
[98] Especially when, in many ways, the synagogue was the only remaining link to the Temple and to corporate worship in Judaism (outside of worship in the home with immediate family).
[99] As suggested by 9:21-22.
[100] On the isolation of the Johannine community, see Meeks, "The Man from Heaven in Johannine Sectarianism," 44–72. This is his particular emphasis in pp. 70–2.

who confessed Jesus to be the Messiah would be put out of the synagogue (ἀποσυνάγωγος γένηται)" (9:22). This same pair of words appears again in 12:42 and the pairing does not appear to be accidental. Martyn emphasizes the apparently novel deployment of the term ἀποσυνάγωγος, which does not appear in any other extant texts previous to or contemporaneous with the Gospel of John. It is clearly spatial and relational in sense and implies excommunication and ejection from the space of rest, dwelling, and belonging. And while γίνομαι is a very common verb and could theoretically be employed banally and without special valence, the early emphasis in the Prologue upon the distinctions of "being" and "becoming" suggests that the employment of γίνομαι with particular emphasis may be intentional. It is possible that the deployment of γίνομαι with ἀποσυνάγωγος connotes a creative act of rejection on the part of the synagogue authorities that results in the casting of the object of excommunication into a new space of dwelling. We will return to the implications for this language below, but suffice to say for now, the excommunication episode of John 9 is replete with imagery of dwelling that is significant to our purpose.

The *Einmalig* Events and the Experience of the Johannine Community

Martyn describes the "two-level drama" as involving, firstly, an *einmalig* event, that is, an "event [which occurred] during Jesus' earthly lifetime."[101] Through the construction of the narrative of the Gospel the author has interwoven with this event, secondly, "actual events experienced by the Johannine church."[102] These two levels of drama create the temporal conflation noted by scores of interpreters. And while this historical conflation is on vivid display throughout the Gospel,[103] Martyn emphasizes it most significantly in John 5, 7, 9, and the Farewell Discourse (14–17). Of the anachronism present in the text that is central to his thesis, the synagogue excommunication pericope, he writes:

> John 9 impresses upon us its immediacy in such a way as strongly to suggest that some of its elements reflect actual experiences of the Johannine community. It does not strike one as artificially contrived, nor does it appear to be composed merely in order to dramatize a theological point of view. At least in part, it seems to reflect experiences in the dramatic interaction between the synagogue and the Johannine church.[104]

This contention regarding the anachronism of John 9 has been the most favorably received of his arguments in *History and Theology in the Fourth*

---

[101] Martyn, *History and Theology*, 30.
[102] Martyn, *History and Theology*, 30.
[103] Martyn, *History and Theology*, 84: "The drama may indeed reflect two levels in general," that is, across the Gospel as a whole, not merely in the specific pericopae considered in his treatment.
[104] Martyn, *History and Theology*, 37.

Gospel.¹⁰⁵ A summary statement in his concluding chapter puts it somewhat more powerfully:

> Theologically the boldest step we have seen John take is the "doubling" of Jesus with the figures of Christian witnesses in his own community. Since we are acquainted with Luke's second volume in which a part of the post-resurrection history of the church is narrated, it strikes us that John could have narrated the history of his own church in a direct and straightforward manner. Instead we find him presenting a two-level drama in which it is not an apostle but rather Jesus himself who ministers to Jews known to John as men who have suffered the fate of excommunication from the synagogue.¹⁰⁶

All this is only to say that the Gospel displays the same phenomenon described by Bachelard in his treatments of the imagination of dwelling: namely, that native to images of dwelling is an unavoidable tendency toward historical conflation. This is a natural phenomenon that accompanies imagery and imagination of dwelling and if, as Martyn believes, the author of the Gospel was not conscious of his (or her) literary practice of historical conflation,¹⁰⁷ he (or she) likely would neither necessarily have been conscious of all the further effects of dwelling imagery on the compilation of the Gospel. Thus, it would seem, from attention to the images present in the

---

[105] Much more than the detailed arguments about Jamnia. Frey (*Theology and History*, 9) states that "the paradigm of the two-level drama is [still] quite perceptive and stimulating. There are, indeed, two levels in John's narration of the Jesus story: the level of the narrated story of the earthly Jesus and the level of the narration, of the author telling his story to his readers or hearers. It is widely accepted that the Johannine narrative is shaped by insights, challenges, and theological terms from the context of the community of addressees. It is also quite likely that some of the elements in the Johannine narration are inspired by experiences from the time between Jesus and the composition of the Gospel." And even those who, like Frey, believe that some of Martyn's suggestions, for instance, regarding the "doubling" of events remain "unconvincing" (Frey, *Theology and History*, 9) and deny the likelihood of events of the Johannine community being the primary focus of the narration, many of them still recognize (e.g., Frey, *Theology and History*, 104) that "in most cases … we can only get back to traditions that are more or less shaped by the language of the Johannine community. … [T]he verdict cannot be avoided that all the words of Jesus in John have undergone a thorough theological transformation, and the claim that they represent the words of the Jesus of history cannot, in most cases, be substantiated." As mentioned previously, even scholarship that has emphasized evidence of synagogue excommunication at the *einmalig* level (Bernier, *Aposunagōgos and the Historical Jesus in John*; Charlesworth, *Jesus as Mirrored in John*, 13 n. 10, 45) does not preclude the legitimacy of the broad outlines of Martyn's observations regarding anachronism in the synagogue expulsion language. As previously mentioned the "two-level drama" thesis is actually buttressed by identification of *einmalig* events.

[106] Martyn, *History and Theology*, 129. He goes on to say, "Jesus also acts the part of the Jewish-Christian preacher who is subjected to arrest and trial as a beguiler. Jesus engages in the debates which John's church has with the Jewish community regarding his own identity as the Mosaic Messiah. It is also the Risen Lord himself who insists that the messianic issue is not midrashic and who terminates these debates with his awesome use of the numinous-laden 'I am.'"

[107] Martyn, *History and Theology*, 89: "I doubt that he was himself *analytically conscious* of what I have termed the two-level drama, for his major concern in this regard was to bear witness to the essential *integrity* of the *einmalig* drama of Jesus' earthly life and the contemporary drama in which the Risen Lord acts through his servants." Emphasis original.

Gospel, the author's memories of home (both good and bad) have become conflated temporally.[108]

Martyn and John's Spatial Conflations

The historical conflation on display in the Gospel is certainly matched by at least an equal level of spatial conflation. To some degree, Martyn's notation of spatial conundrums[109] and dwelling themes in the Gospel, developed *in nuce*, has been overlooked. These initial forays into the subject matter made by Martyn in his final chapter suggest some of the connections hypothesized in this chapter, but he does not develop them. Here they are more fully developed.

The main thrust of Martyn's final chapter has to do with the solution of apparent locational conflicts implied by the two-level drama through the action of the Paraclete. Is Jesus in heaven with the Father (e.g., John 3:13) or on earth with believers (e.g., John 14:23)? Should believers look forward to heavenly habitations (e.g., John 14:2) or to mystical union with a heavenly Jesus (e.g., John 3:13)? Martyn claims that the action of the Paraclete solves these conundrums in the Gospel through immediacy of access, putting off the distant, future, or speculative solutions in favor of that provided by the indwelling. Though Martyn denies that this is ultimately a "mystical" solution,[110] the way this solution is articulated in John suggests very clearly a mysticism of spatial conflation. The meanings of the heavenly habitations (14:2) become, to a significant degree, associated with the new dwelling of the believer (14:23). Instead of the believer speculating about union with God in God's heavenly home, the Father and Jesus come and make their home in the believer. In this way the images of heavenly dwellings on display in the *Parables of Enoch*, and of mystical union described in countless examples of "religious literature of the Hellenistic age,"[111] are actually caught up into the expression of dwelling on display in the Farewell Discourse (*pace*, Martyn) rather than contradicted. No only so, but, contra Martyn, the heavenly dwellings are not made irrelevant nor is mystical union. Rather, these layers of experience of God receive an additional layer of meaning and reinterpretation through the indwelling. Martyn wants to reduce the complexities of locational "conundrums" to a logical "solution," but

---

[108] Frey describes this as the "fusion of horizons" (*Theology and History*, 9). He intimates agreement with Martyn's general conclusions about the instances of anachronism in his questions: "How are these two (or even more) levels connected in the Johannine text? Can we still separate them and determine what is historically true and what is mere interpretation or theology? Or are they connected in an almost inseparable unity so that the insights and fears of the community of addressees are introduced into the narration of the history of Jesus, and, consequently, the earthly Jesus is presented in the light of later Christological insights as a divine being? And if this is true, what is the function of that fusion of levels or horizons which makes John and his representation of the history of Jesus so unique among the Gospels?" For further explorations of the complicated nature of memory with respect to purported *einmalig* events, see Dale C. Allison, Jr., *Constructing Jesus: Memory, Imagination, and History* (Grand Rapids, MI: Baker Academic, 2010).

[109] This is the term he uses for apparently contradictory spatial data in the Gospel, which in his analysis is nearly exclusively confined to treatments of the location of Jesus.

[110] As Martyn, *History and Theology*, 147–8, refers to them.

[111] Martyn, *History and Theology*, 147.

the complexity of the data prevents this spatial harrowing.[112] The indwelling does not abrogate the other, apparently conflicting, imagery of dwelling spaces but augments the values of their reality. Clearly a phenomenology of dwelling-image conflation is at work in the Gospel, even as Martyn views this, rather, as a "conundrum" that requires "solution."[113]

Fascinatingly, Martyn does not seem to have realized that some of the best, and earliest, support for his theory of the two-level drama in the Gospel comes from John 1:14. He repeatedly renders this verse "the word became flesh and dwelt among us."[114] Yet a rendering of "the word became flesh and dwelt *in* us" allows for a fuller appreciation of the two-level drama and the sequential "dwelling" experienced first on the *einmalig* level (the λόγος becoming, or dwelling in, σάρξ) and then on the level of the experience of the Johannine community (the λόγος tenting, or dwelling, in us).[115]

To be perfectly explicit, the second half of the phrase can be understood either at the *einmalig* level or at the level of the Johannine community. In this sense it would

---

[112] As may be recalled from the previous discussion of Bachelard's emphasis on the "complexity" and conflation of dwelling imagery.

[113] Philo's *Leg.* 3.1 is illustrative here. He employs the imagery of home in various ways in a single paragraph. From a strictly geometric perspective, many of these are "at odds" locatively. However, Philo's deployment of the imagery of home is not accidental and does not require "solution." All the various images contribute to an overall picture of wisdom as it relates to "dwelling." See Philo, *Leg.* 3.1 (Colson and Whitaker, LCL): "'And Adam and his wife hid themselves from the presence of the Lord God in the midst of the forest of the garden' (Gen. iii. 8). He introduces a doctrine showing that the bad man is an exile. For if virtue is a city peculiar to the wise, the man who has no capacity to partake of virtue has been driven away from the city, in which the bad man is incapable of taking part. It is accordingly the bad man only who has been driven away and sent into exile. But the exile from virtue has by incurring such exile hidden himself from God. For if the wise, as being His friends, are in God's sight, it is evident that all bad men slink away and hide from Him, as is to be expected in men who cherish hatred and ill-will to right reason. The prophet, moreover, finds proof that the bad man is without city or dwelling-house, in the account of Esau, the hairy man, crafty in wickedness, when he says, 'Esau was skilled in hunting, a countryman' (Gen. xxv. 27); for vice, that hunts after the passions, is by nature unfit to dwell in the city of virtue. Rather, in utter senselessness, it follows after rustic grossness, the life of the untrained. Jacob, the man full of wisdom, belongs to a city, and as a dwelling-house he occupies virtue. The prophet says of him: 'But Jacob was a simple man dwelling in a house' (ibid.). It accords with this too that the midwives, since they feared God, made houses for themselves (Exod. i. 21); for such (souls) as make a quest of God's hidden mysteries—and this is what is meant by 'saving the males' lives' or 'bringing the males to the birth'—build up the cause of virtue, and in this they have elected to have their abode. By these instances it has been made clear how the bad man is without a city or home, being an exile from virtue, while the good man has received it as his lot to have wisdom for both city and dwelling."

[114] See, for example, Martyn, *History and Theology*, 141, 150.

[115] The idea is not unique to John (see, e.g., Col 3:16: ὁ λόγος τοῦ Χριστοῦ ἐνοικείτω ἐν ὑμῖν πλουσίως ἐν πάσῃ σοφίᾳ). The same idea is present in *Odes of Solomon* 12:12: "For the dwelling place of the Word is man" (trans. Charlesworth, OTP 2:747). This composition likely shares the same milieu as the Gospel of John, possibly being written in the "Johannine School." For further observations on the shared milieu, see the chapter "The Odes of Solomon and the Gospel of John," in Charlesworth, *Jesus as Mirrored in John*, 315–39. See also the language of Sir 24:8 in which wisdom "tents" in "Jacob" (ἐν Ἰακὼβ κατασκήνωσον).

employ the typical Johannine device of double entendre.¹¹⁶ The Gospel in general is a "two-level" drama because it ostensibly narrates the life of Jesus¹¹⁷ but is simultaneously relevant for the current experience of the community, even to the point of narrating an event in the current life of the community rather than one that occurred in the distant past. The first half of the phrase (ὁ λόγος σὰρξ ἐγένετο) is clearly referring to the *einmalig* level event of the incarnation.¹¹⁸ The second half (ἐσκήνωσεν ἐν ἡμῖν) is understood as either "lived among us" referring to the *einmalig* or "lived in us" referring to the experience of the indwelling in the Johannine community.¹¹⁹ Thus, it can be viewed as operating at "two levels" because the whole phrase is able to be understood exclusively either at the *einmalig* level or at both levels of the two-level drama. So, the "in us" alternative is not meant to be an exclusive alternative, but rather the ambiguity of the phrase is important for its utility to the two-level drama.

This observation, about the two valences of 1:14, is only possible through attention to the full spectrum of dwelling imagery that pervades the Gospel. Martyn, in spite of his brilliantly subtle work, appears to have missed the subtle interpenetration of the two layers of the drama on display in John 1:14. We find here conflations not only of historical periods (the *einmalig* with that of the Johannine community) but of key spaces associated with those periods (Jesus' body/home for the λόγος with the believer's body/home for the λόγος). The latter is accomplished partly through the use of the ambiguous ἐν.

Compensatory Dwellings and Response to Trauma

While Martyn rightly recognizes some of the traumas experienced by the Johannine community, he has not fully grasped the importance of these traumas for their generative impact on the dwelling imagery of the Fourth Gospel nor for its theology generally. The aspects of these issues in the Gospel of John that require further attention and development are the "world negating" response to loss of home, the compensatory

---

[116] For instance, the narrative of John 3 is dependent on the double meaning of being born ἄνωθεν, that is, either "from above" or "again." John 4:10 turns on a misunderstanding over whether with ὕδωρ ζῶν Jesus means "running water" or "living water," that is, water that imparts supernatural life. The high priest's statement in 11:50 regarding the death of one man to save many does not in his mind mean the Christian confession, but the author has phrased his statement of pragmatic statecraft to simultaneously suggest that confession. Many other examples appear throughout the text, not least of which are the serial, plausibly innocent, Ἐγώ εἰμι statements, which, with varying degrees of subtlety, also declare the divine name (e.g., 4:26; 6:20, 35; 8:12; 10:7, 11; 11:25; 13:19; 14:6; 15:1; 18:5).

[117] And has a likely generative referent in the life of Jesus.

[118] Though even here one could argue that Jesus/ὁ λόγος becomes flesh in the current experience of the community through dwelling in the σὰρξ of the believer.

[119] That the verb ἐσκήνωσεν is aorist does not detract from the operation of the "two-level drama" here. Even if the dwelling of the Holy Spirit in the Johannine community is understood as "present" there was a point at which that reality was instantiated, which was in the past. A present verb would prevent the plausible operation of the phrase at both levels. It is also possible that the "present" aspect of the drama here could refer to the eucharist, as suggested to me by George L. Parsenios *viva voce*, but that does not obviate the likelihood of the importance of the Holy Spirit in the "present" life of the community as well.

nature of dwelling imagery in John, and the co-magnifying effect of these two phenomena on the development of Johannine sectarianism. It is clear from the Gospel that the Johannine community has experienced multiple traumas, including at the very least the departure of Jesus,[120] the excommunication from the synagogue, and the loss of the "beloved disciple." The first two of these are germane to our discussion here.

It is very clear that in the Fourth Gospel the indwelling works as a compensatory substitute for the literal, material presence of the bodily Jesus.[121] The Paraclete is a replacement in every sense for the loss of Jesus. The loss of one as important as Jesus would have been interpreted by the disciples, or the Johannine community, as just as important as the loss of a family member. Jesus had imparted to the disciples the understanding that they have been born of God (John 1:12-13) and were members of God's household (cf. 1 John 3:1-2; 5:1). The loss of Jesus as foremost member of this household was a crisis which has a clear relation to the constellation of home imagery we have been considering in this study. The incorporation into God's household that the disciples felt in the presence of Jesus would have been a vivid experience of home, the loss of which would be brutal. The sending of the Paraclete as a surrogate is a compensatory act, inaugurating new experiences of participation in God's household and of a new home.

The second trauma, the excommunication of some of the Johannine community from the synagogue, would similarly have been felt as a loss of home, both with respect to the place of the synagogue itself and the rupture to familial relations that would have occurred. And the language attributed to Jesus in the Gospel may be indicative here of the further compensatory relation of the indwelling to this additional loss. In the Farewell Discourse Jesus is portrayed as suggesting what the solution would be for him: "The hour is coming, indeed it has come, when you will be scattered, each one to his home, and you will leave me alone. Yet I am not alone because the Father is with me" (16:32). The rest of the context of the Farewell Discourse makes clear that this relation to the Father as the permanent home, accessible regardless of circumstance, is available to the believer through the indwelling.

While we may be inclined to view the compensatory dwelling language of the Gospel in an entirely valorized light, as the Gospel indicates we should, there are many problematic aspects of the phenomena of dwelling that contributed to generating this beautiful and inventive imagery.

The locus of the indwelling, that is, the individual believer as the home for the Spirit of God, indeed one of the homes of Jesus and the Father as well, becomes problematic

---

[120] Frey, *Theology and History*, 154–5: "Jesus' departure and alleged absence obviously continued to provide a source of trouble and distress for his disciples even in the post-Easter period. Thus, the farewell discourses present the lament of Jesus' disciples about his imminent departure (13:33, 36; 14:5) as an image of the tribulations and distress of the post-Easter community in view of his apparent absence. While the community of disciples is troubled by Jesus' invisibility (16:10), feels left behind as 'orphans' (14:18), and feels alone amid an unbelieving and sometimes hostile world (15:18), its most prominent aim is in providing readers with a truthful understanding about Jesus' departure, the coming of the Spirit-Paraclete, and the hope for a reunion with Jesus."

[121] For this theme as developed in the Farewell Discourse, see esp. George L. Parsenios, *Departure and Consolation: The Johannine Farewell Discourses in Light of Greco-Roman Literature*, SNT 117 (Boston: Brill, 2005).

as a dominated space. The space of the individual body, even as purported to be under the guidance of the Holy Spirit, is otherwise subject only to the whim of the individual and the controls of his or her community. To retreat into a miniature, dominated world, as Bachelard says,[122] is a comfort and is restful.[123] It is a retreat from the threatening world, but it is a simplified world that can become perilous in its own way.

An aspect of intimate worlds of retreat, literal or figurative "corners" if you will, is that the imagination they generate typically takes on a highly oppositional form with regard to the surrounding world. The corner of retreat, the place of refuge, operates, on the level of imagery, as a foil against the rest of the world. And what the refuge provides in terms of shelter, support, protection, and nourishment, it constructs in reaction and opposition to the real or imagined failings of the world outside. Thus, the compensatory home, imagined, constructed, and experienced in response to a loss of home, typically shelters a deeply negative imaginative reaction to the surrounding world. This phenomenon is certainly on display in the Gospel of John.[124]

It is strange then to see the heavy emphasis that Martyn puts on the "missional" aspects of the Johannine community[125] when so many indications suggest that it had become rather insular and sectarian by the time of the composition of the Gospel as we have it. This is certainly on display in the Letters of John (e.g., 1 John 2:15, 18-19; 3:10-16; 4:6; 2 John 10; 3 John 5). Martyn even seems to see the data, noting the "remarkable polarity of John's thought"[126] but does not connect it with the constellation of dwelling imagery. For instance, he notices that "the connection between the Eucharist and predestination [is] unmistakably clear. Basically, it is this connection which is so offensive both to 'the Jews' in the synagogue (vv. 41–59) and to 'many of the disciples' in the church (vv. 60–71)."[127] But he does not seem to recognize that these statements, which seem designed to goad those who disagreed with the community, not to welcome, evangelize, or enfold them, would likely have been produced in reaction to the trauma of losing the synagogue as a *home*.[128]

---

[122] Bachelard, *The Poetics of Space*, 161.

[123] That is to say, when it is dominated by the one resting or retreating.

[124] From John 9 alone, there is ample evidence of the phenomenon of "cornering." There is evidence of excommunication to a contingent experience outside the synagogue, but there is also a clear lack of freedom to flee, shown by the ongoing desire of attachment to the synagogue. The ability to write (the Gospel) clearly shows a new experience of protected rest for the fruition of the literary imagination, but the formation of this new "space" certainly occurred under duress, and textual clues suggest it was not the preferred dwelling or resting option nor the previous normative space of dwelling. So, logically, the new contingent space of the "cornering" of the community is implied by the text.

[125] For example, Martyn, *History and Theology*, 64, 65, 66, 67, 81, 82, 85, 90, 91.

[126] Martyn, *History and Theology*, 119.

[127] Martyn, *History and Theology*, 124.

[128] It should be noted that the Qumran community displays indications of all of these same phenomena but at a heightened level. The sectarian polemic there is even stronger. The missional impulse there is nonexistent. There are at least strong vestiges of universal interest and care for others in John. At Qumran the reactively oppositional impulse has taken hold to an almost unprecedented degree, and if we can say that there is a Qumran influence in the Johannine community, we can also at least say that it did not manifest with anywhere near the same level of hatred and separation. In John these phenomena are still, presumably, moderated somewhat by the kerygma.

Interestingly, Martyn's emphasis on the importance of "Son of Man" traditions, if developed further, points to the connection between these issues. He notes that the Son of Man traditions highlight the two-level drama, that is, the historical anachronism; they also highlight the spatial conundrums[129] which are ultimately resolved, in Martyn's mind, by the indwelling. However, it is the very use of the Son of Man traditions as carried forward in the Paraclete that suggest the relevance of the Johannine dwelling imagery to the ubiquitous polemical language reserved in the Gospel for "the world."

One of the key roles of the Son of Man is as judge of the world.[130] The Paraclete, as the ongoing representative of Jesus, "somehow"[131] continues his "[law]suit with the world,"[132] judging it for rejection of Jesus and his Gospel. However, it is this very felt-operation of the Paraclete within the believer through the indwelling that contributes to the freedom with which the author of John judges the world.[133] As the Paraclete dwells in the believer, the believer becomes the agential locus of the judgment function of the Son of Man! Thus, the retreat from the home of the synagogue to the compensatory dwelling with God made possible by the Paraclete actually serves to encourage the vituperative judgment of the Johannine believers against those who caused their excommunication. The imagination of a compensatory dwelling fueled a pejorative and oppositional response to the outside world. There seems little remaining sense of mission. The community is opposed to those outside it (2 John 10). In the epistles, the love command is reserved for brothers, not extended to all (1 John 3:10-11, 14, 16; 1 John 4:6; 3 John 5). This phenomenon as it appears in the Gospel simply constitutes a normative operation of the human imagination of dwelling when confronted with a loss of home and retreat to a "corner."[134] In opting for the flexible compensatory dwelling imagery of the indwelling the Johannine community may have proleptically heeded the wisdom of Bachelard when he wrote, "It is better to live in a state of impermanence than in one of finality,"[135] but in so doing, they confidently consigned their foes to the finality of their judgment.

---

[129] For example, Martyn, *History and Theology*, 129–30: "At first glance it might seem that the Christology of the drama is a rather 'low' one. If the part of Jesus can be acted on the contemporary level by persons in John's church, then the church's Lord would scarcely appear to be an unapproachable figure who dwells outside the world of men. On the other hand, one might say that the Christology of the two-level drama, like that of John's Gospel as a whole, is quite 'high,' and that it is precisely the movement from the *einmalig* level of the drama to its contemporary level which makes it so. Jesus' identity is not an issue which can be decided by asking who he was. Quite the contrary. He is *present*, and he makes his presence known by pronouncing an extremely high Christological claim: 'I am the bread of life ... come down from heaven'" (6:35, 38). Emphasis original.

[130] As seen in, for example, the *Parables of Enoch*; Matt 16:27; 19:28; 25:31-46; Mark 8:38; Luke 9:26; 21:34-46; John 5:27; Rev 1:12-18.

[131] Martyn, *History and Theology*, 141.

[132] Martyn, *History and Theology*, 145.

[133] Martyn misses this point.

[134] Bachelard, *The Poetics of Space*, 143: "The dreamer in his [or her] corner wrote off the world in a detailed daydream that destroyed, one by one, all the objects of the world."

[135] Bachelard, *The Poetics of Space*, 61.

Conclusion

The fact that the Gospel is dripping with home imagery suggests that a psychology of dwelling is a dominant shaping force in the Gospel and would explain why not only spatial but historical conflation is pervasive. It also serves to explain the oppositional and judgmental sectarian theology of reaction against "the world" that pervades the Gospel. Martyn, in attributing to the Paraclete the solution to the various conundrums of the two-level drama, highlighted a key element of the generative background. But in neglecting the full constellation of home imagery present in the Gospel,[136] the "ecology" if you will, he missed the signposts pointing to the phenomenologies of dwelling that are jointly and severally responsible for much of the shape of the Gospel as we have it today. This Gospel, more than any other, employs vivid images to communicate. Is it any wonder then that the so-called "history" that appears in the Gospel seems to act in service to the images employed?[137] Nevertheless, an awareness of the importance of spatial imagery does not invalidate "history" in the Gospel, as "theological" interpretations[138] of it have been want to do, but rather help place its role and validity appropriately. Among these vivid recurring images of light, bread, and living water can certainly be counted the compelling images of "dwelling" in all their manifestations. These images, and the phenomena lying behind them, have shaped the current form of the Gospel perhaps even more than the aforementioned, better-known images. And while, with Bachelard, we may find warning in the statement that a "dreamer of houses sees them everywhere, and anything can act as a germ to set him [or her] dreaming about them,"[139] hopefully in this instance of analysis of the Fourth Gospel, we can, with Alexander Pushkin, rather say: "Il vaut mieux avoir rêvé mille rêves qui ne se sont jamais réalisés que de n'avoir jamais rêvés."[140]

---

[136] In attempting to show this I hope I have, with Bachelard (*The Poetics of Space*, 29), "retained the coalescence of images that refuse an absolute anatomy."

[137] Rather than vice versa. See Bachelard, *The Poetics of Space*, 33: "Great images have both a history and a pre-history; they are always a blend of memory and legend, with the result that we never experience an image directly. Indeed, every great image has an unfathomable depth to which the personal past adds special color. Consequently, it is not until late in life that we really revere an image, when we discover that its roots plunge well beyond the history that is fixed in our memories ... [into] the realm of absolute imagination."

[138] There are too many commentators to list who, throughout history, have suggested that the Johannine emphasis is not "historical" but rather "theological" or "spiritual." In antiquity, we know this from as early as Clement of Alexandria. In modernity, some who have emphasized this perspective include David Flusser (*Jesus*, trans. R. Walls [New York: Herder and Herder, 1969], esp. 7–8), Geza Vermes (*The Passion* [New York: Penguin, 2006], esp. 130–2), and Joseph Klausner (*Jesus of Nazareth*, trans. H. Danby [New York: Macmillan, 1944], 125). Even as we may be able to say with Ferdinand C. Baur (*Kritische Untersuchungen über die kanonischen Evangelien* [Tübingen: F. L. Fues, 1847], 137–8) that the Fourth Gospel is not "a strictly historical gospel" it does not mean that there is no history. But as we have seen, these categories are not entirely helpful and must be expanded to include the influence of spatial hermeneutics. The importance of vivid imagery can suggest the subversion of historical concerns to spatial ones. Much of the language in the Gospel that has in the past been regarded as indicating a "theological," "spiritual," or "mystical" emphasis can more accurately be described as "spatial."

[139] Bachelard, *The Poetics of Space*, 55.

[140] At least, this saying is typically attributed to Alexander Pushkin, though I cannot discover the original source.

2

Space Matters for Scripture and Ecology Matters for Space: Critical Observations from John 4

The Samaritan Interlude in the Gospel of John has often been taken as ground zero for mooting the significance of space in the Christian tradition[1] (particularly the verses "you will worship the Father neither on this mountain nor in Jerusalem ... [and] God is spirit, and those who worship him must worship in spirit and truth" [John 4:21, 24]). Origen, for one, in linking his interpretation of this passage to 1 Kgs 19, suggested that God is not to be found in any created thing or place. Many other commentators have taken some kind of similar, physical space-devaluing approach,[2] whether they argue for a largely symbolic significance to place in the Gospel,[3] or for heavenly derivation and world condemnation as the primary valence,[4] or for transferring to Jesus all

---

[1] Many early interpreters of John 4 set the tone for such an approach including Ambrose, *Spir.* 3.11.82 in NPNF 2 10:146: "He does not abide, indeed, as a body in a body, for God is not a body"; Origen, *Princ.* 1.1.4-5, in ANF 4:243: "the Savior answered that anyone who would follow the Lord must lay aside all preference for particular places"; Theodore of Mopsuestia, *Commentary on John* 2 4.23-24, in CSCO 4 3:91: "God is of an incorporeal nature and cannot be circumscribed into any one place. Rather, he is everywhere, and it is necessary that he be worshiped according to this understanding"; Hilary of Poitiers, *On the Trinity* 2.31, in NPNF 2 9:60-61: "For the Spirit cannot be shut up, as if in a cabin, or confined. It is omnipresent in space and time, and under all conditions it is present in its fullness. Therefore he said that they are the true worshipers who shall worship in the Spirit and in truth."

[2] Among both philosophical theologians such as Thomas Aquinas in *Summa Theologiae* 1a.8.3 or Anselm of Canterbury in *Monologion* 20 and among ancient commentators on John such as Heracleon and Origen. For a good discussion of their allegorical interpretation of the spiritual nature of spatial data, see Elaine Pagels, *The Johannine Gospel in Gnostic Exegesis: Herecleon's Commentary on John*, SBLMS (Nashville: Abingdon, 1973).

[3] R. H. Lightfoot, *St. John's Gospel: A Commentary* (Oxford: Clarendon Press, 1956); Wayne Meeks, "Galilee and Judea in the Fourth Gospel," *JBL* 85.2 (1966): 159-69; Robert Fortna, "Theological Use of Locale in the Fourth Gospel," *ATRSup* 3 (1974): 95-112; Jouette Bassler, "The Galileans: A Neglected Factor in Johannine Community Research," *CBQ* 43 (1981): 243-57; Jerome Neyrey, "Spaces and Places, Whence and Whither, Homes and Rooms," in *The Gospel of John in Cultural and Rhetorical Perspective*, ed. Jerome Neyrey (Grand Rapids, MI: Eerdmans, 2009), 58-84.

[4] R. Bultmann, *The Gospel of John: A Commentary*, trans. G. Beasley-Murray, R. W. N. Hoare, and J. K. Riches (Philadelphia: Westminster, 1971); Leander Keck, "Derivation as Destiny: 'Of-ness' in Johannine Christology, Anthropology, and Soteriology," in *Exploring the Gospel of John*, eds. R. Alan Culpepper and C. Clifton Black (Louisville, KY: Westminster/John Knox, 1996), 274-88.

the significance of particular places.⁵ There is, however, a good deal of data in the Samaritan Interlude that militates against the kind of sweeping, overgeneralized, and over-spiritualized interpretations of space that appear in both early Christian theology and modern critical study that lean too far toward a theological "transparency" of space. John 4, rather, may be taken as an example of a subtler and materially oriented spatial practice, and a useful pericope for analysis and discussion of early Jewish/Christian literary spatial practice.

A key initial question is whether the Samaritan Interlude preserves any historical residue of Jesus' activity in Samaria.⁶ Does this pericope represent a Samaritan perspective, possibly indicating that John affirms experiences of Jesus beyond the Jewish one?⁷ It has been well established that John's Gospel preserves accurate material knowledge of the Palestinian terrain and built-environment from the first century CE.⁸ But many interpreters have struggled with whether the story of John 4 is largely mythic (as far back among modern interpreters as David Fredrich Strauss).⁹ If the Samaritan Interlude is largely mythic how is this geographic data to be interpreted? Karl Kundsin[10] believed it hearkened back to the concerns of the local communities from which the gospel stories arose—that is, in this case, Samaritan ones. Further, even if the story is largely mythic, J. L. Martyn's landmark observations on the social location of the later Johannine community for interpretation of the Gospel as a whole suggest that we must at least consider the possibility of a social location among a later "Samaritan" cohort as the generative background for John 4 even if we ultimately dismiss it.[11]

The text of the Samaritan Interlude is indeed not marked by all the same spatial language and emphases that appear prominently in much of the rest of the Gospel. There is comparatively little derivation language,[12] ascent and descent language, or

---

⁵ W. D. Davies, *The Gospel and the Land: Early Christianity and Jewish Territorial Doctrine* (Berkeley: University of California Press, 1974); Gary Burge, *Jesus and the Land: The New Testament Challenge to "Holy Land" Theology* (Grand Rapids: Baker Academic, 2010); Richard Hays, *Reading Backwards: Figural Christology and the Fourfold Gospel Witness* (Waco, TX: Baylor University Press, 2014); C. H. Dodd, *Interpretation of the Fourth Gospel* (Cambridge: Cambridge University Press, 1968); Raymond Brown, *The Gospel According to John*, Vols. 1 and 2 (Garden City, NY: Doubleday, 1966 and 1970).

⁶ Particularly at the *einmalig* level, which is to say that "unique" to the life and ministry of Jesus, to use Martyn's terminology from *History and Theology in the Fourth Gospel*, 2nd ed. (Nashville, TN: Abingdon, 1979).

⁷ A Samaritan spatial practice if you will.

⁸ James H. Charlesworth, "Can Archaeology Help Us See Jesus' Shadows in the Gospel of John?" in *Jesus Research: The Gospel of John in Historical Inquiry*, eds. James H. Charlesworth with Jolyon G. R. Pruszinski (London: T&T Clark, 2019), 168–86; John M. Vonder Bruegge, *Mapping Galilee in Josephus, Luke, and John: Critical Geography and the Construction of an Ancient Space*, Ancient Judaism and Early Christianity 93 (Leiden and Boston: Brill, 2017); Urban C. von Wahlde, *The Gospel and Letters of John*, Vol. 2 (Grand Rapids, MI: Eerdmans, 2010); Shimon Gibson, *The Final Days of Jesus: The Archaeological Evidence* (New York: HarperCollins, 2010).

⁹ See David Friedrich Strauss, *The Life of Jesus Critically Examined*, ed. Peter C. Hodgson, trans. George Eliot (Philadelphia: Fortress, 1972), 308.

¹⁰ Karl Kundsin, *Topologische Überlieferungsstoffe in Johannes-Evangelium* (Göttingen: Dandenhoek and Ruprecht, 1925).

¹¹ If the Samaritan option there fails, the Johannine community remains a possibly fruitful interpretive milieu.

¹² The language of "derivation as destiny" is explored in Leander Keck, "Derivation as Destiny," 274–88.

dualistic cosmological language.[13] If, as Urban von Wahlde and many others believe,[14] a core of John 4 belongs to one of the earliest strata of the Gospel, then does it preserve a spatial practice that differs from those generated by the social location of the Johannine community itself? A spatial-critical reading of the text brings out the distinctive emphases and key facets of the spatial practice present in the Samaritan Interlude. Evaluation of a possible Samaritan *einmalig*[15] event or later Samaritan social location as the generative impetus behind this text then requires that we first determine whether the data in the Samaritan Interlude are indeed derived from Samaritans. At first blush, things do not look so sanguine for that possibility.

We will begin with an analysis of the plausibility of either an *einmalig* Samaritan experience or a later Samaritan social location behind the spatial practice of John 4, concluding that the data from the Samaritan Interlude suggest that the story may not be, in fact, significantly Samaritan in origin.[16] This indicates that attention to "spatial practice," that is, how the "social practice" of the author's own community is inscribed on the spaces of the text, is necessary. We will continue with a consideration of the implications of the possible generative background in the largely Jewish Johannine community, considering the following key questions related to the utility of "spatial practice" to our larger project. Does attention to the possible spatial practice of the Johannine community allow the common interpretive conclusion that Jesus is supplanting the Temple according to John 4? Does consideration of spatial practice from the perspective of the Johannine community allow any possible conclusions regarding the proper interpretation of the "mythic" outlines of the well-meeting narrative? Is space really spiritualized or mythicized, and if not, how does material space continue to matter? These analyses will indicate the importance of domestic and quotidian space as an "ecogenic"[17] background to the texts in question and the most important aspect of analysis of spatial practice.

Samaritan in Name Only: Spatial Language and Spatial Practice

Beginning with a hodological[18] analysis, we are told early in the pericope that Jesus, upon leaving Judea for Galilee, "had to pass through Samaria" (4:4). On its face, this

---

[13] These latter two categories have been highlighted by Bultmann as "gnostic."
[14] Full documentation of the major positions on what portions of chapter 4 belong to which redactional stages appears in Teresa Okure, *The Johannine Approach to Mission: A Contextual Study of John 4.1–42*, WUNT 2/31 (Tübingen: Mohr Siebeck, 1988), Tables 1a-1b, 61–2. See also von Wahlde, *The Gospel and Letters of John*, 2:176-92 (pre-Johannine stratum: John 4:1-3 [minus vv. 1a, 2], 4-9, 16-18, 25-30, 39; second stratum: 4:10-15, 19-24, 31-34; third stratum: 4:1a, 2, 35-38[?], 40-42).
[15] That is, a "unique" or "singular" event, employing the usage of J. L. Martyn from *History and Theology in the Fourth Gospel*, meaning an event dating to the life of the historical Jesus.
[16] Pace M.-É. Boismard, *Moses or Jesus*, trans. B. T. Viviano (Minneapolis: Fortress, 1993).
[17] Literally, "oikogenic." For the employment of this term in a similar but somewhat less literal manner, see Kenneth Maly, "*A Sand County Almanac*: Through Anthropogenic to Ecogenic Thinking," in *Rethinking Nature: Essays in Environmental Philosophy*, eds. Bruce V. Foltz and Robert Frodeman (Bloomington, IN: Indiana University Press, 2004), 291.
[18] That is, an analysis of route.

is geographically false. There were several routes between Judea and Galilee. The mountain path through Samaria was only one.[19] Jesus is apparently coming from Aenon near Salim (3:23), where he was baptizing.[20] This location has not been definitively agreed upon, but the best candidates are a site just southwest of Scythopolis and a site near where the Jordan River enters the Dead Sea.[21] Neither of these sites require travel through Samaria to reach Cana (4:46) and certainly not the extra thousands of vertical feet climbed and descended and many extra miles of circuitous travel required to pass by the foot of Mt. Gerizim.[22] Certainly, this fact would preclude the

Figure 2.1 The Lower Jordan Valley from the Western Highlands. (Photograph from the G. Eric and Edith Matson Collection titled "Road to Jericho, Jordan, etc. The Jordan Valley from Monastery of Quarantana." Used with permission. Edited for publication.)

[19] There is excellent archaeological evidence from well before 70 CE for a robust Roman road from Scythopolis to Tiberias as detailed in James H. Charlesworth and Mordechai Aviam, "Reconstructing First Century Galilee: Reflections on Ten Major Problems," in *Jesus Research: New Methodologies and Perceptions, The Second Princeton-Prague Symposium on Jesus Research, Princeton 2007*, eds. James H. Charlesworth, with Brian Rhea, and Petr Pokorný (Grand Rapids, MI and London: Eerdmans, 2014), 114. For documentation of another north–south road between Legio (near Megiddo) and Sepphoris, see Mordechai Aviam, "Two Roman Roads in the Galilee," in *Jews, Pagans, and Christians in the Galilee*, Land of Galilee 1 (Rochester, NY: University of Rochester Press, 2004), 133–8.

[20] Or "not" baptizing, according to the likely emendation at 4:2.

[21] von Wahlde, *The Gospel and Letters of John*, 2:151.

[22] Even the fact that Cana (4:46) was likely in the Galilean interior does not require a journey through Samaria. Any journey to Cana from "Aenon" that went through Sychar (4:5) could not possibly be viewed as a necessity according to topographic realities. One simply does not add an unnecessary and strenuous loop southwest to Sychar (assuming a location for Aenon just south of Scythopolis) and then northwards again back in the direction of Cana, including a 2500-foot climb and twenty-mile traverse through mountainous terrain (assuming either location for Aenon).

description of the journey accurately representing the geography of an *einmalig* event and the discrepancy would have been obvious to any Samaritans if they were present in the Johannine community. Many interpreters have solved this difficulty by stating that the requirement was theological or missiological, not geographic.[23] However, the appearance of very similar wording in Josephus (*Vita* 52)[24] for a particular route between Jerusalem and Galilee (not from Judea generally or Aenon near Salim in particular) suggests that what is presented here is a Judean literary trope, or a Jewish imagined geography, regarding the relationship between Judea and Galilee, not necessarily a report of the actual itinerary of an *einmalig*-level journey on foot.[25]

The problems for defending an actual Samaritan event or social location for our text mount as we move through it. The location of the meeting outside "Sychar" (Συχὰρ) is also difficult, as record of such a town in antiquity is not well established.[26] The possibility of a Judean slang name for Shechem as "Sychar," that is, connoting "drunkenness,"[27] has been raised by many interpreters and seems not unlikely here.

The subsequent statement that "Jews have no dealings with Samaritans" (4:9) is remarkably restrained and neutral, nigh euphemistic, given the history of internecine conflict between these two branches of Israel,[28] but the moral tropes in the rest of the story suggest a generally negative stereotype of Samaritans.[29] The woman in the story

---

[23] For example, Lightfoot who suggests that John is the Gospel writer most likely to subvert physical topographic realities for doctrinal purposes. See R. H. Lightfoot, *Locality and Doctrine in the Gospels* (London: Hodder & Stoughton, 1938), 145.

[24] "It was essential to take that route, by which Jerusalem may be reached in three days from Galilee" (*Vita* 52 [Thackeray, LCL]). John 4:4 reads:"Ἔδει δὲ αὐτὸν διέρχεσθαι διὰ τῆς Σαμαρείας while *Vita* 52.269 reads ἔδει τοὺς ταχὺ βουλομένους ἀπελθεῖν δι' ἐκείνης πορεύεσθαι· τρισὶν [γὰρ] ἡμέραις ἀπὸ Γαλιλαίας ἔνεστιν οὕτως εἰς Ἱεροσόλυμα καταλῦσαι.

[25] Though an actual historical journey may have occurred, the phrasing according to a Judean geographic trope suggests a Judean provenance for the story.

[26] U. C. von Wahlde, *The Gospel and Letters of John*, 2:170, notes this, as does John Lightfoot, *A Commentary on the New Testament from the Talmud and Hebraica, Vol. 1: Place Names in the Gospels*, trans. John Strype (Peabody, MA: Hendricksen, 1997), 358–9. Jerome corrects Sychar to Shechem in his Gospel texts (e.g., *Epistles* 108.16) because he thought it was a scribal error and knew of no actual village by that name. Brown makes this correction as well (*The Gospel According to John*, 1:169) in spite of the overwhelming manuscript evidence in favor of Συχὰρ. Jörg Frey (*Theology and History in the Fourth Gospel: Tradition and Narration* [Waco, TX: Baylor University Press, 2018], 107) indicates that this is the first historic attestation of "Sychar" for this location. Codices *Syrus Curetonianus* and *Syrus Sinaiticus* present Συχεμ.

[27] This idea relies on the association of Samaria with "Ephraim" as portrayed in Isa 28, which repeatedly mentions the "drunkards [שכרי]" of Ephraim" and their associated debauchery. John Ashton, *Understanding the Fourth Gospel*, 2nd ed. (Oxford: Oxford University Press, 2007), 99, notes semantically similar epithets for the "foolish people who dwell in Shechem" (in Sir 50: 25-6) and Shechem itself as the "'City of the Senseless' (πόλις ἀσυνέτων)" in T. Levi 7:2.

[28] One could argue that this aside is a later insertion to aid the understanding of gentile believers of an otherwise rather impenetrably Jewish (or Judean) text.

[29] Negative portrayals of Samaria appear throughout 1 and 2 Kings, 2 Chronicles, Isa 7–10, Isa 36, and in several others of the prophets. Jeremiah 23:13 is illustrative: "In the prophets of Samaria I saw a disgusting thing: they prophesied by Baal and led my people Israel astray." Samaria has such a connotation of wickedness that it is used for obvious rhetorical effect in Ezek 16. In 1 Macc 3 Samaria is depicted as having opposed the rebellion of Judas Maccabeus. In 4 Bar 8 an etiology of Samaria appears, suggesting that Samaria was founded by those returning exiles who refused to

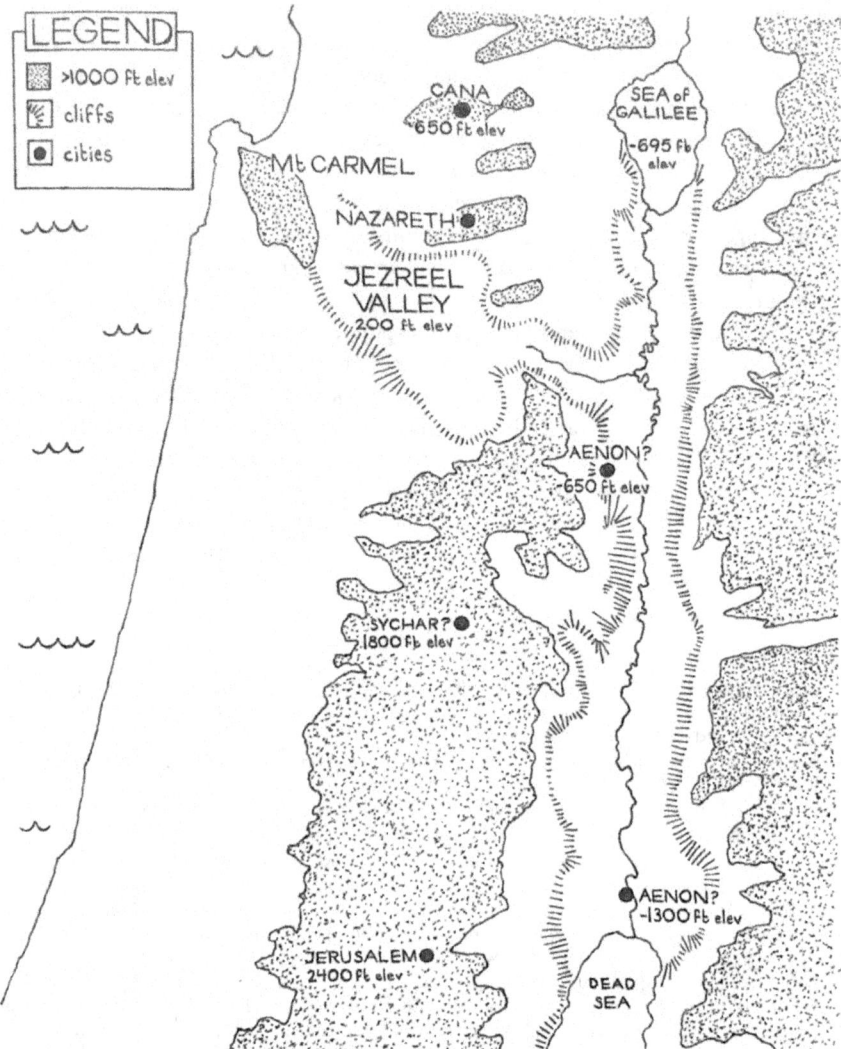

Figure 2.2 Topography of the Jordan Valley and Samaria. (Artist's rendering by K. N. Pruszinski. Used with permission.)

abandon their Babylonian spouses. The portrayal of Samaritans in Luke—the Gospel most likely to have been written by a non-Jew—is instructive. In 9:52-54 Luke writes: "On their way they entered a village of the Samaritans to make ready for [Jesus]; but they did not receive him … When his disciples James and John saw it, they said, 'Lord, do you want us to command fire to come down from heaven and consume them?'" The parable of the Good Samaritan (Luke 10:25-37) is similarly dependent on an understanding of this animosity. In John 8:48 those opposing Jesus say, "Are we not right in saying that you are a Samaritan and have a demon?" Obviously, both of these things are considered to be bad.

is the representative Samaritan. She is portrayed as approaching a place without the protection of fellow women or kinsfolk and conversing with a strange man alone. Either of these actions would have been viewed as socially unacceptable at the time.[30] The estrangement or separation evident in the time of the well meeting further emphasizes disrepute.[31] The subsequent revelation of the woman's marital history and status (4:17-18) amplifies this negative stereotype of Samaria.[32] The further past tense[33] statement that "our fathers *worshiped* on this mountain" (4:20), that is, Gerizim, suggests a view that worship was defunct at this cultic site in Samaria after the desecration of Gerizim by John Hyrcanus[34] in the second century BCE. This is in line with a Jewish polemical (anti-Samaritan) view on the subject,[35] as opposed to a Samaritan position, as it appears[36] worship continued, at least periodically, on the site after its desecration.[37] Beyond these issues, it strains credulity that the word of a woman, whose actions and history are couched as they are, would have been immediately and unquestioningly received by other Samaritans (4:30, 39-42).[38] Further, the Samaritan woman employs Jewish language when she speaks of the Μεσσίας (4:25) and, surprisingly, does not protest to Jesus' statement that ἡ σωτηρία ἐκ τῶν Ἰουδαίων ἐστίν.[39]

This brief outline of some of the main points of issue suggests that the text as we have it now seems to preserve more a stereotyped Jewish view of Samaritans and Samaria than a view that Samaritans would have themselves affirmed, a rather good example of Edward Said's "Imaginative Geography." According to such a geography, "other" groups are presented as exotic and different, and are typically only used as a literary device to further the ends of the author with the author's audience.[40] This observation is buttressed by the fact that according to the most prominent redactional analyses of the pericope, from von Wahlde back to Bultmann, the earliest core of the text, the

---

[30] The author of Sirach warns in Sir 26:9-12 that "the haughty stare betrays an unchaste wife … As a thirsty traveler opens his mouth and drinks from any water near him, so she will sit in front of every tent peg and open her quiver to the arrow."

[31] Normal water-drawing would occur communally and either early or late in the day, temporally removed from the heat of the sun. It is possible, however, that the timing indicates a counterpoint to Nicodemus' coming at night. Nevertheless, in both instances the timing allows for separation/privacy of interaction and is a temporal statement indicating a spatial and social reality.

[32] Even this "unfaithful" portrayal is a typical metaphorical literary trope to represent those who diverge from true worship of God, language that is often applied by Judeans to Samaritans. On "Samaritan" as just such an insult, see Bultmann, *The Gospel of John*, 299 n. 4.

[33] προσεκύνησαν is aorist active indicative, third plural.

[34] According to Josephus, *Ant.* 13.3.4, but according to b. Yoma 69a it was Simeon the Just.

[35] As is clear in Josephus' portrayals of purported Samaritan attempts to desecrate the Jerusalem Temple and attack Jewish pilgrims: *Ant.* 18.2.2, 20.6.1.

[36] See the collection of teachings from the Babylonian Talmud in *Masechtot Qetanot Kutim* (*De Samaritanis*). See also James H. Charlesworth, *Jesus as Mirrored in John: The Genius in the New Testament* (London: T&T Clark, 2018), xii, 47–8.

[37] Some archaeologists do not think the site ever actually held a Samaritan temple building per se but was rather a dedicated location of worship. For example, Robert T. Anderson, "The Elusive Samaritan Temple," *Biblical Archaeologist* 54.2 (1991): 104–7.

[38] This reception seems oriented toward interpreting the positive valence to the whole story, as opposed to the ambiguous (or negative) valence to the Nicodemus story.

[39] "Salvation is from the Jews." See also Frey, *Theology and History*, 32.

[40] Edward Said, *Orientalism* (New York: Vintage, 1979), 49–72.

"pre-Johannine *Vorlage*," appears to have largely mythic outlines.[41] Both the Hebrew Bible literary precedents for well meetings[42] and the woman's rather outlandish serial marital history—the perfect seventh man [husband] in line is clearly implied to be Jesus[43]—suggest that, even when stripped to its most basic elements, the main components of the story suggest genesis neither from a Samaritan *einmalig* event nor social location.[44]

The Samaritan Interlude and the Johannine Community

So, if, in attending to the spatial data of John 4, we cannot with confidence look back to a Samaritan *einmalig* event or social location for the genesis of the Samaritan Interlude, we

---

[41] See von Wahlde's *The Gospel and Letters of John*, 2:176-84, 191-96, and Okure, *The Johannine Approach to Mission*, 61.

[42] In two important instances a marginalized woman experiences a kind of saving theophany. Hagar is met by an angel of the Lord at a spring/well in Gen 16 when she is fleeing the harsh treatment of Sarah. Hagar names the well "well of the living one who sees me." Later, in chapter 21 of Genesis, an angel of the Lord speaks to Hagar at another well when she is in distress, having been cast out of the household of Abraham. She is delivered through this encounter. In three instances a marriage results from a meeting at a well. The relation between these texts and the Gospel of John is so significant that Jocelyn McWhirter refers to the phenomenon as a "tumult of reverberations." See Jocelyn McWhirter, *The Bridegroom Messiah and the People of God: Marriage in the Fourth Gospel*, SNTS Monograph 138 (Cambridge: Cambridge University Press, 2006), 4. In Gen 24 Abraham's servant meets Rebekah at a well and procures her as a wife for Isaac. The intertextual echoes here were noted as early as Origen in *Hom. Gen.* 10.5, in *Homilies on Genesis and Exodus*, trans. Ronald E. Heine, FC 71 (Washington, DC: The Catholic University of America Press, 1982), 167. In Gen 29 Jacob meets his wife-to-be Rachel at a well. In Exod 2 Moses meets his wife-to-be Zipporah at a well in Midian. Origen notes echoes in John 4 with these other two well-meeting-leading-to-marriage texts as well. See Origen, *Comm. Jo.* 13.175-78, in *Commentary on the Gospel According to John: Books 13–32*, trans. Ronald E. Heine, FC 89 (Washington, DC: The Catholic University of America Press, 1993), 105–6. To these add Songs 4:13-15, which suggests, discretely in the NRSV, that the lover's "channel is ... a garden fountain, a well of living water." The sexual connotation is present in other passages as well, including Prov 5:15 in which the reader is exhorted to "drink water from [his] own cistern, flowing water from [his] own well" and Prov 23:26 that notes that "a prostitute is a deep pit; an adulteress is a narrow well." Similarly, the author of Sirach warns in Sir 26:9-12 that "the haughty stare betrays an unchaste wife ... As a thirsty traveler opens his mouth and drinks from any water near him, so she will sit in front of every tent peg and open her quiver to the arrow." From this non-exhaustive catalog, it is clear that even those with the faintest of familiarity with the broad outlines of the cherished stories of the patriarchs would recognize the significance of a man meeting a woman at a well. The clear implication is that marriage may result. Those with a closer knowledge of the scriptures would certainly note the perilous sexual implications of the meeting. The connotation is quite clear from the outset but becomes inescapably so as the woman's history becomes known. Many commentators recognize this wayward valence including R. Alan Culpepper, *Anatomy of the Fourth Gospel: A Study in Literary Design* (Philadelphia: Fortress, 1983), 136, and George L. Parsenios, "Jesus and Divine Adaptability in Chrysostom's Interpretation of John 4," in *Jesus Research: New Methodologies and Perceptions, The Second Princeton-Prague Symposium on Jesus Research, Princeton 2007*, eds. James H. Charlesworth, with Brian Rhea and Petr Pokorný (Grand Rapids, MI and London: Eerdmans, 2014), 868.

[43] Many interpreters come to this conclusion including Mary L. Coloe, *God Dwells with Us: Temple Symbolism in the Fourth Gospel* (Collegeville, MN: The Liturgical Press, 2001), 99.

[44] Ben Witherington, III, *John's Wisdom: A Commentary on the Fourth Gospel* (Louisville, KY: Westminster John Knox Press, 1995), 119: "Here is a narrative loaded with artistic skill and irony, which Jewish listeners especially were likely to appreciate because of its echoes of early stories and ideas from the Hebrew scriptures .... It is, then, a story not about Samaritans as examples of Christian faith, or Samaritans who have joined the Johannine community."

must consider the social location of the Johannine community[45] as evidenced elsewhere in the Gospel of John and as described, in broad-brush strokes, by J. L. Martyn[46] and Wayne Meeks in their respective works *History and Theology in the Fourth Gospel* and "The Man from Heaven in Johannine Sectarianism."[47] This is to say, in interpreting the spatial data of the Samaritan Interlude, we must attend to a particular Jewish-Christian spatial practice.[48] We must look at how a small, sectarian Jewish community that has experienced rejection from the broader Jewish community on account of belief in Jesus envisions and constructs space. We must look at how a community which believes it has experienced the indwelling of the Holy Spirit is able to conflate its own experience of God with that of the time of Jesus' physical earthly ministry. We must look at what spaces had been most crucial to that community's history and how those relate to the spaces of its own experience at the time of the composition of the Gospel. The aforementioned anachronisms of the text highlight these. This is what is called "reflexive space" by Rush Rehm in his spatial analysis of Greek dramas: *The Play of Space*, but is simply another way of referring to textual ecology.[49]

For a Jewish Christian in the Johannine community there were many important experiences of space that must be considered in order to interpret properly the spaces present in the Gospel.[50] Some of the most important spaces in this context (not in any particular order) would seem to be Judea (e.g., 3:22),[51] the body (e.g., 2:21; 19:38-40), the home (e.g., 14:23), one's own community,[52] the common public living spaces in

---

[45] As concluded by John Ashton, *Understanding the Fourth Gospel*, 99, even as he still thinks that the background is in an experience of the Johannine community with a Samaritan mission.

[46] I recognize that many scholars of late have questioned the accuracy of Martyn's reconstruction of a Jamnia decision against Jewish Christians and the use of the *Birkat Ha-Minim*, being skeptical of the ability to reconstruct a defensible history of this proposed event. Other scholars have eschewed Martyn's conclusions due to concerns either to preserve the "history" of the ostensible account of Jesus' life presented in the Gospel or to focus on the narratological unity of the Gospel. In spite of these protests, I am convinced that the broad outlines of Martyn's thesis hold. As previously mentioned, Joel Marcus, "*Birkat Ha-Minim* Revisited," *NTS* 55 (2009): 523–51, is of this opinion and his historical arguments have not been refuted or even meaningfully challenged.

[47] Wayne A. Meeks, "The Man from Heaven in Johannine Sectarianism," *JBL* 91.1 (1972): 44–72.

[48] Not only because it is likely the same as that at work in the rest of the Gospel, but for the simple reason that what Martyn and Meeks suggest as the primary proper interpretive approach for the Gospel as a whole is identical to that prescribed by Lefebvre for interpretation of spatial literary data: the social experience of the community is inscribed in its spatial language. That is an aspect of its spatial practice.

[49] Rush Rehm, *The Play of Space: Spatial Transformation in Greek Tragedy* (Princeton: Princeton University Press, 2002), 23–4.

[50] As previously mentioned, a useful tool for thinking through these kinds of issues is what is sometimes known in social-science circles as the "gravity model," developed most famously in William J. Reilly, *The Law of Retail Gravitation* (New York: Knickerbocker Press, 1931). In gravitational theory, the more massive two objects are, or the closer they are, the greater is the force of attraction between them. It is even so with the social-science gravity model: the more populated two cities are, or the closer they are, the more travel will be made between them. The gravity model thus explains the relative importance of relationships. This idea relates to understanding the spatial practice in our text in the following way: the more important, or the closer together, two spaces are, the more relationship they will have. And while the gravity model clearly does not allow for scientific precision in literary application, the principles are nevertheless instructive.

[51] Or the homeland.

[52] This particular location has not been definitively identified.

that community, the synagogue (e.g., 9:22; 12:42; 16:2; 18:20), the temple (e.g., 2:14-21; 5:14; 7:28; 8:2; 10:23; 18:20), and heaven (e.g., 1:32, 51; 3:13, 6:22-59; 17:1). The interpretation of each of *the spaces present in the text* must be performed predominantly in relation to *the important spaces of the life of the Johannine community* and secondarily to spaces less relevant to the community. Less important spaces must be interpreted in light of the important spaces, even if those important spaces do not appear particularly proximate[53] in a given text (for instance, Judean concerns in an ostensibly Samaritan passage).[54] The clear history of interconnection[55] of many of the above listed spaces in Jewish and Christian writings supports the validity of this approach to interpretation.

The Temple and the Body: The Primacy of Quotidian Space

A few main points will suffice to establish the importance of attending to these experiential domestic and quotidian (ecological) factors as significant shaping influences of Johannine spatial practice. Firstly, it is regularly argued,[56] usually in the

---

[53] Rehm's "extrascenic space." In Rehm, *The Play of Space*, 20-1: This is space "lying immediately offstage, behind and contiguous to the façade." This space is assumed in the narrative without always being explicit.

[54] Eternal realities/spaces theoretically outweigh temporally fleeting realities/spaces but do not obviate them. Our understanding of these, largely imagined, spaces is based almost entirely on our lived experiences of material space. Further, all the spaces in our text have become "eternal" and important by their very inclusion in the scripture.

[55] Sometimes even conflation or synonymy. Clearly the Hebrew Bible and New Testament are rife with language of the Temple as the "house" of God. Similarly, the idea of the body as a temple was increasingly commonplace in this period (e.g., John 2:21; 1 Cor 6:19). A cursory examination of Philo's works suggests close relationships between these various spaces including language of one's village or city as equated with home: *Sacr.* 5.32, *Gig.* 15.67, *Her.* 58.287, *Somn.* 1.8.45-46, *Abr.* 18.85-86, *Flacc.* 14.123; the body as a house or home: *Agr.* 14.65, *Conf.* 17.82, *Somn.* 1.20.122, *Abr.* 16.72-74, *Spec.* 1.29.146; body as temple: *Opif.* 47.137; heaven as home: *Her.* 22.110, *Virt.* 11.73; heaven as temple: *Opif.* 18.55, *Mos.* 2.36.194; earth generally as home (and even house of God): *Her.* 22.110, *Virt.* 11.73, *Flacc.* 14.123, *Post.* 2.5, *Plant.* 12.50, *Somn.* 1.32.185; Judea or the native country is equated with home: *Her.* 58: 287, *Fug.* 14:76, *Somn.* 1.8.46, *Abr.* 18.85-86, *Praem.* 3.17; Jerusalem particularly as country: *Legat.* 36.278; temple as home/house of God: *Cher.* 29.100, *Somn.* 1.23.149, *Somn.* 2.41.272, *Legat.* 36.290, *Sacr.* 20.72; whole world or earth as temple: *Plant.* 30.126, *Somn.* 1.37.215, *Spec.* 1.12.66; Jerusalem itself as a temple: *Spec.* 3.23.130; the private home as a temple: *Spec.* 2.27.148. Similarly, the synagogue and Temple are closely linked (see Charlesworth, *Jesus as Mirrored in John*, 176). Mark Smith has some interesting things to say about many of these intertwined meanings in *Where the Gods Are: Spatial Dimensions of Anthropomorphism in the Biblical World*, Anchor Yale Bible Reference Library (New Haven: Yale University Press, 2016), 5: "Modeled on human spaces of home and palace, divine spaces of shrines and temples are literally in-formed by human form."

[56] See Hays, *Reading Backwards*, 75; Neyrey, "Spaces and Places," 71; Dodd, *Interpretation of the Fourth Gospel*, 313-17; Brown, *The Gospel According to John*, 180. Richard Hays has perhaps the most exaggerated position, stating his contention very plainly (it serves as a forceful representative of the position). He writes: "In John ... the identity of Jesus is deeply imbedded [sic] in Israel's texts and traditions—especially the traditions centered on the Temple and Israel's annual feasts ... [indeed] for John, Jesus becomes, in effect, the Temple." Hays, *Reading Backwards*, 82; emphasis added. Coloe, *God Dwells with Us*, 13-14, comes to this conclusion at the *einmalig* level but concludes that this emphasis is in fact mooted by the transference of this very language and emphasis to the community of believers through the operation of the Holy Spirit.

context of assertions about the Christian de-emphasis of space, that in John 4, Jesus is portrayed as supplanting the Temple. Does the data of the text support this conclusion? Do the social location and spatial practice of the Gospel indicate that such a conclusion is merited? The answer must be "No." The Samaritan Interlude does not portray Jesus as supplanting the Temple. How can we conclude this?[57] Most importantly, we must remember that heavy redaction of the Gospel, if not its entire composition, occurred well after the Temple was already destroyed.

While the Temple is portrayed as still existent in John 4,[58] it is simultaneously portrayed as already[59] mooted by "worship in spirit and in truth." This is a big cue. The author, while uncomfortable with the obvious anachronism of portraying the Temple as already destroyed in Jesus' day, is *not* uncomfortable with the anachronism of the Spirit already having been given. On multiple occasions in this pericope there are indications that the time of the giving of the Spirit is what is in mind.[60] Obviously, according to the narrative action of the Gospel, that has not yet occurred, but from the point of view of the Johannine community, it has.[61] In the form of the Gospel as we now have it, the heavy emphasis on the giving of the Spirit in the Farewell Discourse anchors the importance of this reality for the community. The body is arguably the most proximate and, as such, most important space for the human.[62] That God, the ultimate being, would dwell in the body of the believer through the Holy Spirit is then likely the most pertinent and important spatial relationship in view here.[63] We must consider just how much weight this may carry, even as it appears only briefly, or indirectly, in our pericope (4:14). The anachronistic "Spirit" language refers to a crucial "reflexive space," that is, the body of the believer from which living water wells up. The Temple is obviously very important to self-identified Jews, but it should be considered most likely that the primary temple relationship in John results from the

---

[57] While we will look here only at the data from John 4, there is a great deal of supporting data that appears throughout the Gospel.

[58] Doing otherwise would be an obvious and inexcusable anachronism.

[59] All the language of "now is" (4:23), "already" (4:35), and current fulfillment (4:26) support this contention.

[60] "The hour is coming ... and now is" (4:21, 23) for the living water and the worship in spirit and truth. The "Messiah is coming" (4:25) and "I who speak to you am he" (4:26). "The fields are already white for the harvest" (4:35).

[61] This accords with much of the work that has been done on the "post resurrection perspective" of the Gospel following Nils Dahl, "Anamnesis: Memory and Commemoration in Early Christianity," in *Jesus in the Memory of the Early Church* (Minneapolis: Augsburg, 1976), 11–29, 167–75.

[62] This is a major conclusion from Maurice Merleau-Ponty, *The Phenomenology of Perception*, trans. Colin Smith (London and New York: Routledge, 1962), 67–199. Increasing attention is being given to this in biblical studies including both Dale Martin, *The Corinthian Body* (New Haven, CT: Yale University Press, 1995), and Troels Engberg-Pedersen, *Cosmology and Self in the Apostle Paul: The Material Spirit* (Oxford: Oxford University Press, 2010).

[63] Even simply the massive difference in the number of verses in the Gospel that give primary attention to the Temple as compared to the number related to the Paraclete and the indwelling indicates this priority for the author.

conflation of the temple with *the body* of the believer individually and the community of believers corporately.[64]

Further, if Jesus' earthly body is no longer present to the community,[65] but God is present through the Holy Spirit, why would the author of John be insisting that Jesus is the new Temple? Obviously, Jesus' body is a vessel of God's Spirit at the level of narrative action, but so now is the body of every believer, even at times anachronistically in the narrative (e.g., 4:23-24). The way in which Jesus could operate as the Temple in a way that supersedes other understandings in the life of the Johannine community is not at all clear.

It should also be noted that the heavenly temple was never destroyed.[66] No Jewish author ever portrayed it as such.[67] The earthly Temple was always depicted as a lesser copy of the heavenly temple, but one in which God nevertheless deigned to dwell.[68] Again, one could certainly say that Jesus' body was a temple of the Holy Spirit during his earthly ministry,[69] but to suggest that all the valences of the Temple are transferred entirely to Jesus[70] seems unwarranted according to a consideration of Johannine spatial practice.[71] If Jesus has returned to heaven that would make two temples in heaven, neither of which has, in the life of the Johannine community, replaced the function of the earthly Temple.[72] Not only so, but early believers in Jesus were regularly portrayed

---

[64] As distinct from the perspective of Revelation. Many interpreters elide the understanding of Revelation with that of the Gospel of John, taking the statement that "I saw no temple in the city, for its temple is the Lord God the Almighty and the Lamb" (Rev 21:22) and imputing the same theology to the Gospel of John. However, the issue of authorship for the two texts is by no means established nor whether they were authored by the same individual (unlikely). 3 Baruch specifically relies on the idea that the heavenly temple is preserved from destruction. Too much concern for "canonical" analysis or *einmalig*-level historicity (see Neyrey, "Spaces and Places") distracts from the rather straightforward observation that the body of the believer as a temple of the Holy Spirit is more relevant to the author than "Jesus as temple." Frey (*Theology and History*, 202), for his part, recognizes the ecclesiological implications. The dynamics at work with respect to the synagogue in early Rabbinic Judaism, particularly transference of temple significance to alternate community space for gathering after the destruction of the Temple in 70 CE, parallel this likely dynamic in the Johannine community.

[65] Except perhaps as understood through the eucharist.

[66] Not that John talks specifically about the heavenly temple, but this is a common enough idea in Judaism at the time that it likely is part of the author's cosmology.

[67] Even as Revelation moots its importance compared to the "new Jerusalem" that has "no temple." In 1 Enoch (Animal Apocalypse) the earthly temple is "folded up" but is immediately replaced with one "higher" than it (the heavenly one?). Other texts that describe a heavenly temple include Hebrews and 3 Baruch.

[68] This picture is best known from Hebrews where the heavenly temple is described according to the archaic language of "the true tabernacle" or tent (τῆς σκηνῆς τῆς ἀληθινῆς, Heb 8:2), but it also appears similarly in Wis 9:8. Other relevant language includes that of the earthly tabernacle or temple being made according to the heavenly pattern (e.g., Exod 25; Ezek 43; Acts 7:44; Heb 8:5).

[69] Indeed, that is all that the temple scene in John 2 explicitly suggests.

[70] As in Neyrey, "Spaces and Places," 70-2.

[71] See Coloe, *God Dwells with Us*, 14: "the community ... displaces the Temple as the *locus* of the divine dwelling" (emphasis original).

[72] Of course, we should not make too much of apparent contradictions in language due to the fact that early believers in Christ were known for their willingness to marshal diverse, and at times contradictory, explanatory paradigms in support of belief in Jesus. See, for example, Larry Hurtado, "Two Case Studies in Earliest Christological Readings of Biblical Texts," in *All That the Prophets*

as continuing to worship in the Temple before it was destroyed,[73] so the idea that Jesus is supplanting the Temple is particularly anachronistic.[74]

Beyond this, the unequal treatment of the two holy places in question (Gerizim and Jerusalem) must be considered. It appears innocently enough that the language "neither on this mountain nor in Jerusalem" (4:21) equates the two places. However, at the likely time of composition the Jerusalem Temple was already destroyed,[75] while worship likely still occurred actively, at least periodically, on Gerizim.[76] It seems, in fact, far more likely that the language of the Samaritan Interlude is tropologically oriented against continued worship on Gerizim, which Jews had always viewed as improper. It is recorded in the Babylonian Talmud[77] that any Samaritan wanting to convert to Jewish worship had, first and foremost, to renounce worship on Gerizim. The language of the Interlude may be specifically directed at undermining said ongoing Samaritan worship,[78] but even if it is not, it still appears to preserve a Jewish tradition related to that theme rather than a Samaritan, or *einmalig*, one. Rather than an attempt to undermine the significance of the Jerusalem Temple, an anti-Samaritan trope may be the more likely import of the language of 4:21, especially considering the other anti-Samaritan stereotypes present in the text.

What is perhaps operative here, in the Samaritan Interlude in particular, is a collection of material not unlike the collections of material—often including contradictory elements—that are present in the current canonical form of many Hebrew Bible narratives. There an event appears to be the magnet that draws various traditions and interpretations of the event into the textual unit. However, in the Samaritan Interlude, what we have appears more to be a geographic organizing core. Samaria-themed traditions seem to have been pulled together to provide a stinging contrast to Nicodemus' dull responses to Jesus (3:4, 9). The background of this, of course, would be the social location of the Johannine community and its polemical

---

Have Declared: The Appropriation of Scripture in the Emergence of Christianity, ed. Matthew R. Malcom (London: Authentic Media, 2015), 23: "I propose that the remarkable and novel readings of … biblical texts … likely emerged early, quickly, and typically in settings of group prayer and worship where the sense of the Spirit's presence and power was strong. Early believers came to their Scriptures with convictions shaped by powerful religious experiences that opened the sacred texts for them in new ways, particularly experiences of the risen and exalted Jesus, and continuing revelations from the Spirit."

[73] For example, Acts 2:46-3:1; 5:20, 42; 21:26.
[74] In addition to being at odds with likely elements of the spatial practice of the Johannine community.
[75] The statement appears to be *vaticinium ex eventu*.
[76] Or that, in spite of Roman persecution, it had not been abandoned.
[77] See the Talmudic Booklet *Masechtot Qetanot Kutim* (*De Samaritanis*), one of the minor extra-talmudic tractates found at the end of the IVth Seder of the Babylonian Talmud. It is a compendium of Talmudic opinions referring to gentiles, which were applied to Samaritans. See also J. A. Montgomery, *The Samaritans, The Earliest Jewish Sect: Their History, Theology and Literature* (Philadelphia: Winston, 1907), 196.
[78] As made even more likely by the fact that worship was active enough on Gerizim after the Jerusalem Temple destruction and before Bar Kokhba that, following Bar Kokhba, Hadrian attempted to displace the Samaritan worship site by erecting a shrine there to Zeus Hypistos, using the bronze doors from the Jerusalem Temple in the construction. Robert J. Bull, "The Excavation of Tell er-Ras on Mt. Gerizim," *Biblical Archaeologist* 31 (1968): 58–72.

backlash against fellow Jews for both rejecting Jesus and expelling them from the synagogue.[79]

Having shown then that a consideration of spatial practice based in the Johannine community does not necessarily result in the conclusion that Jesus himself is exclusively supplanting the Temple, the apparent tension between reliable historical geographic data present elsewhere in the Gospel and the "mythical" character of the narrative of the Interlude should receive some attention. In short, how can we interpret "mythic" spatial data as indicating anything other than a spiritualizing tendency in the spatial practice of the Gospel? Does material space not matter?[80] Further, how might interpretation of John 4 be shaped by a consideration of the Johannine community's lived experience of particular physical spaces? It is to these questions that we now turn.

The Significance of the Well: The Perspective of Experience

Like the geographic stereotypes of Samaria typical of a Jewish community at the time, the mythic elements of the Interlude must have resonated within the Johannine community in order for the story to be received. If the Johannine Jews had been kicked out of the synagogue or were at least on rather combative terms with other Jews who did not believe in Jesus,[81] then it would make sense that the Johannine community would easily identify with the social isolation of the Samaritan woman because of their own experience. Those of the community who had been condemned for their belief in Jesus may even have been called "Samaritans" by Jews who did not believe in Jesus.[82] An examination of both the timing of the well meeting and the various words used here for "well," that is, the distinction between πηγή and φρέαρ, may also be instructive for understanding the presence of ostracization themes and the relevance of those themes to the material spatial reality of the Johannine community.

Many interpreters have noted the strange timing of the meeting.[83] The isolation of the woman is obvious, first, from the transparent fact that she arrives unaccompanied. In antiquity, trips outside the city limits to a communal water source would almost always have been communal. But the isolation of the woman is buttressed by the temporal language. Here the temporal cue "it was the sixth hour" (noon) acts as

---

[79] Making use of traditionally Jewish anti-Samaritan polemics to shame *Judeans* by showing that *even Samaritans* embraced Jesus.

[80] As suggested repeatedly by Neyrey, "Spaces and Places," 66, 70, 71, 76, 77, 80, 81, 82. He does not seem to see the irony that the de-emphasis of space for which he is arguing is utterly dependent on and informed by all manner of physical spatial data.

[81] As shown by Martyn.

[82] In accordance with its generic use as an insult suggesting waywardness from proper worship or righteous living. See Bultmann, *The Gospel of John*, 299 n. 4.

[83] For example, Brown, *The Gospel According to John*, 1:169; von Wahlde, *The Gospel and Letters of John*, 2:171; Robert Kysar, *Augsburg Commentary on the New Testament: John* (Minneapolis: Augsburg, 1986), 62–3: "The time notation of the sixth hour (about noon) makes for a difficulty with the woman's arrival to get water, for the women of the village would not usually come in the heat of the day to draw their supply of water."

language of estrangement, that is, relational distance.[84] Normally a trip for water would have occurred early or late in the day, to avoid the heat of the sun. It seems obvious here that the rest of the Samaritan townsfolk go to the well at a different time of day. Interpreters have certainly proposed alternate interpretations of the temporal cue in the text,[85] but for our purposes, it seems clear that the time of the meeting operates to separate the woman from others.[86]

With respect to the well: English translations[87] of John 4 almost universally render both πηγή (4:6a, 6b, 14) and φρέαρ (4:11, 12) interchangeably as "well." This is not necessarily unfounded, as there is precedent for apparently interchangeable use in the LXX of Genesis 16 and 24. However, the occurrence of the two words in John 4 is dependent on who is speaking. The narrator uses only πηγή (4:6). Jesus uses only πηγή (4:14). The woman, on the other hand, uses φρέαρ exclusively (4:11, 12). This distinction in word choice, especially the distinction between the usage in 4:6 and in 4:11-12, in describing the same location is usually a good cue for some significant discrepancy among the accumulated layers of meaning of a place.[88]

πηγή is not typically understood to have a negative valence in the New Testament.[89] It usually refers to a fountain or spring that wells up or gushes out, though it can also

---

[84] See Tuan, *Space and Place*, for nonspatial language standing in for spatial matters.

[85] Which occurs in broad daylight (in contrast to Nicodemus' meeting at night) to lay bare all in the woman's life. Interestingly, Nicodemus' separation from others (the privacy of his visit) is indicated by the timing of his meeting with Jesus. He is a "respectable" citizen yet comes to Jesus at a time suggesting the "shame" of the visit and his unwillingness to be seen in public with Jesus. The woman happens upon Jesus at a time indicating "shame" but the trajectory of her story is toward public testimony regarding Jesus, something considered honorable by the Johannine community. See, for example, 9:22 (also 2 John 7-8) for "shame" associated with unwillingness to acknowledge Jesus publicly.

[86] See, for example, Bruce J. Malina and Richard L. Rohrbaugh, *Social-Science Commentary on the Gospel of John* (Minneapolis: Fortress, 1998), 98: "The fact that the woman at the well is alone and that she comes at midday when the other village women are not there suggests that she has been shunned by the other women. She is perhaps seen as socially deviant (4:16-18). ... She appears to be either an adulteress or a 'mistress' a fact that the author presumes to have been known to her audience." So also, Witherington, *John's Wisdom*, 120; Jerome Neyrey, "What's Wrong with This Picture? John 4, Cultural Stereotypes of Women, and Public and Private Space," in *The Gospel of John in Cultural and Rhetorical Perspective* (Grand Rapids, MI: Eerdmans, 2009), 143–71, esp. 155.

[87] Of the major English translations only the New American Bible makes any real distinction, rendering πηγή in 4:6 as "well," φρέαρ in 4:11-12 as "cistern," and πηγή in 4:14 as "spring." The King James Version, American Standard Version, and New American Standard Bible use "well" throughout. The NRSV, Revised Standard Version, Common English Bible, English Standard Version, New International Version, and New King James Version use "well" for both πηγή and φρέαρ in 4:6 and 4:11-12 respectively. However, in 4:14 they render πηγή differently, in the New King James Version as "fountain" and the others as "spring." To be fair, the latter instance (4:14) is not referring to Jacob's well but the internal πηγή of living water welling up to eternal life.

[88] Mark Wynn notes not only that "a place-relative gesture may enable some sort of ... directedness toward God, or an encounter with God," but that knowledge of place itself is analogous to knowledge of God. As with knowledge of God, in the same way, any single person's knowledge of a place is partial compared to the totality of human knowledge of that place, and the experienced knowledge of that place is a combination of the distinctly individual and the corporately shared. In this instance we are investigating both the individually distinct knowledges of place and the attendant implications for knowledge of God. See Wynn, *Faith and Place: An Essay in Embodied Religious Epistemology* (Oxford, UK: Oxford University Press, 2009), 71–100, 135.

[89] The only possible exception occurs in Mark 5:29 in which the flow of blood from the hemorrhaging woman is referred to as a πηγή. Outside the NT it is used very generally to refer to "streams" including streams of tears (e.g., in Aeschylus, *Ag.* 888), but also running water (e.g., Homer, *Il.* 20.9), milk (e.g., Plato, *Menex.* 237e), and so on.

refer simply to a source.[90] In New Testament usage it can have a neutral connotation as in John 4:6 (and Rev. 8:10; 14:7; 16:4) but often has a very positive connotation, similar to that found in John 4:14 (see also Rev 7:17; 21:6). Such a positive understanding draws on the precedent of Isaiah 12:3 in the LXX which suggests that the righteous will draw water ἐκ τῶν πηγῶν τοῦ σωτηρίου (from the wells of salvation).

φρέαρ, on the other hand, does not have such a univocally positive valence in the New Testament. In fairness, its primary connotation is that of a "construction consisting of a vertical shaft, covered with a stone, for water supply," that is to say, a "well."[91] This is its simple meaning in Luke 14:5 for instance. However, φρέαρ has an additional, and not-insubstantial, negative connotation: that of "an opening that leads to the depths of the nether world."[92] This is the meaning implied by the usage in Revelation 9:1 in which an angel is given ἡ κλεὶς τοῦ φρέατος τῆς ἀβύσσου (the key of the shaft of the abyss). It is even possible, based on the woman's emphasis that the φρέαρ is deep, that the spatial connotation to this different word emphasizes the inaccessibility of the water to the woman, whereas Jesus' use of πηγή emphasizes the accessibility of the living water which wells up.[93]

The fact that the narrator and Jesus use πηγή and that the woman uses φρέαρ does not appear to be accidental. Is it significant that the aforementioned odd timing of the meeting suggests social isolation? Is the traumatic experience of the Johannine community with respect to the broader Jewish community possibly in play here? Would it be a surprise, in light of the preceding analysis, if the Samaritan woman viewed the well in a negative light?[94] It does not seem to be a stretch to expect that a woman in such a situation, confronted daily in this place with the trauma of her estrangement from her own society, would come to view the place negatively. The place would come to signify, for her, her own relational estrangement. She herself admits that she would prefer not to come back there (4:15).[95]

The emphasis on the part of the woman that she too is a daughter of Jacob would seem to parallel the experience of the Johannine community.[96] Jews who, because of belief in Jesus, were ostracized from the broader Jewish community would have felt this way. We can also imagine, without much difficulty, that Jews who did not believe in Jesus may have accused those who did of being apostate Samaritans. This is not hard to imagine since in the Gospel Jesus himself is accused of being a Samaritan (John 8:48). It is even possible to envision daily trips by members of the Johannine

---

[90] BDAG, 810-11.
[91] BDAG, 1065.
[92] BDAG, 1065.
[93] Thanks to Nate C. Johnson who shared this idea with me.
[94] Augustine views it negatively: "The water in the well is the pleasure of the world in its dark depth: from this people draw it with the vessel of lusts." Augustine, *Tract. Ev. Jo.* 15.16 in NPNF 1 7:102-3.
[95] While this kind of analysis could be considered "psychologizing," the mythic characteristics of the narrative preclude its basis in the events of the life of Jesus. Even a "theological" reading requires that the data from the narrative make significant sense *both* internally *and* to the immediate community of reception.
[96] Tod Swanson, "To Prepare a Place: Johannine Christianity and the Collapse of Ethnic Territory," *JAAR* 62.2 (1994): 261, concludes that it was "the Samaritan woman who represented the Johannine community."

community to their local well, experiencing it as a location of social ostracization from other Jews. Johannine Jews might have gone to such a well at a different time from synagogue Jews in order to avoid confrontation. Such a place would have negative experiences associated with it but would also likely develop an association with the welling up of the Spirit within the Christ-believer. Even as it is empirically verifiable that Jacob's well exists, it seems possible that the proper interpretation of the Samaritan Interlude may require imagining experiences at another well, namely the local well of the Johannine community.[97]

Conclusions Regarding the Samaritan Interlude

Having thus plausibly shown that the Samaritan Interlude may not contain data of Samaritan provenance, but rather seems to indicate a spatial practice based in the Johannine community, we can begin to see just how parochial and imagined the expressions of universality and plurality may be in the Gospel of John.[98] It is in the Samaritan Interlude that we notice just how non-Samaritan the Gospel is. Rather, the interests of the author and the author's immediate community of reception seem, unsurprisingly, oriented around Jewish believers in Jesus, as they themselves were.[99] This appears to be a group with expectations of divine access made great by their felt experience of the indwelling and made polemical by their experience of rejection by their fellow countrymen. It is a rather insular group, aware of its out-status with respect to its own Jewish identity, seeking to craft a narrative that affirms, supports, and strengthens its own experience.

In this sense, both the dominating and the domination-subverting tendencies of the spatial practice[100] of the Johannine community are on display. "Samaritanism" is appropriated by the Jewish Johannine community for its utility in their dispute with other Jews. The Samaritans are possibly little more than an oversimplified trope, but

---

[97] This is, of course, a speculation. However, if it is defensible that we must look to a social location in the Johannine community as the most relevant explanation for some Johannine data, then we cannot rule out the likelihood that other pieces of data may also be explained by that social location, even if the connection cannot be proven. It certainly seems likely that the members of the Johannine community themselves would have connected the meanings of their experiences at their local well with the description of the well in John 4. We should not foreclose the possibility of lived experiences of the local well of the Johannine community having an "ecogenic" effect on the text of the Samaritan Interlude.

[98] But the author does appear to be trying, in spite of the prejudicial baggage.

[99] This interest and coloring of narrative with respect to the interests of the Jewish Johannine community has been recognized by many scholars. See, for example, Frey, *Theology and History*, 104: "In most cases ... we can only get back to traditions that are more or less shaped by the language of the Johannine community. ... [T]he verdict cannot be avoided that all the words of Jesus in John have undergone a thorough theological transformation, and the claim that they represent the words of the Jesus of history cannot, in most cases, be substantiated."

[100] As previously mentioned, Lefebvre wrote that "spatial practice consists in a projection onto a [spatial] field of all aspects, elements and moments of social practice." Lefebvre, *The Production of Space*, 8.

one the reader is meant to identify with as faithfully responding to Jesus.[101] Space is highly spiritualized but simultaneously unbreakably anchored to the physical realities of human experience—here, that of the largely Jewish but marginalized Johannine community and their own embodied experience.

It is true that the text appears to teach a theology of space that allows detachment from or reinterpretation of dominated, traumatized spaces[102] (such as the Jerusalem Temple, Mt. Gerizim, and the well) while seeming to emphasize a spiritualizing tendency. However, the embedded spatial data of the text may provide an example of the ways in which the experiences of human material spatiality, including those of domination and trauma, may have been reappropriated and "redeemed" through imagination of new modes of access to God considered available through the indwelling of the Holy Spirit.

In this sense Lefebvre is not really fair to the spatial practice of the Gospel of John.[103] It is not all idealized, theoretical *logos*. As in any spatial practice there is no *logos* without *sarx*.[104] John may be saying that neither on this mountain nor in Jerusalem will the true worshipers worship and that such as these will worship in spirit and in truth, but the material world is not spiritualized away. It is not mooted by the spiritual reality the Gospel claims to point to. Embodiment is *not* spiritualization, even as the means by which that embodiment is achieved is the Spirit.[105] Rather, through the spatial practice on display in the Samaritan Interlude it can be said that, according to John, not only metonymically but also literally, Jesus acts as a savior of the *cosmos* (4:42).[106] The fields—literally, the spaces (*tas khoras*)—are ready to harvest (4:35), that is, they are ready to be interpreted. The material reality matters. And interpretation is not just spiritual but is based on the material reality of experience, a theme that will be confirmed repeatedly throughout this book from the earliest text (*Parables of Enoch*) to the latest (Augustine's *De Trinitate*).

Analysis of the spatial practice here shows that pitting the "historical" against the "theological" in Johannine studies is perhaps unnecessary. Theological interpretation is utterly dependent on both historical context and quotidian personal experience,[107] especially for understanding why a text would be compelling enough to write and be favorably received. It is not a-historical. The space of life is the tool by which the

---

[101] Interestingly, through the rather coarse Jewish representation and appropriation of Samaritanism in this text the reader or hearer is actually encouraged to identify with the Samaritan, that is, with the one who is both an outcast and a, seemingly, faithful disciple.

[102] As in Jerusalem as dominated by Rome and suffused with trauma from the events of 70 CE, Gerizim as dominated by successive imperial powers and layered with traumatic meaning from their desecrations, and the well, as proposed in this study, as a space dominated by the social structure and stigma that arguably traumatizes the Samaritan woman.

[103] He, in truth, is responding to a dogmatic Catholic, scholastic appropriation of the Gospel rather than the Gospel directly.

[104] The verse "the flesh is useless" (6:63) does not subvert the significance of the *sarx* language in the prologue nor even the language in that very pericope. Otherwise the crucifixion is useless.

[105] No one refers to the Jerusalem Temple as "spiritualized space" even as the mechanism by which its holiness was understood was through its operation as a dwelling-place for the *spirit* of God.

[106] Devotion to Jesus allows the preservation of a text that itself preserves evidence of a material spatial practice—a valuation of the *cosmos*—in spite of the overt Johannine polemics against the *cosmos*.

[107] The history of the author and immediate community of reception especially.

spiritual, theological, or mythical is interpreted. Similarly, the historical perspective is utterly tied to the concerns and experience of the writer's own community, to their own experience in their own space.[108] Neither interpretive approach can escape the "ecology"[109] of the text, that is, what is important in the ground of lived experience in the spaces of intimate knowledge for the author and his or her community. But inasmuch as interpreters are concerned about the historicity of the Johannine depictions at the *einmalig* level, consideration of "spatial practice" as an approach to analysis is more likely to return conclusions germane to the experience of the Johannine community than to the time of Jesus' ministry. Such conclusions are of course still deeply valuable, as one could argue that the *einmalig* narrative may have been mythicized for the very purpose of better reflecting the historical and material experience of the Johannine community.[110]

A spatial-critical reading of John 4, then, highlights the ways in which this marginal Jewish community not only imagined spaces of trauma[111] but reimagined them,[112] enabling that community to appropriate those spaces for their redemption and flourishing.[113] It further shows that accurate interpretation requires attention to spatial practice and textual ecology.

What has been suggested by the preceding analysis is that consideration of spatial language in the Gospel of John must certainly involve attention to historical and literary contextual concerns, but, more than this, must be at least equally attentive to the actual spatial practice on display in the text and to the experiential spatial background that has contributed to producing the text. Another way of saying this is that *responsible literary analysis cannot be accomplished without attention to the phenomenology of quotidian and domestic space in the experience of the author*. This is the dynamic we see at play in John 4, wherein a narrative ostensibly about Samaritans, the Temple, Jacob's well, and spiritualizing space is likely actually about Judeans, the body of the believer, and perhaps even the Johannine community's local well, while remaining dependent on the importance of material space. Human experience of domestic and quotidian space is a critical πηγή, or source, of literary productions of space, especially productions of ideal space. This is not only so in a positive sense but, as we have seen and will continue to see, the lived experience of suffering, the φρέαρ of home life if you will, can be an equally powerful generative source. And as we will see in the following chapters, these very materially spatial concerns are broadly and directly relevant to the proper interpretation of early Jewish and Christian literature generally.

---

[108] Even what is emphasized from the *einmalig* level.
[109] "Ecology" meaning literally "oikology," or the logic of the text's native home or habitat.
[110] This is no different from the dynamic at work in Daniel or 4 Ezra, according to which the texts tell much more about their milieu of composition than about the historical events they purport to describe.
[111] That is, the temple, their own bodies, their landed identity as Jewish, even the spatially "other" Samaritan as faithful.
[112] For one view of this transformation, see Neyrey's assessment ("What's Wrong with This Picture?" 161) that "the space in which she and Jesus have intercourse [that is, the well,] is ceasing to be 'public' and becoming 'private.' She is being transformed into an 'insider,' one whom Jesus receives into his fictive-kinship 'private' world."
[113] As shown in Chapter 1.

3

The Undisputed Pauline Corpus and Gentile Believers as the Dwelling of God

Having explored some of the interpretive possibilities of considering the constellation of ideas involving home, the Holy Spirit, and "indwelling" in the Gospel of John, it is perhaps natural to consider the same constellation as it appears in other New Testament literature, namely within the undisputed letters of Paul. What we can know of Paul's background and circumstances suggest that they are somewhat different from those of the author(s) of the Gospel of John, but the hermeneutical implications of considering this classic constellation of ideas through a spatial-critical approach are no less important for understanding Pauline ideas. In this chapter we will consider how a spatial-critical consideration of Paul's main concern, his gentile Christ-believer communities, and their fundamental experience of divine dwelling—or "indwelling"— through the Holy Spirit can meaningfully inform interpretation of Pauline soteriology and sacrificial theology.

Paul's great concern is his end-of-the-age gentile mission, and the content of his correspondence is, for the most part, concerned with the salvation of gentile Christ-believers.[1] This predominating interest matters a great deal because it means that as we consider the "ecology" of these texts we must consider the concerns that might arise for a Jew (Paul) who is trying to advocate for, and identify with the experience of, gentiles.[2] Paul's statement that "to those outside the law I became as one outside the law" (1 Cor 9:21) suggests that for him this is at least a significant intention. We must further, if we are to take seriously the prevalence of language about the indwelling of the Holy Spirit in gentile bodies, consider the reality of the body as a space, or a home, in which the divinity could dwell. As such, our ecological concern takes on two dimensions here: an interest in a theological ecology (the dwelling of God) and an interest in a human ecology (the gentile body). These two ecological concerns of course meet most prominently in Paul's Letters in the language of the indwelling of the

---

[1] In general, regarding interpretation of the undisputed Pauline corpus, I follow the conclusions of John Gager, *Reinventing Paul* (Oxford: Oxford University Press, 2000).

[2] There is not enough space here to consider all aspects of Pauline ecology, but further analytical work on the carceral ecology of his letters is certainly warranted.

Holy Spirit in gentile bodies and have bearing on a wide swath of Pauline interpretive issues. Thus, consideration of an issue so generally considered important as Paul's soteriology requires attention to this ecological profile. And we will see that a *spatial* approach to understanding the sacrificial language employed by Paul may best align with this aforementioned ecological profile and have the most explanatory utility for Paul's language and purpose.

The multivalent usage of sacrificial terminology in Paul is also, of course, well established.³ However, debate has continued over whether the proper paradigm for understanding "sacrifice" in Paul comes from the Levitical tradition or even whether the idea of "atoning sacrifice" is a concept germane to Paul at all.⁴ For the most part scholars seem to have split between those defending a traditional and more "canonical" reading of Paul as dependent on Levitical traditions for a personal "atoning sacrifice" understanding of Christ's death on the one hand,⁵ and those who believe that neither "atoning sacrifice"⁶ nor Levitical traditions are relevant to Paul's understanding on the other.⁷ This chapter seeks to show that a third possibility may be posited: Paul's understanding of Christ's death as sacrifice may have been partially dependent on interpretations of the Levitical tradition of the *ḥaṭṭa't* as a sacrifice that operated to purify the *place* for the Deity.⁸ Especially Paul's pneumatology points in this direction,

---

3   Hans-Josef Klauck, "Kultische Symbolsprache bei Paulus," in *Gemeinde Amt Sakrament: Neutestamentliche Perspektiven*, ed. Hans-Josef Klauck (Würzburg: Echter, 1989), 348–58.
4   As perhaps indicated by some of Harry Attridge's comments at the 2016 Princeton-Prague Symposium on the historical Jesus that appear in Jolyon G. R. Pruszinski, "Roskovec, Daise, and a Developing Consensus: Discussion of Papers IV," in *Jesus Research: The Gospel of John in Historical Inquiry*, eds. James H. Charlesworth and Jolyon G. R. Pruszinski, Jewish and Christian Texts 26 (London: T&T Clark, 2019), 252: "The *tamid* is the daily offering. The *hattat* offering would be an offering for sin. There was a set of explicit offerings for sin. And the *tamid* is sometimes associated with the *hattat* offerings. So there are specific offerings that are made to take away sin and one might say that Jesus died for us like one of those offerings in some sort of sacrificial metaphor. But if you say, like Paul, that Christ our Passover has been sacrificed, you are not immediately calling up a sacrifice of atonement for sin, you are calling up a sacrifice that liberates or marks a people."
5   For example, Richard H. Bell, "Sacrifice and Christology in Paul," *Journal of Theological Studies* 53.1 (2002): 1–27. See also Simon Gathercole, *Defending Substitution: An Essay on Atonement in Paul* (Grand Rapids, MI: Baker Academic, 2015).
6   For example, Ernst Käsemann, *Perspectives on Paul*, trans. Margaret Kohl (Philadelphia: Fortress, 1971), 42–5.
7   For example, Bradley H. McLean, "The Absence of an Atoning Sacrifice in Paul's Soteriology," *New Testament Studies* 38 (1992): 531–53.
8   "Milgrom has argued that this sequence of the graded usage of blood in respect to the grid of the sacred shrine shows that what is being purged is not the sin from the sinner, but the effects of sin, i.e. cultic impurity, from the sanctums within the sanctuary. Since the blood is understood to be a purging agent, one would expect the sinner to receive this material if the primary intention of the ritual were to eliminate his/her sinful condition. Such an understanding would accord well with what is said about the purificatory role of the *ḥaṭṭa't* blood in the case of those suffering from discharge: 'Thus you shall keep the people of Israel separate from their uncleanness lest they die in their uncleanness by defiling my tabernacle that is in their midst' (Lev 15:31; cf. Num 19:13). Impurity, conceived in this fashion, becomes 'a physical substance, an aerial miasma which possessed magnetic attraction for the realm of the sacred' (Milgrom 1983: 77). The purification offering is designed to remove this maleficent material from the sanctuary itself. If the impurity is allowed to accumulate, the deity will be forced to leave the sanctuary." So, Gary A. Anderson, "Sacrifice and Sacrificial Offerings (Old Testament)," in *The Anchor Bible Dictionary*, Vol. 5, ed. David N. Freedman (New York: Doubleday, 1992), 879–80.

suggesting that the tradition of Christ's sacrificial death can be traced at least as far back as the point at which it became clear to Paul that the gentiles were, or needed to be understood as, "temples" of God, vessels purified for the presence of the Holy Spirit.

Attention to Paul's writings in this direction is particularly warranted by the fact that, as previously mentioned, spatial concerns have generally been ignored in historical scholarship. Critical theorists of space, such Michel Foucault, have suggested that undue attention to history has hampered attention to spatial realities.[9] Edward Soja echoes these concerns and suggests that spatial hermeneutics must be developed and employed for responsible analysis.[10] He writes, "We must be insistently aware of how space can be made to hide consequences from us, how relations of power … are inscribed into the apparently innocent spatiality of social life." Yi Fu Tuan has written, "Every activity generates a particular spatio-temporal structure, but this structure seldom thrusts to the front of awareness."[11] As a writer with well-established apocalyptic bona fides,[12] Paul's writings merit attention in this direction, especially in light of Rowland's observations[13] that eschatological or temporal concerns are not inherently germane to the apocalyptic genre.[14] Such observations suggest the possibility that

---

[9] Michel Foucault, "Of Other Spaces," trans. Jay Miskowiec, *Diacritics* 16 (1986): 22: "The great obsession of the nineteenth century was, as we know, history: with its themes of development and of suspension, of crisis and cycle, themes of the ever-accumulating past, with its great preponderance of dead men and the menacing glaciations of the world … The present epoch will perhaps be above all the epoch of space. We are in the epoch of simultaneity: we are in the epoch of juxtaposition, the epoch of near and far, of the side-by-side, of the dispersed. We are at a moment, I believe, when our experience of the world is less that of a long life developing through time than that of a network that connects points and intersects with its own skein. One could perhaps say that certain ideological conflicts animating present-day polemics oppose the pious descendants of time and the determined inhabitants of space."

[10] Edward W. Soja, *Postmodern Geographies: The Reassertion of Space in Critical Social Theory* (London and New York: Verso, 1989), 2. He goes on to say: "The historical imagination is never completely spaceless and critical social historians have written, and continue to write, some of the best geographies of the past. But it is always time and history that provide the primary 'variable containers' in these geographies … This [essay] does not deny the extraordinary power and importance of historiography as a mode of emancipatory insight, but identifies historicism with the creation of a critical silence, an implicit subordination of space to time that obscures geographical interpretations of the changeability of the social world and intrudes upon every level of theoretical discourse, from the most abstract ontological concepts of being to the most detailed explanations of empirical events" (14–15).

[11] Yi Fu Tuan, *Space and Place: The Perspective of Experience* (Minneapolis and London: University of Minnesota Press, 1977), 130.

[12] For example, Lisa M. Bowens, *An Apostle in Battle: Paul and Spiritual Warfare in 2 Corinthians 12:1–10*, WUNT 2/433 (Tübingen: Mohr Siebeck, 2017); Harold Attridge, "Reflections on Research into Q," *Semeia* 55 (1992): 229; J. Louis Martyn, "Apocalyptic Antinomies in Paul's Letter to the Galatians," *NTS* 31 (1985): 410–24; M. C. de Boer, "Paul and Apocalyptic Theology," in *Origins of Apocalypticism in Judaism and Christianity*, ed. John J. Collins (New York: Continuum, 1998), 345–83.

[13] Rowland concludes, contra the *Semeia* 14 definition, that literary forms and eschatological concerns are not defining characteristics. Rather, he writes that "apocalyptic" is best defined by "the belief that God's will can be discerned by means of a mode of revelation which unfolds directly the hidden things of God. To speak of apocalyptic, therefore, is to concentrate on the theme of the direct communication of the heavenly mysteries in all their diversity." C. Rowland, *The Open Heaven, A Study of Apocalyptic in Judaism and Early Christianity* (London: SPCK, 1982), 14.

[14] Though John Collins considers this rejection a bridge too far, he rightly recognizes the helpful contribution made by Rowland's work. John J. Collins, *The Apocalyptic Imagination: An Introduction to the Jewish Matrix of Christianity* (New York: Crossroad, 1987), 8, and many endnotes.

crucial spatial realities are often hidden from view, or at times, hidden in plain sight. This chapter will attempt to draw out just such subtle and unconsidered data that has been rather buried in over-contentious debate.[15]

Because the argument of this chapter is based significantly on subtle and circumstantial evidence, little can be said *conclusively* on the subject at hand. However, the purpose of this chapter is to argue for continued *consideration* of explanatory options that should not yet be foreclosed regarding Paul's sacrificial theology, soteriology, and pneumatology, based on what we can surmise regarding a Pauline "ecology." The goal is not to prove the influence of a space-sanctifying, Levitical sacrificial tradition on Pauline soteriology, but rather to investigate its utility as an explanatory paradigm and determine whether it merits further attention and inclusion in the ongoing conversation. To begin, we must consider some of the key issues related to "sacrifice" in Paul.

Milgrom, McLean, and Sacrifice in Paul

Jacob Milgrom has on numerous occasions[16] argued that the *ḥaṭṭa't* sacrifice in the Levitical system did not purify the one offering the sacrifice but rather the place of sacrifice from the sin of the one offering.[17] At its most basic, this assertion is based on the observation that the blood of the sacrifice is the "ritual detergent"[18] that effects

---

[15] Especially the Bell ("Sacrifice and Christology in Paul") versus McLean dimension.
[16] McLean, "Absence," 534, contains a helpful list, including Jacob Milgrom, "Israel's Sanctuary: The Priestly 'Picture of Dorian Gray,'" *RB* 83 (1976): 390–9; J. Milgrom, "Sacrifices and Offerings, OT," in *The Interpreter's Dictionary of the Bible, Supplementary Volume*, eds. K. Crim et al. (Nashville: Abingdon, 1976), 766–7; J. Milgrom, "The Day of Atonement," in *The Encyclopedia of Judaism, Vol. 5*, ed. Geoffrey Wigoder (New York and London: Macmillan, 1989), 1375–87; J. Milgrom, "Sin-Offering, or Purification-Offering?" *Vetus Testamentum* 21 (1971): 237–9; J. Milgrom, *Studies in Priestly Theology and Terminology* (Leiden: Brill, 1982), 75–6; J. Milgrom, "The Function of Ḥaṭṭa't Sacrifice," *Tarbiz* 40 (1970): 1–8.
[17] Anderson, "Sacrifice," 879, summarizes Milgrom's findings very helpfully: "The purificatory function of the *ḥaṭṭa't* challenges us to reconsider the role of the *ḥaṭṭa't* in rituals that seem to have an atoning function. Can these rituals also be understood in a purificatory sense? Milgrom has argued the affirmative on the basis of the atonement rituals found in Leviticus 4:1-5:13 and Leviticus 16. Milgrom pays particular attention to the role of blood manipulation in each of the rituals described here, for it is the blood itself which acts as the purging agent. In light of this fact, it is significant to note that the blood is never placed upon the individual. If the individual himself was being cleansed, one would expect the blood to be placed on him or her. Instead the blood is placed on various cultic appurtenances. Even more telling is the variability of this blood ritual with respect to the status of the sinner. Leviticus 4 makes very careful distinctions between the status of various classes of people. The inadvertent sins of the priest and community as a whole are more serious than the sins of the individual, be he a commoner or a ruler. Most serious of all are the advertent offenses of any kind. In each of these cases, as the seriousness of the sin becomes more pronounced, the blood is brought closer to the very inner sanctum of the holy of holies. Thus the blood used for the commoner is placed on the altar of the burnt offering *outside the sanctuary* per se (Lev 4:30). The blood used for the sin of the priest or of the community as a whole is placed *within the sanctuary* itself, sprinkled on the veil separating the holy of holies from the outer chamber and placed on the incense altar. Finally, the blood of the purification offering on Yom Kippur, which atones for advertent sins (so would seem the sense of *peša'* in Lev 16:16), is sprinkled 'in front of the mercy seat' within the holy of holies itself (Lev 16:14)."
[18] Milgrom, "Israel's Sanctuary," 391.

purification and that the manipulation of the blood occurs with respect to various locations, not at all with respect to any humans. This is on display in the fourth chapter of Leviticus:

> The anointed priest shall take some of the blood of the bull and bring it into the tent of meeting. The priest shall dip his finger in the blood and sprinkle some of the blood seven times before the LORD in front of the curtain of the sanctuary. The priest shall put some of the blood on the horns of the altar of fragrant incense that is in the tent of meeting before the LORD; and the rest of the blood of the bull he shall pour out at the base of the altar of burnt offering, which is at the entrance of the tent of meeting.[19]
>
> (Lev 4:5-7, NRSV)

This function appears again in Lev 8:15 when "Moses took the *ḥaṭṭaʾt* blood and with his fingers put some on each of the horns of the altar, thereby decontaminating (*wayᵉḥaṭṭē*) the altar."[20]

One would then best understand the function of the sacrifice as removing the accumulated effects of sin from the place of worship so that the deity could dwell there. Clearly this assertion has been somewhat contentious, and Milgrom himself acknowledges the fraught nature of attempting to disentangle the cultic rites present in the Hebrew Bible.[21] However, Bradley McLean has taken some of this reasoning a step further and asserted that, at least in the writings of Paul, there is no evidence at all that Levitical sacrificial traditions have any connection to the view that Christ's death acts as a sacrifice atoning for personal sin.[22]

At the outset it should be noted that McLean seems to interpret Milgrom's statements to suggest that the *ḥaṭṭaʾt* does not accomplish atonement at all.[23] This seems to be an extreme interpretation with which Gary Anderson, for one, does

---

[19] See nearly identical language present also in Lev 4:16-18, 25, 30, 34; 5:9. While Lev 5:10 and 5:13 might be taken to connect the sacrifice with personal atonement and forgiveness, the contention made by Milgrom is that guilt is only attached to actions upon realization of the sin and that the individual forgiveness of the sin is the result of contrition gained apart from the manipulations of the sacrificial ceremonies. Further, the operations in question here pertain to the effects of sin and forgiveness upon the cultic spaces as the result of individual sin, and the atonement and forgiveness are for the spatial contamination that has resulted, not the personal contamination.

[20] Milgrom's translation from "Israel's Sanctuary," 391.

[21] Jacob Milgrom, *Cult and Conscience: The Asham and the Priestly Doctrine of Repentance* (Leiden: Brill, 1976), 3. Christophe Nihan ("The Templization of Israel in Leviticus: Some Remarks on Blood Disposal and *Kipper* in Leviticus 4," in *Text, Time, and Temple: Literary, Historical and Ritual Studies in Leviticus*, ed. Francis Landy, Leigh M. Trevaskis, and Bryan D. Bibb, HBM 64 [Sheffield: Sheffield Phoenix, 2015], 96–120), for one, has suggested that the place of offering cannot have been what is purified, but rather, the individual. Christian A. Eberhart, however, has pointed out some of the problems with Nihan's perspective in "To Atone or Not to Atone: Remarks on the Day of Atonement Rituals According to Leviticus 16 and the Meaning of Atonement," in *Sacrifice, Cult, and Atonement in Early Judaism and Christianity: Constituents and Critique*, ed. Henrietta L. Wiley and Christian A. Eberhart, Resources for Biblical Study 85 (Atlanta: SBL Press, 2017), 197–231.

[22] McLean, "Absence," 531–53. See also his 1989 Toronto dissertation and the book in which much of the material later appeared: *The Cursed Christ: Mediterranean Expulsion Rituals and Pauline Soteriology*, JSNTSup 126 (Sheffield: Sheffield Academic Press, 1996).

[23] In this he mistakenly equates "atonement" with "personal forgiveness for personal sin."

not concur.²⁴ Anderson interprets Milgrom's contention to be that the atonement accomplished in the *ḥaṭṭa 't* is not one for the personal sin of the one offering sacrifice but is rather an atonement that purifies the temple as a dwelling for the deity from the effects of the sin of the one making the offering. The distinction is key. McLean's interpretation of Milgrom suggests that atonement is largely alien to the Levitical traditions of sacrifice²⁵ while Anderson's reading suggests that Milgrom is arguing for a spatial—rather than personal—understanding of the atonement accomplished in the *ḥaṭṭa 't*. The more important issue is how these sacrifices were interpreted in the time of Paul. McLean, based on his interpretation of Milgrom's work and the data in the undisputed Pauline Letters, goes on to conclude that Paul's theology does not rely on Levitical sacrificial tradition at all. Rather, he claims that Paul's understanding of personal atonement and forgiveness is based exclusively in the Greco-Roman world of expiatory, substitutionary expulsion rituals.²⁶

The questions at issue then are: (1) Does Paul view Christ's death as a sacrifice in any way at all? (2) If so, is there any evidence that Paul draws on Levitical sacrificial tradition, specifically the *ḥaṭṭa 't*, in his understanding of Christ's death? Which is to say, might Paul view Christ's sacrificial death as an atonement purifying a place for the dwelling of God? As we shall see, the evidence from Paul's writings does not fully support McLean's—very extreme—contention²⁷ that Jewish sacrificial traditions do not provide any background for the Pauline understanding of Christ's death. Rather, it appears that there is significant evidence within Paul's writings to suggest that his understanding of Christ's death was influenced by Levitical sacrificial traditions as interpreted according to Milgrom's space-sanctifying model.

The Undisputed Letters and Christ as Sacrifice

There is, admittedly, little direct evidence in Paul's writings from which to understand a possible sacrificial aspect to his soteriology. The passages usually considered most relevant come from Galatians (3:13), 1 Corinthians (5:7; 9:13-15; 10:14-33; 11:23-31; 15:3), and Romans (3:25; 5:5-11; 8:30-33; 15:16-21).

---

²⁴ Anderson, "Sacrifice," 880: "This understanding of the process of atonement is quite distinct from the previous theories … which hold that the process is primarily concerned with removing sin from the sinner. Whereas the latter stress the role of substitutionary death in the atoning process, Milgrom stresses the role of purification."

²⁵ Confirmed by Bell, "Sacrifice and Christology in Paul," 4–5. On its face this interpretation seems rather extreme in light of, for instance, Lev 5:10-13.

²⁶ This is deeply problematic for a number of reasons, not least of which is McLean's seeming return to the approach of the *religionsgeschichtliche Schule* that devalues Paul's Judaism and Jewish context. For just such a critique, see Joan F. Gormley, "The Cursed Christ: Mediterranean Expulsion Rituals and Pauline Soteriology," *CBQ* 59.4 (1997): 780–2.

²⁷ McLean, "Absence," 531–2, argues that "1) sacrifice does not atone for personal sin; 2) a sacrificial victim becomes neither sinful nor accursed, but remains holy; 3) there are no explicit textual references in Paul's letters to Christ's death as an atoning sacrifice; 4) references to Christ's blood in Paul's letters cannot be interpreted as implicit references to an atoning sacrifice; 5) Paul's interpretation of the suffering and death of Christ is incompatible with sacrificial theology."

The Galatians passage[28] is rather inconclusive, as Christ is described as having become "a curse for us" though no explicit mention of sacrifice is made. It is clear from this passage that, to Paul, Christ's death is effective in some way for others, as might be expected with a sacrifice according to a personal atonement model, but it appears that the dynamic of this passage is more indicative of the scapegoat ritual, as accurately indicated by McLean.[29]

1 Corinthians 5:7 at first seems similarly inconclusive. The mention that τὸ πάσχα ἡμῶν ἐτύθη Χριστός seems confusing since neither was the Passover originally considered to be a sacrifice nor an atonement,[30] nor does θύω necessarily mean "to sacrifice"[31] but can simply mean "to kill ceremonially."[32] It must however be noted, with Dunn,[33] that by the time Paul is writing, the Passover had already begun to develop the connotation of sacrifice despite its original freedom from this meaning, and Paul's usage generally need not exclude the influence of separate Levitical tradition, even if this specific instance does not connote it. Likewise, even if the specifics of the particular verse were to be decided against a "sacrificial" reading, one cannot escape the overall sense that Christ is the living thing whose death precipitates the deliverance of those who are covered by his blood (according to the Passover paradigm). The death of Christ is still effective "for" believers, just as a sacrifice is effective in some way[34] for those who offer or are identified with it.[35]

In 1 Cor 9:13-15 Paul identifies himself and his ministry with the temple service of priests and the temple sacrifice. This is a rather loose identification that is one in a long list of reasons Paul musters in the service of financial support for ministers of the Gospel. This may be taken as a connection between the temple and the body of believers, but the relationship between the temple sacrifice and any particular parallel in the community of believers is not explicit enough in this passage to allow a definitive identification.

---

[28] Χριστὸς ἡμᾶς ἐξηγόρασεν ἐκ τῆς κατάρας τοῦ νόμου γενόμενος ὑπὲρ ἡμῶν κατάρα, ὅτι γέγραπται, Ἐπικατάρατος πᾶς ὁ κρεμάμενος ἐπὶ ξύλου (Christ redeemed us from the curse of the law by becoming a curse for us—for it is written, "Cursed is everyone who hangs on a tree," NRSV).

[29] McLean, in "Absence," 539, does fail to note the inconvenient fact that since the scapegoat ritual does not involve the death of both of the animals, while in this passage it is clear that Christ's death, not simply his banishment, is involved, the scapegoat ritual cannot be the only contributory tradition. The passage seems to indicate that multiple strands of tradition are woven together rather than that Paul is dependent upon on a single strand. He brings up the problem in *The Cursed Christ*, suggesting that Greco-Roman rituals involve killing the scapegoat figure to prevent its return (but the killing is not originally or integrally part of the rituals).

[30] See, as an example of this long-appreciated reality, Otto Schmitz, *Die Opferanschauung des späteren Judentums und die Opferaussagen des Neuen Testaments* (Tübingen: Mohr, 1910), 51, 161.

[31] In spite of the NRSV translation: "Our paschal lamb, Christ, has been sacrificed."

[32] Though the valence does tend toward "sacrifice." See BDAG, 463.

[33] James D. G. Dunn, "Paul's Understanding of the Death of Jesus," in *Reconciliation and Hope: New Testament Essays on Atonement and Eschatology Presented to L.L. Morris on His 60th Birthday*, ed. Robert Banks (Carlisle: Paternoster, 1974), 132–3.

[34] Even if it is to allow God to dwell nearby rather than specifically absolve personal guilt.

[35] It should be noted that if the Passover has taken on the idea of sacrifice in this period, the "sacrifice" would operate to protect through manipulation of its blood upon the space of dwelling.

The eucharistic passages in 1 Corinthians provide some useful fodder for interpretation. It seems clear from 10:16-18[36] that the partaking of the eucharist is equated with partaking of the meat sacrificed in the temple service. It would seem clear then that here Paul does, albeit indirectly, identify Christ's death as a sacrifice according to the Levitical tradition. The words of institution in 1 Cor 11:24, Τοῦτό μού ἐστιν τὸ σῶμα τὸ ὑπὲρ ὑμῶν (this is my body that is for you), clearly connote Christ's death[37] and the sense that it is effective in some way for those who participate in the eucharist out of faith. This is the dynamic one would expect from an understanding based, to some degree, on Levitically derived sacrificial traditions.

In a similar way, in 1 Cor 15:3, without specifically referencing sacrifice, Paul manages to describe one of the dynamics of sacrifice that Christ fulfills, namely that ἀπέθανεν ὑπὲρ τῶν ἁμαρτιῶν ἡμῶν ("[he] died for our sins"). This is obviously one of the key dynamics at work in sacrifice: namely, that a living thing dies as a result of, and for the sake of, the sins of another. He also identifies this as a received tradition.[38]

The English of Rom 3:25 suggests the most explicit support for Christ being "a sacrifice of atonement." However, many commentators for well over one hundred years have questioned this interpretation, suggesting that ἱλαστήριον is more likely, in light of the Septuagint witness, to mean that Christ is the *place* of sacrifice, the mercy seat itself,[39] as it were.[40] This issue is by no means settled, but it does seem likely that regardless of the details, Christ's death is in view[41] and is in some way "effective"[42] for those who believe, as would be the case with a sacrifice. Exactly what is accomplished is less clear, but it does seem less likely from the wording that Christ's death here atones for personal sin since the specific language used suggests not that a transactional individual atonement has been made, but rather that God has already shown "his divine forbearance" by the fact that he had "passed over the sins previously committed."[43] This seems more akin to fiat forgiveness separately accomplished not unlike the contrition-based forgiveness described by Milgrom.[44]

---

[36] τὸ ποτήριον τῆς εὐλογίας ὃ εὐλογοῦμεν, οὐχὶ κοινωνία ἐστὶν τοῦ αἵματος τοῦ Χριστοῦ; τὸν ἄρτον ὃν κλῶμεν, οὐχὶ κοινωνία τοῦ σώματος τοῦ Χριστοῦ ἐστιν; ὅτι εἷς ἄρτος, ἓν σῶμα οἱ πολλοί ἐσμεν, οἱ γὰρ πάντες ἐκ τοῦ ἑνὸς ἄρτου μετέχομεν. βλέπετε τὸν Ἰσραὴλ κατὰ σάρκα· οὐχ οἱ ἐσθίοντες τὰς θυσίας κοινωνοὶ τοῦ θυσιαστηρίου εἰσίν; ("The cup of blessing that we bless, is it not a sharing in the blood of Christ? The bread that we break, is it not a sharing in the body of Christ? Because there is one bread, we who are many are one body, for we all partake of the one bread. Consider the people of Israel; are not those who eat the sacrifices partners in the altar?" [1 Cor 10:16-18]).

[37] τὸν θάνατον τοῦ κυρίου (1 Cor 11:26).

[38] As in verse 11:23, though here the source of the tradition is not identified, while in 11:23 it is ἀπὸ τοῦ κυρίου (from the Lord).

[39] See B. Janowski, *Sühne als Heilsgeschehen: Studien zur Sühnetheologie der Priesterschrift und zur Wurzel KPR im Alten Orient und im Alten Testament*, WMANT 55 (Neukirchen-Vluyn: Neukirchener Verlag, 1982), 353. See also Hans-Josef Klauck, "Sacrifice and Sacrificial Offerings (New Testament)," trans. Reginald H. Fuller, in *The Anchor Bible Dictionary*, Vol. 5, eds. David N. Freedman et al. (New York: Doubleday, 1992), 889.

[40] The NRSV notes this alternate reading as "place of atonement."

[41] As suggested by "ἐν τῷ αὐτοῦ αἵματι," or "by his blood" (NRSV).

[42] NRSV. Only implied by "διὰ."

[43] τὴν πάρεσιν τῶν προγεγονότων ἁμαρτημάτων.

[44] Milgrom, "Israel's Sanctuary," 390.

The language of Rom 5:8 and 8:32, without being specifically or technically sacrificial, reiterates the role of Christ's death as being somehow "for" those who believe. This, as mentioned before, is the dynamic that might be expected from a Levitical sacrificial tradition. It is also possible that the language of 8:32, that God "gave him up,"[45] could likewise echo a sacrificial understanding of Christ.

Finally, in Rom 15:16 Paul identifies himself as "a minister of Christ Jesus to the gentiles in the priestly service."[46] As noted previously, Paul considers his service within the temple of the body of believers to be a kind of "priestly service." The following phrase, "the offering of the gentiles," is vague and could refer to the gentiles themselves or their lives as a sacrifice, as in Rom 12:1. It certainly does not refer directly to Christ, but due to Paul's—not infrequent—emphasis on believers identifying with Christ it is likely that the language assumes some understanding of Christ's life as sacrifice to God in an ethical sense. This is less relevant to our inquiry but does, helpfully, suggest the multivalent nature of sacrificial traditions.

Thus, in spite of the limited direct data, it would seem that the preponderance of evidence in Paul's undisputed letters confirms the contention that Paul understood Christ's death to be a sacrifice in some sense, if not necessarily a sacrifice atoning for personal sin. This data set is not robust enough to determine whether Paul understood Christ's sacrifice as a space-purifying act enabling the dwelling of God in a particular location, but an examination of Paul's pneumatology will provide key "circumstantial" evidence.

Spatial Purification and the Undisputed Pneumatological Phenomena

It is clear from reading the undisputed letters that the presence and action of the Holy Spirit in the believer is very important to Paul. Paul views the believer individually and believers generally as a temple of the Holy Spirit. Both individual and corporate ideas are in play and are not viewed as mutually exclusive.[47] And in light of Paul's general concern and emphasis, we must understand this temple imagery to have a primarily *gentile* valence in his writings. One would also expect this if Paul thought that the indwelling of the gentiles was made possible by the space-sanctifying nature of Christ's sacrificial death. In such a situation one would also expect that the presence of God in the bodies of those purified would be noted from the outset: not occurring in later stages of initiation but at the very beginning. Again, this is in fact what we find in the undisputed letters,[48] and most clearly in Gal 3:3 in which believers are described as "having started with the Spirit." There is not language of a staged indwelling or later

---

[45] παρέδωκεν αὐτόν. Similar to Eph 5:25.
[46] λειτουργὸν Χριστοῦ Ἰησοῦ εἰς τὰ ἔθνη ἱερουργοῦντα.
[47] This idea of the body as a temple or dwelling of the Holy Spirit is present or clearly implied in Rom 5:5; 8:9-11; 1 Cor 3:9-17; 6:13-19; 9:13; 14:25; 2 Cor 4:7; 5:1-5; and 6:16.
[48] This language of initial indwelling is present in some form in Rom 8:23: "we ourselves, who have the first fruits of the Spirit," 1 Cor 12:13: "in the one Spirit we were all baptized into one body," 2 Cor 1:22: "his Spirit in our hearts as a first installment," Gal 3:3: "having started with the Spirit," Gal 4:29, and 1 Thess 1:5-6.

indwelling preceded by other stages in the faith.[49] One would also expect that such an indwelling as a result of sacrificial purification might not be instantialized until the remorse-based forgiveness that Milgrom describes[50] had also occurred. This occurs, according to Paul, at the time of proclamation of the good news. It is new awareness that allows "the repentance that leads to salvation."[51] Regularly Paul notes that the reception of the Holy Spirit occurs at the time of the first hearing of the good news.[52] Beyond these factors one would also expect that Paul would link the new indwelling of God in believers closely with his language of soteriology. This he does as well,[53] most obviously in Rom 8:13-14: "for if you live according to the flesh, you will die; but if by the Spirit you put to death the deeds of the body, you will live. For all who are led by the Spirit of God are children of God."[54]

Beyond these expectations being met, which does not in itself prove anything, we would expect, if Paul's sacrificial understanding were based in the space-purifying role of the *ḥaṭṭā't*, to see some explicit language describing Christ's death as effecting the receipt of the Holy Spirit. Interestingly, such language is indeed present in both Galatians and Romans. In the Galatians passage referenced earlier regarding Christ bearing our curse in death, Paul suggests that this accursed death allows "the blessing of Abraham [to] come to the gentiles, so that we might receive the promise of the Spirit through faith" (Gal 3:14).[55] Even more compelling is Paul's claim in Rom 5 that "God's love has been poured into our hearts through the Holy Spirit that has been given to us. For while we were still weak, at the right time Christ died for the ungodly" (Rom 5:5-6).[56]

Finally, the key link in this chain of logic has to do with whether Christ's sacrificed body could be understood to purify other bodies which were not explicitly sacrificed. Again in Romans Paul writes: "by sending his own Son in the likeness of sinful flesh, and to deal with sin, he condemned sin in the flesh, so that the just requirement of the law might be fulfilled in us, who walk not according to the flesh but according to the Spirit"

---

[49] Acts 19:2 notwithstanding.
[50] Milgrom argues "that the purification offering has no role whatsoever in removing human sin ... [But] scripture itself says that the purification rite is performed so that the sinner may be forgiven (Lev 4:20, 26, 31). Yet Milgrom contends that the forgiveness is not for the sinful act per se but rather for the *consequence* of the act, the contamination of the sanctuary. How then is the actual act of the individual sinner forgiven? Milgrom argues that the forgiveness of the original sin itself is accomplished by a feeling of remorse." Anderson, "Sacrifice," 880.
[51] 2 Cor 7:10.
[52] For example, 1 Cor 2:4: "My speech and proclamation were not with plausible words of wisdom, but with a demonstration of the Spirit and of power."
[53] Passages with a clear link between the presence of the Holy Spirit and soteriological concerns are Rom 8:13-14, 16; 1 Cor 2:12-16; 2 Cor 1:21-22; 3:16-18, Gal 4:6; 5:24-25; 6:8; 1 Thess 4:8.
[54] εἰ γὰρ κατὰ σάρκα ζῆτε μέλλετε ἀποθνῄσκειν, εἰ δὲ πνεύματι τὰς πράξεις τοῦ σώματος θανατοῦτε ζήσεσθε. ὅσοι γὰρ πνεύματι θεοῦ ἄγονται, οὗτοι υἱοὶ θεοῦ εἰσιν. This also suggests the idea that the purification of the space happened regardless of ethical or moral purity (e.g. Torah observance) in gentiles.
[55] εἰς τὰ ἔθνη ἡ εὐλογία τοῦ Ἀβραὰμ γένηται ... ἵνα τὴν ἐπαγγελίαν τοῦ πνεύματος λάβωμεν διὰ τῆς πίστεως.
[56] ἡ ἀγάπη τοῦ θεοῦ ἐκκέχυται ἐν ταῖς καρδίαις ἡμῶν διὰ πνεύματος ἁγίου τοῦ δοθέντος ἡμῖν, ἔτι γὰρ Χριστὸς ὄντων ἡμῶν ἀσθενῶν ἔτι κατὰ καιρὸν ὑπὲρ ἀσεβῶν ἀπέθανεν.

(Rom 8:3-4)[57] ... "since the Spirit of God dwells in you" (Rom 8:9).[58] Here the link seems clear. It is made even clearer by the identification that Paul makes, for himself and for other believers, with Christ as crucified: "I have been crucified with Christ" (Gal 2:19)[59] and "those who belong to Christ Jesus have crucified the flesh with its passions and desires" (Gal 5:24).[60] Even further, recalling the long debate over Rom 3:25, the interpretation of Christ as the mercy seat, the location purified, might support the contention that Paul viewed Christ's body as representative of all bodies, able to purify the human body generally, and able to purify the gentile body specifically as a dwelling for God.

Possible Qumran Precedents

The community at Qumran provides an additional precedent for the particular constellation of ideas that are currently being considered. The community, which saw a רוח קודש (spirit of holiness) as being in them, also clearly saw itself as operating in a priestly capacity in spite of its separation from the Jerusalem Temple and the operation of the Temple cult. This is indicated very clearly in the *Damascus Document*'s interpretation of Ezek 44:15, in which it is asserted that "'the priests' are the penitents of Israel who depart(ed) from the land of Judah, ('the Levites' are those) who accompany them, and the 'Sons of Zadok' are the chosen ones of Israel, those called by name, who stand in the end of days" (CD MS A 4.3-4).[61] The community is portrayed as still performing the cultic sacrificial rituals,[62] even as they must be understood to be metaphorical or ethical. This is made even more pertinent by the evidence from *The Rule of the Community* that the religiously observant and ethical life of the community—the sacrifice, if you will—was atoning *for the earth*:

> When these become in Israel—the Council of the Community being established in truth—an eternal plant, the House of Holiness consisting of Israel, a most holy assembly for Aaron, (with) eternal truth for judgment, chosen by (divine) pleasure to atone for the earth and to repay the wicked their reward.[63]
>
> (1QS 8:4-7)

---

[57] τὸν ἑαυτοῦ υἱὸν πέμψας ἐν ὁμοιώματι σαρκὸς ἁμαρτίας καὶ περὶ ἁμαρτίας κατέκρινεν τὴν ἁμαρτίαν ἐν τῇ σαρκί, ἵνα τὸ δικαίωμα τοῦ νόμου πληρωθῇ ἐν ἡμῖν τοῖς μὴ κατὰ σάρκα περιπατοῦσιν ἀλλὰ κατὰ πνεῦμα.
[58] εἴπερ πνεῦμα θεοῦ οἰκεῖ ἐν ὑμῖν.
[59] Χριστῷ συνεσταύρωμαι.
[60] οἱ δὲ τοῦ Χριστοῦ [Ἰησοῦ] τὴν σάρκα ἐσταύρωσαν σὺν τοῖς παθήμασιν καὶ ταῖς ἐπιθυμίαις.
[61] Joseph M. Baumgarten and Daniel R. Schwartz, "Damascus Document (CD)," in *The Dead Sea Scrolls: Hebrew, Aramaic, and Greek Texts with English Translations, Volume 2; Damascus Document, War Scroll and Related Documents*, ed. James H. Charlesworth (Tübingen and Louisville: Mohr Siebeck and Westminster John Knox, 1995), 19.
[62] Indicated by CD 4.2: "they shall present to me fat and blood."
[63] Elisha Qimron and James H. Charlesworth, "Rule of the Community (1QS; cf. 4QS MSS A-J, 5Q11)," in *The Dead Sea Scrolls: Hebrew, Aramaic, and Greek Texts with English Translations, Volume 1; Rule of the Community and Related Documents*, ed. James H. Charlesworth (Tübingen and Louisville: Mohr Siebeck and Westminster John Knox, 1994), 35.

These emphases in the sectarian documents at Qumran suggest that not only did they view some version of sacrifice as place-purifying, but that the effectiveness of sacrifices—ethical or otherwise—made by a human could be transferred to other spaces besides their own person. Whether Paul was aware of the Qumran perspectives on this subject is not important. That this particular constellation of ideas had crystallized at Qumran, however, makes it more plausible that a similar constellation could crystallize elsewhere in the Jewish world as well.

Possible Evidence to the Contrary

Due to the contentious nature of this debate over sacrificial themes in Paul,[64] and also simply in the name of due diligence, we must examine putative contrary evidence. However, in spite of McLean's protestations,[65] the existence of contrary evidence does not prevent the presence of influence from a Levitical sacrificial tradition. It simply suggests the presence of other additional traditions. Nor does possible evidence suggesting a function of personal atonement in sacrificial death prevent the influence of a Levitical sacrificial tradition that is largely space purification-oriented.[66] We would expect some degree of conceptual conflict if multiple traditions were being drawn on for their explanatory power.[67] In this case the scapegoat traditions and Passover traditions show some conflict with Levitical sacrificial traditions as defined by Milgrom. Should we be surprised? This cannot but be the case if multiple distinct traditions are being marshaled to explain a single person or event. The unity of the person or event is the focal point for contradictions between the diverse explanatory traditions.

---

[64] Bell's ripostes to McLean are certainly highly charged, if not always entirely defensible.
[65] McLean, "Absence," 548–52.
[66] Although problems do remain with Milgrom's theory. See Anderson, "Sacrifice," 880: "Stated in this general way, Milgrom's argument is very persuasive. Things become more difficult when Milgrom attempts to argue that the purification offering has no role whatsoever in removing human sin. Indeed scripture itself says that the purification rite is performed so that the sinner may be forgiven (Lev 4:20, 26, 31). Yet Milgrom contends that the forgiveness is not for the sinful act per se but rather for the *consequence* of the act, the contamination of the sanctuary. How then is the actual act of the individual sinner forgiven? Milgrom argues that the forgiveness of the original sin itself is accomplished by a feeling of remorse. This feeling is indicated in the biblical text by the use of the verb '*āšēm* (Lev 4:13, 22, 27), which Milgrom translates 'to feel guilty.' But there are problems. If such an important atoning function is present in the act of feeling remorse, why is this term absent in Num 15:22-31? Or why is it absent in the case of the priest (Lev 4:1-12)? This situation is complex and does not offer any easy solution. Certainly Milgrom's work is an important contribution, but loose ends still abound." If the role of sacrifice in Paul is confusing and contested, the understanding of the Levitical traditions themselves is certainly no less so.
[67] See Dunn, "Paul's Understanding," 133: The "tendency to run together different metaphors and descriptions of Jesus' death so that old distinctions are blurred and lost is clearly evident elsewhere in the early Church (1 Pet 1:18 f.; [John] 1:29), and Paul's language ... hardly suggests that it was otherwise with him." Eberhart ("To Atone or Not to Atone") describes some of this complex conceptual conflict both among Hebrew Bible sacrificial traditions and in the New Testament writers' usage of them.

McLean argues that:

1. sacrifice does not atone for personal sin;
2. a sacrificial victim becomes neither sinful nor accursed but remains holy;
3. there are no explicit textual references in Paul's letters to Christ's death as an atoning sacrifice;
4. references to Christ's blood in Paul's letters cannot be interpreted as implicit references to an atoning sacrifice;
5. Paul's interpretation of the suffering and death of Christ is incompatible with sacrificial theology.[68]

Regarding point two, Paul clearly does not believe that Christ became exclusively unholy or entirely accursed,[69] but, much like a sacrifice as described by McLean himself,[70] took on the sin and accursedness of others while still remaining holy. Point three is, at best, debatable in light of Rom 3:25, though I tend to agree with McLean's use of the word "explicit." While we may be inclined to concede McLean's point four in light of 1 Cor 5:7,[71] passages such as Rom 5:8-9[72] may militate against this idea. Also, Anderson's aforementioned interpretation of Milgrom prevents this conclusion. McLean's fifth point is his weakest because the presence of ideas in Paul's soteriology of Christ's death that do not derive from Levitical sacrificial traditions does not prove that he is not influenced by Levitical sacrificial traditions, but only that he is influenced by other ideas as well. Further, McLean's entire argument in favor of the exclusive explanatory power of scapegoat traditions[73] is rather hamstrung by Paul's emphasis on Christ's death.[74] And though we are inclined to grant McLean's first point for the sake of argument in light of Milgrom's work, whether Paul's letters support a personal sacrificial atonement as is traditionally held remains the key issue requiring further attention.

In chapter 5 of the letter to the Romans, more than any other passage, Paul uses language that seems to suggest some degree of a personal atonement role to sacrifice:

---

[68] McLean, "Absence," 531–2.
[69] As indicated by 1 Cor 12:3.
[70] McLean, "Absence," 538–42.
[71] "Clean out the old yeast so that you may be a new batch, as you really are unleavened. For our paschal lamb, Christ, has been sacrificed."
[72] "But God proves his love for us in that while we still were sinners Christ died for us. Much more surely then, now that we have been justified by his blood, will we be saved through him from the wrath of God."
[73] Or similar Greco-Roman traditions.
[74] And while it had become the practice to kill the scapegoat in order to prevent its return in Greco-Roman rituals of the time, and possibly even at times in first-century Judaism (McLean, *The Cursed Christ*, 70–87), the biblical precedents make no mention of this at all and it is a clear departure from the biblical witness.

God proves his love for us in that while we still were sinners Christ died for us. Much more surely then, now that we have been justified by his blood, will we be saved through him from the wrath of God. For if while we were enemies, we were reconciled to God through the death of his Son, much more surely, having been reconciled, will we be saved by his life.[75]

(Rom 5:8-10)

Here we appear to see the death of Christ—which we have shown Paul believed to be a sacrifice—seeming to effect justification and reconciliation. This sounds a good deal like forgiveness and not very much like purification. However, a few things must be noted here. Firstly, the language here is corporate, not individual. This is likewise the case in every single passage previously noted. This suggests that a personal atonement is not primarily in view but rather some kind of corporate one. Secondly, elsewhere Paul is more delicate in his formulations, such as in Rom 4:25 where he separates Christ being "handed over"[76] to death for our trespasses" and subsequently being "raised for our justification."[77] This alternate formulation is more in line with what we would expect according to Milgrom's *ḥaṭṭā't* function. The variability in the formulation also suggests that we cannot rely on the precision of any single formulation in isolation but should look to the whole witness of the undisputed letters for clarity. Thirdly and perhaps most importantly is the complicating issue of experiential phenomena.

Repeatedly Paul describes the action and indwelling of the Spirit not in theoretical terms but in a language of phenomenal experience.[78] There are clear evidences to him of the Spirit's presence and power. His explanations appear not to have been contrived by logic but rather to have been cobbled together as by one trying to make sense of confusing experiences. This is likewise true of much of the language of forgiveness that is used.[79] Paul does not describe a tidy theory, or a measured transaction, but rather an incredible and—to him—empirically verifiable phenomenon: the gentiles must have been purified and forgiven, because it is clear that God is dwelling in them. This incredible fact is clear evidence to Paul of the proximity of the *eschaton*. If the gentiles were filled for the first time with the Holy Spirit—a phenomenon foretold in the apocalyptic section of Joel[80] and reiterated at the beginning of Acts[81]—then the gentile believers must have been newly sanctified as proper vessels for the dwelling of God.[82] This purification would have been attributed to the sacrifice of Christ and appropriated by gentile believers through contrition and faith—not obedience to the

---

[75] συνίστησιν δὲ τὴν ἑαυτοῦ ἀγάπην εἰς ἡμᾶς ὁ θεὸς ὅτι ἔτι ἁμαρτωλῶν ὄντων ἡμῶν Χριστὸς ὑπὲρ ἡμῶν ἀπέθανεν. πολλῷ οὖν μᾶλλον δικαιωθέντες νῦν ἐν τῷ αἵματι αὐτοῦ σωθησόμεθα δι' αὐτοῦ ἀπὸ τῆς ὀργῆς. εἰ γὰρ ἐχθροὶ ὄντες κατηλλάγημεν τῷ θεῷ διὰ τοῦ θανάτου τοῦ υἱοῦ αὐτοῦ, πολλῷ μᾶλλον καταλλαγέντες σωθησόμεθα ἐν τῇ ζωῇ αὐτοῦ.

[76] Or "given up."

[77] ὃς παρεδόθη διὰ τὰ παραπτώματα ἡμῶν καὶ ἠγέρθη διὰ τὴν δικαίωσιν ἡμῶν.

[78] For example, 1 Thess 1:5-6, Gal 3:2-5, and 1 Cor 14:25.

[79] For example, Rom 3:25, 15:8-9, 1 Cor 6:11, and all of the passages about forgiveness as a "free gift" that do not indicate a transactional understanding of forgiveness, such as Rom 5:15-17 and 6:23.

[80] Joel 2:28: "at that time I will pour out my spirit on all flesh."

[81] Acts 2:17-21.

[82] For a rather exhaustive catalog of Jewish texts indicating this expectation, see Dale C. Allison, *Constructing Jesus: Memory, Imagination, an History* (Grand Rapids, MI: Baker Academic, 2010), 49.

law or heritage. Christ's death would have been seen to have cleansed the spaces of the gentiles' bodies for the presence of God. This passage is clearly in Paul's mind as he cites Joel 2:32, "All who call on the name of the LORD will be saved," in Rom 10:13 while discussing God's saving presence among gentile believers.

A further eschatological consideration must be made as regards gentile access to God. Access to God would certainly have been of great concern for Paul, in light of, for instance, his quotation of Lev 26:11 in 2 Cor 6:16, "I will live in them and walk among them." But that passage refers specifically to Israel, not to gentiles. According to Isa 56 gentiles will be able to access God in the Temple through conversion and legal obedience:

> And the foreigners who join themselves to the LORD, to minister to him, to love the name of the LORD, and to be his servants, all who keep the sabbath, and do not profane it, and hold fast my covenant—these I will bring to my holy mountain, and make them joyful in my house of prayer; their burnt offerings and sacrifices will be accepted on my altar; for my house shall be called a house of prayer for all peoples. Thus says the Lord GOD, who gathers the outcasts of Israel, I will gather others to them besides those already gathered.
>
> (Isa 56:6-8)

But Paul's entire mission is based in the idea that gentiles do not need to abide by traditional forms of Jewish legal observance.[83] Without that, according to the traditional understanding, there was no access to God for gentiles because there was no access to the Temple. This was, of course, still enforced in Paul's day, even as he saw it as the end of the age. So clearly, a key cornerstone of Paul's gentile mission is his conviction that God is newly accessible to gentiles through Christ's death.[84] Concern for the gentile experience of access to God, as indicated by a Pauline theological ecology, suggests that a primary role of Christ's death for Paul would have been that it enabled gentile access to God and circumvented the problem of Isa 56. In light of the preceding discussion of Paul's pneumatology, it is undeniable that, for Paul, Christ's sacrificial death had purified gentile bodies as appropriate dwelling places for the divinity.

If a spatial soteriology of sacrificial purification influenced Paul, and he had the conviction[85] that the gentiles had become (or needed to be understood as) sanctified vessels of the Holy Spirit of God, then the belief in Jesus' death as a uniquely sacrificial/purifying act would go back, *at the very latest,* to the point[86] at which it was clear either that God had come to dwell in the gentiles *en mass* via the Holy Spirit or that such a theological position was required for his mission. Such a phenomenon would require both the conclusion that the *eschaton* was at hand and that something unique had precipitated it. What we see in Paul may be *ex post facto* explanations and rationalizations for the change of situation. He may be scrambling to explain something that must be explained because it has occurred, but which was not exactly expected or exhaustively thought through ahead-of-time. Or he may be scrambling to explain something that he had come to feel was a necessary but

---

[83] Gager, *Reimagining Paul.*
[84] Hence the context in which 2 Cor 6:16 appears: a discussion of the body as the temple of the Holy Spirit.
[85] As in Acts 10:45.
[86] Which would be a very early point.

complicated theological position. Paul does his best to explain but appears to be struggling with the facts on the ground as much as anyone else.

Essentially, it seems that evidence of doctrinal messiness or contradictions in Paul may be evidence of reactions to the messiness of reality. Larry Hurtado has recently put this idea into helpful words:

> I propose that the remarkable and novel readings of … biblical texts … likely emerged early, quickly, and typically in settings of group prayer and worship where the sense of the Spirit's presence and power was strong. Early believers came to their Scriptures with convictions shaped by powerful religious experiences that opened the sacred texts for them in new ways, particularly experiences of the risen and exalted Jesus, and continuing revelations from the Spirit.[87]

It seems clear then that contradictions between possible traditional influences in Paul's view of Christ's death do not require decision for one or the other. These influences need not be mutually exclusive. In fact, it seems least likely that they were so. It is more likely that when confronted with the perceived fact that the Spirit of God was, or needed to be, present in gentiles, Paul, and others, had to think fast and drew on all explanatory paradigms available to them. Levitical sacrificial thinking and Passover traditions may have bled into the scapegoat traditions, but only because all of these different traditions had useful explanatory power. Evidence for the influence of one need not overrule evidence for the influence of another.

Conclusion

Based on the explicit and circumstantial evidence from the undisputed Pauline Letters, and a consideration of aspects of his theological ecology, it seems plausible that Paul may have been influenced in his understanding of the efficacy of Christ's death by Levitical sacrificial traditions that, according to Milgrom, emphasized the purification of space for the dwelling of God.[88] In Paul, this space would be the bodies/temples

---

[87] Larry W. Hurtado, "Two Case Studies in Earliest Christological Readings of Biblical Texts," in *All That the Prophets Have Declared: The Appropriation of Scripture in the Emergence of Christianity*, ed. Matthew R. Malcom (London: Authentic Media, 2015), 23.

[88] Interestingly, the witness from the disputed Pauline Letters is very different. Ephesians seems to affirm an explicit association between Christ's sacrifice and personal atonement, as seen in 1:7: "In him we have redemption through his blood, the forgiveness of our trespasses." See also Eph 2:16, 5:1-2, 25. For the most part though the understanding of the Holy Spirit described in Ephesians is not at odds with the descriptions noted in the undisputed letters. Colossians is even further removed. While reconciliation is effected by Christ's death (1:20), it appears that in some way Christ's sacrifice is not fully effective and needs to be supplemented by "Paul's" (1:24). Further, there is little if any talk of the Holy Spirit but rather of "Christ" in the believer, and the transformation of said gentile believers appears to be less instantaneous and more incremental, and the change effected (forgiveness, purification) by baptism rather than Christ's sacrifice (2:12-13). These differences indicate to me a clear division between the likelihood of authorship for Ephesians and Colossians as compared to the undisputed letters. Colossians being very significantly different from the theology and content of the undisputed letters.

of the gentiles shown to be newly sanctified for the presence of God through the phenomenon of the indwelling of the Holy Spirit.[89]

It *cannot* be claimed that the understanding of Levitical sacrifice suggested in this chapter as a possible operating assumption for Paul is the only appropriate understanding. There is much evidence that supports multivalent understandings of Christ's death and of the salvation that believers in him thought occurred as the result of it. The imagery of legal language used to describe justification, of redemption language related to slavery, and of scapegoat/scape-man imagery to suggest atonement all have a role in the complex tapestry of interconnected meanings that Paul weaves.[90]

This plausible reading of Paul's soteriology may help make better sense of some of Paul's language concerning what the law was able to do and not able to do. It may have been functionally clear to him that the law had not been able to purify the gentiles, *en mass*, to be dwelling places for God and that, on the contrary, the death of Christ had been able. It is not intended as a criticism of the law, which Paul loved, valued, and kept but may simply have been an observation based on experience.

It is also possible that the theological innovation of Christ's death as a (space-purifying) sacrifice enabling God's dwelling in gentile bodies/temples may have been a functional workaround to allow gentile access to God without legal observance. Temple authorities of the time, who could not have been expected to allow gentile access to God through the Temple without full legal obedience and conversion, would have been an obstacle to Paul's eschatological mission. The innovation of Christ's death as sacrifice fits Paul's particular need extremely well, though whether it is a Pauline innovation cannot be determined. It does not seem to appear yet in the pre-Pauline Philippians hymn (2:6-11).

The reading of Paul suggested in this chapter also allows room for reconsideration of the theologies that prevent God from loving humanity without killing God's own son. A metaphysical, personal, substitutionary atonement theory is not a necessary component of the *ḥaṭṭa't* and may not be explicitly supported by the undisputed Pauline correspondence. This theory also has the potential to contribute to the decolonizing of Pauline interpretation, in allowing for more agency of the believer in Pauline soteriology. According to the reading of Paul set forward, in line with Milgrom's conclusions,[91] God could forgive gentiles by fiat upon repentance rather than requiring death and blood.[92] According to *ḥaṭṭa't* traditions, Christ's death would not be mechanistically necessary for the forgiveness of gentiles. At the same time, Jesus is able to give

---

[89] This conclusion is part of a broader movement to recognize the crucial importance of the "body" in Paul. See Dale Martin, *The Corinthian Body* (New Haven, CT: Yale University Press, 1995); See also Troels Engberg-Pedersen, *Cosmology and Self in the Apostle Paul: The Material Spirit* (Oxford: Oxford University Press, 2010).

[90] If Paul can exhort believers παραστῆσαι τὰ σώματα ὑμῶν θυσίαν ζῶσαν ἁγίαν εὐάρεστον τῷ θεῷ (present your bodies as a living sacrifice, holy and acceptable to God [Rom 12:1]), then it seems clear that his idea of sacrifice cannot be based exclusively in Levitical traditions.

[91] Milgrom, "Israel's Sanctuary," 390.

[92] There is no need for "cosmic child abuse" as in Rita Nakashima Brock, *Journeys by Heart: A Christology of Erotic Power* (New York: Crossroad, 1988), 56.

himself freely[93] in order to accomplish something new—the purification of the body for the dwelling of God—not required to die that humanity might be loved by God.[94]

Having seen some of the fruitful possibilities raised through applying spatial analysis and a concern for theological ecology to an apocalyptic thinker like Paul, who reimagined reality in light of his convictions regarding the end of the age, we turn now to an apocalypse proper: the *Parables of Enoch*. Here we will see not so much a reimagination of the dwelling of God with faithful humans, though that does appear in this early Jewish apocalyptic text, but what happens when an experience of marginal dwelling becomes appropriated literarily—and valorized.

---

[93] As in Eph 5:2: καθὼς καὶ ὁ Χριστὸς ἠγάπησεν ἡμᾶς καὶ παρέδωκεν ἑαυτὸν ὑπὲρ ἡμῶν προσφορὰν καὶ θυσίαν τῷ θεῷ (as Christ loved us and gave himself up for us, a fragrant offering and sacrifice to God).

[94] This, of course, does not address the possibility of personal atonement as derived from other traditions.

4

Identification with a Marginal Home: Waters of Judgment as the Oppressed in the *Parables of Enoch*

Scholars have long recognized that apocalypses are not simply eschatological in spite of how they are popularly understood.[1] As mentioned in the preceding chapter on Paul, Christopher Rowland has pushed this observation even further[2] to suggest that eschatological or temporal concerns are not integral to the genre.[3] Further examination of the spatial dimensions of the apocalypses is warranted to better understand this less-considered aspect of their meaning. This imperative is buttressed by many of the aforementioned observations of postmodern philosophers of space,[4] but Tuan's

---

[1] For example, see the *Semeia* 14 definition of an apocalypse reproduced in John J. Collins, *The Apocalyptic Imagination: An Introduction to the Jewish Matrix of Christianity* (New York: Crossroad, 1987), 4: "A genre of revelatory literature with a narrative framework, in which a revelation is mediated by an otherworldly being to a human recipient, disclosing a transcendent reality which is both temporal, insofar as it envisages eschatological salvation, and spatial insofar as it involves another, supernatural world."

[2] Rowland concludes, contra the *Semeia* 14 definition, that literary forms and eschatological concerns are not defining characteristics. Rather, he writes that "apocalyptic" is best defined by "the belief that God's will can be discerned by means of a mode of revelation which unfolds directly the hidden things of God. To speak of apocalyptic, therefore, is to concentrate on the theme of the direct communication of the heavenly mysteries in all their diversity." Christopher Rowland, *The Open Heaven, A Study of Apocalyptic in Judaism and Early Christianity* (London: SPCK, 1982), 14.

[3] Though John Collins considers this rejection a bridge too far, he rightly recognizes the helpful contribution made by Rowland's work. Collins, *The Apocalyptic Imagination*, 8–9, 220 nn.18–24.

[4] Michel Foucault, "Of Other Spaces," trans. Jay Miskowiec, *Diacritics* 16 (1986): 22: "The great obsession of the nineteenth century was, as we know, history: with its themes of development and of suspension, of crisis and cycle, themes of the ever-accumulating past, with its great preponderance of dead men and the menacing glaciations of the world ... The present epoch will perhaps be above all the epoch of space. We are in the epoch of simultaneity: we are in the epoch of juxtaposition, the epoch of near and far, of the side-by-side, of the dispersed. We are at a moment, I believe, when our experience of the world is less that of a long life developing through time than that of a network that connects points and intersects with its own skein. One could perhaps say that certain ideological conflicts animating present-day polemics oppose the pious descendants of time and the determined inhabitants of space." And Soja, *Postmodern Geographies*, 2: "We must be insistently aware of how space can be made to hide consequences from us, how relations of power ... are inscribed into the apparently innocent spatiality of social life." Further, "the historical imagination is never completely spaceless and critical social historians have written, and continue to write, some of the best geographies of the past. But it is always time and history that provide the primary

observations are especially relevant for apocalyptic hermeneutics: "Every activity generates a particular spatio-temporal structure, but this structure seldom thrusts to the front of awareness … What compels us to reflect on experience? Untoward events."[5] It has been a commonplace for decades to note that apocalypses (e.g., The Book of the Watchers, Daniel, 4 Ezra, 2 Baruch, 3 Baruch), especially early ones,[6] often arose out of just such a traumatized environment. That such events facilitate consideration of previously neglected spatial phenomena militates further in favor of attending to the role of space in such works.

In the first chapter of this book the Gospel of John was analyzed for clues regarding the generative background of its composition, namely the importance of "home" as both a positive and negative shaping influence. In this chapter we will consider the semi-contemporaneous *Parables of Enoch* (1 En. 37–71) and a likely generative spatial locus: the dwelling-place of farmers who had been consigned to marginal, wet lands in the aftermath of the consolidation of the better "dry" lands in the hands of Herodian sympathizers. The *Parables* share a significant similarity with the Gospel of John with respect to the author's interest in the heavenly habitations of the righteous—though what is an interest for John seems to be an obsession for the author of the *Parables*.[7] This pervasive dwelling-related theme, which can be understood as a compensatory reimagination of home in light of a traumatized environment, suggests the importance of an ecological analysis of the *Parables* and of consideration for how this authorial interest in dwelling may relate to other, ostensibly unrelated themes. One such theme that many interpreters have suggested is awkwardly interpolated, and not obviously related to the predominating themes of the *Parables*, is that of "waters of judgment." The following analysis, however, will show that the anthropomorphic language of waters of judgment that appears in *Parables of Enoch* indicates a valorized[8] spatial identification

---

'variable containers' in these geographies … This [essay] does not deny the extraordinary power and importance of historiography as a mode of emancipatory insight, but identifies historicism with the creation of a critical silence, an implicit subordination of space to time that obscures geographical interpretations of the changeability of the social world and intrudes upon every level of theoretical discourse, from the most abstract ontological concepts of being to the most detailed explanations of empirical events" (14–15).

[5] Yi Fu Tuan, *Space and Place: The Perspective of Experience* (Minneapolis and London: University of Minnesota Press, 1977), 130–1. He goes on to say, "In non-technological societies the forces of nature often seem unpredictable: they are untoward events that intrude on human lives and command attention. They can be 'tamed' by being made a part of a cosmology or world view." This is precisely what is occurring in apocalypses.

[6] For example, Martha Himmelfarb, *The Apocalypse: A Brief History* (Malden, MA: Wiley-Blackwell, 2010), ix–x; Anathea Portier-Young, *Apocalypse against Empire: Theologies of Resistance in Early Judaism* (Grand Rapids, MI: Eerdmans, 2011); idem, "Jewish Apocalyptic Literature as Resistance Literature," in *The Oxford Handbook of Apocalyptic Literature*, ed. John J. Collins (Oxford and New York: Oxford University Press, 2014), 145–62, esp. 145–50; Richard A. Horsley, *Revolt of the Scribes: Resistance and Apocalyptic Origins* (Minneapolis: Fortress, 2010); David Flusser, "The Four Empires in the Fourth Sibyl and in the Book of Daniel," *Israel Oriental Studies* 2 (1978): 148–75.

[7] Indicated by as many as twenty-eight references to the heavenly habitations in the *Parables*.

[8] In line with Gaston Bachelard's observations regarding the "auto-valorizing" effect of even marginal spaces of dwelling, for example, Gaston Bachelard, *The Poetics of Space*, trans. Maria Jolas (Boston: Beacon Press, 1994), 12: "I shall therefore put my trust in the power of attraction of all the domains of intimacy. There does not exist a real intimacy that is repellent. All the spaces of intimacy are designated by an attraction. Their being is well-being. In these conditions, topoanalysis bears the stamp of a topophilia, and shelters and rooms will be studied in the sense of this valorization."

between the oppressed peoples of the region and the "waters" to which they had been consigned, even as this identification is not an "ideal" relationship. The appropriation of judgment language associated with water in the Noah story allows those who have been marginalized by the politically powerful to harness their identification with their new surroundings in an inspiring transformative vision for the "dry land" and "those who rule it."

With regard to this idea of valorization, I draw again on the work of Gaston Bachelard, from *The Poetics of Space*. As briefly mentioned in Chapter 1, he describes a normative feature of the phenomenology of dwelling being that of "auto-valorization." This is to say, the act of dwelling in a place, of resting there, of being sheltered there, typically attaches to that space a positive connotation, without regard for how humble or marginal the dwelling may be. He writes:

> I shall ... put my trust in the power of attraction of all the domains of intimacy. There does not exist a real intimacy that is repellent. All the spaces of intimacy are designated by an attraction. Their being is well-being. In these conditions, topoanalysis bears the stamp of a topophilia, and shelters ... will be studied in the sense of this valorization.[9]

Introduction

A convincing case has been made, based partly on the presence of polemics against landowners in the *Parables of Enoch*, for determining the date and setting of a late redactional stage of the work.[10] This setting can be deduced to have been near the Huleh Valley in Galilee during the period detailed in Josephus' *Antiquities* 17 that saw many of the ancestrally held lands of farmers in the region consolidated in the hands of the ruling elite.[11] If this location of the text and its concerns is correct, then it is also possible that the insertion of the Noachian interpolations into *Parables of Enoch* dates to this redactional stage. The association of the oppressors to be judged with the dry lands they rule suggests a logically parallel association between the righteous oppressed and the watery places to which they had been relegated. The likelihood of these parallel associations is buttressed by the fact that the judgment of "those who rule the dry land" is associated with the judgment that comes by means of the anthropomorphic waters of the flood—waters that have "souls" (1 En. 69:22).[12] Moreover, by the time of this redactional stage, "waters of judgment" had become a rather common literary

---

[9] Bachelard, *The Poetics of Space*, 12.
[10] James H. Charlesworth, "The Date and Provenience of the Parables of Enoch," in *Parables of Enoch: A Paradigm Shift*, eds. Darrell L. Bock and James H. Charlesworth (New York: T&T Clark, 2013), 37–57.
[11] Josephus, *Ant.* 17.304-314.
[12] Translation from E. Isaac, "1 (Ethiopic Apocalypse of) Enoch: A New Translation and Introduction," in *The Old Testament Pseudepigrapha: Volume I, Apocalyptic Literature and Testaments*, ed. James H. Charlesworth (Peabody, MA: Hendrickson Publishers, 1983), 5–89.

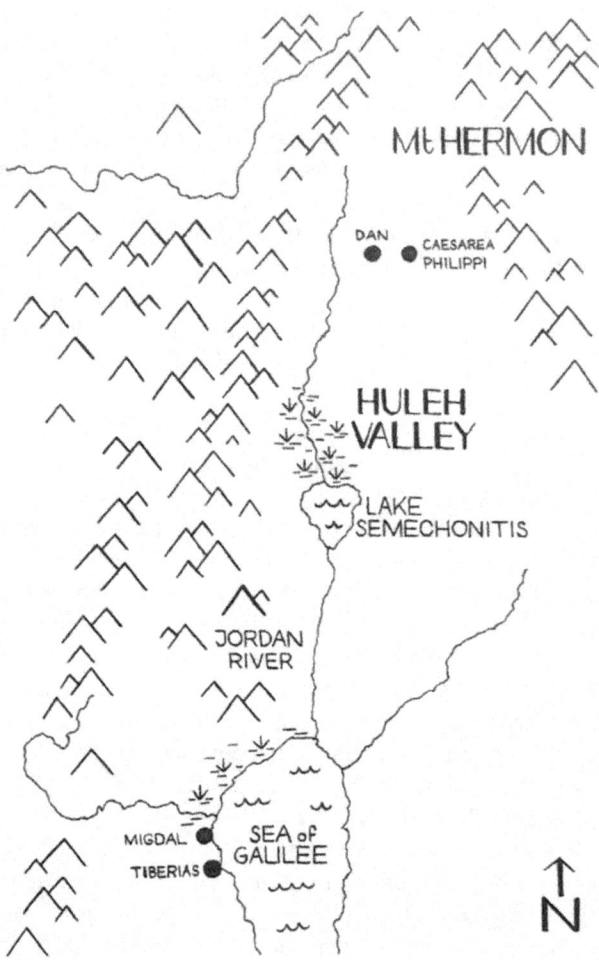

Figure 4.1 Map of the Huleh Valley and the Kinnereth/Sea of Galilee. (Artist's rendering by K. N. Pruszinski. Used with permission.)

trope used figuratively to represent human agents effecting drastic change whether as invading armies, oppressed peoples, or both.[13]

"Those Who Rule the Dry Land" Place the Text

In *Parables of Enoch: A Paradigm Shift*, James Charlesworth outlines[14] several factors contributing to a likely dating of the text to the late Herodian period in Galilee. The most significant innovation present in this contribution is his identification of the prominence of polemics against landowners in *Parables of Enoch*.

"Landowners," or designations of similar import, regularly appear at the end of the lists of oppressors who will be judged in *Parables of Enoch*. E. Isaac's translation in *OTP* represents these lists as shown in Table 4.1.

The designation of powerful oppressors who are condemned is a common trope in the Hebrew Bible and early Jewish literature. Charlesworth notes that such condemnations appear in Exod 22:28, 1 Kgs 21:10, 13, Isa 8:21, and Eccl 10:20.[15] This is by no means an exhaustive list as any student of the relevant literature will recognize. It is also typical for such ruling persons to appear in lists of the powerful oppressors who are categorically punished or judged (see Table 4.2 for examples).

Usually these lists are not long, often only rhetorical pairs as in Job 3:14 and Luke 21:12, and usually they do not involve a specific designation with respect to the earth or land. However, many texts do refer to "kings of the earth" or similar nonspecific, but generally earth/land linked, plural designations without necessarily presenting a list of such persons. Included among these are the designations shown in Table 4.3.

Table 4.1 E. Isaac's "Landowner" Designations in *Parables of Enoch*

1 En. 48:8	"the kings of the earth and the mighty landowners"
1 En. 53:5	"the kings and the potentates of this earth"
1 En. 55:4	"kings, potentates, dwellers upon the earth"
1 En. 62:1	"the kings, the governors, the high officials, and the landlords"
1 En. 62:3	"the kings the governors, the high officials, and the landlords"
1 En. 62:6	"(these) kings, governors, and all the landlords"
1 En. 62:9	"the kings, the governors, the high officials, and those who rule the earth"
1 En. 63:1	"the governors and the kings who possess the land"
1 En. 63:12	"the governors, kings, high officials, and landlords"
1 En. 67:8	"the kings, rulers, and exalted ones, and those who dwell on the earth"
1 En. 67:12	"the kings and the rulers who control the world"

---

[13] As this chapter will show.
[14] Charlesworth, "The Date and Provenience of the Parables of Enoch," 37–57.
[15] Charlesworth, "The Date and Provenience of the Parables of Enoch," 48.

Table 4.2 Powerful Oppressors in Jewish and Christian Scripture

Neh 9:34	מְלָכֵינוּ שָׂרֵינוּ כֹּהֲנֵינוּ וַאֲבֹתֵינוּ	our kings, our officials, our priests, and our ancestors …
Jer 2:26, 32:32	מַלְכֵיהֶם שָׂרֵיהֶם וְכֹהֲנֵיהֶם וּנְבִיאֵיהֶם	their kings, their officials, their priests, and their prophets …
Dan 9:8	לִמְלָכֵינוּ לְשָׂרֵינוּ וְלַאֲבֹתֵינוּ	on … our kings, our officials, and our ancestors …
Bar 1:16	τοῖς βασιλεῦσιν ἡμῶν καὶ τοῖς ἄρχουσιν ἡμῶν καὶ τοῖς ἱερεῦσιν ἡμῶν καὶ τοῖς προφήταις ἡμῶν καὶ τοῖς πατράσιν ἡμῶν	on our kings, our rulers, our priests, our prophets, and our ancestors …
Rev 6:15	οἱ βασιλεῖς … καὶ οἱ μεγιστᾶνες καὶ οἱ χιλίαρχοι καὶ οἱ πλούσιοι καὶ οἱ ἰσχυροί	the kings … and the magnates and the generals and the rich and the powerful …
Luke 21:12	βασιλεῖς καὶ ἡγεμόνας	kings and governors …

Table 4.3 Land-Linked Oppressors in Jewish and Christian Scripture (Not in List)

מַלְכֵי הָאֲדָמָה	"kings of the earth"	Isa 24:21
מַלְכֵי הָאֲרָצוֹת	"kings of the lands"	Ezra 9:7
מַלְכֵי־אֶרֶץ	"kings of [the] land"	7 times[16]
מַלְכֵי הָאָרֶץ	"kings of the land"	5 times[17]
שֹׁפְטֵי אֶרֶץ	"rulers of the land"	Isa 40:23
κρίνοντες τὴν γῆν	"rulers of the earth"	Wis 1:1
βασιλεῖς τῆς γῆς	"kings of the earth"	12 times[18]
βασιλεῖς τῆς οἰκουμένης ὅλης	"kings of the whole world"	Rev 16:14
reges terrae	"kings of the earth"	4 Ezra 15:20

There are, however, a few instances, in what became the canonical Jewish and Christian literature,[19] where such designations of oppressors do appear both in a list and with a general link to the land in a way similar to the lists of *Parables of Enoch*. These are included in Table 4.4:

---

[16] Ezek 27:33; Ps 2:2; 76:13 (v. 12, NRSV); 89:28 (v. 27, NRSV); 138:4; 148:11; Lam 4:12.
[17] 1 Kgs 5:14 (4:34, NRSV); 10:23; 2 Chr 9:22-23; Ps 102:16 (102:15, NRSV).
[18] 1 Macc 1:2; 1 Esd 8:74 (8:77, NRSV); Rev 1:5; 6:15; 17:2, 18; 18:3, 9; 19:19; 21:24; Matt 17:25; Acts 4:26.
[19] Although, rather strikingly, there are no instances of this language in the rest of 1 Enoch outside of *Parables of Enoch*.

Table 4.4 Land-Linked Oppressor Lists in Jewish and Christian Scripture

Job 3:14	מְלָכִים וְיֹעֲצֵי אָרֶץ	kings and counselors of the earth ...
Ps 2:10	מְלָכִים הַשְׂכִּילוּ הִוָּסְרוּ שֹׁפְטֵי אָרֶץ	O kings, be wise; be warned, O rulers of the earth ...
Ps 148:11	מַלְכֵי־אֶרֶץ וְכָל־לְאֻמִּים שָׂרִים וְכָל־שֹׁפְטֵי אָרֶץ	Kings of the earth and all peoples, princes and all rulers of the earth!
Rev 6:15	οἱ βασιλεῖς τῆς γῆς καὶ οἱ μεγιστᾶνες καὶ οἱ χιλίαρχοι καὶ οἱ πλούσιοι καὶ οἱ ἰσχυροί	The kings of the earth and the magnates and the generals and the rich and the powerful ...
Rev 19:17-19	συνάχθητε εἰς τὸ δεῖπνον τὸ μέγα τοῦ θεοῦ, ἵνα φάγητε σάρκας βασιλέων καὶ σάρκας χιλιάρχων καὶ σάρκας ἰσχυρῶν καὶ σάρκας ἵππων καὶ τῶν καθημένων ἐπ' αὐτῶν καὶ σάρκας πάντων ... Καὶ εἶδον τὸ θηρίον καὶ τοὺς βασιλεῖς τῆς γῆς ...	Gather for the great supper of God, to eat the flesh of kings, the flesh of captains, the flesh of the mighty, the flesh of horses and their riders—flesh of all ... Then I saw the beast and the kings of the earth ...

Of the texts presented in this list only those in Revelation are linked explicitly with judgment. What should also be clear from this list is the fact that it is shorter in its entirety than the list from *Parables of Enoch* alone. Though oppressor lists and general locative markers for rulers often appeared separately, their combination is comparatively unusual, and their constant combined presence in *Parables of Enoch* is very distinctive. This suggests, at the very least, a stylistic tick, but it more likely signals a particular significant concern of the author.

It becomes clearer that the mentions of oppressive landowners in *Parables of Enoch* are not accidental, but rather quite historically relevant when viewed in light of the rash of land confiscations that began under Herod the Great and continued after his death. Charlesworth notes[20] Josephus' account in *Antiquities* 17.304-14 regarding Herod's confiscations. Indeed, "he was wont to kill members of the nobility upon absurd pretexts and then take their property for himself."[21] But not only was his program against the wealthy nobility, including the Hasmoneans, but also against all who were liable to tax or who had any property at all:

> While many had perished through forms of destruction that had never been witnessed before, those who still lived were much more unfortunate in their suffering than these others because they were not only distressed by the wrongs that they witnessed and reflected upon, but also by the loss of their property.[22]

---

[20] Charlesworth, "The Date and Provenience of the Parables of Enoch," 51.
[21] Josephus, *Ant.* 17.307 (translation Marcus and Wikgren, LCL): τῶν τε εὐπατριδῶν, ὁπότε κτείνειεν αὐτοὺς ἐπ' ἀλόγοις αἰτίαις, τὰς οὐσίας ἀποφερόμενον.
[22] Josephus, *Ant.* 17.305 (translation Marcus and Wikgren, LCL): πολλῶν γοῦν ὄντων οἳ ὀλέθροις ἀπολώλοιεν οἵους οὐχ ἱστορῆσθαί πω πρότερον, πολλῷ δυστυχεστέρους τοῦ πάθους ἐκείνων τοὺς ζῶντας εἶναι, οὐ μόνον ὧν ὄψει καὶ διανοίᾳ ἐπ' αὐτοῖς ἀνιαθεῖεν ἀλλὰ καὶ ὧν ταῖς οὐσίαις.

"Through taxation and intrigue, Herod and his hierarchy eventually controlled virtually two-thirds of the fertile land by the time he died."[23] This kind of rule continued under his descendants and was marked by the relegation of the owners of ancestral lands to tenant-farmer status, or other marginal employment, due to either bankruptcy or outright seizure and the transference of land into the ownership of, often foreign, Herodian cronies.[24]

While this identification of polemics against landowners begins to make sense of some of the data of *Parables of Enoch*, it does not go quite far enough. Charlesworth notes that those who had lost their "dry land" would have been relegated to the dangerous and less productive marshy lands of the Huleh Valley, "the large swampy

Figure 4.2 Huleh Valley Wet Lands Prior to Reclamation. (Photograph by Zoltan Kluger from January 1940 titled "Members of Kibbutz Amir, their heads covered with netting against malaria flies, working in the Hula swamps." From Wikimedia commons. Used with permission. Edited for publication.)

---

[23] Charlesworth, "The Date and Provenience of the Parables of Enoch," 51.
[24] Charlesworth, "The Date and Provenience of the Parables of Enoch," 51.

area from Dan or Banias to Bethsaida or Capernaum."[25] However, just as the oppressive rulers were associated with the land they had appropriated, so it seems likely that the righteous oppressed would in some way identify with the watery lands to which they had been relegated. These Galileans would not have exclusively remained farmers, as the wetlands were not as productive. Rather they would have taken up other occupations, including fishing in the Sea of Galilee or working in the fish-processing industry located at Migdal (known in Greek as *Tarichaea*, or "Processed-Fishville").[26] This would create an even closer identification between the oppressed and the waters to which they had been consigned. Not only so, but the possible location of composition at Migdal[27] would allow for the influence of a topographic environment marked by the marshy northwest Sea of Galilee and the immediate presence of the sea itself. The logically parallel associations of the oppressors with the dry land and the oppressed with the waters are able to explain much more about *Parables of Enoch*, including possibly the Noachian interpolations, than can the sole association of the oppressors with the dry land.

Conflation of Identities in *Parables of Enoch*

From the outset it must be noted that the judgments against landowners are a theme that runs throughout *Parables of Enoch* in its current form. Any interpolation into the work would have had to make sense with this theme were it already present. Or, on the other hand, interpolations of landowners into the text would have had to make sense with the whole text as it already stood, since oppressor lists including landowners appear throughout. Thus, we are left with three options: (1) landowner passages preceded Noachian interpolations, but Noachian interpolations made sense in the overall context; (2) Noachian interpolations preceded landowner interpolations, but landowner interpolations made sense in the overall context; or (3) landowner and Noachian interpolations were made at the same time and both make sense with each other and in the overall preexisting context (or some other simultaneous redaction theory). In any of these options the landowner interpolations have to make sense besides the Noachian interpolations. Similarly, any interpolations must make sense beside the statement at the beginning of *Parables of Enoch* that "one should not withhold the beginning of wisdom from those of latter days" (1 En. 37:3). That is to say, what is written at any stage of the redaction is written for its relevance to issues of concern for the current redactor, as is the case with all apocalypses.[28]

---

[25] Charlesworth, "The Date and Provenience of the Parables of Enoch," 54.
[26] K. C. Hanson, "The Galilean Fishing Economy and the Jesus Tradition," *BTB* 27 (1997): 99–111.
[27] James H. Charlesworth, "Did Jesus Know the Traditions in the Parables of Enoch?" in *Parables of Enoch: A Paradigm Shift*, eds. Darrell L. Bock and James H. Charlesworth (New York: T&T Clark, 2013), 186–91.
[28] All other major apocalypses clearly respond to issues of their day, often through a reimagined past and prophecy *ex eventu*. See Daniel, Revelation, 2 Baruch, 4 Ezra, and so forth.

By the time the bulk of the redactions were completed on the version of the text we have now, the identities of the judged oppressors in *Parables of Enoch* had all been conflated. Not only is there significant variability in the exact language used for the oppressors (evidenced in Table 4.1), but the equation of these various designations through their inclusion in interchangeable lists causes a conflation across the entire document, even to the point of including the very generic designation those "who dwell upon the earth."[29] This phrase, were it not conflated with the wicked rulers and landowners, would not carry such a negative connotation. However, due to its usage in 55:4 and 67:8, it must be considered often (though not always) to have this negative valence throughout the work. It is certainly negative in the Noachian sections.

Not only are these various designations of the judged conflated, but the judged oppressors are likely conflated to a degree with the judged angels. This is confirmed by the initial flood-judgment scene in chapter 54:

> And in those days, the punishment of the Lord of the Spirits shall be carried out, and they shall open all the storerooms of water in the heavens above, in addition to the fountains of water which are on earth. And all the waters (*māyāt*) shall be united with (all) other waters .... And they shall obliterate all those that dwell upon the earth as well as those that dwell underneath the ultimate ends of heaven. On account of the fact that they did not recognize their oppressive deeds which they carried out on the earth, they shall be destroyed by the Flood.[30]
>
> (54:7-10)

This is further confirmed by the judgment through the burning waters in chapter 67:

> I also saw that valley in which there took place a great turbulence and the stirring of the waters ... the valley of the perversive angels shall (continue to) burn punitively underneath that ground; in respect to its troughs, they shall be filled with rivers of water by which those angels who perverted those who dwell upon the earth shall be punished. Those waters shall become in those days a poisonous drug of the body and a punishment of the spirit unto the kings, rulers, and exalted ones, and those who dwell on the earth; lust shall fill their souls so that their bodies shall be punished.[31]
>
> (67:5-8)

From these texts it is clear that the judgment of the angels and the judgment of the landowners, both accomplished through the waters of the flood, have been conflated by the author. Simultaneous judgment of heavenly and earthly beings is not an innovation. It appears in other prior texts, including Isa 24:21:

---

[29] This phrase appears in 1 En. 37:2, 5; 38:2; 40:6, 7; 43:4; 48:5; 53:1; 54:6, 9; 55:1, 2, 4; 60:5, 22; 65:6, 10, 12; 66:1; 67:7, 8; 69:1, 7; 70:1.

[30] Isaac, "1 Enoch," 38.

[31] Isaac, "1 Enoch," 46. And while many commentators believe this to be a reference to the springs of Kallirrhoë where Herod sought healing late in his life, it cannot be denied that the scene serves to accomplish other symbolic ends as well.

In that day the LORD will punish	וְהָיָה בַּיּוֹם הַהוּא יִפְקֹד יְהוָה
the powers in the heavens above	עַל־צְבָא הַמָּרוֹם בַּמָּרוֹם
and the kings on the earth below.	וְעַל־מַלְכֵי הָאֲדָמָה עַל־הָאֲדָמָה

There is a clear relationship between the kind of evil knowledge imparted by the evil angels and the usage of this kind of knowledge by the wealthy ruling class.[32] All of the skills and innovations attributed to the evil angels are associated with decadence and depravity, which are nearly universally associated with wealth and power. Nickelsburg and VanderKam conclude that "the interpolation enhances the Parables' relatively minor interest in the sin of the fallen angels [connecting it with] its major interest in the kings and mighty."[33]

These various relationships that suggest conflation of the judged are only buttressed by the fact that the Noachian sections were interpolated in the first place. The necessity of their relevance to the situation of the author's community (37:3) requires that they be viewed in the context of, and as pointing to, the judgments against the oppressive rulers.

However, this is not the only identity conflation that occurs in the work. There is much to suggest that the identities of the various righteous ones involved in performing the judging are somewhat conflated as well. At the beginning of *Parables of Enoch* it is the righteous who appear to be doing the judging: "When the congregation of the righteous shall appear, sinners will be judged for their sins" (38:1).[34] Then it appears that the Lord of the Spirits will judge: "He will judge the sinners" (38:3).[35] But then the judgment appears to shift back to being the work of the righteous: "the kings and rulers shall perish, they shall be delivered into the hands of the righteous and holy ones" (38:5).[36] In various places the righteous angels[37] and the Son of Man[38] act as judges. However, this last figure[39] must be recognized to function generically and in a sense that is representative of all righteous ones.[40] These conflated relations suggest that at any given point in the narrative the judgment accomplished by one figure must

---

[32] See 1 En. 65:6, in Isaac, "1 Enoch," 45: "An order has been issued from the court of the Lord against those who dwell upon the earth, that their doom has arrived because they have acquired the knowledge of all the secrets of the angels."

[33] George W. E. Nickelsburg and James C. VanderKam, *1 Enoch 2: A Commentary on the Book of 1 Enoch, Chapters 37–82*, Hermeneia, ed. Klaus Baltzer (Minneapolis: Fortress, 2012), 296.

[34] Isaac, "1 Enoch," 30.

[35] Isaac, "1 Enoch," 30.

[36] Isaac, "1 Enoch," 30.

[37] 1 En. 62:11.

[38] 1 En. 46:3 and 62:9.

[39] Even if expressly titular and associated with Enoch himself at the end of *Parables of Enoch*.

[40] If only due to the Hebrew Bible background of the phrase and the conflation of functions that occurs in *Parables of Enoch*.

necessarily have in view, and implicate, the judgment accomplished by another. All are co-judges. In this way it seems clear that not only are the righteous ones partly responsible for judgment,[41] but they can be seen to be involved in any act of judgment in the work.

A further conflation at work in *Parables of Enoch* is between the various words for earth and land. The two used throughout are *medr* and *yabs*. These are employed in equal proportion[42] and in often interchangeable ways. For instance, in the polemical lists they are used interchangeably (*medr* in 38:4; 48:8; 53:5; 62:1, 3, 6; and *yabs* in 48:8; 55:4; 62:9; 63:1, 12; 67:8, 12), much as are the designations for oppressive rulers/landowners. *Medr* means "earth," "ground," "soil," "land," "district," or "country."[43] It is typically used to translate γῆ in the Bible.[44] *Yabs* is more specifically translated as "dry land" or "dry ground."[45] It is etymologically related to the Aramaic יביש and to the Hebrew יבשה and is used most frequently to translate ξήρα in the Bible.[46] Clearly in other usage these terms are distinct, but in *Parables of Enoch* the author has blended their use to suggest overlapping ideas. We cannot really separate the specificity of implications of *yabs*, which most clearly depicts the detail of appropriated farmland, from the generality of *medr*. Nickelsburg and VanderKam write that at times distinctions can be drawn in the usage of *yabs* between a connotation of "dry land" as opposed to water (53:1; 60:9, 11; 61:10) and a connotation of "earth" as opposed to heavens (45:4-5; 55:2; 58:5; 60:11; 69:4).[47] However, even this distinction appears to be overwrought. The heavens throughout *Parables of Enoch* are identified with the waters that proceed from them and are identified in the Genesis account itself as a kind of waters (Gen 1:7). The distinction made by Nickelsburg and VanderKam appears to be more of a modern construction than one well founded in the concepts as deployed in *Parables of Enoch* or other antique literature. Charlesworth dismisses the likelihood of *yabs* being linked in meaning to mythological representations of the flood due to his conviction that other traditions are more important in shaping *Parables of Enoch*.[48] However, in light of the conflations across *Parables of Enoch* on multiple fronts and how that conflationary phenomenon functions to spread meaning across the work, it seems more likely that any flood valence to *yabs* in *Parables of Enoch* is not diluted by other traditions. On the contrary, it would appear that its conflation in usage with *medr* causes the echoes of the flood imagery to reverberate more widely across the work.[49]

---

[41] They are also responsible for judgment in 1 En. 48:9 and in other parts of 1 Enoch outside of *Parables of Enoch* as well. See, for instance, 1 En. 95:3 and 98:12.

[42] *Medr* is used forty-three times and *yabs* is used forty-two. See Nickelsburg and VanderKam, *1 Enoch 2*, 89–90, for a useful excursus on the usage of these words in *Parables of Enoch*.

[43] Thomas O. Lambdin, *Introduction to Classical Ethiopic (Geʽez)*, Harvard Semitic Studies 24 (Missoula, MT: Scholars Press, 1978), 413.

[44] Nickelsburg and VanderKam, *1 Enoch 2*, 89.

[45] Lambdin, *Introduction to Classical Ethiopic*, 447.

[46] Nickelsburg and VanderKam, *1 Enoch 2*, 89.

[47] Nickelsburg and VanderKam, *1 Enoch 2*, 89.

[48] Charlesworth, "The Date and Provenience of the Parables of Enoch," 49.

[49] *Yabs* is almost exclusively used by the author for the phrase translated as "those that dwell on the earth" or similar in Nickelsburg and VanderKam, *1 Enoch 2*, 89. This is the most common designation for those judged in the Noachian interpolations (appearing at least nine times) and must necessarily carry this connotation over into its usage elsewhere in *Parables of Enoch*.

Water Data in *Parables of Enoch*

E. Isaac's translation of *Parables of Enoch* is of particular interest for our purposes as he brings out the text's anthropomorphic language to describe the waters. In verse 16 of chapter 69, the author begins a poetic recitation of the secret oath of the angels. The poetic structure is maintained through verse 21 and at the beginning of verse 22 it ends, though the oath apparently continues until the end of verse 25. Isaac renders this latter section of the oath as follows:

> By the same oath the stars complete their courses of travel; if they call their names, he causes them to respond from the beginning (of creation); and forever! ^{22} Likewise the waters and their souls, all the winds and their paths of travel from all the directions of winds; ^{23} the voice of the thunder and the light of the lightning are kept there; ^{24} the reservoirs of hail, the reservoirs of frost, the reservoirs of mist, the reservoirs of rain and dew are kept there; ^{25} All these believe and give thanks in the presence of the Lord of the Spirits; they glorify with all their might, and please him in all this thanksgiving; they shall thank, glorify, exalt the Lord of Spirits forever and ever!
>
> (69:21-25)[50]

The sections of the oath preceding this are without anthropomorphisms. From the text quoted above it seems that Isaac interprets the textual evidence to suggest that the earliest reading is likely one that attaches an anthropomorphic quality to the waters ("and their souls," v. 22) but not as directly to any other natural elements following.[51] All commentators struggle with verses 22-24 of chapter 69.[52] Most, relying typically on the Princeton Ethiopic 3 manuscript in the Garrett collection or the EMML 2080 manuscript (and similar manuscripts), attach the idea of souls or spirits to the other elements listed subsequently in verse 22.[53] This seems to be the result of smoothing out the flow of the passage and likely does not preserve the difficulty of the earliest text. The preferred reading preserves the singular anthropomorphism of the waters.[54]

---

[50] Isaac, "1 Enoch," 48–9.
[51] Olson agrees. See Daniel Olson, *Enoch: A New Translation* (North Richland Hills, TX: Bibal, 2004), 131: "And the same is true for the spirits of the water, all of the winds, and their pathways according to the different varieties of the winds" (1 En. 69:22).
[52] Matthew Black believes the text of verse 22 may be corrupt. See M. Black, *The Book of Enoch or 1 Enoch: A New English Translation* (Leiden: Brill, 1985), 249.
[53] See Richard Laurence, *The Book of Enoch the Prophet* (London: Kegan, Paul, Trench & Co., 1883), according to his numbering 1 En. 68:31: "All of them have spirits." See also R. H. Charles, *The Book of Enoch the Prophet* (London: Oxford University Press, 1912), 1 En. 69:22: "the spirits of the water, and of the winds, and all zephyrs." Michael Knibb follows Charles in M. Knibb, *The Ethopic Book of Enoch: A New Edition in the Light of the Aramaic Dead Sea Fragments Vol. 2* (Oxford: Clarendon, 1978), 165. See also Black, *The Book of Enoch*, 66: "And likewise, with regard to the waters, to their winds, and to all spirits and their courses from all regions of spirits" (1 En. 69:22); and finally, Nickelsburg and VanderKam, *1 Enoch 2*, 304: "And likewise the spirits of the water, of the winds, and all the breezes and their paths, from all the quarters of the winds" (1 En. 69:22).
[54] The "voice" of verse 23 does not inherently connote personification and with thunder usually does not so. See August Dillman, *Lexicon linguae aethiopicae cum indice latino* (Lipsiae: T. O. Weigel, 1865; reprinted, New York: Ungar, 1955), 450–1.

This conclusion is further complicated, but not voided, by the statement in verse 25: "All these believe and give thanks." However, most commentators[55] view verses 22-24 as an insertion and argue that verse 25 was the original conclusion to the oath, following directly from verse 21. This would make for a smoother original flow—before the interpolation of verses 22-24—and would attach an unsurprising anthropomorphic quality to the stars specifically, which often represented angels in this period. In this earlier form of the text the natural conclusion of the angelic oath is the praise of the stars (which represent angels) for the Lord of the Spirits. The awkwardness of the waters, but none of the other elements, having souls, and yet all the elements praising the Lord of the Spirits, as opposed to only those that would have been viewed as animate, likely represents the stage of redaction that we are interested in. This is likely the stage at which concerns about oppressive landowners, and judgment of the oppressors by the waters, are being combined in the text. The reading offered by Isaac and Olson, based on the Kebran/Tanasee 9 manuscript, is both the most difficult reading in terms of the immediate context and the most compelling in terms of the broader sociological context of the late ancient redaction of *Parables of Enoch*.

What is of particular interest regarding the anthropomorphic waters of 69:22 is that anthropomorphic elements largely do not appear in the rest of *Parables of Enoch*. In fact all of the elemental anthropomorphisms in *Parables of Enoch* relate to the water.[56] The waters of judgment in chapter 54 are gendered: "That which is from the heavens above is masculine water, (whereas) that which is underneath the earth is feminine" (54:8).[57] Later it is stated that from the seed of the Lord of Spirits "will emerge a fountain (*naq*ʾ)[58] of the righteous and holy ones without number forever" (65:12).[59] Tellingly, the main Noachian judgment follows immediately upon this equation of the righteous with water. These statements, combined with the anthropomorphism of 69:22, suggest that the waters of judgment in *Parables of Enoch* are specifically associated with the righteous oppressed, even as the dry land is associated with the oppressors. This cue from the very sparse, yet focused, anthropomorphic language of *Parables of Enoch* is made even clearer by its striking contrast with the constant presence of anthropomorphic language for the elements in the rest of 1 Enoch, which is otherwise absent in *Parables of Enoch*.[60]

---

[55] Such as Nickelsburg and VanderKam, *1 Enoch 2*, 310.

[56] Though some commentators do see a personification of the earth in 65:5, but it is very minimal. See Andreas G. Hoffman, *Das Buch Henoch: In vollständiger Übersetzung mit fortlaufendem Commentar, ausführlicher Einleitung und erläuternden Excursen* (Jena: Croeker, 1833–1838), 2:515, and August Dillman, *Liber Henoch Aethiopice, ad quinque codicum fidem editus, cum variis lectionibus* (Leipzig: Vogel, 1851), but reprinted as August Dillman, *The Ethiopic Text of 1 Enoch*, Ancient Texts & Translations (Eugene, OR: Wipf & Stock, 2005), 35.

[57] Isaac, "1 Enoch," 38. This is a feature of the Kebran/Tanasee 9 manuscript. See Siegbert Uhlig, *Das Äthiopische Henochbuch*, JSHRZ 5/6 (Gütersloh: Mohn, 1984), 599, for a discussion on the textual issues with this section of *Parables of Enoch*.

[58] Johannes Flemming, *Das Buch Henoch: Äthiopischer Text*, Texte und Untersuchungen n.s. 7.1/22.1 (Leipzig: Hinrichs, 1902), 78.

[59] Isaac, "1 Enoch," 45.

[60] For examples of anthropomorphic language for the elements and other entities, see 1 En. 6:3; 7:6; 9:2; 14:8; 18:15; 21:6; 72:3; 75:1-2; 81:7; all of chapters 85–90; 100:11; 101:7; and 108:5-6.

Textual Precedents

The main question now is whether the posited social setting of *Parables of Enoch*, the presence of the Noachian elements in the text, and the identified anthropomorphisms of the waters in *Parables of Enoch* add up to a clear identification between the righteous oppressed and the waters of judgment. This question is best answered through a consideration of the precedents for the symbolic usage of water in the Hebrew Bible, LXX, and other early Jewish writings.

Anthropomorphic waters, as it so happens, do appear at times in the Hebrew Bible. Psalm 77:16 provides an excellent example:[61]

When the waters saw you, O God,	רָא֬וּךָ מַּ֨יִם ׀ אֱלֹהִ֗ים
when the waters saw you, they were afraid;	רָא֣וּךָ מַּ֣יִם יָחִ֑ילוּ
the very deep trembled.	אַ֝֗ף יִרְגְּז֥וּ תְהֹמֽוֹת

Anthropomorphic language is, of course, very common in the Hebrew Bible, so it is no surprise that such language would at times be used for so common an element as water. Such anthropomorphic language for water continues up through the period of the composition of *Parables of Enoch*, appearing in Wisdom (5:22; 19:20), Sirach (43:20), the Prayer of Azariah (1:38), and even the Gospel of Luke (8:25), among other places.

Water can however be associated even more closely with human and divine beings. The association is strong between heavenly voices, whether of God (Jer 10:13; 51:16, 4 Ezra 6:17), angels, or the heavenly righteous, and the "sound of many waters" (Rev 14:2; 19:6). The "glory of God" is described as being like the "sound of mighty waters" (Ezek 43:2) and "the Lord sits enthroned over the flood" (Ps 29:10). Identification with humans also appears in passages where blood is being "poured out like water" (Ps 79:2-3) according to which usage the "watercourses will be filled with you" (Ezek 32:6). Even more explicitly: "the roar of the nations" is like "the roaring of mighty waters" (Isa 17:12) and "you shall be … like a spring of water" (Isa 58:11). More striking still is the statement in 4 Ezra, a text in which anthropomorphic language and symbolic representation are very heavily employed, that literal waters are "dumb and lifeless" (4 Ezra 6:48),[62] suggesting that any waters that appear to be different from that characterization are in fact symbolic of something beyond themselves.

Water, however, is not simply *associated* with humans and divine beings but often *representative* of them as well. In Jer 46 the "word of the LORD" that came to Jeremiah "concerning the nations" equates the people of Egypt with the Nile:

---

[61] Verse 17 in the Masoretic text.
[62] Bruce Metzger, "The Fourth Book of Ezra with the Four Additional Chapters: A New Translation and Introduction," in *The Old Testament Pseudepigrapha: Volume I, Apocalyptic Literature and Testaments*, ed. James H. Charlesworth (Peabody, MA: Hendrickson Publishers, 1983), 536.

Who is this, rising like the Nile,	מִי־זֶה כַּיְאֹר יַעֲלֶה
like rivers whose waters surge?	כַּנְּהָרוֹת יִתְגָּעֲשׁוּ מֵימָיו
Egypt rises like the Nile,	מִצְרַיִם כַּיְאֹר יַעֲלֶה
like rivers whose waters surge.	וְכַנְּהָרוֹת יִתְגֹּעֲשׁוּ מָיִם
It said, Let me rise, let me cover the earth,	וַיֹּאמֶר אַעֲלֶה אֲכַסֶּה־אֶרֶץ
let me destroy cities and their inhabitants.	אֹבִידָה עִיר וְיֹשְׁבֵי בָהּ

(Jer 46:7-8).

The language of Hos 6:3 is similarly evocative, describing God as coming "like the spring rains that water the earth." Wisdom 13:2 opines: "they supposed that [the] … turbulent water[s] … were the gods that rule the world." And in Sirach, personified wisdom speaks claiming, "I was like a canal from a river, like a water channel into a garden" (Sir 24:30).

Waters have obviously, by the time of *Parables of Enoch*, also come to symbolize judgment. This can be seen in Ezekiel: "when I make you a city laid waste … and the waters cover you … Now you are wrecked by the seas in the depths of the waters" (26:19; 27:34); in Hosea: "I will pour out my wrath like water" (5:10) and "Samaria's king will perish like a chip on the face of the waters" (10:7); in Amos: "Let justice roll down like waters, righteousness like an ever-flowing stream" (5:24); in Habakkuk: "You split the earth with rivers. The mountains saw you and writhed; a torrent of water swept by; the deep gave forth its voice … you trampled nations" (3:9-10, 12); and in the aforementioned Psalm 77 in the judgment of the Egyptians by the waters of the Red Sea.

The judgments in apocalyptic literature are particularly vivid. In Revelation they occur through the pouring of the golden bowls in chapter 16. Not only is judgment poured out like a liquid, but bowls two, three, and six all pertain to transformation of earthly waters for judgment. It appears that because the oppressors of the earth bloodied the waters of the earth—figuratively—through their oppression, their punishment is a literal bloodying of the waters of earth. Another apocalyptic work that employs this same trope is 2 Baruch. In the vision of chapter 36 the waters of judgment destroy a forest, which is later interpreted to be the "fourth kingdom" (2 Bar 39:5): "that fountain came to the forest and changed into great waves, and those waves submerged the forest and suddenly uprooted the entire forest and overthrew all the mountains which surrounded it" (2 Bar 36:4).[63] The theme is further expanded in the concluding vision Baruch receives that involves the outpouring of alternating dark and light waters in a storm (2 Bar 53). The interpretation of this vision occupies 2 Bar 54–74 and indicates that the waters are closely associated with judgment, starting with the equation of the first dark waters with the Noachian flood (56:15-16). And while

---

[63] A. F. J. Klijn, "2 (Syriac Apocalypse of) Baruch: A New Translation and Introduction," in *The Old Testament Pseudepigrapha: Volume I, Apocalyptic Literature and Testaments*, ed. James H. Charlesworth (Peabody, MA: Hendrickson Publishers, 1983), 632.

the waters of judgment are not always explicitly equated with peoples, they are equated with historic periods characterized according to the actions of alternatingly righteous and unrighteous people.[64]

The waters representing humans and the waters representing judgment come together in several texts in which waters explicitly represent humans involved in judgment scenarios. The earliest of these appears in Isaiah:

> Therefore, the Lord is bringing up against it the mighty flood waters of the River, the king of Assyria and all his glory; it will rise above all its channels and overflow all its banks; it will sweep on into Judah as a flood, and, pouring over, it will reach up to the neck; and its outspread wings will fill the breadth of your land, O Immanuel.
>
> (8:7-8)

Later in Isaiah the same confluence of themes reappears: "See, the Lord has one who is mighty and strong ... like a storm of mighty, overflowing waters; with his hand he will hurl them down to the earth" (28:2). The same themes recur in Jeremiah:

> See, waters are rising out of the north and shall become an overflowing torrent; they shall overflow the land and all that fills it, the city and those who live in it. People shall cry out, and all the inhabitants of the land shall wail. At the noise of the stamping of the hoofs of his stallions, at the clatter of his chariots, at the rumbling of their wheels.
>
> (47:2)

Clearly these texts identify a threatening human army with waters of judgment. Similar motifs continue to appear in later texts as well. In Greek Esther this occurs when Mordecai dreams of the perils of his people: "At their outcry, as though from a tiny spring, there came a great river, with abundant water; light came, and the sun rose, and the lowly were exalted and devoured those held in honor" (11:10-11). Later

---

[64] The closest equations between waters and judgment occur with the "sixth bright waters," which represent "the time in which David and Solomon were born" who effected the "shedding of much blood of the nations which sinned at that time" (2 Bar 61, *OTP* 1:642); the "seventh black waters," which represent the time in which the Assyrians "came and carried [the nine and a half tribes] away into captivity" (2 Bar 62, *OTP* 1:642); the "ninth black waters" during which time "judgment went out against the two and a half tribes so that they also should be carried away into captivity" (2 Bar 64, *OTP* 1:643); the "tenth bright waters," which represent the "purity of the generation of Josiah" who "killed the impious" (2 Bar 66, *OTP* 1:643-44); the "eleventh black waters," which represent "the disaster which has befallen Zion now" and includes Jerusalem being "trodden down" by "the nations" and the rise of the "king of Babylon" who has "destroyed Zion" and "boast[ed] over the people" (2 Bar 67, *OTP* 1:644); the "twelfth bright waters," which represents a time when the enemies of the faithful will "fall before them" (2 Bar 68, *OTP* 1:644); the "last black waters," after the twelfth, which represent a period of tumult when "the many will be delivered over to the few ... some of them will fall in war ... [and the nations] will come and wage war" (2 Bar 70, *OTP* 1:644-45); and the final "bright waters," which represent a time when "all those, now, who have ruled over you ... will be delivered up to the sword" (2 Bar 72, *OTP* 1:645); trans. Klijn, "2 (Syriac Apocalypse of) Baruch."

it becomes clear to him, after the deliverance of his people, that "the river is Esther, whom the king married and made queen" (Greek Esther 10:6).

Revelation 17 begins with an angel saying, "Come, I will show you the judgment of the great whore who is seated on many waters" (17:1). The intervening verses contain further details of the vision, including the explanatory note that "the waters that you saw, where the whore is seated, are peoples and multitudes and nations and languages" (Rev 17:15). The whore of Babylon is subsequently judged. It is not inconsequential that this scene occurs in a work of the same genre as *Parables of Enoch*.

4 Ezra also contains an extensive judgment scene of "Babylon." In this vision tempests associated with peoples—or rather, armies—from various locales threaten Babylon. In the end:

> The winds from the east shall prevail ... and the tempest that was to cause destruction by the east wind shall be driven violently toward the south and west. Great and mighty clouds, full of wrath and tempest, shall rise and destroy all the earth and its inhabitants, and shall pour out upon every high and lofty place ... floods of water, so that all the fields and all the streams shall be filled with the abundance of those waters. They shall destroy cities and walls, mountains and hills, trees of the forests, and grass of the meadows, and their grain. They shall go on steadily to Babylon and blot it out.[65]
>
> (4 Ezra 15:39-43)

Again, in an apocalyptically oriented document, we see human armies represented as waters of judgment.

From these examples it is clear that waters representative of humans are a common literary trope by the time of the writing of *Parables of Enoch*. Even more relevant is the fact that this trope appears frequently in scenes of judgment. It should not be surprising that the motif of judgment through water would be a typical literary device due to the compelling nature of the Noah account in Genesis. Neither, however, should it be surprising that its literary employment is universally metaphorical, representing a judging agent other than literal water, as God promised never again to destroy the world in a flood (Gen 9:11). As such, the employment of the theme of judgment by water, for a text intended to apply to the circumstances of the audience and the author (37:3), requires that the waters signify something other than themselves. Since this combination of themes is employed so commonly in well-known Jewish literature it would appear that the employment of Noachian judgment tropes in *Parables of Enoch* would likely connote an identification between the righteous oppressed and the waters of judgment, parallel to the identification between the oppressive rulers and the dry land present throughout the work. The waters of judgment signify the dispossessed.

---

[65] Metzger, "The Fourth Book of Ezra," 556–7.

Conclusion

The Noachian interpolations in the current form of *Parables of Enoch* effect the judgment of the oppressive rulers through flood, including landowners who had confiscated the "dry land." These landowners, in the Herodian period and thereafter, had relegated the righteous oppressed to the status of tenant farmers on their own ancestral lands or had kicked them off the "dry land" entirely, leaving them only the marshlands of the Huleh Valley and the Sea of Galilee from which to make their living. The anthropomorphic language for water employed by the author of *Parables of Enoch* suggests an association of the righteous oppressed with the waters of judgment (logically parallel to that between the oppressing landowners and the dry land). This association was a well-known literary trope, especially in apocalyptic literature of the time. It was likely known enough that the connections between the righteous oppressed and the waters could be largely veiled or implied. Such built-in plausible deniability would be necessary for a document challenging the powerful rulers who benefitted from the status quo. Still, the document would clearly provide much-needed encouragement to the dispossessed through the identifications suggested. However, the textual cue that finally confirms the likelihood of this hypothesis comes from another part of 1 Enoch entirely, namely, the vision that comes to Enoch in Dan. There he says, "I went and sat down upon the waters of Dan—in Dan which is on the southwest of Hermon—and I read their memorial prayers until I fell asleep. And behold a dream came to me and visions fell upon me" (1 En. 13:7-8).[66] Here the identification of the recipient of visions is already explicitly made with the "waters of Dan," that is, the Huleh Valley. It does not seem hard to imagine a later writer, inspired by the visions of Enoch and his (or her) own identification with the waters of Dan,[67] composing or redacting an apocalyptic text that challenges the mighty interloping landowners while affirming the struggle of the righteous oppressed through identification with the waters of judgment. Such an identification would be made all the more straightforward by the likely locus of dwelling of the marginalized at this time being among the "wet" lands. It might be too much to say that *Parables of Enoch* is a direct call to arms for the oppressed,[68] but it is certainly a subversive text that was redacted to provide support for the oppressed in their time of struggle and suffering.

A case has been made for strong identification between the people who have come to dwell in marginal circumstances, in the "watery" lands of the Huleh Valley and Sea of Galilee, and the "watery" locus of their dwelling. That this identification was useful from a literary standpoint does not undermine its reality. Even if this identification

---

[66] Isaac, "1 Enoch," 19–20.
[67] The kind of phenomenology of spatial experience that is suggested as being operative here is described in detail in Maurice Merleau-Ponty's *The Phenomenology of Perception*, trans. Colin Smith (London and New York: Routledge, 1962).
[68] Such a direct call might come in more explicit terms, such as is evidenced in the lanrguage of a campaign note published on Facebook by "The People for Bernie Sanders 2016 Political Organization," which asserted: "Each one of us is a rain drop. Together we are a monsoon" (Facebook.com, April 24, 2016); or more recent political language of a "blue wave" in the 2018 U.S. election.

was made only in the mind of the author (or redactor) of *Parables of Enoch*, he (or she) furnished his (or her) contemporaries with a compelling vision of their spaces of experience and the possibility of their transformation and redemption.

As was seen in the previous analysis of the Gospel of John (Chapter 1), even difficult[69] experiences of home or its loss[70] can foster the production of alternate, hopeful, and even redeemed spaces.[71] The formerly valorized "dry lands" became places of oppression and expulsion. Those who dwell there are demonized. The formerly pejoratively understood "watery lands" have been positively appropriated for their association with potential to judge the mighty. The act of dwelling in these marginal places has had an auto-valorizing effect.[72] They have become idealized, even in their marginality.

The outlines of this conclusion accord with Bachelard's observations regarding the psychology of dwelling: even marginal dwelling spaces (e.g., the *Parables*' watery areas) are often valorized, the loss of ideal dwelling (e.g., the *Parables*' ancestral dry lands) typically fosters new dreams of home (e.g., the *Parables*' heavenly habitations of the righteous), and experiences of marginal dwelling often result in polemical reaction to the outside world (e.g., the *Parables*' polemics against wealthy landowners). The following chapters on the book of Revelation and the *History of the Rechabites* will further examine this generative effect of marginal spaces of dwelling in the production of both ideal spaces and spaces of judgment.

---

[69] And sometimes especially difficult ones.
[70] Bachelard, *The Poetics of Space*, 7: "Being is already a value. Life begins well, it begins enclosed, protected, all warm in the bosom of the house. From my viewpoint, from the phenomenologist's viewpoint, the conscious metaphysics that starts from the moment when being is 'cast into the world' is a secondary metaphysics. It passes over the preliminaries, when being is being-well, in the well-being originally associated with being. To illustrate the metaphysics of consciousness we should have to wait for the experiences during which being is cast out, that is to say, thrown out, outside the being of the house, a circumstance in which the hostility of men and of the universe accumulates. But a complete metaphysics, englobing both the conscious and the unconscious, would leave the privilege of its values within. Within the being, in the being of within, an enveloping warmth welcomes being."
[71] Bachelard (*The Poetics of Space*, 56) claims that "the houses that were lost forever continue to live on in us" and that "we must lose our earthly Paradise in order actually to live in it, to experience it in the reality of its images, in the absolute sublimation that transcends all [suffering]" (*The Poetics of Space*, 33). This experience of being cast out spurs an even deeper and more vital imagination of home.
[72] Bachelard, *The Poetics of Space*, 12.

5

Prison and Pit, Doors and Dwelling: Phenomenologies of the Familiar in the Book of Revelation

Following the fruitful consideration of the textual ecology of the *Parables of Enoch*,[1] this chapter examines another apocalypse, the book of Revelation, using a similar spatial hermeneutic. This analysis is based in a consideration of Revelation's carceral ecology and involves comparison to the *Parables of Enoch*, which was also likely the product of a marginal experience of dwelling.[2] Analyzing ostensibly similar spaces that are presented divergently, the chapter focuses particular attention on "doorway" phenomena in Revelation.[3] Recent research in cognitive psychology[4] suggests that passing through a doorway has a measurable cognitive effect, inducing forgetfulness of prior thoughts. Revelation employs doorway and gateway language repeatedly, while *Parables of Enoch* does not. The respective spatial emphases of Revelation and *Parables of Enoch* suggest diverging engagements with a traumatized material world. References in *Parables of Enoch* to oppressive landowners and transformative goals

---

[1] And, again, considering Christopher Rowland's observations that apocalypses are not necessarily temporal according to which he concludes, contra the *Semeia* 14 definition, that literary forms and eschatological concerns are not defining characteristics. Rather, he writes that "apocalyptic" is best defined by "the belief that God's will can be discerned by means of a mode of revelation which unfolds directly the hidden things of God. To speak of apocalyptic, therefore, is to concentrate on the theme of the direct communication of the heavenly mysteries in all their diversity." Christopher Rowland, *The Open Heaven, A Study of Apocalyptic in Judaism and Early Christianity* (London: SPCK, 1982), 14. Considering, again, also Foucault's contention that historical analyses have diverted attention from spatial phenomena (Michel Foucault, "Of Other Spaces," trans. Jay Miskowiec, *Diacritics* 16 [1986]: 22).
[2] Especially in light of the fact that they share much in terms of language and background, as detailed in James H. Charlesworth, "The Parables of Enoch and the Apocalypse of John," in *The Pseudepigrapha and Christian Origins*, eds. G. S. Oegema and J. H. Charlesworth (New York: T&T Clark, 2008), 193–242.
[3] For particular attention to this theme, see Jolyon G. R. Pruszinski, "The Cognitive Phenomenology of Doors in the Book of Revelation: A Spatial Analysis," *Religions* 10.194 (2019): 1–14. doi:10.3390/rel10030194.
[4] Gabriel A. Radvansky, Sabine A. Krawietz, and Andrea K. Tamplin, "Walking Through Doorways Causes Forgetting: Further Explorations," *The Quarterly Journal of Experimental Psychology* 64 (2011): 1632–45.

for the earth suggest a continuing critical engagement with the material world. The lack of comparable language in Revelation may suggest a comparatively more escapist perspective. Revelation combines polemic against all the "inhabitants of the earth," an emphasis on the replacement of the old order, and the use of compensatory cultic language to orient the reader away from the existing material world. The parallel narrative employment of doorway language, coming as it does from a carceral generative background, that is, one of a marginal experience of dwelling, suggests an operative governing psychology of separation and forgetfulness in Revelation.

Introduction to Revelation's Carceral Background

There should really be no doubt that the reference to Patmos in Rev 1:9 is a reference to a kind of imprisonment. That the word "prison" is not used is irrelevant. This is not unlike how today one might say "I was at Alcatraz" or "I was at Rahway" or "I was at San Quentin." In our parlance there is no need to say "imprisoned" because these place names are synonymous with "prison." Both Tacitus (*Annals* 3.68, 4.30, 15.71) and Pliny (*Natural History* 12:4-13, 23) refer to Patmos as a location of forced exile for political prisoners.[5] Thus when the author writes "I ... was on the island of Patmos on account of the word of God" (Rev 1:9) he assuredly means "I was incarcerated." So, our consideration of this setting is the result of the author's own claim.

Whether the author was actually imprisoned is another question entirely. Justifiably, one could view his statement of location with some suspicion, as it is also a key component of his claim for authority.[6] The author, in part, bases the claim for the authority of his work on the fact that he is an authentic witness—a claim that, he knows, is buttressed by his purported suffering "on account of the word of God." There is no direct way to know inescapably whether this claim is valid, though the circumstantial evidence from the Apocalypse suggests the validity of the traditionally held claim, as we will see. If we begin with this supposition we should consider again what characteristics might be expected to appear in a work produced in response to just such an experience of marginal dwelling. The observations of Gaston Bachelard, first mentioned in Chapter 1, regarding marginal or traumatized experiences of dwelling, are of especial relevance and bear repeating here.

---

[5] J. Massyngberde Ford, *Revelation: A New Translation with Introduction and Commentary*, Anchor Bible 38 (Garden City, NY: Doubleday, 1975), 384.

[6] See Elaine Pagels, *Revelations: Visions, Prophecy, and Politics in the Book of Revelation* (New York: Viking, 2012), 8, 183; Adela Yarbro Collins, *Crisis and Catharsis: The Power of the Apocalypse* (Philadelphia: Westminster, 1984), 25–53; David E. Aune, *Revelation 1–5*, WBC 52a, eds. Bruce M. Metzger et al. (Dallas: Thomas Nelson, 1997), xlvii–xc; Leonard L. Thompson, *The Book of Revelation: Apocalypse and Empire* (New York: Oxford University Press, 1990); and Paul B. Duff, "Was There a Crisis Behind Revelation? An Introduction to the Problem," in *Who Rides the Beast? Prophetic Rivalry and the Rhetoric of Crisis in the Churches of the Apocalypse* (Oxford: Oxford University Press, 2001), 3–82, on the possible invention of this background.

Bachelard's Observations Regarding Marginal Dwelling

In *The Poetics of Space* Bachelard emphasizes the responsiveness of the imagination of home to experiences of trauma, or as he says, being "cast" out of the home and "into the world."[7] In some ways an experience of the fullness of the image of home is not possible without serious loss. Bachelard writes that "we must lose our earthly Paradise in order actually to live in it, to experience it in the reality of its images, in the absolute sublimation that transcends all [suffering]."[8] Such loss[9] or trauma, in opposition to a previous experience of safety and rest, fosters a more robust imagination of home.

Beyond this, experiences of marginal dwelling, "meager" experiences,[10] or experiences of being "cornered," as he calls them, are also generative of the imagination of dwelling. As previously mentioned, when humans have been forced out of the comfort or shelter of their dwelling or repose, the corner to which they retreat, or into which they are cast, becomes a new and powerful locus for dreaming new dreams of dwelling and repose. Such a distressed retreat to a materially "meager" though imaginatively rich[11] experience of dwelling is typically associated with reaction against the world[12] outside of the "corner." The new, ideal dreams of home coexist with and co-inform "world-negating"[13] emotions formed from the experience of trauma: "the corner becomes a negation of the universe."[14]

---

[7] Gaston Bachelard, *The Poetics of Space*, trans. Maria Jolas (Boston: Beacon Press, 1994), 7: "Being is already a value. Life begins well, it begins enclosed, protected, all warm in the bosom of the house. From my viewpoint, from the phenomenologist's viewpoint, the conscious metaphysics that starts from the moment when being is 'cast into the world' is a secondary metaphysics. It passes over the preliminaries, when being is being-well, in the well-being originally associated with being. To illustrate the metaphysics of consciousness we should have to wait for the experiences during which being is cast out, that is to say, thrown out, outside the being of the house, a circumstance in which the hostility of men and of the universe accumulates. But a complete metaphysics, englobing both the conscious and the unconscious, would leave the privilege of its values within. Within the being, in the being of within, an enveloping warmth welcomes being."

[8] Bachelard, *The Poetics of Space*, 33.

[9] Bachelard, *The Poetics of Space*, 100: "the home of other days has become a great image of lost intimacy."

[10] Bachelard, *The Poetics of Space*, 137: "Every retreat on the part of the soul possesses, in my opinion, figures of havens. That most sordid of all havens, the corner, deserves to be examined. To withdraw into one's corner is undoubtedly a meager expression. But despite its meagerness, it has numerous images, some, perhaps, of great antiquity, images that are psychologically primitive. At times, the simpler the image the vaster the dream."

[11] Bachelard, *The Poetics of Space*, 142: "From the depths of his [or her] corner, the dreamer sees an older house, a house in another land, thus making a synthesis of the childhood home and the dream home."

[12] Bachelard, *The Poetics of Space*, 46: "Such a [space] invites mankind to heroism of cosmic proportions. It is an instrument with which to confront the cosmos." See also ibid., 143: "The dreamer in his [or her] corner wrote off the world in a detailed daydream that destroyed, one by one, all the objects of the world."

[13] Bachelard, *The Poetics of Space*, 136: "Every corner in a house, every angle in a room, every inch of secluded space in which we like to hide, or withdraw into ourselves, is a symbol of solitude for the imagination; that is to say, it is the germ of a room, or of a house .... Also, in many respects, a corner that is 'lived in' tends to reject and restrain, even to hide, life. The corner becomes a negation of the Universe."

[14] Bachelard, *The Poetics of Space*, 136.

Thus, if we are to ask whether a particular text bears the marks of a generative background in a carceral experience of dwelling, that is to say, a marginal experience, a traumatized experience, or to use Bachelard's term, an experience of being "cornered," we would look for certain things. On the one hand, we might expect to see elements of an ideal, imagined dwelling space that includes positive aspects of previous ideas or experiences of dwelling appearing as an amalgam, generated in compensatory response to the experience of incarceration.[15] And, on the other hand, we might see evidence of deeply condemnatory or destructive emotional language for the world outside the "corner," that is, the world that consigned the author to the corner. Beyond these suggestions from Bachelard, we would, of course, also look for further evidence of an authorial interest in incarceration. So, the question remains, do we see these characteristics manifested in the book of Revelation?

Evidence from Revelation Suggesting a Carceral Background

The first instance of the language of incarceration that appears in Revelation comes as the ostensible author refers to dwelling in a state of imprisonment on Patmos (Rev 1:9) at the time of his vision, as previously mentioned. This initial reference is followed by frequent further references to imprisonment, whether directly (2:10; 20:7-8)[16] or indirectly (1:18; 3:7; 9:1-2; 16:10; 20:1-3, 10).[17] It should be understood that any language of the "pit" (6:15-16; 11:7; 17:8)[18] would also have been understood at the time to conjure the idea of prison.[19] And of course, the Apocalypse itself makes this equation:

---

[15] For example, images that are complex, involve rest, and evidence spatial and temporal amalgamation or conflation.

[16] "Behold, the devil is about to throw some of you into prison" (2:10); "And when the thousand years are ended, Satan will be loosed from his prison and will come out to deceive the nations which are at the four corners of the earth" (20:7-8).

[17] For example: "I have the keys of Death and Hades" (1:18); "the true one, who has the key of David, who opens and no one shall shut, who shuts and no one opens" (3:7); "he was given the key to the shaft of the bottomless pit; he opened the shaft of the bottomless pit, and from the shaft rose smoke like the smoke of a great furnace, and the sun and air were darkened with the smoke from the shaft" (9:1-2); "the fifth angel poured his bowl on the throne of the beast, and its kingdom was in darkness; men gnawed their tongues in anguish" (16:10); "then I saw an angel coming down from heaven, holding in his hand the key of the bottomless pit and a great chain. And he seized the dragon, that ancient serpent, who is the Devil and Satan, and bound him for a thousand years, and threw him into the pit, and shut it and sealed it over him, that he should deceive the nations no more, till the thousand years were ended. After that he must be loosed for a little while" (20:1-3); "the devil who had deceived them was thrown into the lake of fire and Sulphur where the beast and the false prophet were, and they will be tormented day and night for ever and ever" (20:10).

[18] For example: "then the kings of the earth and the magnates and the generals and the rich and the powerful, and everyone, slave and free, hid in the caves and among the rocks of the mountains, calling to the mountains and rocks, 'fall on us'" (6:15-16); "when they have finished their testimony, the beast that ascends from the bottomless pit will make war upon them and conquer them and kill them" (11:7); "the beast that you saw was, and is not, and is to ascend from the bottomless pit and go to perdition; and the dwellers on earth whose names have not been written in the book of life from the foundation of the world, will marvel to behold the beast" (17:8).

[19] See Matthew D. C. Larsen, *Early Christians and Incarceration: A Cultural History* (New Haven, CT: Yale University Press, forthcoming), on carceral geographies.

> Then I saw an angel coming down from heaven, holding in his hand the key to the bottomless pit and a great chain.² He seized the dragon, that ancient serpent, who is the Devil and Satan, and bound him for a thousand years,³ and threw him into the pit, and locked and sealed it over him, so that he would deceive the nations no more, until the thousand years were ended. After that he must be let out for a little while ....⁷ When the thousand years are ended, Satan will be released from his prison⁸ and will come out to deceive the nations at the four corners of the earth, Gog and Magog, in order to gather them for battle; they are as numerous as the sands of the sea.
>
> (Rev 20:1-8)

Of particular interest here is Rev 6:15-16, where the location of punishment seems to be in caves or underground,[20] but then Rev 9:1-2 is also indicative of the general explicit mentions of the pit:

> And the fifth angel blew his trumpet, and I saw a star that had fallen from heaven to earth, and he was given the key to the shaft of the bottomless pit (ἡ κλεὶς τοῦ φρέατος τῆς ἀβύσσου);² he opened the shaft of the bottomless pit (τὸ φρέαρ τῆς ἀβύσσου), and from the shaft rose smoke like the smoke of a great furnace, and the sun and the air were darkened with the smoke from the shaft.
>
> (Rev 9:1-2)

Further, the frequent reference to keys, doors, gates, and locks[21] (not to mention binding, loosing, sealing, etc.) is possibly indicative of an experience of incarceration.[22]

Language of an Ideal Dwelling

Returning specifically to the characteristics suggested by Bachelard, we can note many instances of imagined ideal dwelling in Revelation. Really the examples are too numerous to count, but it is obvious to any reader that the Apocalypse describes detailed visions of both the heavenly dwelling of God and the ideal dwelling of the righteous in the new Jerusalem. These dwellings are elevated (the dwelling of God is in the heavens; the new Jerusalem comes from the heavens and descends but is still over a thousand miles tall [Rev 21:16]). These ideal dwellings are also bereft of suffering and pain, and indeed previous experiences of pain are "wiped" (Rev 21:4). The familiar description of the final state of affairs in the new Jerusalem is illustrative:

---

[20] Rev 6:15-16: "Then the kings of the earth and the magnates and the generals and the rich and the powerful, and everyone, slave and free, hid in the caves (σπήλαια) and among the rocks of the mountains [read: underground],¹⁶ calling to the mountains and rocks, 'Fall on us and hide us from the face of the one seated on the throne and from the wrath of the Lamb.'"
[21] Explicit mentions of these occur frequently. Keys: 1:18, 3:7, 9:1, 20:1; Doors: 3:8, 3:20, 4:1; Gates: 21:12, 21:13, 21:15, 21:21, 21:25, 22:14; Locks: 20:3.
[22] Though of course could at times be indicative of secret divine knowledge hidden and revealed.

"See, the home of God is among mortals. He will dwell with them; they will be his peoples, and God himself will be with them;[4] he will wipe every tear from their eyes. Death will be no more; mourning and crying and pain will be no more, for the first things have passed away." ...[10] And in the spirit he carried me away to a great, high mountain and showed me the holy city Jerusalem coming down out of heaven from God ....[23] And the city has no need of sun or moon to shine on it, for the glory of God is its light, and its lamp is the Lamb.[24] The nations will walk by its light, and the kings of the earth will bring their glory into it.[25] Its gates will never be shut by day—and there will be no night there.[26] People will bring into it the glory and the honor of the nations .... Then the angel showed me the river of the water of life, bright as crystal, flowing from the throne of God and of the Lamb[2] through the middle of the street of the city. On either side of the river is the tree of life with its twelve kinds of fruit, producing its fruit each month; and the leaves of the tree are for the healing of the nations.

(Rev 21:3-4, 10, 23-25; 22:1-2)

Clearly this is like the kind of ideal, compensatory dwelling language described by Bachelard.

Language of World Condemnation

In addition to this ideal language of utopic dwellings there is also, of course, a great deal of language related to spaces of judgment, condemnation, and punishment and the people who are consigned to them. We have already looked at some of the language associated with "the pit" and with locations of judgment, but beyond this condemnatory language, it is necessary to consider exactly who is being condemned and for what. In short, the condemned are encompassed very broadly.

The most specific and clearly described judged parties are the spiritual forces of evil: angels, Satan, evil beasts, and so forth. The beasts are typically understood to be representative in some way of the leaders of Rome (Rev 17:9), which is the "whore of Babylon" itself (Rev 17:18), but the "kings of the earth" are also depicted separately and judged for their "fornication" with the whore (Rev 17:2). But beyond these figures the descriptions of the condemned are staggeringly generic and all-inclusive. Among the condemned are "merchants," which is to say anyone who benefited from any kind of trade under the Pax Romana (Rev 18:3) and even any who buy or sell at all (13:7)! In addition to these are all "the inhabitants of the earth" (Rev 17:2) "with the wine of whose fornication" they have become drunk. The wine is the blood of the saints (17:6) and the suggestion seems to be that if you are not one of the persecuted saints (2:10, 20:4) then you are among those who have participated in their persecution. You are one of those who do not "come out from her" (Rev 18:3) and are therefore condemned.[23]

---

[23] This is not to say that there is no evidence of some of the kings of the earth and the people of the nations being saved in the end (e.g., Rev 5:13; 21:24), but only to indicate that there is a lot of very generic (and recklessly polemical) language against what appears to be basically everyone outside the author's "corner."

This pervasive, blanket condemnation of all who are not among the persecuted righteous (1:7; 6:10, 15; 8:13; 11:10; 13:3, 8, 12, 14; 14:8), indeed the whole inhabited world (19:15, 18-21), and even the earth itself (13:12; 19:2)[24] seems to accord with the logic of "world negation," which is a common feature of experiences of marginal (and specifically, incarcerated) dwelling according to Bachelard. The literary evidence for a carceral ecological background to Revelation having been outlined, a comparative analysis of the spaces that appear in Revelation and the *Parables of Enoch* will better enable interpretation of unique elements of Revelation's textual ecology.

A Spatial Comparison of Revelation and the *Parables of Enoch*

At the outset it must be noted that some degree of selectivity is necessary in analyzing the spaces important to the authors of *Parables of Enoch* and Revelation. Both apocalypses are rife with spatial imagery, too much in fact for exhaustive close analysis herein. For the purposes of this examination we have chosen to consider spaces that appear in both apocalypses but with significantly different descriptive language. Certainly, each author has distinctive spatial interests. *Parables of Enoch* has extended discourses on the geography of the heavens and the habitations of the holy. This is not a concern of the author of Revelation. Conversely, the author of Revelation addresses several geographically identified churches, which do not appear in *Parables of Enoch*. These issues merit consideration elsewhere but will not enter our analysis. Rather we will examine discrepancies between the apocalypses in descriptions of the same spaces. For instance, polemics against landowners, while important for understanding the world of the author of *Parables of Enoch*, do not appear in Revelation even in similar judgments against the powerful of the earth. The heavenly temple is very prominent in Revelation while effectively nonexistent in *Parables of Enoch*, in spite of the presence of descriptions of God's court, throne, and house. Perhaps even more telling is the usage of the doorway/gateway theme in Revelation in heavenly descriptions and its complete absence in *Parables of Enoch*.

Comparison of "Same" Spaces

As apocalypses, *Parables of Enoch* and Revelation both clearly involve commerce between the earthly and heavenly spheres. These relationships between the heavens and earth drive both narrative action and theological priorities. Typical apocalyptic spatial themes appear in both texts, including Hades/Sheol;[25] the abyss of condemnation;[26] the wilderness/desert;[27] other earthly places (mountains, valleys, the sea, islands, waters, etc.); and heavenly places (moon, sun, stars, the paths, storehouses of the winds and

---

[24] Except perhaps Rev 12:16, which has an explicitly positive valence for the earth.
[25] See Rev 1:18; 6:8; 20:13; 20:14; and 1 En. 51:1; 56:8; 63:10.
[26] Which in both is described as being like a furnace. See Rev 9:1-2, 11; 11:7; 17:8; 20:1-2; and 1 En. 53:1; 54:5-6; 56:3; 67:4.
[27] See Rev 12:6, 14; 17:3; and 1 En. 42:3; 60:8-9; 61:5.

rains, etc.). There is attention to the earth, its inhabitants,[28] and its seats of oppressive powers in both apocalypses, as well as to the heavenly dwelling of God and God's throne. Thus, one might be inclined to believe that *Parables of Enoch* and Revelation feature similar constructions of space. The commonality of imagery has often been pointed out,[29] yet the descriptions and usages of the spaces employed by the different authors suggest rather different understandings of space and its significance.

Earth-Linked Oppression

Much of the language related to the earth[30] in Revelation is general, often indicating concern for oppression and evil overall but rarely indicating specifics. Beyond the fact that Jesus Christ is identified as the "ruler of the kings on earth" (Rev 1:5)[31] there is precious little positive identification attached to specifics. In fact, οἱ κατοικοῦντες ἐπὶ τῆς γῆς[32] are never mentioned in a positive light. They are known exclusively for persecuting the saints, allying themselves with the harlot Babylon, and being judged. This characterization, caricature even, suggests that the author's attitude toward the existing earth is entirely negative: that it is irredeemably evil and worthy of destruction, incapable of being transformed for the better.

In language that is almost as totalizing, the "kings of the earth" are described negatively throughout the Apocalypse, except at the very outset[33] and in the concluding discussion of the light of the new Jerusalem: "The nations will walk by its light, and the kings of the earth will bring their glory into it" (Rev 21:24).[34] The most significant language regarding the kings comes in the discussion of the harlot Babylon in chapters seventeen and eighteen: "And the woman that you saw is the great city which has dominion over the kings of the earth" (Rev 17:18).[35] They have partaken fully of her evil.

An interesting addition to the polemics against the kings of the earth is that against merchants, as hinted at above. In chapter eighteen the author of Revelation has included merchants in the denunciation of the kings: "the kings of the earth have committed fornication with her, and the merchants of the earth have grown rich with the wealth of her wantonness" (Rev 18:3).[36] These men are the beneficiaries of the evil practices of those who dominate the earth. At the destruction of Babylon, their sponsor, "the

---

[28] "Those who dwell upon the earth" or similar wording.
[29] For example, see David E. Aune, "The Apocalypse of John and Palestinian Jewish Apocalyptic," in *The Pseudepigrapha and Christian Origins: Essays from SNTS*, eds. G. S. Oegema and J. H. Charlesworth (New York and London: T&T Clark, 2008), 169–92, esp. 172–92.
[30] Usually γῆ.
[31] ὁ ἄρχων τῶν βασιλέων τῆς γῆς.
[32] RSV: "those who dwell upon the earth"; NRSV: "the inhabitants of the earth." This is a designation found in some form in Rev 3:10; 6:10; 11:10; 13:8, 12, 14; 14:6; 17:2.
[33] As previously mentioned in Rev 1:5.
[34] NRSV translated from: καὶ περιπατήσουσιν τὰ ἔθνη διὰ τοῦ φωτὸς αὐτῆς· καὶ οἱ βασιλεῖς τῆς γῆς φέρουσιν τὴν δόξαν αὐτῶν εἰς αὐτήν.
[35] See also Rev 17:1-2; 18:2-3, 9-11.
[36] οἱ βασιλεῖς τῆς γῆς μετ' αὐτῆς ἐπόρνευσαν, καὶ οἱ ἔμποροι τῆς γῆς ἐκ τῆς δυνάμεως τοῦ στρήνους αὐτῆς ἐπλούτησαν.

merchants of the earth will weep and mourn for her ... for thy merchants were the great men of the earth, and all nations were deceived by thy sorcery" (Rev 18:11, 23).[37] One may be inclined to think that the polemic against merchants is indicative of a particular historical problem or concern, but the condemnation is more likely a literary trope[38] against an easy target than a grievance based on particular historical events.[39]

Though filled with much similar language, *Parables of Enoch* deals very differently with the earth,[40] those who dwell in it, and those who exercise dominion on it. Even more than the author of Revelation, the author of *Parables of Enoch* exhibits significant interest in "those who dwell upon the earth."[41] Rather than a univocal condemnation, like the author of Revelation, the author of *Parables of Enoch* moves back and forth between intercessory concern (e.g., 1 En. 40:6-7) and judgment (e.g., 1 En. 54:9; 65:10; 66:1). The inhabitants of the earth are not one-dimensional. There is clear divine care for them (1 En. 40:6-7; 55:2; 60:5, 22). They are the recipients of revelation (1 En. 37:2, 5; 38:2). They also are judged for evil and are accountable for their actions (1 En. 53:1-2; 54:9; 55:1). They are led astray (1 En. 54:6; 67:7; 69:1). At times they are described as participating in oppression (1 En. 55:3-4; 65:6, 12; 67:8).[42]

This last category is of particular interest because it coincides with a very unique emphasis made by the author of *Parables of Enoch*, as discussed in chapter four. In 1 En. 55:4 and 67:8, "those who dwell upon the earth" are included in a list of oppressors who will be judged.[43] In E. Isaac's translation this list appears in other places with the alternate, and more specific, designations: "landowners,"[44] "landlords,"[45] "those who possess the earth,"[46] "those who rule the earth,"[47] and ones "who possess the land."[48]

---

[37] Καὶ οἱ ἔμποροι τῆς γῆς κλαίουσιν καὶ πενθοῦσιν ἐπ' αὐτήν ... ὅτι οἱ ἔμποροί σου ἦσαν οἱ μεγιστᾶνες τῆς γῆς, ὅτι ἐν τῇ φαρμακείᾳ σου ἐπλανήθησαν πάντα τὰ ἔθνη.

[38] A very similar trope appears in Ezekiel (e.g., 16:29).

[39] The trope appears in various Greek (e.g., Hesiod, *Op.* 286; Philostratus *Vita. Apoll.* 4.32) and Latin authors (e.g., Cicero, *Off.* 1.150; and Seneca, *Med.* 361). A rather exhaustive summary appears in David E. Aune, *Revelation*, WBC 52c, eds. Bruce M. Metzger et al. (Dallas: Thomas Nelson, 1997), 988-9. But one need look no further than the classical role of the god Mercury as patron of both merchants and *thieves*.

[40] Ethiopic is *"yabs"* or *"medr."*

[41] "Those who dwell upon the earth" (and closely related expressions) appears at least twenty-four times in Isaac's translation of *Parables of Enoch*. See E. Isaac, "1 (Ethiopic Apocalypse of) Enoch," 5-89: 1 En. 37:2, 5; 38:2; 40:6, 7; 43:4; 48:5; 53:1; 54:6, 9; 55:1, 2, 4; 60:5, 22; 65:6, 10, 12; 66:1; 67:7, 8; 69:1, 7; 70:1. In this designation, "earth" represents the Ethiopic *"yabs"* in every instance. See Nickelsburg and VanderKam, *1 Enoch 2*, 89, for alternate use of *"medr."*

[42] Nickelsburg and VanderKam compose a similar list: *1 Enoch 2*, 90.

[43] This is a stock phrase that refers to all enemies of God, a similar version of which is used in Rev 6:15. See David E. Aune, *Revelation 6-16*, WBC 52b, eds. Bruce M. Metzger et al. (Dallas: Thomas Nelson, 1997), 419. The author of *Parables of Enoch* adds his or her own particular emphasis in other instances of the usage of this phrase.

[44] 1 En. 48:8 in *OTP* 1:37. "The strong who possess the land" in Nickelsburg and VanderKam, *1 Enoch 2*, 166.

[45] 1 En. 62:1, 3, 6; and 63:12 in *OTP*, 43-44. Those "who possess the land" in Nickelsburg and VanderKam, *1 Enoch 2*, 254-5.

[46] 1 En. 38:4 in *OTP* 1:30. "The exalted who possess the land" in Nickelsburg and VanderKam, *1 Enoch 2*, 95.

[47] 1 En. 62:9 in *OTP* 1:43. "Those who rule the land" in Nickelsburg and VanderKam, *1 Enoch 2*, 254.

[48] 1 En. 63:1 in *OTP* 1:44. Same reading in Nickelsburg and VanderKam, *1 Enoch 2*, 255.

In this usage, "those who dwell upon the earth" is not general in scope but specific to those who oppress others by their dominion over the land. As previously mentioned, in a recent examination[49] of questions related to the dating of *Parables of Enoch*, James Charlesworth highlights the significance of this polemical language against landowners. In his estimation the intentional addition of "those who possess the dry ground"[50] to a normal polemical list[51] is indicative of a specific historical-political concern: namely, the appropriation of ancestral lands in the Huleh Valley by Herod and Herodian sympathizers[52] and the disinheritance of a whole region of farmers. According to this assessment, the author or redactor of *Parables of Enoch* is thoroughly engaged with this specific problem of the day,[53] in apparent contrast to the author of Revelation who seems more content to deal in generalities.

Heavenly Temple

Perhaps an even more striking difference between *Parables of Enoch* and Revelation is the depiction of the heavenly dwelling of God, specifically the area in the vicinity of the throne. In *Parables of Enoch* this area, the heavenly locus of God's presence, is described with various permutations of the generic designation "before the Lord of Spirits." Much less frequently employed specific terms describe the area as "underneath the wings of the Lord of Spirits,"[54] "the court of the Lord,"[55] or in its fullest description:

> He carried me off my spirit, and I, Enoch, was in the heaven of heavens. There I saw—in the midst of that light—a structure built of crystals, and between those crystals tongues of living fire. And my spirit saw a ring which encircled this structure of fire. On its four sides were rivers full of living fire which encircled it. Moreover, seraphim, cherubim, and ophanim—the sleepless ones who guard the throne of his glory—also encircled it. And I saw countless angels—a hundred thousand times a hundred thousand, ten million times ten million—encircling

---

[49] James H. Charlesworth, "The Date and Provenience of the Parables of Enoch," in *Parables of Enoch: A Paradigm Shift*, eds. Darrell L. Bock and James H. Charlesworth (New York: T&T Clark, 2013), 37–57.
[50] 1 En. 48:8 from the translation by Michael Knibb, *The Ethiopic Book of Enoch*, Vol. 2 (Oxford: Clarendon Press, 1978).
[51] Usually "kings, governors and high officials" in E. Isaac's translation in *OTP*.
[52] As described in Josephus, *Ant.* 17.304-314, and referenced by Charlesworth, "The Date and Provenience of the *Parables of Enoch*," 51.
[53] Charlesworth, "The Date and Provenience of the *Parables of Enoch*," 48. He writes of further language in *Parables of Enoch* indicative of this concern: "After a discourse on the desired place to dwell, the author notes that the Chosen One will make the ground a blessing so that the 'chosen ones' may finally dwell on it (45:5). When the Son of Man appears he will destroy 'the kings and the powerful from their resting places' who along with 'the strong' will be punished (46:4). When the Son of Man appears 'the kings of the earth and *the strong who possess the dry ground* … will not save themselves'" (48:8). Emphasis original.
[54] 1 En. 39:7, E. Isaac's translation in *OTP* 1:31. "Beneath the wings of the Lord of Spirits" in Nickelsburg and VanderKam, *1 Enoch 2*, 111.
[55] 1 En. 65:6, E. Isaac's translation in *OTP* 1:45. "The presence of the Lord" in Nickelsburg and VanderKam, *1 Enoch 2*, 273.

that house. Michael, Raphael, Gabriel, Phanuel, and numerous (other) holy angels that are in heaven above, go in and out of that house.

(1 En. 71:5-8)[56]

What is most striking here and most at odds with the description of the same location in Revelation, that is, in the presence of God at the throne, is the complete lack of any language related to a temple or cultic practice in *Parables of Enoch*.[57] Revelation, on the contrary, is overflowing with cultic language for this place. On fifteen separate occasions this area is referred to as "the" temple.[58] It is filled with all the cultic appurtenances: the altar,[59] the Ark of the Covenant,[60] and incense.[61] Worship goes on there nearly constantly. This temple is never described as being replaced with a new version along with the "new heavens," "new earth," and "new Jerusalem." One might argue that the referents to "that house"[62] in *Parables of Enoch* suggest the technical phrase "house of God"[63] used often in the Hebrew Bible for the Temple, but an Ethiopic corollary of the technical phrase "house of God" never appears. The difference between the two apocalypses in this area could not be starker. The temple does not seem to be a crucial concern to the author of *Parables of Enoch*, or if it is, it is dealt with by a literary strategy of avoidance.[64]

Doors and Gates

Perhaps the most telling aspect of the differentiated spatial depictions in *Parables of Enoch* and Revelation is the regular notation, emphasis even, of doors and gates in Revelation and their parallel utter absence of notation in *Parables of Enoch*. Though some do not consider doorways to be a space in and of themselves, they do in fact constitute a meaningful liminal and quotidian space. Moreover, their very nature, of connecting other spaces, bears significantly on spatial analysis. *Parables of Enoch* is bereft of any language specifically referencing doors or gates. They are clearly not important to the author's vision of heaven or to the world produced by the apocalypse. This is especially significant when considered in light of the fact that heavenly doors and

---

[56] E. Isaac translation's in *OTP* 1:49–50.
[57] Martha Himmelfarb has argued that the Enoch corpus was oriented polemically against the temple cult due to the profane actions of the priests. This would explain the lack of cultic language related to the "heaven of heavens." See Martha Himmelfarb, *Ascent to Heaven in Jewish and Christian Apocalypses* (New York: Oxford University Press, 1993), 20; idem, *A Kingdom of Priests: Ancestry and Merit in Ancient Judaism* (Philadelphia: University of Pennsylvania Press, 2006), 21–2.
[58] Rev 3:12; 7:15; 11:1, 2, 19; 14:15, 17; 15:5, 6, 8; 16:1, 17; 21:22.
[59] See Rev 6:9; 8:3, 5; 9:13; 11:1; 14:18; 16:7.
[60] Rev 11:19.
[61] Rev 5:8; 8:3, 4.
[62] Ethiopic: *we'etu sete*. See Johannes Flemming, *Das Buch Henoch: Äthiopischer Text*, Texte und Untersuchungen n.s. 7.1/22.1 (Leipzig: Hinrichs, 1902), 88.
[63] בֵּית אֱלֹהִים.
[64] Again, see Martha Himmelfarb's work for a plausible explanation: *Ascent to Heaven in Jewish and Christian Apocalypses*, 20; also, *A Kingdom of Priests: Ancestry and Merit in Ancient Judaism*, 21–2.

gates (or the gates of the renewed temple and Jerusalem) are important themes in both apocalyptic and non-apocalyptic sections of the Hebrew Bible and intertestamental literature including Gen 28:17, Ps 78:23, Isa 54:12, 60:11, Ezek 10:19, 40:6-43:12 (most prominently of all), Tob 13:16-17, 3 Macc 6:18, and 4 Ezra 3:19.

Conversely, the author of Revelation uses the door/gate theme repeatedly. At its first explicit appearance, in the proclamation to the church in Philadelphia, it is said: "Look, I have set before you an open door, which no one is able to shut" (Rev 3:8).[65] The implication in the passage is that the door is open to heaven for the hearers and shut to those who are disobedient. The next proclamation, to the church in Laodicea, also includes doorway language: "Listen, I am standing at the door, knocking; if you hear my voice and open the door, I will come in to you and eat with you, and you with me. To the one who conquers, I will give a place with me on my throne, just as I myself conquered and sat down with my Father on his throne" (Rev 3:20-21).[66] Here the state of fellowship with Christ is defined by whether one permits Christ to enter through the door. The implication of not allowing Christ to pass through is that judgment will remain upon those within, whereas, if he is allowed to enter, the judgment is forgotten and full fellowship granted. The transition between the messages to the churches and the subsequent "heavenly journey" occurs at the beginning of chapter four with "After this I looked, and there in heaven a door stood open" (Rev 4:1).[67] In this instance the door marks an explicit separation between the earthly temporal concerns of the first three chapters and the heavenly transcendent language of the subsequent ones. After the door, not only does the Apocalypse shift in tone,[68] but much of the language of exhortation and contingency from chapters two to three is forgotten in favor of ekphrastic and definitive language.[69]

One could also argue that much of the language of the opening of the heavens that appears throughout the Apocalypse carries the implication of a door in the heavens,[70] in which case the instances of employment of doorway imagery are even more numerous. Consider, for example, "then God's temple in heaven was opened, and the ark of his covenant was seen within his temple" (11:19); "the temple of the tent of witness in heaven was opened" (15:5); "then I saw heaven opened" (19:11).

The remainder of the language on this theme concerns the twelve gates of the new Jerusalem described at the end of Revelation.[71] The gates are always open, but only

---

[65] ἰδοὺ δέδωκα ἐνώπιόν σου θύραν ἠνεῳγμένην, ἣν οὐδεὶς δύναται κλεῖσαι αὐτήν.

[66] ἰδοὺ ἕστηκα ἐπὶ τὴν θύραν καὶ κρούω· ἐάν τις ἀκούσῃ τῆς φωνῆς μου καὶ ἀνοίξῃ τὴν θύραν, [καὶ] εἰσελεύσομαι πρὸς αὐτὸν καὶ δειπνήσω μετ' αὐτοῦ καὶ αὐτὸς μετ' ἐμοῦ. ὁ νικῶν δώσω αὐτῷ καθίσαι μετ' ἐμοῦ ἐν τῷ θρόνῳ μου, ὡς κἀγὼ ἐνίκησα καὶ ἐκάθισα μετὰ τοῦ πατρός μου ἐν τῷ θρόνῳ αὐτοῦ.

[67] Μετὰ ταῦτα εἶδον, καὶ ἰδοὺ θύρα ἠνεῳγμένη ἐν τῷ οὐρανῷ.

[68] Here begins the "ascent to heaven" or "otherworldly journey" section of Revelation, which is a common feature of many apocalypses, including *Parables of Enoch*. See Aune, *Revelation 1-5*, xciii.

[69] This is the tone of the apocalypse right up until the hortatory language returns again at the very end in Rev 22:17, immediately following the final discussion of gates. See Robin J. Whitaker, "The Poetics of Ekphrasis: Vivid Description and Rhetoric in the Apocalypse," in *Poetik und Intertextualität in der Apocalypse*, eds. Stefan Alkier, Thomas Hieke, and Tobias Nicklas, WUNT 1 (Tübingen: Mohr Siebeck, 2015), 227-40.

[70] As Rowland does.

[71] See Rev 21:12-13, 15, 21, 25; 22:14-15.

the righteous may enter. The gates mark the boundary between those who enter into blessed communion with God and those left outside in judgment, that is, the "sorcerers and fornicators and murderers and idolaters, and everyone who loves and practices falsehood" (Rev 22:15).[72] The gate of the city as a normative locus of judgment according to the judicial practices of the time further enriches this symbolism: upon the judgment of a case, the concerned parties would depart from the gate, entering a new reality shaped by the judgment, functionally forgetting the reality that came before.

The Significance of the Door/Gate/Threshold in Antiquity

The cognitive phenomenology of doorways may hold an important key to interpreting the significance of the doorway and gateway language in Revelation. Of course, it has long been recognized by scholars of religion that thresholds have an important liminal function in the demarcation of sacred space. The Hebrew Bible and Hellenistic-era Jewish literature clearly preserve interest in the doors and gates of the Temple, Jerusalem, and heaven (Gen 28:17; Ps 78:23; Isa 54:12; 60:11; Ezek 10:19; 40:6-43:12; Tob 13:16-17; 3 Macc 6:18; 4 Ezra 3:19; T. Ab. 11:1-4). We find repeated mentions of "those who guard the threshold" of the Temple (2 Kgs 22:4; 23:4; 25:18; 1 Chr 9:19; 2 Chr 34:9; Jer 35:4; 52:24). In 1 Sam 5:1-5, the god Dagon was discovered broken upon the threshold.[73] The theophany of Isa 6 involves the shaking of the threshold.[74] Both 1 Kgs 14:17 and Zeph 1:9 suggest that the threshold represents a significant event horizon.[75] And certainly one need look no further than the Rabbis for extensive discussions of just what happens at the threshold or gate with respect to purity and sanctity.[76] Indeed, the cognitive phenomenology of doorways is so extensive and

---

[72] οἱ φάρμακοι καὶ οἱ πόρνοι καὶ οἱ φονεῖς καὶ οἱ εἰδωλολάτραι καὶ πᾶς φιλῶν καὶ ποιῶν ψεῦδος.
[73] "When the Philistines captured the ark of God, they brought it from Ebenezer to Ashdod; then the Philistines took the ark of God and brought it into the house of Dagon and placed it beside Dagon. When the people of Ashdod rose early the next day, there was Dagon, fallen on his face to the ground before the ark of the LORD. So they took Dagon and put him back in his place. But when they rose early on the next morning, Dagon had fallen on his face to the ground before the ark of the LORD, and the head of Dagon and both his hands were lying cut off upon the threshold; only the trunk of Dagon was left to him. This is why the priests of Dagon and all who enter the house of Dagon do not step on the threshold of Dagon in Ashdod to this day."
[74] Isa 6:4.
[75] 1 Kgs 14:17: "Then Jeroboam's wife got up and went away, and she came to Tirzah. As she came to the threshold of the house, the child died." Zeph 1:9 references devotees of Dagon: "On that day I will punish all who leap over the threshold, who fill their master's house with violence and fraud."
[76] See, for example, the discussions in b. Šabb 6a, 8b, 9a. See also b. Šabb 91b, here verse 4 "GEMARA: The Gemara begins by asking: What is the nature of this threshold in terms of Shabbat? If you say that it is a threshold that has the legal status of the public domain, in that it does not extend above nine handbreadths, and its area is four by four handbreadths, and it is suitable for use by the multitudes, why is he exempt? Didn't he carry out food from the private domain to the public domain? Rather, say that it is a threshold that has the legal status of the private domain, in that it extends above ten handbreadths, and its area is four by four handbreadths. In that case, why does the mishna say: Whether he then carried it out from the threshold into the public domain or another person carried it out, he is exempt? Why should he be exempt? Didn't he carry out food from the private domain to the public domain?" (trans. *The William Davidson Talmud* [Sefaria.org]).

opens so many possibilities for analysis that Gaston Bachelard, in his rather exhaustive treatment of the phenomenology of intimate spaces, in *The Poetics of Space*, decides that he must deal with doorways only briefly due to the too-extensive possibilities.[77] An open door can express potentialities or a closed one limitations. It can operate to include or exclude. And he writes, "Is he [or she] who opens a door and he [or she] who closes it [even] the same being?"[78]

Cognitive Phenomenology of Doorways in Recent Scholarship

While many options could be considered, a recent study of the cognitive phenomenology of doorways by researchers at the University of Notre Dame[79] is likely instructive for our purposes. This study, published in 2011 and entitled "Walking Through Doorways Causes Forgetting: Further Explorations," confirmed a long-suspected correlation[80] between the action of passing through a doorway and the precipitation of befuddlement or forgetfulness relating to what one was thinking about before passing through the door.

The researchers ran tests on subjects using a virtual environment similar to a video game in which participants attempted to memorize the characteristics of a particular digital "object" and then used their digital avatar to "travel" to another location in the digital environment. Once in the new location the test subjects were quizzed for how much they remembered about the object characteristics and how quick their recall was (Figure 5.1b). The study found that in this digital environment, the process of moving from one virtual room to another through a virtual "door" induced a statistically significant drop in recall speed and content compared with recall for object transport to another location within a virtual room, that is, without transiting a door (Figure 5.1a).

The experiment was repeated with various monitor sizes used to display the digital environment to approximate a varying degree of "immersion" in the virtual environment, but there were only small differences recorded between measured degrees of "immersion." The experiment was also repeated in like terms in the non-virtual physical environment of the lab with, once again, similar but somewhat more dramatic results. Memory of object characteristics was quicker and better within the room (Figure 5.1a) and dropped off significantly after having passed through a doorway (Figure 5.1b).

In order to determine whether recall was affected mainly by the location of memorization and recall, the researchers used a virtual environment to allow subjects

---

[77] Bachelard, *The Poetics of Space*, 222–4.
[78] Bachelard, *The Poetics of Space*, 224.
[79] Radvansky et al., "Walking Through Doorways Causes Forgetting," 1632–45.
[80] Christopher A. Kurby and Jeffrey M. Zacks, "Segmentation in the Perception and Memory of Events," *Trends in Cognitive Sciences* 12 (2008): 72–9. See also Khena M. Swallow, Jeffrey M. Zacks, and Richard A. Abrams, "Event Boundaries in Perception Affect Memory Encoding and Updating," *Journal of Experimental Psychology: General* 138 (2009): 236–57. And further, see Jeffrey M. Zacks, Nicole K. Speer, and Jeremy R. Reynolds, "Segmentation in Reading and Film Comprehension," *Journal of Experimental Psychology: General* 138 (2009): 307–27.

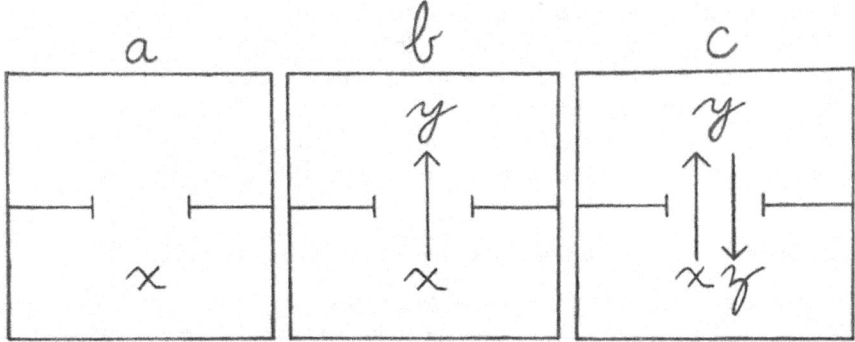

Figure 5.1 Schematic of the Radvansky et al. Doorway Experiment. (Artist's rendering by K. N. Pruszinski. Used with permission.)

to memorize object characteristics, leave the room through a virtual doorway, and then return back through the doorway to the original virtual location to attempt to remember the object characteristics (Figure 5.1c). Interestingly, recall remained depressed even when attempted in the original location, isolating the memory effect to transiting the doorway rather than simple location alteration.

To quote the authors: "when people pass through a doorway to move from one location to another, they forget more information than if they do not make the shift."[81] This is thought to occur either to prepare the mind for perception of new information or stimuli, or as a simple result of the experience of new stimuli driving previous thoughts away. The results clearly indicated that transit through a doorway had a similar cognitive effect, whether in a "real" material environment or in a virtual "imagined" one, without much effect from the degree of immersion in the "virtual" environment.

This observation of the equivalency of effects between "real" and "imagined" environments, extensible to at least partial equivalency between material and textual ones, should not be surprising in light of observations made at least as early as the work of Maurice Merleau-Ponty. He wrote:

> The essence of consciousness is to provide itself with one or several worlds, to bring into being its own thoughts before itself, as if they were things, and it demonstrates its vitality indivisibly by outlining these landscapes for itself and then by abandoning them. The world structure, with its two stages of sedimentation and spontaneity, is at the core of consciousness.[82]

---

[81] Radvansky et al., "Walking Through Doorways," 1632.
[82] Maurice Merleau-Ponty, *The Phenomenology of Perception*, trans. Colin Smith (London and New York: Routledge, 1962), 130.

The analysis of this chapter assumes that this equivalency of effects between the "real" and "imagined" is extensible to at least partial equivalency between material and textual "imagined" environments. As such, among the associations with doorways that we must consider relevant for our analysis of Revelation is this one, according to which passing through a doorway, gateway, or similar portal, or even just imagining such, is highly associated with the cognitive function, or induction, of forgetfulness.

Plausible Function of the Doorway Cognitive Phenomenon in Antiquity

One objection to making much of this association is the protest that Revelation is largely derivative of Ezekiel. Gates appear frequently in Ezekiel, so is it not likely that their presence in Revelation simply indicates employment of a literary trope, that is to say, rote borrowing from Ezekiel? Though Revelation certainly draws on Ezekiel, militating against this objection is the relative prominence of doorways and gates in Revelation compared to Ezekiel. In Ezekiel there are exhaustive and detailed descriptions of the whole built environment of the Temple, not just the gates. The gates are included but do not seem to receive really special attention. Conversely, in Revelation the gates are more prominent compared to the total picture of descriptive language, which largely focuses on actions. Also, in Ezekiel there is not the same emphasis on replacing the existing reality of Jerusalem or the Temple. They are improved, in some ways miraculously, but they are the same city and Temple. In Revelation the emphasis is on a new one. The old earthly spaces all pass away. The slate is wiped clean. In Ezekiel there is separation that occurs between the sides of the gates, but those outside the gates are still involved in the function of the Temple. In Revelation those outside are utterly excluded.

Another possible objection to the relevance of this cognitive phenomenon for the interpretation of Revelation is related to the protest that this study was only completed in 2011. How could early Jews have possibly been aware of this phenomenon? Certainly they had not made a scientific study of this phenomenon, but they may have been consciously or unconsciously aware of it.[83] Several biblical passages may allude indirectly to the operation of the phenomenon, including discussion of "forgetting God" after being delivered from the "house of Egypt,"[84] Pharaoh's cupbearer forgetting

---

[83] See P. M. Phillips, *The Prologue of The Fourth Gospel* (London and New York: T&T Clark, 2006), esp. 139–40, for speculation on textual prologue as threshold/doorway and the usage of ambiguity and befuddlement by the author of the Fourth Gospel to induce readers to forget their previous understandings of the *logos* in favor of a Christological one. His work suggests that this phenomenon may have been known and extended metaphorically to textual applications. The extension need not only be metaphorical, as Merleau-Ponty's phenomenology has suggested that perceptual phenomena are authentic whether in observing the quotidian material world or a textually produced world. See Merleau-Ponty, *The Phenomenology of Perception*, 130. As previously mentioned, even the Notre Dame study found similar effects when they compared an "actual" environment and a simulated "virtual" environment. See Radvansky et al., "Walking Through Doorways," 1632. This avenue of inquiry, namely the phenomenology of reading a *biblos* as it pertains to apocalypses, particularly *Parables of Enoch* and Revelation, deserves additional scholarship. *Parables of Enoch*'s polemic against "books" stands in sharp contrast to Revelation's apparent total embrace. The book as place or "world" in this context is a fertile area of inquiry.

[84] Deut 6:12; 8:14.

Joseph when he exited the prison,[85] the foolish man in James forgetting what he looks like in a mirror immediately upon "going out" from there,[86] or even Peter's immediate forgetfulness of Jesus' warning to him at the last supper, only remembered when the cock crows.[87]

Admittedly, the apparently glancing similarities of these passages may only strain credulity. However, definitive evidence for the phenomenon lies in Philo. In his discussion of the Temple, in *De ebrietate*, he writes:

> To [a perfect man] it is permitted to enter once a year and behold the sights which are forbidden to others, because in him alone of all resides the winged and heavenly yearning for those forms of good which are incorporeal and imperishable. And so … when he approaches … ignorance and the condition of the uninstructed are forgotten … when [he] enter[s] into the tabernacle of testimony.
> (*Ebr.* 34.136-138 [Colson and Whitaker, LCL])

Here, we clearly see forgetfulness of what was in the mind before passing a doorway and the changing of attention to other things in light of that passing. This becomes even clearer in a passage from *De somniis II*. Philo, in describing the actions of the high priest, writes:

> About the high priest: "When *he enters* … into the Holy of Holies, he …" *forgets all else, forgets [him]self*, and [*the mind*] fixes its thoughts and memories on [God] alone Whose attendant and servant it is, to whom it dedicates not a palpable offering, but incense, the incense of consecrated virtues.
> (*Somn.* 2.34.230-232 [Colson and Whitaker, LCL]; emphasis added)

Here we see again a clear cognitive effect of forgetfulness operative in the priest as a result of passing through the entrance to the Holy of Holies. It would appear then that the operation of the phenomenon in question, an association of passing a doorway with forgetfulness, is at least represented in Philo and was, as such, likely operative in antiquity.[88] This increases the likelihood that the author of Revelation may have been shaped, at least unconsciously or unwittingly, by the phenomenon. This is not to suggest that there is explicit evidence of the phenomenon in Revelation, as in Philo, but rather that, in light of the indirect evidence, it is likely to be operative and, to some degree, hermeneutically explanatory.

---

[85] Gen 40:23.
[86] Jas 1:24.
[87] Matt 26; Mark 14; Luke 22.
[88] The fact that the operation of the phenomenon in this instance is related to the unique space of the Holy of Holies does not actually detract from the relevance of the phenomenon in Revelation since a door in the heavens would certainly be similarly distinctive or atypical.

Discussion of Interpretive Implications

It seems likely that the presence of the very significant language of doorways and gates in Revelation and the deployment of that language in concert with its theological interests suggest a subtle but important theological distinction between Revelation and *Parables of Enoch* in their respective orientations toward the material world and its concerns.[89]

It is becoming increasingly common for scholars with postcolonial interests to emphasize the political commitments of Revelation and anti-empire polemic. This is not unimportant. But the spatial-thematic differences between Revelation and *Parables of Enoch* (particularly the roles of doorways and gates in Revelation) may make it likely that the author of Revelation is somewhat more disengaged from the quotidian struggles of earthly reality than is the author of *Parables of Enoch*. It would be unfair to argue that the author of Revelation is not at all interested in the political concerns of that time and place.[90] This is an issue of degree of interest more than kind. Perhaps the traumas that had occurred between the writing of the respective texts were too overwhelming to the author of Revelation. Specific concerns that appear in the direct addresses to individual congregations (Rev 2:1-3:22) do not seem obviously, or primarily, politically oriented. They are spiritual and, as previously mentioned, directed toward enabling escape from the existing, traumatized world. The author of *Parables of Enoch* appears to be very interested in remembering the injustice done, seeing it judged, and seeing the *existing* earth and heaven fixed.[91] The author of Revelation seems more interested in forgetting the memory. The existing, traumatized heaven and earth vanish.[92] They are replaced with a new heaven, new earth, and new Jerusalem.[93] The old simply pass away. In the process of reading or hearing the Apocalypse, the reader imagines passing through the successive doors and gates with the author, ending up in the new Jerusalem, forgetting what lies behind. Even the emotions associated with those previous places "have passed away" when God "will wipe away every tear from their eyes, and death shall be no more, neither shall there be mourning nor crying nor pain any more" (Rev 21:4).[94] "Wipe" is the operative word here, as those punished outside the gates at the denouement of Revelation receive barely even a mention. The

---

[89] Even the specific concerns of the direct addresses to individual congregations (Rev 2:1–3:22) are not overtly politically oriented. They are more obviously spiritual and, as previously mentioned, directed toward enabling escape from the existing, traumatized world.

[90] Studies of these issues have certainly been made. See, for example, E. Pagels, *Revelations*, and E. Schussler-Fiorenza, *The Book of Revelation: Justice and Judgment* (Philadelphia: Fortress, 1985).

[91] For example: "On that day, I shall cause my Elect One to dwell among them. I shall *transform* heaven and make it a blessing of light forever. I shall also transform the earth and make it a blessing" (1 En. 45:4-5). E. Isaac's *OTP* translation, emphasis added.

[92] See Rev 6:12-14: "When he opened the sixth seal … the sky vanished like a scroll rolling itself up, and every mountain and island was removed from its place." See also 20:11: "Then I saw a great white throne and the one who sat on it; the earth and the heaven fled from his presence, and no place was found for them," and 21:1: "the first heaven and the first earth had passed away."

[93] See Rev 21:1-2: "Then I saw a new heaven and a new earth … and I saw the holy city, the new Jerusalem, coming down out of heaven from God."

[94] ἐξαλείψει πᾶν δάκρυον ἐκ τῶν ὀφθαλμῶν αὐτῶν, καὶ ὁ θάνατος οὐκ ἔσται ἔτι οὔτε πένθος οὔτε κραυγὴ οὔτε πόνος οὐκ ἔσται ἔτι. See also Rev 7:17: "God will wipe away every tear from their eyes."

generic and totalized enemies of the middle of Revelation are essentially forgotten except for a very brief tropological vice list, ending in the "second death" (Rev 21:8).

There is a good deal of support for the idea that the author of Revelation and the communities that received it favorably had suffered greatly and were mourning the loss of the Temple.[95] The heavenly temple and the heavenly Jerusalem of Revelation function to console[96] and compensate.[97] But it cannot be denied that the tone of the Apocalypse leans toward forgetting and disengagement with the known, and traumatized, material world, especially when compared with *Parables of Enoch*. The author of Revelation seems to have abandoned attention to the earthly details of oppression. The focus is on the memory wipe that will occur with the institution of the new Jerusalem.

Dwelling on the Context of a Carceral Geography

At this point it is important to remember that the purported location of reception for the author's vision in the book of Revelation, as noted earlier in the chapter, is when the ostensible author "John" is dwelling in a state of imprisonment on Patmos (Rev 1:9). The language of the Apocalypse seems to have been significantly shaped by this experience, as seen by the frequent references to the experience of imprisonment, whether directly (2:10; 20:7-8)[98] or indirectly (1:18; 3:7; 6:15-16; 9:1-2; 11:7; 16:10; 17:8; 20:1-3, 10).[99] From this language we can see that the author has constructed what appears to be a compensatory response to the lived experience of imprisonment. This is a normative psychological function of dwelling as we know from Bachelard.

---

[95] Little else can explain the prominence of the temple imagery when earlier Palestinian-inspired apocalypses like *Parables of Enoch* can leave it out entirely.

[96] George L. Parsenios, *Departure and Consolation: The Johannine Farewell Discourses in Light of Greco-Roman Literature*, SNT 117 (Brill: Boston, 2005), 96–8: Of the classical modes of consolation both the Peripatetic approach, that what truly matters is still intact and that there is no cause for deep grief, and the Epicurean perspective, that the grieved should fill the void with some token or substitute, are on display. Both are relevant for the loss of sacred space or country as indicated by Cicero's understanding of consolation "*de interitu patriae*," that is, "concerning destruction of one's homeland," as one of the standard "textbook" types of consolation. See Paul A. Holloway, "Left Behind: Jesus' Consolation of His Disciples in John 13:31-17:26," *ZNW* 96 (2005): 4.

[97] Foucault refers to these types of places as heterotopias of compensation. See Foucault, "Of Other Spaces," 27.

[98] "Behold, the devil is about to throw some of you into prison" (2:10); "And when the thousand years are ended, Satan will be loosed from his prison and will come out to deceive the nations which are at the four corners of the earth" (20:7-8).

[99] For example: "I have the keys of Death and Hades" (1:18); "the true one, who has the key of David, who opens and no one shall shut, who shuts and no one opens" (3:7); "he was given the key to the shaft of the bottomless pit; he opened the shaft of the bottomless pit, and from the shaft rose smoke like the smoke of a great furnace, and the sun and air were darkened with the smoke from the shaft" (9:1-2); "the fifth angel poured his bowl on the throne of the beast, and its kingdom was in darkness; men gnawed their tongues in anguish" (16:10); "then I saw an angel coming down from heaven, holding in his hand the key of the bottomless pit and a great chain. And he seized the dragon, that ancient serpent, who is the Devil and Satan, and bound him for a thousand years, and threw him into the pit, and shut it and sealed it over him, that he should deceive the nations no more, till the thousand years were ended. After that he must be loosed for a little while" (20:1-3); "the devil who had deceived them was thrown into the lake of fire and sulphur where the beast and the false prophet were, and they will be tormented day and night for ever and ever" (20:10).

What the author of Revelation has done then is to produce an alternate, literary reality where he and his fellow righteous ones are liberated and their unrighteous oppressors are imprisoned and punished. The compensatory nature of the vision is perhaps most vividly seen in the geographic juxtaposition of the identification of "the beast" with "the abyss" or "pit" at the bottom of the φρέαρ (9:1-2), while the final locus of revelation for the author is on "a great, high mountain" where the "holy city Jerusalem" can be seen "coming down out of heaven" (21:10). The author is translated from his own "pit" of imprisoned experience to a redeemed and ideal, opposite location. The elevated position of his oppressors is also reversed to be one of associations with the pit (e.g., 6:15-16).[100]

This carceral spatial context is relevant for interpretation of the aforementioned doorway phenomenology that is likely operative in the Apocalypse. The literary production of spaces of reversal in Revelation relies on this very function of doorways. That is, the vivid portrayal of the ideal, ultimate, and permanent space of dwelling in the new Jerusalem for the righteous is aided by the ability to forget or "wipe" the space of suffering that the author has experienced. The parallel consignment of enemies to spaces of imprisonment and suffering, where they will be forgotten, is aided by this same doorway phenomenology. One could argue that the phenomenology of doorways, as previously examined, is inherent to the psychology of imprisonment. The prisoner behind the door feels forgotten, and indeed society and those responsible for the imprisonment are free to forget the prisoner behind the door.[101] The author's vision works against this experience by indicating that he is not forgotten by God, but the vision replicates the function of the carceral experience for those who will be judged. Fundamentally, this carceral context supports the likelihood of an operative narrative doorway phenomenology in Revelation. The author is undeniably already, by virtue of his imprisonment, forcibly disengaged from the rest of the world! Further, the doorway phenomenology that likely operates here can be seen within a complex, mutually reinforcing amalgam of psychologies of dwelling, all of which work simultaneously to produce the spaces of the apocalypse in the mind of the reader: that is, spaces of disengagement with the material world and forgetfulness of its experience of suffering.

Caveats to Observations

However, one must not argue too forcefully for the development of an ethic[102] of disengagement and forgetting in Revelation. It does represent a departure from the mindset that generated *Parables of Enoch*, but only of degree, not of kind. Apocalypses,

---

[100] The idea of underground imprisonment is connoted by the verse: "then the kings of the earth and the magnates and the generals and the rich and the powerful, and everyone, slave and free, hid in the caves and among the rocks of the mountains, calling to the mountains and rocks, 'fall on us'" (6:15-16).

[101] There are, of course, alternate optics to be considered, such as the function of imprisonment as "spectacle" to ensure certain patterns of behavior in society. But the psychology of imprisonment is complex and certainly involves the operation of both of these, apparently conflicting, phenomena, among others (e.g., Bentham's panopticon).

[102] Or anti-ethic.

by their very phenomenology, are productions of alternate worlds[103] that transcend[104] but also inherently inform engagement with the preexisting world. In this sense, *Parables of Enoch* produces an alternate—idealized—world that could be deemed escapist, even as it seeks to critique and judge the depredations of the known world. Conversely, Revelation, though very plausibly escapist, still alters the existing material world through the production of an alternate world of critique[105] and healing.[106] This alternate vision was clearly effective and cherished by many who were exposed to the Apocalypse.[107] Furthermore, the reader or hearer "returns" to the known world after reading or hearing and must decide what to do. It should also be noted that neither of these texts was intended to be read in isolation but are productions for religious communities shaped by other religious texts. To think that the perspective of one apocalypse was ever intended to obliterate the previous perspectives of honored scripture is injudicious. The departure of Revelation is marked but not complete.

---

[103] Carol Newsom, "The Rhetoric of Jewish Apocalyptic Literature," in *The Oxford Handbook of Apocalyptic Literature*, ed. John Collins (Oxford and New York: Oxford University Press, 2014), 203.

[104] Newsom, "The Rhetoric of Jewish Apocalyptic Literature," 211.

[105] The contribution of Revelation, or any apocalypse for that matter, to the sense of an impending *eschaton* would likely have further encouraged moral engagement with the known world. See Paul Magdalino, "The History of the Future and Its Uses: Prophecy, Policy and Propaganda," in *The Making of Byzantine History, Studies Dedicated to Donald M. Nicol*, eds. Roderick Beaton and Charlotte Roueché (London: Variorun, 1993), 6, where he recounts the description of events surrounding the Constantinople earthquakes of 557 found in Agathias' *Historiae*, V. 5: ed. R. Keydell (Berlin, 1967), 169–70: "At the time, however, there was no-one who was not greatly shocked and afraid. Litanies and hymns of supplication were everywhere to be heard, with everyone joining in. And things which are always promised in words, but never carried out in deeds, were at that time readily performed. Suddenly all were honest in their business dealings, so that even public officials, putting aside their greed, dealt with law-suits according to the law, and other powerful men contented themselves with doing good and abstaining from shameful acts. Some, changing their life-style completely, espoused a monastic and mountain way of life, renouncing money and honours and all the other things most pleasing to men. Many gifts were brought to the churches, and by night the most powerful citizens frequented the streets and cared for those wretched and pitiful people who lay crippled on the ground, providing all that they needed in food and clothing. But all this was limited to that fixed space of time in which the terror was endemic. As soon as there was some respite and relief from danger, most people reverted to their normal ways."

[106] A significant dynamic at play is likely related to the psychology of trauma healing. The author of Revelation, in describing several idealized, and non-traumatized, spaces is giving the reader who has suffered trauma the opportunity to form a new, non-traumatized attachment relationship. The work of psychologist Jon Allen suggests that such relationships can be developed with places in addition to people. See Jon G. Allen, *Coping with Trauma: Hope Through Understanding*, Second Edition (Washington, DC: American Psychiatric Publishing, Inc., 2004), 40: "In thinking about the diversity of attachments that can form over the lifetime, we should not overlook the importance of attachments to familiar places and inanimate objects. This phenomenon of bonding to places has been called site attachment. Children coping with trauma invariably seek a safe place in the environment, such as their room, their closet, their bed, or a spot in the woods. Just as children rely on familiar inanimate objects … so too, do adults. It's important to be able to go to a tangible place of safety. But it's also possible to seek shelter in your imagination. Traumatized individuals often find it helpful to visualize an imagined or actual safe place. Relaxation and hypnosis can be used to enhance such visualization, which can be enormously powerful. Picturing oneself in a safe place can be a key component of self-soothing."

[107] Judith Kovacs and Christopher Rowland, *Revelation: The Apocalypse of Jesus Christ* (Oxford: Blackwell, 2004), 250.

Conclusion

The spatial emphases of the author of Revelation suggest a differing mode of engagement with a traumatized material world from that suggested by the spatial language employed by the author of *Parables of Enoch*. In *Parables of Enoch* the author's references to oppressive landowners and transformative goals for the heavens and earth suggest a meaningful and critical engagement with particular social struggles in the material world.[108] The lack of similar specific language in Revelation, combined with (1) the author's polemic against all "those who dwell upon the earth," (2) the emphases on the disappearance of the old order and its replacement with a new one, (3) the compensatory cultic language, (4) the carceral geographic background, and most especially (5) the significant use of doorway language, interwoven with themes of both exclusion and forgetfulness, suggests an orientation toward the existing world that is comparatively less engaged and more escapist. That doors and gates appear so prominently, and that the reader or listener is invited to pass through them, implicates the cognitive phenomenological processes suggested in the studies by Radvansky et al., according to which, the passing of a doorway, whether physical or imagined, induces forgetfulness in the subject. The operation of this phenomenon appears consonant with the narrative logic, spatial structure, theology, and textual ecology of Revelation. The differences between the respective generative domestic environments for *Parables of Enoch* and Revelation may best account for the observed differences in their spatial practice. While both likely spring from marginal and traumatized experiences of dwelling, the comparatively more extreme and restricted experience of imprisonment behind Revelation may explain its more escapist tone. The hermeneutical value of attention to spatial analysis, and particularly analysis of the phenomenology of domestic, or quotidian, spaces, even for interpreting marginal spaces, is clearly shown.

It is too much to say that Revelation is entirely escapist. That would be to misread the genre (as many modern readers are wont to do). However, it seems safe to say that the differences in spatial emphases between *Parables of Enoch* and Revelation indicate possibly significant discrepancies between the respective authors' approaches to engagement with the existing, traumatized world. Maurice Merleau-Ponty famously suggested that one cannot imagine a place without imagining oneself in that place.[109] If so, the cognitive phenomenology of the doorway[110] may provide a helpful interpretive guide to understanding not only the mindset of the author (or authors) of Revelation and the initial community of reception but also the modern communities of reception,

---

[108] Thus, it is not so much that *Parables of Enoch* may be considered superior to Revelation in its response to trauma because its alternate vision of the world is transformative and engaged, having produced a "realistically alternative possible future" compared to that envisioned by Revelation. This is indeed paramount for effective trauma healing (see Allen, *Coping with Trauma*, 292). Rather, the differences may be accounted for by variance in the extremity of their respective generative environments of dwelling. *Parables of Enoch*'s experience seems to be one of economic distress and marginalization from ancestral lands. Revelation's is one of outright imprisonment. Escape and forgetting are actually contextually relevant and important in such a setting.

[109] Merleau-Ponty, *The Phenomenology of Perception*, 101.

[110] Radvansky et al., "Walking Through Doorways Causes Forgetting," 1632–45.

who in passing the gates of the Apocalypse themselves often appear forgetful both of earthly concerns and of those they believe will suffer judgment outside the gates. And while the modern scholarly production of responsible postcolonial readings is perhaps made more challenging by the phenomenologies shown by this study to be operative in the book of Revelation,[111] such characteristics of the text actually indicate the necessity of further analysis along these very lines, specifically with respect to its carceral geography.

---

[111] That is, of an escapist tone, as opposed to the rather transparently proto-Marxist interpretations available for *Parables of Enoch*.

6

"Real" Visions of the Ideal Home: From Ascetic Dwellings to the Isle of the Blessed Ones in the *History of the Rechabites*

Introduction

Having considered two apocalypses produced from a traumatized experience of marginal dwelling (*Parables of Enoch* and Revelation) we turn now to an apocalypse likely produced, in part, from an experience of marginal dwelling willingly chosen: the *History of the Rechabites*. The narrative describes two dwelling places, the cave of the hermit Zosimus and the Isle of the Blessed Ones, the Rechabites. Many Greek and Latin texts describe the Isles of the Blessed, but the *History of the Rechabites* is the first known Jewish or Christian appropriation (Josephus' mention of Essene appropriation [*Jewish War*, 2.8.154–58] is essentially a rumor). While Zosimus' experience of dwelling is harsh and spare, the Rechabites' experience is one of idyllic ease. Previous chapters have shown how experiences of dwelling, especially marginal ones, can be generative of alternate, utopic, imagined visions of dwelling. While most commentators would perhaps expect a similar dynamic to be at play in the *History of the Rechabites*, this chapter will examine the, admittedly rather speculative, possibility of the marginal locus of dwelling being the place not of imagination exclusively but of imagination and unusual literal vision.[1] Scholars have long attempted to locate the Isle of the Blessed Ones but, from antiquity, vague and mythic descriptions have eluded any definitive identification. However, this chapter shows that it may have been unusual visions of Cyprus from the biblical Mt. Zaphon that provided the spark for literary appropriations of the Greco-Roman Blessed Isle legend in the popular, late-antique, pseudepigraphic text *History of the Rechabites*.

Under rare astronomical and meteorological conditions, a visual phenomenon known as the "Canigou Effect" allows a viewer from Marseille, France, to see the Mt. Canigou Massif, a mountain in the Pyrenees. Otherwise the mountain is totally

---

[1] For an explication of this phenomenon with less emphasis on textual ecology, see Jolyon G. R. Pruszinski, "Visions of Cyprus: A Phenomenological Background to Jewish and Christian Scripture," in *Cyprus within the Biblical World: Are Borders Barriers?* eds. James H. Charlesworth and Jolyon G. R. Pruszinski, Jewish and Christian Texts 32 (London: T&T Clark, 2021).

obscured by the ocean due to the curvature of the earth. These rare conditions allow for the sudden "appearance" of an otherwise *invisible island* silhouetted against the setting sun. A nearly identically congruent geographic relationship exists between the biblical Mt. Zaphon, or "Jebel Aqra" as it is now known, on the Turkish-Syrian border, and Cypriot Mt. Olympus. The same visual phenomenon—the appearance to a viewer on the slopes of Mt. Zaphon of an otherwise *invisible island* in the sunset (actually the summit of Cypriot Mt. Olympus)—could thus be produced under similar, rare conditions. It is even possible that some of the Mt. Zaphon traditions that appear in the Hebrew Bible may themselves preserve traces of evidence of just such a phenomenon.

In the text of *History of the Rechabites* the Isle of the Blessed Ones is described as an intermediary state between the world of corruption and heaven, thus allowing the faint but real possibility of glimpsing it (1:2). The Blessed Isle legends place it in the west, corresponding to an alignment with the setting sun. The Isle is located across the "great sea" (2:6) just as Cyprus is from Syria. A pillar of cloud rises from the island (2:8; 10:8) just as orographic lift produces the same visual effect from Mt. Olympus. The waters surrounding the island rise up around it (10:7), obscuring it, just as the ocean obscures Cyprus from Syria under normal conditions. Further, the island is always bathed in light (11:5), and a "Canigou Effect" allows the sun, as it leaves the rest of the world in darkness, to appear to set into the location of the island and join it.

The psychology of dwelling operative in the experience of an ascetic hermit would have fostered the interpretation of an unusual vision in idealized terms. The proposed phenomenon would have provided just the kind of environmental catalyst necessary to spark the Jewish/Christian appropriation of the Greco-Roman legend of the Blessed Isle. And the nearby city of Antioch was home to the kind of robust Jewish and Christian communities in Late Antiquity that might have popularized a text such as the *History of the Rechabites*. The analysis of this chapter must, due to the nature of the material, take a rather speculative tone, but the possibilities suggested by the spatial relationships highlighted below merit consideration nevertheless.

The Search for the Isle of the Blessed Ones

The legend of the Isle of the Blessed Ones appears in many of the classic Greek works that have been preserved extant from antiquity. Hesiod writes that to some very fortunate ancients:

> Zeus the father, Cronus' son, bestowed life and habitations far from human beings and settled them at the limits of the earth; and these dwell with a spirit free of care on the Islands of the Blessed beside deep-eddying Ocean—happy heroes, for whom the grain-giving field bears honey-sweet fruit flourishing three times a year.[2]

---

[2] Hesiod, *Op.* 168-173 (Most, LCL).

In other texts, such as Pindar's *Olympian Odes*[3] and Plato's *Gorgias*,[4] the righteous dead are assigned a life of ease and reward in the Blessed Isles.

However, the attempt to locate the Isle of the Blessed Ones has ever been inconclusive. Various locations have been proposed, based mostly on reports of mild climate, including Sicily, the Aeolian Islands, the Aegadian Islands, other small Sicilian islands, Bermuda, the Lesser Antilles, the Azores, Madeira, Cape Verde, and the Canary Islands. Indeed, the collective name for these latter four archipelagos, "Macaronesia," is derived specifically from the association with the Blessed Isles made by Greek geographers of antiquity.[5] Why, however, would Jews or Christians, who had known of this renowned legend for centuries[6] without ever making it their own literarily,[7] incorporate it into their own devotional literature in the *History of the Rechabites*?

---

[3] Pindar, *Ol.* 2.61-78 (Race, LCL): "But forever having sunshine in equal nights and in equal days, good men receive a life of less toil, for they do not vex the earth or the water of the sea with the strength of their hands to earn a paltry living. No, in company with the honored gods, those who joyfully kept their oaths spend a tearless existence, whereas the others endure pain too terrible to behold. But those with the courage to have lived three times in either realm, while keeping their souls free from all unjust deeds, travel the road of Zeus to the tower of Cronos, where ocean breezes blow round the Isle of the Blessed, and flowers of gold are ablaze, some from radiant trees on land, while the water nurtures others; with these they weave garlands for their hands and crowns for their heads, in obedience to the just counsels of Rhadamanthys, whom the great father keeps ever seated at his side, the husband of Rhea, she who has the highest throne of all."

[4] Plato, *Gorg.* 523a (Lamb, LCL): "Socrates: Give ear then, as they say, to a right fine story, which you will regard as a fable, I fancy, but I as an actual account; for what I am about to tell you I mean to offer as the truth. By Homer's account, Zeus, Poseidon, and Pluto divided the sovereignty amongst them when they took it over from their father. Now in the time of Cronos there was a law concerning mankind, and it holds to this very day amongst the gods, that every man who has passed a just and holy life departs after his decease to the Isles of the Blest, and dwells in all happiness apart from ill; but whoever has lived unjustly and impiously goes to the dungeon of requital and penance which, you know, they call Tartarus. Of these men there were judges in Cronos' time, and still of late in the reign of Zeus—living men to judge the living upon the day when each was to breathe his last; and thus the cases were being decided amiss. So Pluto and the overseers from the Isles of the Blest came before Zeus with the report that they found men passing over to either abode undeserving."

[5] Certainly, there is also some literary conflation with the Elysian Plain, Hades, the White Isle, and Atlantis.

[6] Perhaps as much as a millennium.

[7] At least, there is no prior appropriation to our knowledge. Atlantis themes are at times conflated with Blessed Isle themes in Greco-Roman sources, but the Jewish and Christian writers who transmit or appropriate Atlantis traditions do not seem to transmit those aspects that relate to the Blessed Isle. Philo refers to the Platonic Atlantis story in *Aet.* 26, but only to relate it to destruction by flood. Jerome refers negatively, and only in passing, to the legend as part of a polemic against those who suggest that the righteous are geographically confined after death (*Vigil.* 6). But there is no suggestion there that Christians have appropriated the legend. Tertullian may refer to the legend in a polemic against those Christian heretics who speculate about the living quarters of the heavens (*Val.* 7). But again, here there is only reference to the legend and not a suggestion that Christians have appropriated it. Hippolytus refers to the legend of Isle of the Blessed Ones to suggest that the Greeks derived it from Jewish Essene traditions (*Haer.* 9.22). This is the text that most suggests a Jewish connection to the legend. The only early Christian writer who makes any reference of any kind to a similar legend, favorably received, is Clement of Rome in 1 Clement 20:8. There he writes vaguely that ὠκεανὸς ἀπέραντος ἀνθρώποις καὶ οἱ μετ' αὐτὸν κόσμοι ταῖς αὐταῖς ταγαῖς τοῦ δεσπότου διευθύνονται (the ocean, impassable to humans, and the worlds in the middle of it, are governed by the same ordinances of the lord). Whether these "worlds" beyond the ocean refer to Atlantis or the Blessed Isle or something else entirely is unclear. What is clear is that this is nothing close to the scale of appropriation of the legend of the Blessed Isle that we find in *History of the Rechabites*.

Introduction to the *History of the Rechabites*

Not much is known about the Rechabites before the revelation of the abode of the Blessed that appears in our text. They are mentioned fleetingly in Jer 35 as those who were faithful to the command of their ancestor Jonadab not to drink wine, nor to build houses, nor to engage in agriculture even when tempted. They are held up by Jeremiah—and indeed God—as an example against the rest of Judah.[8] The text of the core of the *History of the Rechabites* is thus something of a midrashic expansion on Jer 35, which explains, among other things, how the Rechabites came to be preserved by God for all time in their blessed abode. Other traditions have been grouped with it, or around it, including the travelogue of the righteous man Zosimus—for whom the work is sometimes named the *Story of Zosimus* or the *Apocalypse of Zosimus* or the *Testament of Zosimus*. As we have the extant text today, in various translations, an angel guides the holy Zosimus to the abode of the Rechabites where he learns of their blessed state and way of life. All commentators recognize the composite nature of the text and there are many speculations regarding the earliest stratum or whether it was a Jewish or Christian text in its earliest form.[9] The question, however, of what would have precipitated the appropriation of the Blessed Isle legend into the amalgamated *History of the Rechabites* remains entirely unanswered. Some data about the Isle from our text may be illuminating.

The Legend in the *History of the Rechabites*

The Isle of the Blessed Ones is described in the text as a physical place, away from the world of corruption, that is, away from the contaminated world of human beings.

---

[8] "Then the word of the LORD came to Jeremiah: Thus says the LORD of hosts, the God of Israel: Go and say to the people of Judah and the inhabitants of Jerusalem, Can you not learn a lesson and obey my words? says the LORD. The command has been carried out that Jonadab son of Rechab gave to his descendants to drink no wine; and they drink none to this day, for they have obeyed their ancestor's command. But I myself have spoken to you persistently, and you have not obeyed me. I have sent to you all my servants the prophets, sending them persistently, saying, 'Turn now every one of you from your evil way, and amend your doings, and do not go after other gods to serve them, and then you shall live in the land that I gave to you and your ancestors.' But you did not incline your ear or obey me. The descendants of Jonadab son of Rechab have carried out the command that their ancestor gave them, but this people has not obeyed me. Therefore, thus says the LORD, the God of hosts, the God of Israel: I am going to bring on Judah and on all the inhabitants of Jerusalem every disaster that I have pronounced against them; because I have spoken to them and they have not listened, I have called to them and they have not answered. But to the house of the Rechabites Jeremiah said: Thus says the LORD of hosts, the God of Israel: Because you have obeyed the command of your ancestor Jonadab, and kept all his precepts, and done all that he commanded you, therefore thus says the LORD of hosts, the God of Israel: Jonadab son of Rechab shall not lack a descendant to stand before me for all time" (Jer 35:12-19, NRSV).

[9] One does wonder about whether there is a connection between prefix *mem* (place of) the *rekabim* (rechabites) and *merkabah* (chariot) mysticism (which was typically oriented around descriptions of inaccessible holy places and which seems to have been increasingly heavily criticized and prohibited in the Talmudim). It is possible that our text comes out of a Jewish background in which *merkabah* legends are increasingly suspect and may have been sanitized through the euphemism of the "Rechabites." However, such an investigation is well beyond the limited scope of this chapter.

And while it is away from the inhabited world and its corruption (Hist. Rech. 1:2), it is not heaven. Zosimus is guided on a journey by an angel (1:3; 2:1). It is not a heavenly journey as in many apocalypses, although by means of two giant trees[10] he is lifted up briefly into the heavens, but this brief elevation is only the means of conveyance from one physical, earthly location to another (3:1-4). This physical-earthly location of the abode of the Blessed allows, presumably, for the faint, but real, possibility of glimpsing it on earth, as does Zosimus.[11]

The Greek Blessed Isle legends place it in the west,[12] and in this detail our extant texts of the *History of the Rechabites* agree, namely that the Isle of the Blessed Ones is across the great sea (2:6 [*Pwqynws*],[13] 2:6-7 [ποταμώδους, ποταμῷ, and ποταμόν][14]), which is considered to be in the west.[15] Significantly, this reckoning corresponds to an alignment with the setting sun.

The abode of the blessed is described as being "in the midst" (*lgw* [2:8a]) of a cloud and that "(something) like a dense bulwark of cloud" (*šwr' lbšd' d'nn'* [2:8]) or "wall" (τεῖχος [2:8]) of cloud extends from the water up to heaven, separating the Isle from those who would see it (10:7; 11:5; 17:3a, 4b, 5b [Syriac]; 4:2, 8-9; 10:8 [Greek]).

Another interesting aspect of the separation of the Isle is that the waters surrounding the island rise up around it (10:7), obscuring it.[16] In the Syriac manuscripts the Rechabites claim that when they were settled in their abode, "God commanded and the waters rose up from the deep abyss and encircled this place" (10:7a).[17] In the Greek recensions the description of this event suggests instead that God miraculously parted the water to expose an island, not unlike the parting of the Red Sea, and that "water came up out of the abyss" (ἀνῆλθεν ὕδωρ ἀπὸ τῆς ἀβύσσου, 10:7). In either case the suggestion is that the Isle is obscured by the water that surrounds it in some supernatural fashion.

Finally, the Isle of the Blessed Ones is described as being always bathed in light. The Rechabites explain "the land in which we are is filled with a glorious light so darkness

---

[10] These trees may refer to the two Edenic trees: that of the knowledge of good and evil and that of life, which were also represented by the pillars at the entrance to the second Jerusalem Temple.

[11] The Isles of the Blessed Ones are also literal places in the Greek and Roman accounts. This element in the text does much to mitigate criticisms, à la D. F. Strauss' criticisms of Eichorn and Paulus in *The Life of Jesus, Critically Examined*, of interpretive approaches that seek to understand possible naturalistic explanations. The *History of the Rechabites* identifies itself as a text that describes seeing a literal, albeit hidden, place.

[12] Ptolemy (*Geogr.* 7.5.14), Plutarch (*Sert.* 8), Strabo (*Geogr.* 3.2.13), and Philostratus (*Vit. Apoll.* 5.3), among others, all agree upon this.

[13] English translations of the Syriac text are from James H. Charlesworth, "The History of the Rechabites: A New Translation and Introduction," in *OTP* 2.443-61. Syriac text comes from manuscript BnF syr. 236.

[14] In Greek traditions the great sea is synonymous with the "encircling river." English translations of the Greek text are from James H. Charlesworth, *The History of the Rechabites*, Volume 1: *The Greek Recension* (Chico, CA: Scholars Press, 1982). Greek text comes from Cod. Par. Gr. 1217 of BnF.

[15] These two words, "west" and "sea," are of course the same in Hebrew: *yam*.

[16] I am not aware of a parallel data point in the Greek legends. Although some kind of separation would be tropologically expected with a holy place.

[17] *OTP* 2:455.

and night do not enter it. And we possess a shining appearance and dwell in light" (11:5a-5b).[18]

Lacking Similar Detail in Greco-Roman Legends

Many of these characteristics indicate a divergence from the most popular versions of the earliest legends of the Blessed Isle. Analysis of these texts is somewhat difficult, as the Blessed Isles legends are often conflated in Greco-Roman sources with legends of Elysium, Hades, Atlantis, and remote geographies like the dwelling of the "Aithiopians."[19] It is true that Greco-Roman legends regularly envision the Blessed Isles as a real earthly place. They are certainly to be found in the west across the great sea (or the encircling river), and antique geographic tropes do make use of the language of inaccessibility for remote or exotic locations.[20] However, it is typical in these traditions that a single Island of the Blessed is not envisioned but rather *islands*.[21] There are similarly no well-established preexisting themes in Greek or Roman sources of constant light in the abode of the blessed,[22] nor shrouding or concealing of the place with a cloud,[23] nor of the surrounding water rising up around the place to protect or conceal it.[24] So where might such ideas about the Blessed Isle that appear in *History of the Rechabites* originate?

---

[18] Syriac translation from *OTP* 2:456.

[19] Ethiopian legends appear in Homer, as noted by Brent Landau, "'One Drop of Salvation from the House of Majesty': Universal Revelation, Human Mission and Mythical Geography in the Syriac Revelation of the Magi," in *The Levant: Crossroads of Late Antiquity. History, Religion and Archaeology*, eds. Ellen Bradshaw Aitken and John M. Fossey (Leiden: Brill, 2013), 98: "The Aithiopians are situated at the boundaries of Okeanos (*Iliad* 23.205), in a land accessible only to the gods. As a sign of their favor in the eyes of the gods, their land is blessed with extreme fecundity and a most pleasant climate."

[20] For example, Atlantis in Plato's *Critias* 113d-e (Bury, LCL): "Poseidon, being smitten with desire for her, wedded her; and to make the hill whereon she dwelt impregnable he broke it off all round about; and he made circular belts of sea and land enclosing one another alternately, some greater, some smaller, two being of land and three of sea, which he carved as it were out of the midst of the island; and these belts were at even distances on all sides, so as to be impassable for man; for at that time neither ships nor sailing were as yet in existence." But even this legend is attributed to the ancient past, and subsequent development of Atlantis as described in *Critias* involves bridging these barriers and cutting shipping channels through them. The base of the outer edges was still walled though and these walls were plated with metals, including brass, "which sparkled like fire" in the sun (Plato, *Critias* 116c [Bury, LCL]). The towers of the temple at the center (and highest point) of Atlantis were coated in gold. These features seem reminiscent of elements of a Canigou Effect, especially the shining through of the sun underneath or at the base of the "island," as we will see.

[21] Plato has it in the plural (*Menex.* 235c; *Gorg.* 523a; 526c; *Symp.* 179e). Others similarly (Strabo, *Geogr.* 3.2.13; Antoninus Liberalis, *Metam.* 33; Athenaeus, *Deipn.* 15.695; Apollodorus, *Library* 3.10.1; Hesiod, *Op.* 155-173; Philostratus, *Vit. Apoll.* 5.3). Only Pindar (*Ol.* 2.55-75), Euripides (*Hel.* 1676), and Herodotus (*Hist.* 3.26.1) envision one island, and Herodotus' account is very garbled.

[22] Though Pindar, *Ol.* 2.55-75, could arguably preserve such a tradition.

[23] Although one could interpret the Greek myths regarding Atlas (Atlantis) as the father of Calypso (literally "I will conceal" or "I will cover") to be a possible indirect suggestion of this idea in a tradition that may sometimes be conflated with the Blessed Isle tradition, the relation is clearly very speculative.

[24] There are, of course, many examples of various kinds of obstacles preventing access to remote, and often sacred, locations. For a discussion of some of these tropes, particularly "extreme inaccessibility," as they pertain to various locales as appearing in late antique texts, see Landau, "One Drop of Salvation from the House of Majesty," 98.

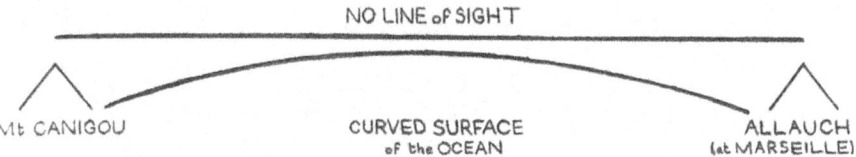

Figure 6.1 Line of Sight without Atmospheric Refraction, Marseille to Canigou. (Artist's rendering by K. N. Pruszinski. Used with permission.)

The "Canigou Effect"

A visual phenomenon known as the "Canigou Effect," which has been observed in the western Mediterranean, provides a possible answer.[25] This atmospheric-astronomical effect allows a viewer from Marseille, France, to see, under unusual conditions, Mt. Canigou, a mountain in the Pyrenees, which is otherwise totally obscured by the ocean due to the curvature of the earth.[26]

These rare conditions allow for the "appearance" of an otherwise invisible "island" silhouetted against the setting sun. This phenomenon is likely a subspecies of the Novaya Zemlya effect,[27] which, through rare conditions[28] of atmospheric refraction, allows the viewing of objects at a distance that are actually below the horizon. When these atmospheric conditions occur during the alignment of the sunset with the Canigou Massif, as seen from Marseille, the local effect is produced.[29]

---

[25] This visual phenomenon has been documented most extensively by Alain Origne, a research engineer at Laboratoire d'Astrophysique de Marseille, at his website: http://canigou.allauch.free.fr/Photos-anims.htm.

[26] Assuming that the radius of the earth is 6371 kilometers, the distance "D" to the visible horizon from a location "h" high above sea level is given by the formula $D = (112.88 \text{ km}) \sqrt{h}$. Thus, from the summit of the Canigou Massif (2.75 km) the horizon across the sea would be 187.19 kilometers distant. From the observation location "Allauch" in Marseille (0.31 km above sea level) without atmospheric refraction the horizon would appear 62.85 kilometers distant. If the sum of these two distances were greater than the distance from Marseille to Canigou (263.1 km), then the mountain would be normally visible. However, the combined horizon viewing distance (250.04 km) is just a little less than the distance between the two locations, thus they are not mutually visible without significant atmospheric refraction.

[27] This effect has been noted, among other instances, during polar expeditions. During the Barentsz expedition in 1597, expedition members observed the sun above the horizon a full two weeks before it would have been visible without atmospheric refraction. Gerrit de Veer, *The Three Voyages of William Barents to the Arctic Regions: 1594, 1595, and 1596*, trans. Charles T. Beke (London: The Hakylut Society, 1876), 143–4.

[28] Namely, atmospheric inversion, which will be described later in the chapter.

[29] This particular local manifestation of the effect is categorized by William R. Corliss, *Rare Halos, Mirages, Anomalous Rainbows and Related Electromagnetic Phenomena: A Catalog of Geophysical Anomalies* (Glen Arm, MD: The Sourcebook Project, 1984), 144, as a "telescopic mirage," though no telescopic effect is required, and in spite of the fact that it is more akin to a "Novaya Zemlya effect," which involves viewing an object below the horizon as a result of highly refracted light. Corliss catalogs a similar observation of Tahiti and surrounding islands from a distance of "210 miles away" (Corliss, *Rare Halos*, 144). In this latter instance, both a telescopic effect and a refraction around the surface of the earth allowed the observation. The whole chapter in Corliss (*Rare Halos*, 137–57) on mirages is instructive, as many of these observed phenomena either defy easy categorization or display characteristics of multiple phenomena simultaneously. A better-known Mediterranean mirage is the "Fata Morgana" occasionally observable in the straits of Messina (Corliss, *Rare Halos*, 139–41), though this mirage shares only some characteristics with that viewable from Marseille.

128   *An Ecology of Scriptures*

Figure 6.2 Canigou Effect. (Artist's rendering by K. N. Pruszinski. Used with permission.)[30]

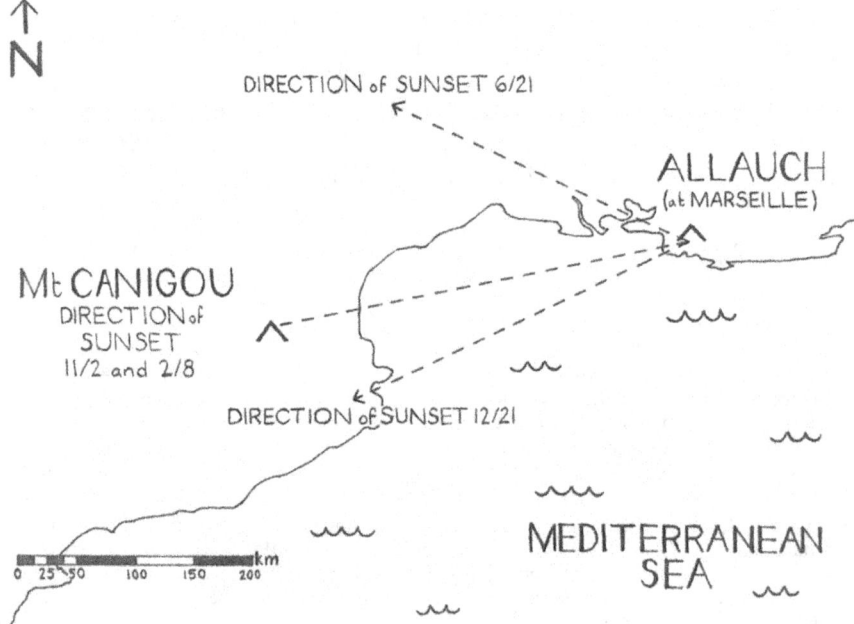

Figure 6.3 Calendrical Conditions for Sunset Alignment, Marseille to Canigou. (Artist's rendering by K. N. Pruszinski. Used with permission.)

---

[30] Sunset over Roc Negre of the Canigou Massif from Allauch, France. Notice that no "island" is visible in the image on the left, before Canigou appears in silhouette. Three renderings based on photographs: "Roc Negre depuis semaphore fevrier 2012 (16)," "Roc Negre depuis semaphore fevrier 2012 (25)," "Roc Negre depuis semaphore fevrier 2012 (33)" by flickr.com user "akunamatata" taken February 17, 2012. Used with permission.

As can be seen from Figure 6.2, even when the sun is very low on the horizon, though not yet behind the massif, there is still no land visible across the ocean. As the sun dips behind the Canigou Massif, the mountain range "appears." Interestingly, the sun continues to shine through "below" the mountain at times.[31] This creates something of a floating effect, where the base of the "island" appears to glow brilliantly as it hovers slightly over the water.[32] Astronomically speaking, the setting sun must align with the mountain (Canigou) and the viewing location (Marseille).[33] Atmospherically, the sky must be crystal clear and the air must be stable over the ocean. This phenomenon typically occurs when the low-altitude air is cold and dry.[34] Under these conditions, in Marseille the optical effect may be observed with the highest probability in November and in February.

Parallel Geography in Eastern Mediterranean

There appear to exist parallel favorable conditions in the eastern Mediterranean as well.[35] Under normal circumstances, due to the curvature of the earth, Cyprus is not

---

[31] See canigou.allauch.free.fr/Anim-16nov08-1.htm for a similar, but animated, sequence that shows this brilliant "base" of the "island" very vividly, as documented by Alain Origne.

[32] This aspect of the effect may result from a "Fata Morgana" mirage coincident with Novaya Zemlya refraction or may be due to some other category of mirage, enabling reflection of differently refracted sunlight on the surface of the water (see the discussion of "multiple mirages" in Corliss, *Rare Halos*, 147–9). The various naming conventions and categories of mirage are not well established and exhibit a good deal of variability of use. At the least it is necessary for two different refraction trajectories to be at work, one for the "island" and a separate one for the "shining base." The latter may be the result of differently, and more strongly, refracted light traveling through the coldest layer of air at the very surface of the water, allowing a sliver of sun to be visible at the base through what is known as a "superior" mirage. The observed effect would require two different superior mirages to be visible, one stacked on top of the other but reversed in order from the actual objects' orientation, likely as a result of multiple atmospheric thermocline ducting effects. This is an otherwise documented phenomenon and not unprecedented: "The Novaya Zemlya Effect … may also be applicable to other optical phenomena occurring near the horizon, which are generally considered to be the consequence of simple refraction by atmospheric strata" (Corliss, *Rare Halos*, 151). The mechanism of the effect, however, is not the primary concern. Rather the fact of its occurrence, the description of it visually, and notation of the conditions under which it occurs are the concerns for this chapter.

[33] However, due to the length of the Canigou Massif range, the array of dates during which the astronomical alignment is in some way possible is rather broad. For instance, perfect alignment of the peak occurs on November 2 and February 8; however, the photos upon which the above drawings in Figure 6.2 were based were taken of the effect over the southeastern spur of the massif on February 17, 2012.

[34] The Novaya Zemlya effect is most frequently observed in polar regions due to this necessity of atmospheric inversion, that is, a temperature gradient from cold in lower elevations to warm in higher elevations. This enables greater concavity of refraction along the curvature of the earth. This effect is visible outside of polar regions when atmospheric inversion is present. See W. H. Lehn, "The Novaya Zemlya Effect: An Arctic Mirage," *Journal of the Optical Society of America* 69 (1979): 776–81.

[35] The phenomenon remains formally undocumented to my knowledge.

directly visible across the Mediterranean from the region of Antioch, now near the border of southern Turkey and western Syria.[36]

However, under similar meteorological[37] and astronomical[38] conditions to those required at Marseille, it should be possible to see across the ocean between the Antioch area and Cyprus due to their similar geographic relationship. These similarities include the time of year of sunset alignment (November 2 and February 8 at Marseille, and November 13 and January 28 in the Antioch region), the distance between the locations in question (263 kilometers from Marseille to Canigou and 306 kilometers from Jebel Aqra to Cypriot Mt. Olympus), and the aforementioned not quite tangential line of sight between respective observation points and mountaintops.

This congruency suggests the likelihood of rare Novaya Zemlya-type apparitions of the summit of the Cypriot Mt. Olympus appearing as a small island visible only in the setting sun, from the Antioch area during the calendrical periods of adequate alignment. As it pertains to our text, the Isle in question would be located across the "great sea" (2:6) just as Cyprus is from Syria.[39] The waters surrounding the island rise up around it (10:7), obscuring it, just as the ocean obscures Cyprus from western Syria under normal conditions. Further, the island is always bathed in light (11:5 [Syriac]), and the proposed visual effect allows the sun, as it leaves the rest of the world in darkness, to appear to set into the location of the island and join it. The island only ever becomes visible in silhouette against the sun.

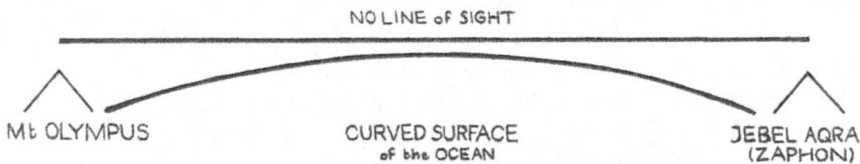

Figure 6.4 Line of Sight without Atmospheric Refraction, Zaphon to Olympus. (Artist's rendering by K. N. Pruszinski. Used with permission.)

---

[36] The summit of Cypriot Mt. Olympus, at 1.952 kilometers, is not visible from sea level beyond 157.71 kilometers without atmospheric refraction. The distance from Mt. Olympus to a comparable viewing location on the Turkish coast near Antioch is approximately 306 kilometers.

[37] Similar meteorological conditions occur in similar seasons due to the relative homogeneity of the Mediterranean climate. The parallel viewing windows for each location are favorable for the occurrence of the necessary conditions of atmospheric inversion.

[38] The range of dates when the astronomical alignment is possible for viewing points in the region of Turkey/western Syria is narrower than the date range for viewing the effect from Marseille. This is because of the different orientation of the Cypriot Olympus range. It presents a narrower viewing cross-section to points to the east-northeast than does the Canigou Massif.

[39] This is basically similar to Greco-Roman accounts.

"Real" Visions of the Ideal Home 131

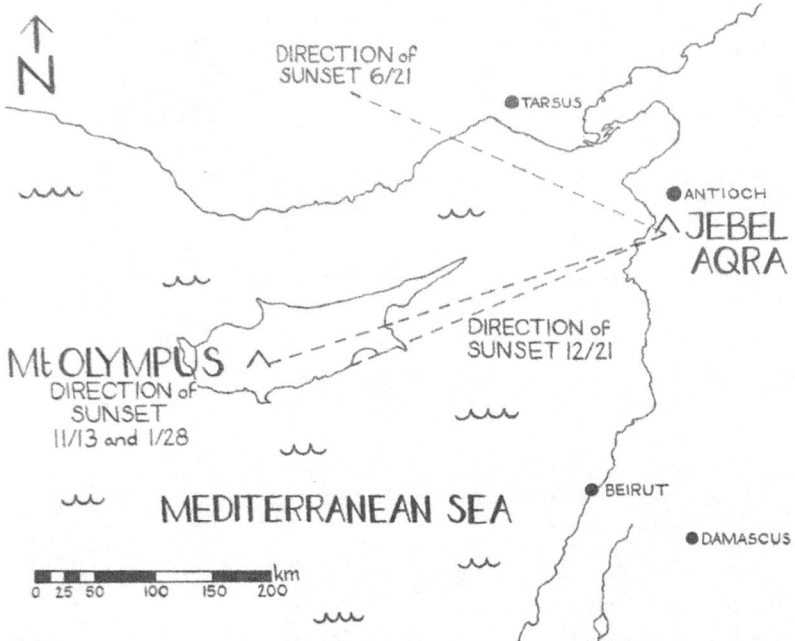

Figure 6.5 Calendrical Conditions for Sunset Alignment, Zaphon to Olympus. (Artist's rendering by K. N. Pruszinski. Used with permission.)

Figure 6.6 Orographic Lift, Santa Lucia Mountains, California. (Photo by Robert Schwemmer, NOAA, NOS, CINMS. Used with permission. Edited for publication.)[40]

[40] Photo by Robert Schwemmer, NOAA, NOS, CINMS. From https://www.flickr.com/photos/51647007@N08/5033367878/. Used with permission. Licensed use: https://creativecommons.org/licenses/by/2.0/. Edited for publication.

Perhaps the most convincing evidence from our text is the fact that a cloud conceals the Island (2:8; 10:8). No one would argue that Cyprus is continually wrapped in cloud, and yet a common phenomenon that might account for the text occurs normally when prevailing winds rise over higher elevations. The phenomenon is known as orographic lift. Air rises as it passes over a mountain. The water vapor present in the air condenses as it chills at elevation to produce clouds, often at heights well above the elevation of the summit. Such clouds then often continue in the direction of the prevailing wind.

If such a mountain was not visible a significant distance downwind due to the curvature of the earth, the clouds produced by it would nevertheless be visible as they rose high above the mountain or continued downwind. Orographic lift produces this exact effect on Mt. Olympus.[41]

Figure 6.7 Dust Storm with Orographic Clouds over Cypriot Mt. Olympus. (Photo by NASA. Used with permission. Edited for publication.)[42]

---

[41] I am not aware of a parallel data point in the Greco-Roman legends. There are, of course, Hebrew Bible precedents for the shrouding of a holy place or thing in cloud, but it is likely that this has phenomenological background in natural summit shrouding.

[42] Original photo by NASA. From https://commons.wikimedia.org/wiki/File:Cyprus.A2002292.1045.500m.jpg. Used with permission. Edited for publication.

And even if the astronomical and other atmospheric factors were otherwise perfectly aligned for a Canigou-Effect type of phenomenon, orographic lift might still cause the peak to be obscured, hiding it within a "bulwark of cloud."

Prior Evidentiary Zaphon/Kasios Traditions

Perhaps most interestingly, the location in the vicinity of Antioch that best matches the geographic parameters necessary for a Canigou-Effect apparition of Cyprus is Jebel Aqra, the biblical Mt. Zaphon, on the modern-day Turkish-Syrian border, on the Mediterranean coast just south of the mouth of the River Orontes.[43]

One might wonder if such a mountain would, in antiquity, have had anyone on it regularly enough to catch the proposed vision of the Blessed Isle. However, Mt. Zaphon, also known (later) as Mt. Kasios, was home in antiquity to a succession of

Figure 6.8 View South to Jebel Aqra/Zaphon/Kasios from Turkey. (Photo by Anthiok at en.wikipedia. Used with permission. Edited for publication.)[44]

---

[43] The horizon from the summit of Jebel Aqra (1.717 km), without atmospheric refraction, is 147.91 kilometers. That distance added to the distance from Cypriot Mt. Olympus to the horizon is 305.62 kilometers. This is almost precisely the distance from Jebel Aqra to Cypriot Mt. Olympus and as such would not allow a viewer to see one from the other under normal, limited refraction, conditions.

[44] Photo by Anthiok at en.wikipedia. https://upload.wikimedia.org/wikipedia/commons/5/5a/Jebel_Aqra_%28Kel_Da%C4%9F%C4%B1%2C_Mount_Casius%29%2C_2008.jpg. Used with permission. Licensed use: https://creativecommons.org/licenses/by/3.0/deed.en. Edited for publication.

cultic practices, including Baal traditions[45] preserved in Ugaritic texts and the Hebrew Bible. While these traditions do not necessarily describe a Canigou Effect-type vision directly, some of the themes and language preserved in the Zaphon traditions could be explained by the proposed phenomenon.[46]

Fascinatingly, the Baal Saphon (Zaphon) cult was active in several locations around the Mediterranean in antiquity, and in every instance there was a relation to a geographic phenomenon that in some way replicated those present at Mt. Zaphon. The instances of worship in the near-environs of the mountain, like at Ugarit and Tyre, require no further explanation than proximity to the mountain itself. The locus of reverence in Egypt was related to a particular "mountain" and the nearby lake, which produced a misty cloud cover reminiscent of that related to Baal's vanquished serpent foe.[47] But most relevantly we have record of recognition of Baal Sapon in *Marseille*,[48] which, as we have already mentioned, is the location in which the Canigou Effect has been observed and which exhibits such a congruency in its geographic relationships to Mt. Zaphon that we may conclude that the two likely produce similar visual phenomena. That Marseille was found to be a suitable location for the cult in the western Mediterranean would seem to confirm the strong connection between the two sites postulated above.

The Hebrew Bible of course has appropriated and transformed many Zaphon traditions and some of these appear to preserve elements of a possible Canigou Effect-type phenomenon from Zaphon. Not only have many scholars suggested that Baal traditions were appropriated and attached, with some alteration, to YHWH in the Hebrew Bible, but holy mountain traditions from Zaphon came to be attached to holy mountains revered in the Hebrew Bible. These Hebrew Bible texts provide the most

---

[45] Mark Smith (*Where the Gods Are*, 5) writes that there is a multiplicity of natural images for Baal/Yahweh. "In this complex of divine imagery, the rainy storm cloud moving eastward is identified as the god's chariotlike vehicle; its lightning is recognized as divine weaponry and its thunder as the god's mighty 'voice' (see Ps 29; Ps 18 = 2 Sam 22:8-10)." This imagery may derive not only from the production of clouds as air rises directly from the ocean up the slopes of Zaphon but also from clouds coming eastward across the ocean toward Zaphon formed from orographic lift at Cypriot Olympus.

[46] A good deal of attention in the Baal cycle is given to deliberation over whether to build a window into Baal's palace. Baal is against it from the beginning, concerned with others looking in upon the palace. Ultimately, he is prevailed upon to allow a single window. Baal's window is not just referred to in typical building terms but also as a "break in the clouds." Interestingly the window is only built after the rest of the construction is completed. The palace is built through a multi-day process of burning during which the ruder elements of construction are transformed into gold, silver, and lapis, all shining brilliantly. Lady Asherah of the sea is instrumental in inciting the building process, and initial concerns regarding the window related to "Pidray, girl of light." However, once the palace is completed and glorious to behold Baal agrees to allow the window, which will allow glimpses of the palace. The narrative does not make sense if the temple to Baal on the summit of Zaphon is in mind. That temple would have been regularly visible from all around. However, a rare vision of an apparently "heavenly" location shining brilliantly where the sea and sun meet through a "window" in the clouds would do better justice to the details of the Baal cycle text.

[47] Robin Lane Fox, *Travelling Heroes in the Epic Age of Homer* (New York: Vintage, 2008), 254.

[48] Smith, *Where the Gods Are*, 88, derives his evidence for this conclusion from Herbert Donner and Wolfgang Röllig, *Kanaanäische und aramäische Inschriften*, 2nd ed. (Wiesbaden: 1966–9), 69.1.

"Real" Visions of the Ideal Home 135

Figure 6.9 The Baal Stele. (Photo by Jastrow from Wikimedia commons. Used with permission. Edited for publication.)[49]

---

[49] Excavated in 1930 from the western wing of the temple of Baal in the acropolis of Ugarit, the Baal stele (also known as "Baal with thunderbolt"), currently housed at the Louvre, provides some additional suggestive data. Here Baal is depicted on a flat platform, clearly engaged in the action of ruling: wielding the mace and growing food out of a planted spear. However, this platform for his governance is supported by the *sea*, as indicated by the waves depicted underneath. Such a depiction could be derived from visions of Baal's palace, shining across the sea, from which he rules. It could alternately depict his victory over the sea and the god of death, Mot, but such a figurative explanation does not detract from the possible literal phenomenal background to the legend: the appearance of an "island" out of the sea that shines and appears on a shining floor. (Baal is often considered to be synonymous with Mt. Zaphon, a "homology" according to Smith, *Where the Gods Are*, 86. So it is possible that the stele preserves evidence of a Canigou Effect–type vision, but it is possible that it simply depicts Baal/Mt. Zaphon looming from the ocean from the perspective of further down the coast.) Some scholars have suggested that the lapis of the palace appeared on the floor (e.g., Smith, *Where the Gods Are*, 132, n. 93), which would support the idea of a shining floor that was laid upon the ocean. Photo by Jastrow, from: https://upload.wikimedia.org/wikipedia/commons/3/35/Baal_thunderbolt_Louvre_AO15775.jpg. Used with permission: https://commons.wikimedia.org/wiki/File:Baal_thunderbolt_Louvre_AO15775.jpg. Edited for publication.

likely basis for a "literary borrowing" explanation[50] of the *History of the Rechabites* data, but these texts are also the ones most dependent on Zaphon traditions. They are not a "clean" source but rather are likely themselves to have been influenced by Zaphon or northern Lebanon range[51] visual phenomena and traditions. The possibly Zaphon-connected Hebrew Bible texts are too numerous to catalog here exhaustively, so a few must suffice. One of the most obvious examples appears in the book of Exodus:

> [9] Then Moses and Aaron, Nadab, and Abihu, and seventy of the elders of Israel went up, [10] and they saw the God of Israel. Under his feet there was something like a pavement of sapphire stone, like the very heaven for clearness. [11] God did not lay his hand on the chief men of the people of Israel; also they beheld God, and they ate and drank. [12] The LORD said to Moses, "Come up to me on the mountain, and wait there; and I will give you the tablets of stone, with the law and the commandment, which I have written for their instruction."[13] So Moses set out with his assistant Joshua, and Moses went up into the mountain of God. [14] To the elders he had said, "Wait here for us, until we come to you again; for Aaron and Hur are with you; whoever has a dispute may go to them."[15] Then Moses went up on the mountain, and the cloud covered the mountain. [16] The glory of the LORD settled on Mount Sinai, and the cloud covered it for six days; on the seventh day he called to Moses out of the cloud. [17] Now the appearance of the glory of the LORD was like a devouring fire on the top of the mountain in the sight of the people of Israel. [18] Moses entered the cloud and went up on the mountain. Moses was on the mountain for forty days and forty nights.
> (Exod 24:9-18)

God and the holy mountain are shrouded in cloud. At the same time the divinity has the appearance of a bright fire and is described as standing on a clear-blue precious stone like lapis. Though not oceanic in location,[52] many later interpretative traditions still attribute the blue pavement under the feet of God as a reference to the waters of the ocean.[53]

Further Zaphon traditions likely appear in the book of Job:

> [5] The shades below tremble, the waters and their inhabitants. [6] Sheol is naked before God, and Abaddon has no covering. [7] He stretches out Zaphon over the void, and

---

[50] As opposed to the proposed "phenomenological background" explanation. There has certainly been significant literary borrowing, but that does not preclude a likely phenomenological explanation.

[51] It is also possible that the proposed phenomenon is viewable from certain northern Lebanon range locations, but the probability is much lower than at Jebel Aqra/Zaphon due to the sunset alignment occurring in warmer months, making the likelihood of favorable atmospheric conditions (i.e., stable cool surface air producing atmospheric inversion) much lower.

[52] Frank Moore Cross, *Canaanite Myth and Hebrew Epic* (Cambridge, MA: Harvard University Press, 1973), 166-7, asserts that previous scholars' contentions of a volcanic eruption as a phenomenological background to texts such as the Exodus 24 theophany are misguided, suggesting instead the mountainous storm imagery of Baal traditions as adequately explanatory. This chapter suggests that Canigou Effect–type phenomena observed from Zaphon may also (or instead) lie behind these appropriated traditions.

[53] See, for example, b. Soṭ. 17a:24.

hangs the earth upon nothing.⁸ He binds up the waters in his thick clouds, and the cloud is not torn open by them.⁹ He covers the face of the full moon, and spreads over it his cloud.¹⁰ He has described a circle on the face of the waters, at the boundary between light and darkness.¹¹ The pillars of heaven tremble, and are astounded at his rebuke.¹² By his power he stilled the Sea; by his understanding he struck down Rahab.¹³ By his wind the heavens were made fair; his hand pierced the fleeing serpent.¹⁴ These are indeed but the outskirts of his ways; and how small a whisper do we hear of him! But the thunder of his power who can understand?

(Job 26:5-14)

Baal traditions are being recycled in Job 26, as is evidenced not only by the use of "Zaphon" but also by the reference to the "thunder of his power" and the Baal legend of the defeat of the Sea/Death/Mot. But beyond this we can note clear resemblances to the Canigou-Effect phenomenon as previously described, namely the effect of obscuring cloud and the reference to the "face of the waters" as "the boundary between light and darkness." But most notable of all is the language of Zaphon stretched "over the void" (i.e., the sea) and the earth hung "upon nothing," as appears to be the case in a Canigou Effect.⁵⁴

Interestingly, the book of Job not only preserves Zaphon traditions but also discusses the inaccessible dwelling-place of wisdom:

> ⁵ As for the earth, out of it comes bread; but underneath it is turned up as by fire.⁶ Its stones are the place of sapphires, and its dust contains gold ....¹² But where shall wisdom be found? And where is the place of understanding?¹³ Mortals do not know the way to it, and it is not found in the land of the living ....²⁰ Where then does wisdom come from? And where is the place of understanding?²¹ It is hidden from the eyes of all living, and concealed from the birds of the air.²² Abaddon and Death say, "We have heard a rumor of it with our ears."²³ God understands the way to it, and he knows its place.²⁴ For he looks to the ends of the earth and sees everything under the heavens.
>
> (Job 28:5-6, 12-13, 20-24)

While, on the one hand, we see again the language of fire, shining blue gems, and gold underneath the earth, not unlike what we have seen earlier, here we also see a further connection to the idea of wisdom being located in a particular, hard to find place and God knowing its location because God "looks to the ends of the earth." One might be inclined to believe that the combination of these themes as preserved in the book of Job could have provided the license to a perceptive ascetic to believe, had they seen a Canigou Effect-type vision from Zaphon, that they had managed to glimpse the dwelling of the wise.⁵⁵

---

⁵⁴ Many further connections can be made between Zaphon traditions and the Hebrew Bible, likely including Ps 48:2; Ps 68; Ps 89; Jer 10:10-13; Ezek 1.
⁵⁵ Ps 107 could have provided some suggestive background for the establishment of the Rechabites in their abode.

The New Testament is not devoid of similar themes. Though it is unlikely that the book of Revelation is the direct result of a vision on biblical Mt. Zaphon,[56] there are many themes that appear in Revelation that are likely received and reinterpreted Zaphon traditions.[57] Chapter 21 is particularly rich in these themes including the victory over the sea, victory over death, a heavenly vision, God as the source of life-giving water, a burning water-surface associated with the abyss or sea, vision from a mountain top, shiningly bright divine residence, and a jeweled foundation of the divine residence.[58] Interestingly, Rev 21 also emphasizes the idea of constant light in the heavenly city (21:23-25), which is very similar to the scenario described in the *History of the Rechabites* and which might be assumed from viewing a Canigou-Effect phenomenon.

The themes preserved in these Jewish and Christian texts, which appear to have some Zaphon-linked background, include descriptions of visually perceived phenomena with marked similarities to those present in a Canigou Effect. The evidence is circumstantial but may suggest support for Zaphon-based viewing of a Canigou-Effect type of phenomenon.

Environmental Phenomena as Literary Catalysts

Though it may seem strange, it is not at all unprecedented for environmental catalysts to act as literary inspiration for the location of mythic spaces. In 1 Enoch, for example, it is likely that the presence of Mt. Hermon suggested to the author the location of the descent of the angels. In 1 Enoch 6 it is written:

---

[56] Though the vision of Rev 21:10 does occur on a mountain top, and I have heard oral reports of similar sunset phenomena in the Southern Sporades.

[57] These would most likely have been received through their use in the Hebrew Bible. See also Smith, *Where the Gods Are*, 37.

[58] Rev 21:1-4, 6-8, 10-11, 18-20, 23-25: "Then I saw a new heaven and a new earth; for the first heaven and the first earth had passed away, and the sea was no more. ² And I saw the holy city, the new Jerusalem, coming down out of heaven from God, prepared as a bride adorned for her husband. ³ And I heard a loud voice from the throne saying, 'See, the home of God is among mortals. He will dwell with them; they will be his peoples, and God himself will be with them; ⁴ he will wipe every tear from their eyes. Death will be no more; mourning and crying and pain will be no more, for the first things have passed away. ... To the thirsty I will give water as a gift from the spring of the water of life. ⁷ Those who conquer will inherit these things, and I will be their God and they will be my children. ⁸ But as for the cowardly, the faithless, the polluted, the murderers, the fornicators, the sorcerers, the idolaters, and all liars, their place will be in the lake that burns with fire and sulfur, which is the second death.' ¹⁰ And in the spirit he carried me away to a great, high mountain and showed me the holy city Jerusalem coming down out of heaven from God. ¹¹ It has the glory of God and a radiance like a very rare jewel, like jasper, clear as crystal. ¹⁸ The wall is built of jasper, while the city is pure gold, clear as glass. ¹⁹ The foundations of the wall of the city are adorned with every jewel; the first was jasper, the second sapphire, the third agate, the fourth emerald, ²⁰ the fifth onyx, the sixth carnelian, the seventh chrysolite, the eighth beryl, the ninth topaz, the tenth chrysoprase, the eleventh jacinth, the twelfth amethyst. ²³ And the city has no need of sun or moon to shine on it, for the glory of God is its light, and its lamp is the Lamb. ²⁴ The nations will walk by its light, and the kings of the earth will bring their glory into it. ²⁵ Its gates will never be shut by day—and there will be no night there."

> The angels … said to one another, "Come, let us choose wives for ourselves from among the daughters of man and beget us children." … And they descended into 'Ardos, which is the summit of Hermon. And they called the mount Armon, for they swore and bound one another by a curse.
>
> (1 En. 6:2-6, *OTP* 1.15)

And elsewhere in 1 Enoch it appears that Hermon suggests the location of the Garden of Eden, paradise, or the throne of God:[59]

> He [Michael] answered, saying, "This tall mountain which you saw whose summit resembles the throne of God is (indeed) his throne, on which the Holy and Great Lord of Glory, the Eternal King, will sit when he descends to visit the earth with goodness. And as for this fragrant tree, not a single human being has the authority to touch it until the great judgment, when he shall take vengeance on all and conclude (everything) forever. This is for the righteous and the pious. And the elect will be presented with its fruit for life. He will plant it in the direction of the northeast, upon the holy place—in the direction of the house of the Lord, the Eternal King."
>
> (1 En. 25:3-5, *OTP* 1.26)

In a similar vein, the tradition of Aphrodite being birthed from the sea off the coast of Cyprus is likely derived from observation of a natural phenomenon near Paphos. The action of crashing waves in a southwest wind forms a feature that "looks exactly like a human figure literally 'rising from the sea' and spreading long hair and dripping arms."[60] Robin Lane Fox's magisterial, if at times speculative, *Travelling Heroes in the Epic Age of Homer* is brimming with further examples of such environmental phenomena. These examples are of exceptional patterns of effect, but as shown in previous chapters, there are a variety of well-documented quotidian environmental phenomena that have at least as significant a contributory generative effect on the production of literary works.

It seems clear then that a Canigou Effect-type vision could have provided a similar kind of environmental catalyst necessary to spark the Jewish and Christian literary appropriation of the legend of the Blessed Isle. But are there any other indications that the Antioch region would have been a likely locus of provenance?

Provenance: Palestine/Syria

While there has been hearty disagreement over whether the earliest parts of the text of the *History of the Rechabites* had a Jewish or Christian origin, most experts have agreed over a Palestinian or near-Palestinian provenance. Similarly, most experts have noted that the ascetic characteristics of the lives of the Rechabites, exaggerated in the

---

[59] 1 En. 25:5; 32:1; 77:4 (*OTP*)/77:3 (in Nickelsburg and VanderKam, *1 Enoch 2*).
[60] J. L. Myres, "Aphrodite Anadyomene," *ABSA* 41 (1945): 99.

descriptions of Zosimus' life at the beginning and end of the text, suggest favorable reception in monastic or ascetic circles if not actual composition therein.[61] While not in Palestine, the Kasios/Antioch region is nearby.[62] Interestingly, the presence of two miraculously tall, heaven-scraping trees, which serve as Zosimus' mode of transport across the ocean, may point to a provenance somewhere north of Palestine in the Lebanon range. Palestine was not known for its large trees, but the enormous "cedars of Lebanon" were renowned and could have inspired an author who had them to hand.[63] Additionally, Antioch was home to the kind of robust Jewish and Christian literary communities in late antiquity that might have generated a popular text like the *History of the Rechabites*.[64]

And while it has been established that there was significant enough cultic activity on Mt. Zaphon in antiquity to allow for possible viewing of the visual phenomenon in question, it is also necessary to consider whether in later years, when known as Mt. Kasios in the Hellenistic and Late Antique eras, the mountain would have had enough activity on it to allow the reasonable possibility for viewing the phenomenon in question.

During the Hellenistic era, Mt. Kasios was a prominent locus in particular of the Olympian cult and was considered (one of) the home(s) of Zeus. The Emperor Julian is even reported, according to Libanius,[65] to have had an epiphanic vision of Zeus on Mt. Kasios in 363 CE. Robin Lane Fox suggests that coinage[66] from Selucia at the time shows the pillared temple on the summit surrounding a conical rock, said to represent perhaps not the mountain per se but Zeus Kasios himself.[67] However, it is certainly

---

[61] James R. Davila, in his paper for the SBL Pseudepigrapha Group at the November 24, 2003, meeting in Atlanta ("Is the Story of Zosimus Really a Jewish Composition"), asserts a monastic/ascetic provenance and notes that both Brian McNeil and Christopher Knights agree concerning the favorable reception such a work would have received in monastic/ascetic communities. See https://www.st-andrews.ac.uk/divinity/rt/otp/abstracts/zosimus/.

[62] The reasons scholars argue for a Palestinian provenance do not rule out Antiochene provenance: there is a setting in a monastic or ascetic community, there is interest in Jerusalem (particularly in manuscript BnF syr. 234 in which Zosimus is described as a monk living in a monastery in Jerusalem, but, as Davila points out, interest in Jerusalem does not necessitate Palestinian provenance), further mention at the end of BnF syr. 234 that Zosimus was ultimately settled in a different non-Jerusalemite *Palestinian* monastery, and the translation history in *OTP*'s manuscript D (British Museum Add. 12174) that suggests that "it was translated from [an original Hebrew] by the Hands of the Reverend Mar Jacob of Edessa" (*OTP* 1:444, 461). These seem to indicate more the provenance of particular manuscript traditions rather than provenance of the first unified Ur-text. While a Palestinian provenance is of course possible, the composite nature of the text, including likely elements that originated in two different languages (chapters 8–12 and 14–16:7 Greek; 1-7, 13, 16:8-18 Syriac; see Davila, "Is the Story of Zosimus Really a Jewish Composition" for helpful demarcation), increases the probability that the text came together as a whole in a more northerly locale like Antioch.

[63] James H. Charlesworth shared this idea with me, *viva voce*, at the 2018 Larnaca conference on Cyprus and the Bible.

[64] See, for example, Charlesworth, *Jesus as Mirrored in John*, 364, 388, 427, n. 13, and for discussion of the library at Antioch dating to 221 BCE, see pp. 525–6.

[65] Libanius, *Or.* 18.172.

[66] K. Butcher, *Coinage in Roman Syria: Northern Syria 64BC-AD253*, Royal Numismatic Society 34 (Ann Arbor: University of Michigan Press, 2004), 413–25.

[67] Fox, *Travelling Heroes*, 282.

possible that the conical rock represents the vision of the distant peak of Cypriot Olympus to the west as only rarely viewable from the summit of Mt. Kasios.

Christian hermits were also very active on the mountain in late antiquity, with a monastery[68] founded near the tree line. They intended to supplant the "pagan" cult and the caves all over the high slopes were occupied by ascetics. Several Christian literary giants, including Diodorus, Chrysostom, and Theodore of Mopsuestia (the latter two of whom also studied under Libanius in Antioch), likely spent time here, as well as Simeon Stylites the Younger.[69]

The data[70] from the text of *History of the Rechabites* really is incontrovertible in its support of an ascetic provenance. Zosimus is described as having lived as a hermit (1:1) in a cave (2:1) in the wilderness (1:1) his whole life, this site being the location of the initial revelatory visit from the angel (1:3). The descriptions of the Rechabites suggest characteristics appealing to an ascetic sensibility including separation (7:3; 9:9; 10:7a), abstinence (7:2b; 8:3, 5; 9:2, 8; 10:7a; 11:7; 13:2), and constant prayer (7:2a; 10:7a; 11:2b; 16:8b). In many ways their life together seems to mimic that of a monastic community. Then, after his journey, Zosimus returns to his cave (18:4). Further information related to the cave appears in the longer Greek text (19:4-8; 21:2, 8), as does narrative about monastic reception (22:1, 4; 23:1). Syriac Manuscript 234 also suggests that Zosimus went to live in a Palestinian monastery upon his return. These data taken together point to a setting of ascetic provenance.

Mt. Kasios was a highly populated mountain at a time when Christian contestation with the traditional practice of Greco-Roman religion was very active. Against this historical background we should recognize that its highly trafficked summit region afforded ample opportunity for the religious in its vicinity to catch a fleeting glimpse of Cyprus (or the Isle of the Blessed Ones), possibly catalyzing its Christian appropriation of the earlier Blessed Isle legend in the *History of the Rechabites*.

Marginal Dwelling as Contributory Generative Background

In previous chapters we have discussed the productive role of experiences of domestic space in generating the texts under consideration. It should be noted clearly that in none of these instances do we posit that phenomenological background as the exclusive generative influence on the text but rather as an important one among many. Certainly, previous religious and textual traditions are highly formative for the Gospel of John, the undisputed Pauline Letters, the *Parables of Enoch*, and Revelation in addition to their spatial influences. In this chapter a proposal has been set forward for a particular, literal vision as a generative influence on the *History of the Rechabites* as a literary product. However, many of the same dynamics previously mentioned remain relevant.

---

[68] St. Barlaam's Monastery.
[69] See the illuminating discussion in Peter Brown, "The Rise and Function of the Holy Man in Late Antiquity," *The Journal of Roman Studies* 61 (1971): 83.
[70] These references pertain to the reconstructed Syriac text as found in *OTP*.

The ascetic, cave-dwelling life of Zosimus, as described in the text, seems to reflect a real background of lived experience. This kind of experience of marginal dwelling has been shown in previous analyses to be adequately fecund, in combination with an active religious life and textual inheritance, to produce the ideal visions of dwelling that appear in the Gospel of John, the undisputed Pauline Letters, the *Parables of Enoch*, and Revelation. The question put forward in this chapter is different: If this kind of marginal experience of dwelling was combined with a rare and wonderful vision, what would happen? The data seem to suggest that the author's chosen marginal experience of dwelling, combined with a rich inheritance of traditions, both biblical and Greco-Roman, sets the stage for a rather novel interpretation of a rare natural phenomenon. This creative interpretation not only made sense of the author's experience but provided an outlet for the author's hopes and dreams. And though the literary synthesis forged by the author is novel, these hopes and dreams share many characteristic similarities with those previously noted in other texts. The ideal locus of dwelling is a place of serenity and ease, there is enduring fellowship among the righteous, and still there is the presence of reactive, world-negating language. The "corner" of marginal dwelling[71] has again produced two worlds, the ideal one of blessing for the righteous and the compromised, condemned world of the judged. Even as a rare natural phenomenon may have sparked the act of production itself, the lived experience of the author[72] seems to have governed the shape and character of the spaces produced.

Conclusion

According to the argument set forth in this chapter, it is likely that a visual phenomenon similar to a "Canigou Effect" is visible from the summit of Jebel Aqra under rare but predictable astronomical and atmospheric conditions.[73] This

---

[71] Gaston Bachelard, *The Poetics of Space*, trans. Maria Jolas (Boston: Beacon Press, 1994), 46, 136, 137, 142,

[72] Which appears to have shared some similarities to that of the authors of other texts we have considered.

[73] It is hypothesized that the effect is visible in many locations, not only those described herein. Due to this likelihood, of the visibility of "Canigou Effect" type phenomena in locations beyond the environs of the Canigou Massif, I propose the generic appellation "Atlantis Effect" for the visual phenomenon, due to its similarity to the description of Atlantis as it appears in Plato's *Critias*. These elements include location in the west, across a large body of water, a brilliantly shining base, and being now, or typically, invisible (in *Critias* this is due to the destructive flood that obliterated the island). This phenomenon would involve several elements: (1) the Atlantis Effect involves the appearance of an island that is not normally visible from the viewing location. The natural curvature of the earth would prevent normal viewing without atmospheric refraction. Typically, the two locations involved would sit just below an ocean-surface-grazing tangential line. This change in visibility would require a Novaya Zemlya refraction effect, a subspecies of a superior mirage, which allows distant objects below the horizon to become visible due to atmospheric inversion. (2) The Atlantis Effect is visible in the setting sun. For most locations this requires twice-yearly predictable but narrow calendrical viewing windows in which there is an alignment of viewing location, target location, and sunset. (3) The Atlantis Effect at its most vivid appears to reveal an island with a brilliantly shining base. This requires refraction of some sunlight to occur differently from the light coming from the rest of the target "island." This effect is likely the result of "stacking" of superior mirages due to differential refraction. Atmospheric inversion would be necessary, but the "shining base" aspect is likely the result of more heavily refracted light moving through the coldest section of air along the ocean reflecting off of the ocean itself.

phenomenon may have led to the development of traditions linked to the site that preserve evidence of the phenomenon, such as in the Baal cycle and the Hebrew Bible. The most compelling language that seems to preserve evidence of the aforementioned visual phenomenon appears in the late antique pseudepigraphic text known as the *History of the Rechabites*. It seems likely, based on the account of the location of the Isle of the Blessed Ones preserved in *History of the Rechabites*, that a Canigou Effect-type vision from the summit of Jebel Aqra may have provided the phenomenological catalyst, which sparked the appropriation of the Blessed Isle legend by a Jewish or, more likely, Christian author, a legend that had otherwise been largely neglected in those traditions.

The primary objection to the proposal set forth in this chapter is the consideration that the description of the location of the Isle in the *History of the Rechabites* may be based solely on literary precedents[74] or tropes and not on an actual environmental-phenomenological spark. Unfortunately, no data, not even modern confirmation of the phenomenon from Jebel Aqra, could definitively prove that the proposed vision led to the appropriation of the legend of the Blessed Isle in the *History of the Rechabites*. Even that confirmation should not be expected any time soon since the summit of Jebel Aqra has been off-limits to civilians for decades due to its designation as a military zone. The recent Syrian conflict has not ameliorated the situation.[75]

One final consideration, however, must be made, and it pertains to the importance of lines of sight in the evaluation of holy space and of the location of temples, in particular. Eleanor Grey, in "Beyond the Temple: Blurring the Boundaries of 'Sacred Space,'" has set forth excellent reasons to consider sacred space in the Greek and Roman cosmology as not simply involving the demarcated precincts of a temple, or holy site, but the spaces that are seen from that site.[76] Fascinatingly, Fox independently confirms this priority in his discussion of the siting considerations made in the construction of the Barlaam Monastery on Jebel Aqra. He writes:

> As [Symeon Stylites the Younger's] blessing and prophecies proved their worth, they attracted important patrons, including the Byzantine emperor Maurice who built the large stone church which still stands around the pillar. The siting is extremely significant: the view through its side chapels aligns exactly with the peak of Jebel Aqra, the demonic backdrop to Symeon's life on high .... [He] stood on high as an alternative Christian focus, contradicting an ancient pagan "high place" in the mountain landscape behind him.[77]

---

[74] Though no source available to us appears to contain all the relevant elements before their usage in the *History of the Rechabites*. It appears to present, for its time, a unique synthesis.

[75] Not only is the site home to a Turkish military installation, but as of 2018 the Rabia (Russian) and Al Zaitwnia (Turkish) military installations were also within 20 kilometers of the summit.

[76] E. Grey, "Beyond the Temple: Blurring the Boundaries of 'Sacred Space,'" in *Proceedings of the Fourteenth Annual Theoretical Roman Archaeology Conference, Durham 2004*, eds. J. Bruhn, B. Croxford, and D. Grigoropoulos (Oxford: Oxbow Books, 2005), 109–18.

[77] Fox, *Travelling Heroes*, 250.

Certainly the vista-related implications of siting were not lost on those who built the cultic sites on the summit either.[78] This crucial dimension to the holiness of cultic sites, that their holiness is not based simply on the site itself but on what can be seen from the site, further militates in favor of the suggested hypothesis of this chapter: that the rare visions of Cyprus possible from the summit of Jebel Aqra not only led to preservation of evidence of this phenomenon in the Baal cycle, Hebrew Bible, and other traditions but, in particular, likely sparked the appropriation of the Blessed Isle legend by the author or redactor of the *History of the Rechabites*. This conclusion provides additional data for discussions of provenance and supports linking a significant stage in the text's production to the Antioch region or western Syria. It is no stretch to say that a hermit, confronted with a rare vision of the kind posited, and subject to the psychologies of marginal dwelling described by Bachelard, even if by his own choosing, may have imagined that his dreams of the ideal dwelling had become fleetingly manifest to him.

---

[78] In fact, there are many indications in the Baal cycle that the views from Zaphon were of particular relevance and importance, as, for example, previously mentioned with respect to the window controversy. This is in spite of protestations against the importance of geographic referents from some scholars such as Simon Parker, *The Pre-Biblical Narrative Tradition*, SBL Resources for Biblical Study 24 (Atlanta: Scholars Press, 1989), 55. For a perspective supportive of the importance of geography and to this issue, see B. Margalit, "The Geographical Setting of the AQHT Story and Its Ramifications," in *Ugarit in Retrospect: Fifty Years of Ugarit and Ugaritic*, ed. D. G. Young (Winona Lake, IN: Eisenbrauns, 1981), 131–58.

7

Augustine's Christological Emphasis in *De Trinitate*: An Affirmation of the Human Ecology

As we come to the penultimate chapter of this book we come to a text that is later than the others, less Jewish than the others, a text neither biblical nor para-biblical, and whose context is better documented and better understood in modern scholarship. *De Trinitate* is Augustine of Hippo's final major work, considered by many to be his magnum opus and his most mature theological production. Augustine looms large over the Christian traditions of interpretation and reception, and ending with Augustine is, admittedly, a broadening of scope. It is an opportunity to test a concern for textual ecology and spatial practice on a larger scale, to see if Augustine's thought can be seen to follow or affirm any of the patterns we have begun to discern.

Trin. itself is an ambitious text in which Augustine leads the reader through a highly structured approach to deeper understanding of God. It is also a commonly misunderstood text, believed by many interpreters to be a failure in its attempt to discern the accurate image of the triune God and a tacit admission that *sapientia* (wisdom) is essentially inaccessible to humans. There is a long history of mistakenly interpreting Augustine to be promulgating a dualistic worldview along Neo-Platonic lines, in which the material world and the body are bad, and the spiritual—the life of the mind—is good.[1] Augustine's own thoughts in *Trin.* are not unmistakably clear on this point, and so confusion is understandable. He goes to great lengths to deny any kind of materiality in God. For example:

> The authority of the apostle as well as plain reason assures us that man was not made to the image of God as regards the shape of the body, but as regards his rational mind. It is an idle and base kind of thinking which supposes that God is confined within the limits of a body with features and limbs.[2]
>
> (*Trin.* 12.12)

---

[1] For example, Oliver du Roy, *L'Intelligence de la Foi en la Trinité selon saint Augustin, genèse de sa théologie trinitaire jusqu'en 391* (Paris: Études augustiniennes, 1966), 456.

[2] All English translations from Edmund Hill, trans., *The Trinity* (Brooklyn: New City Press, 1991). Here, 331. "Non solum ueracissima ratio sed etiam ipsius apostoli declarat auctoritas, non secundum formam corporis homo factus est ad imaginem dei sed secundum rationalem mentem. cogitatio quippe turpiter uana est quae opinatur deum membrorum corporalium lineamentis circumscribi atque definiri" (CCSL 50: 366.70-75).

This statement, taken out of context, seems almost to go so far as to deny the incarnation!

Indeed, when Augustine discusses the higher and greater reality of divine *sapientia*, contrasted with the "lower" and "lesser" reality of material *scientia* (knowledge), he cannot help but describe them at times with valued language: "Behold piety is wisdom, while to abstain from evil things is knowledge ([Job] 28:28)" (*Trin.* 12.22).[3] Here he affirms a positive, or engagement-oriented, value to *sapientia* while suggesting a negative, or abstinence-oriented, value to *scientia*. This spiritual/*sapientia* versus material/*scientia* divide is reiterated frequently in *Trin*. At times he even seems to go so far as to suggest that *sapientia* has no embodiment in and no commerce with the material realm (*Trin.* 12.23).[4] However, when the entire scope of *Trin*. is considered, it appears not only that Augustine affirms the value of materiality and *scientia*, but that its affirmation plays a key part in the success of the purpose of *Trin*. While the image of God in the human mind does not finally succeed in revealing the triune God completely, this failure serves only to point back to the mode of access that Augustine believes humans *do* have to God, namely the material experience and received historical understanding (*scientia*) of the incarnation of Christ and the mission of the Holy Spirit in both the individual and the holy scriptures. In other words, it is an affirmation of a meaningful material ecology.

Even from the period immediately following his conversion, Augustine took the value of the created order seriously.[5] This emphasis, clearly on display in the *Confessions*, is at issue in *Trin*. Has Augustine indeed continued this theme of emphasis or jettisoned it in favor of a more dualistic interpretation of reality? Is the goal of the Christian life for Augustine to escape materiality in the bliss of eternal contemplation? Goulven Madec insists[6] that Augustine has not attempted to defend a Platonic dualism in *Trin.*, in spite of protestations to the contrary. Rather, he asserts that (most specifically in Books 13 and 14) Augustine is setting out the principle of coherence to his theology: that in Christ there is a union of the apparent dualistic elements of Platonism—the material and the spiritual, *scientia* and *sapientia*.[7] As Rowan Williams writes, "[Augustine's] rhetoric remains Platonic and dualistic even when the substance of his thought is moving in a quite other direction."[8] The incarnation is crucial to *sapientia*

---

[3] Hill, *The Trinity*, 337. "Ecce pietas est sapientia; abstinere autem a malis scientia est" (CCSL 50: 375.19-20).

[4] Hill, *The Trinity*, 338: "The word of wisdom ... is concerned with things that neither were nor will be but just are, and which because of the eternity in which they are, are talked about as having been and being and going to be without any change of real tense ... They do not abide fixed locally in space like bodies, but in non-bodily nature; thus as intelligible they are available to the inspection of the mind just as bodies are visible or touchable to the body's senses ... [But] few have the acuteness of mind to reach these ideas, and when someone does manage as far as possible to attain them he does not abide in them, because his very acuteness of mind gets blunted so to say and beaten back, and there is only a transitory thought about a non-transitory thing."

[5] Marie-Anne Vannier, "Saint Augustin et la création," *Augustiniana* 40 (1990): 349.

[6] Goulven Madec, "Christus, scientia et sapientia nostra: le principe de cohérence de la doctrine augustinienne," *Recherches Augustiniennes* 10 (1975): 78 n. 2.

[7] Madec, "Christus, scientia et sapientia nostra," 81 n. 2.

[8] Rowan Williams, "Sapientia and the Trinity: Reflections on the *De Trinitate*," *Augustiniana* 40 (1990): 318.

and knowledge of God. It is the essential principle through which, Madec asserts, all Augustine's works should be interpreted. As an affirmation of the necessity of faith in the *scientia* of the incarnation specifically (and materiality generally) in order to attain any accurate knowledge of God, *Trin.* succeeds. It is not based on a single quotation from Book 13 that we can make this assertion but from the overall structure of the work, its repeated emphases, and its subsequent reception.

The purpose, then, of concluding with Augustine is to show that even for this massively important figure in the Christian theological tradition, the material experience of humans, and by extension, the ecological basis for hermeneutics, is crucial to his theological program. This is not a novel observation, though it is perhaps not adequately acknowledged with respect to *Trin.* What later becomes an established medieval mode of thinking about God, the "analogical" approach, which affirms the material and experiential even while acknowledging their limitations,[9] is here thought through carefully and, finally, affirmed. Augustine's "spatial practice" is dependent on the material realities of the scriptures and the incarnation—the dwelling of God respectively in texts and in a human body. He cannot depart from a fundamentally human ecology, not only because his scholarship (σχολή) is produced by his attention to the scriptures and the incarnation but also because it is produced by his own material experience of a protected world of rest (also σχολή).[10] For Augustine, in the pursuit of understanding God, the *scientia* of material human life—its ecology—is neither irrelevant, nor corrupt, nor transcended, but rather utterly necessary. What follows is an exegesis of his thought.

Introduction to *Trin.*

If Augustine's entire purpose in writing *De Trinitate* was to discern the accurate image of the triune God, not only in the material realm but also in the highest and most Godly function of the human mind, many readers may interpret the work as a failure. However, upon considering the general emphasis and purpose of Augustine's theology, as interpreted by Goulven Madec in his 1975 lecture "*Christus, scientia et sapientia nostra: le principe de cohérence de la doctrine augustinienne*,"[11] it appears that Augustine successfully affirms the necessity of Christ for interpreting God the Trinity. In fact, it seems that Augustine's goal is to suggest that without the *scientia* of the incarnation, natural reason cannot attain to an understanding of God the Trinity, whereas natural reason coupled with that *scientia* can attain to deeper understanding. Contrary to the common misconception, Augustine does not devalue materiality. Rather, he suggests that the incarnation—God's self-revelation in Christ—endows value to both the created order and created beings, enabling them to witness to the truth of God the

---

[9] Elizabeth A. Johnson, *She Who Is: The Mystery of God in Feminist Theological Discourse* (New York: Crossroad Publishing, 2018), 117–22.
[10] As we have seen from Bachelard.
[11] Madec, "Christus, scientia et sapientia nostra," 77–85.

Trinity. Likewise, the ongoing experience of the indwelling in the believer witnesses to the nature of God the Trinity by enabling receipt and accurate interpretation of the *scientia* of the incarnation. Without the incarnation and indwelling, without the impartation of interpretive value to materiality and *scientia*, Augustine claims humans could neither know God the Trinity, nor rise to fleeting glimpses of God's *sapientia* (*Trin*. 8.3), nor be capable to criticize the clouded impressions of natural reason as Augustine does so persistently in Books 9–15.

Confusions Regarding *Trin.*

By the time readers of *Trin*. reach the fifteenth book, some may be wondering if Augustine is going to succeed in his plan "to train the reader, *in the things that have been made* (Rom 1:20), for getting to know him by whom they were made" (*Trin*. 15.1).[12] Augustine himself appears less than confident about the potential success of finding a Trinity in the human mind that illumines God's nature. "Whether this nature is a triad we ought to demonstrate, not merely to faith on the authority of divine scripture, but also to understanding, if we can, by some evidence of reason. Why I say 'if we can' will appear well enough as our investigation of the subject proceeds" (*Trin*. 15.1).[13] Later, in the Book 15 prologue, he goes on to say, "Now it would seem that what is always being sought is never being found" (*Trin*. 15.2)[14] and then enters into what appears to be a rationalization of this concern.

A skeptical reader might suspect Augustine of attempting to soften the blow of failure to his audience. He insists on having discovered trinities in the created order (*Trin*. 15.10),[15] but it seems clear by the end of the book that he views his attempts to discern a trinity in the mind that is accurately representative of the Divine Trinity as inadequate (*Trin*. 15.45).[16] The reader might justifiably consider Augustine to have failed in his purpose, if his sole purpose is finding a trinity in the created order or

---

[12] Hill, *The Trinity*, 395, emphasis original. "In rebus quae factae sunt ad cognoscendum eum a quo factae sunt exercere lectorem" (CCSL 50A: 460.1-2).

[13] Hill, *The Trinity*, 395. "Quae utrum sit trinitas non solum credentibus diuinae scripturae auctoritate, uerum etiam intellegentibus aliqua si possumus ratione iam demonstrare debemus. cur autem 'si possumus' dixerim res ipsa cum quaeri disputando coeperit melius indicabit" (CCSL 50A: 460.11-15).

[14] Hill, *The Trinity*, 395. "Uidetur enim quod semper quaeritur numquam inueniri" (CCSL 50A: 461.5-6).

[15] Hill, *The Trinity*, 402–3: "To be sure, we plainly see some evident trinities … We found a … trinity in man, namely the mind, and the knowledge it knows itself with, and the love it loves itself with."

[16] Hill, *The Trinity*, 435: "I have been acutely conscious of the enormous difficulty of the effort to perceive this, and I have no doubt that my careful and intelligent readers will be equally conscious of it. So great has this difficulty been, that every time I wanted to bring out some comparative illustration of this point in that created reality which we are, having promised in the second book of this work that I would talk about the matter later on, I found that no adequate expression followed whatever understanding I came to; and I was only too well aware that my attempt even to understand involved more effort than result. In the one person which a man is I did indeed find an image of that supreme trinity; and it was my purpose, above all in the ninth book, to point out those three in a changeable object, to enable us the more easily to comprehend them as deployed through intervals of time. And yet the three things of one person were quite unable to match those three persons in the way our human plan requires, as we have been demonstrating in this fifteenth book."

in the image of God in the human that fully and accurately illuminates God's triune nature. However, it seems that this is not his overarching goal in *Trin*. Even as he was preparing his audience for the failure of reason to discover an accurately illuminative trinity in the created order, Augustine was suggesting that such a failure did not prevent the success of the work. In the beginning of Book 15 he also states, "The God himself we are looking for will help us, I confidently hope, to get some fruit from our labors" (*Trin*. 15.2).[17] Clearly the fruit of his labors must not depend on the success of natural reason alone.

Does Augustine still not leave the reader at an impasse in pursuit of God due to this "failure" of the created order? Does Augustine's demonizing language regarding creation and materiality suggest such an impasse toward any further success in accessing knowledge of God "who is spirit?"

The Structure and Emphasis of *Trin*.

The Early Books

At the most basic level, the very outline of *Trin*. supports the thesis that Augustine affirms the necessity of the *scientia* of the incarnation and scriptures specifically (and materiality generally) in order to attain closer apprehension of God. The first seven books emphasize, nearly exclusively, the scriptures and arguments springing from them as revealing the triune God. At the outset of the work, Augustine insists that the human cannot hope for a better understanding of the triune God without faith; the understanding sought must proceed directly from faith. He writes, "The reader of these reflections of mine on the Trinity should bear in mind that my pen is on the watch against the sophistries of those who scorn the starting-point of faith, and allow themselves to be deceived through an unseasonable and misguided love of reason" (*Trin*. 1.1).[18] He goes on to describe the ways in which humans are deceived by reason and then to emphasize the necessity of God's condescension to them in the scriptures (*Trin*. 1.2). The following books, through Book 4, are all focused on the testimony of scripture: the proofs of the Trinity from scripture (the rest of Book 1), the Old Testament theophanies (Book 2), and the missions in the scriptures (Books 3 and 4).[19] Books 5–7 present a section of reasoning about the Trinity based on scripture and solving the relevant difficulties

---

[17] Hill, *The Trinity*, 395. "Deus quippe ipse quem quaerimus adiuuabit, ut spero, ne sit infructuosus labor noster" (CCSL 50A: 460.1-2).

[18] Hill, *The Trinity*, 65. "Lecturus haec quae De Trinitate disserimus prius oportet ut nouerit stilum nostrum aduersus eorum uigilare calumnias qui fidei contemnentes initium immaturo et peruerso rationis amore falluntur" (CCSL 50: 27.1-4).

[19] An excellent observation of relevant themes in Book 4 comes from Lewis Ayers, "The Christological Context of Augustine's De Trinitate XIII: Toward Relocating Books VIII–XV," *Augustinian Studies* 29.1 (1998): 125, "Because we cannot any longer perceive God through those things which were made 'in the Word', the heavens and the earth (the structure of our incapacity), the Incarnate Christ provides 'smaller' signs and testimonies which will enable us to move to the 'bigger' signs and testimonies (the structure of the Incarnation)."

from scripture. This heavy emphasis on the scriptural foundations (*scientia*)[20] of the pursuit of understanding the triune God provides the basis for the rest of the work.

The Centrality of Book 8

Book 8 is the central focus of the chiastic structure to *Trin*. Augustine begins 8.4 by emphasizing the accessibility of knowledge of good things in the material sphere. He breaks into a beautiful paean to what it is one loves when one loves created things (*Trin*. 8.4). Thus he makes clear his confidence in access to God through love of the good in the created order, especially by loving the Good in all good which is God. Even as he points to the spiritual reality beyond the physical, he strongly affirms the value of the material.

The next significant theme of Book 8 is concern over whether one can be confident that one is actually loving God when one thinks one is loving God. Even as Augustine affirms some level of access to and understanding of God through knowing and loving good, he recognizes the limitation of this love (*Trin*. 8.6).[21] This nagging concern about how one can love and what one can know, though it will continue for the rest of *Trin*., points to a key assertion in the very center of this central book:

> When we believe some material or physical facts we read or hear about but have not seen, we cannot help our imaginations fabricating something with the shape and outline of bodies as it may occur to our thoughts, and this will either not be true, or if it is true, which can only happen extremely rarely, this is not what it profits us to hold on faith ... Nor as regards the faith we have in the Lord Jesus Christ is it in the least relevant to salvation what our imaginations picture him like, which is probably quite different from the reality. What does matter is that we think of him specifically as a man; for we have embedded in us as it were a standard notion of the nature of man, by which whenever we see some such thing we immediately recognize it as a man, or at least as the shape of a man.
>
> It is in terms of this sort of notion that our thoughts are framed when we believe that God became man for us as an example of humility and to demonstrate God's love for us. This indeed it is useful for us to believe and to hold firm and unshaken in our hearts, that the humility thanks to which God was born of a woman, and led through such abuse at the hands of mortal men to his death, is a medicine to heal the tumor of our pride and a high sacrament to break the chains of sin. So too with his miraculous powers and his resurrection; we know what omnipotence is and so we believe these things of the omnipotent God, and we think about them in terms of the species and genera of things which are either connatural to us or

---

[20] Which are part of the *material* world.
[21] Hill, *The Trinity*, 247: "But we also have to stand by and cling to this good in love, in order to enjoy the presence of him from whom we are, whose absence would mean that we could not even be. For since *we are still walking by faith and not by sight* (2 Cor. 5:7) we do not yet see God, as the same apostle says, *face to face* (1 Cor. 13:12). Yet unless we love him even now, we shall never see him. But who can love what he does not know?"

gathered from our experience of this sort of facts, and in this way our faith is not fabricated .... So then, since we desire to understand as far as it is given us the eternity and equality and unity of the trinity, and since we must believe before we can understand, we must take care our faith is not fabricated.[22]

(*Trin.* 8.7-8)

At the very core of this text is the incarnation. It is by the general *scientia* of the physical created world, the dwelling place of humanity, that one can begin to understand the *scientia* of received revelation concerning the incarnation. Furthermore, it is through this appreciation for God which comes through the incarnation, according to Augustine, that one can love God and seek deeper understanding of God. All of *Trin.* up until this point is pointing in this direction, and all the rest of it afterwards will point back. This central core of the central book affirms the value and necessity of the material, the space and data of creation, in light of Augustine's view of the fundamentality of the incarnation and of the *scientia* humans may receive of the incarnation through transmission by the Holy Spirit.

Augustine's final concern in this passage—that faith be not fabricated—is an important one and might be a useful way to interpret much of Books 9–15. But his most pressing interest is how one loves God in light of the knowledge gained of God through the incarnation. Those who would seek him must seek him inwardly and with humility:

For *love is not inflated* (1 Cor. 13:4), and *God is love* (1 [John] 4:8), and *those who are faithful in love will repose with him* ([Wisd. of Sol.] 3:9), called away from the din outside to the joys of silence. There you are, *God is love*. Why should we go running round the heights of the heavens and the depths of the earth looking for him who is with us if only we should wish to be with him?[23]

(*Trin.* 8.11)

Here it seems Augustine is introducing the inward emphasis of the latter books of *Trin.*, laying the ground for the contemplation necessary properly to discern the nature of the triune God. The emphasis is not inexorably inward but constantly pulled back to the physical, relational world:

Let no one say "I don't know what to love." Let him love his brother, and love that love; after all, he knows the love he loves with better than the brother he loves. There now, he can already have God better known to him than his brother, certainly better known because more present, better known because more inward

---

[22] Hill, *The Trinity*, 247–9.
[23] Hill, *The Trinity*, 254–5, emphasis original. "Dilectio enim non inflatur, et deus dilectio est, et fideles in dilectione adquiescunt illi reuocati ab strepitu qui foris est ad gaudia silentia. ecce, deus dilectio est. utquid imus et currimus in sublimia caelorum et ima terrarum quaerentes eum qui est apud nos si nos esse uelimus apud eum?" (CCSL 50: 286.57-62).

to him, better known because more sure. Embrace love which is God, and embrace God with love ... And if a man is full of love, what is he full of but God?[24]

(*Trin.* 8.12)

This mode of knowing God and pursuing God is not one that eschews the creation but one which is bound up in the relationships, difficulty, and necessary humility of dwelling in a messy world. Of course, Augustine's most compelling example in this context comes in the *scientia* of the incarnation, which he suggests points to the eternal spiritual reality of God as love:

So it is from what we see that we love the man we believe to have lived like that; and unless above all we loved this form which we perceive always enduring, never changing, we would not love him merely because we hold on faith that his life when he lived in the flesh was harmoniously adjusted to this form.[25]

(*Trin.* 8.13)

It seems clear that the content of Book 8, the crucial book for the whole work, supports the affirmation of the material and the plausible success of the general endeavor. Why then does Edmund Hill, the translator and commentator for what was long the best regarded modern scholarly English version of the text, read the text so differently? Hill picks up on most of the key factors we have mentioned, but in spite of his excellent work seems not to see the forest for the trees. He notes the Platonic language of forms, recognizing that it does not suggest a dualistic interpretation, but rather what later becomes a normative Christian one;[26] he recognizes that for Augustine faith based on the *scientia* of the incarnation is the solution to the problem of knowing and loving an unknown God;[27] he even recognizes that Augustine suggests that we have direct access to God via our love of "the Good;"[28] but he cannot seem to accept these realities as truly valuable. He views the Platonic language as inaccessible; he refers to faith based on the incarnation as an "ad hoc" solution (as if the only solution available to humans must be not very great since he thinks it won't be permanent); and he simply dismisses direct access to God now as incorrect, even as Augustine makes no clear disavowal.[29] It seems then that Hill has taken up the contemplative work of the

---

[24] Hill, *The Trinity*, 255. "Nemo dicat: 'non noui quod diligam.' diligat fratrem et diligat eandem dilectionem; magis enim nouit dilectionem qua diligit quam fratrem quem diligit. ecce iam potest notiorem deum habere quam fratrem, plane notiorem quia praesentiorem, notiorem quia interiorem, notiorem quia certiorem. amplectere dilectionem deum et dilectione amplectere deum ... et quo nisi deo plenus est qui plenus est dilectione" (CCSL 286.1-7, 287.11).

[25] Hill, *The Trinity*, 257. "Illum ergo quem sic uixisse credimus ex hoc quod uidemus diligimus, et nisi hanc formam quam semper stabilem atque incommutabilem cernimus praecipue diligeremus, non ideo diligeremus illum quia eius uitam cum in carne uiueret huic formae coaptatam et congruentem fuisse fide retinemus" (CCSL 50: 290.22-27).

[26] Hill, *The Trinity*, 240 n. 1.

[27] Hill, *The Trinity*, 237-8 n. 1.

[28] Hill, *The Trinity*, 238 n. 1.

[29] Hill, *The Trinity*, 238 n. 1: "That knowledge of these values does not give us direct knowledge of God is clear, in spite of the way in which in the first two chapters Augustine eagerly identifies truth and the good with God."

latter half of *Trin.*, of discovering by natural reason a trinity in the created order that is accurately revelatory of the triune God, not as secondary to or supportive of the real purpose of the work but as the entire purpose of the work.

The emphases of Book 8 can only be viewed as inadequate and limited if we view the main themes of Books 9–15 as what *Trin.* is really about. Hill's apparent periodic confusion regarding Augustine's approach in the latter books, suggested by some of his chapter introductions, confirms this misinterpretation. However, we will see that Augustine did not view the work of the latter books of *Trin.* as the exclusive goal but as serving the overarching goal of the work, which is to affirm the value of the material creation, the *scientia* we derive from it, and the incarnation and the indwelling of the Holy Spirit (through faith). These are not simply the starting place for theology and knowledge of God for Augustine but are necessary and constant reference points for informing better knowledge of the triune God. He suggests that it is only through knowledge based in the dwelling of God—where and as humans dwell—that immediate access is possible both to the ability to love and to God's divine *sapientia*. Without these humans cannot succeed in the quest to know God.

The Later Books

On the surface, it seems that the content of Books 9–15 of *Trin.* is composed largely of successive attempts to discern an accurately illuminative Trinitarian image in some aspect of the created order—most significantly the human mind—which are each in turn rejected as inadequate. It is this repetition of failed attempts, culminating in Book 15, which leads many readers to believe that Augustine has failed in his general argument in *Trin.* A simple question is pertinent here. Why would Augustine, one of the most brilliant men in history, take up the task of writing an entire book over the course of years and then publish it if he truly believed that it had failed in its purpose? It seems more likely that he viewed the book as a success even as the latter chapters seem a failure (when taken out of context). They are only truly a failure if their failure does not serve the success of the whole work. In fact the "failure" of the latter books does support this overall success, as we will see in our examination of Books 9–15.

Amid all the concern about the problems stemming from the material order (the distractions it causes, its erstwhile inability accurately to illumine the triune God, etc.), Augustine simultaneously makes repeated affirmations of its benevolence in seeking what is spiritual and of eternal value. He does this in 11.2.10 and again in 12.3.20. In this latter instance he is affirming even the sensuous, more animal, elements of the soul as part of paradise. Later he questions whether one could ever conceive of the spiritual without the physical: "The non-bodily and unchanging idea of a square body, for example, may abide forever the same; but a man's thought does not abide in it in the same way, if that is to say he could ever attain to it without a spatial image" (*Trin.* 12.23).[30]

---

[30] Hill, *The Trinity*, 339–40. "Neque enim sicut manet uerbi gratia quadrati corporis incorporalis et immutabilis ratio sic in ea manet hominis cogitatio, si tamen ad eam sine phantasia spatii localis potuit peruenire" (CCSL 50: 377.68-71). It doesn't get much clearer than this.

By the time we reach Book 13 Augustine is in full swing: parsing the mental faculties of humans, rejecting inadequate trinities of the mind, and seeking some trinity of mental function that reveals the triune God accurately. He continues this endeavor at the beginning of Book 13 by parsing the Johannine prologue. This focus on John 1, as a model for parsing the eternal and temporal, the physical and spiritual, has at its back one key fact: that through the incarnation of Christ, the dwelling of God in a human body amid the material world of humanity, these natures are unified, comingled, and co-magnified in their effect and glory. The *sapientia* of God, present in the Word eternally, is only made accessible to mankind through the *scientia* of the human Christ. In this way, Augustine's emphasis affirms material experience and shows its necessity for appreciating the spiritual.[31]

Augustine continues to meditate on the work of Christ in Book 13 and by the end of the book reaches a doctrinal summit. Whereas previously he had attempted to separate the realms of *scientia* and *sapientia*, here Augustine asserts their union in Christ (*Trin.* 13.24).[32] Here also we find the core text of Madec's thesis, his suggested "key" to Augustine's theology, in which Madec claims that "Augustin a considéré la doctrine qu'il a élaborée comme intégralement chrétienne, entièrement christologique."[33]

> Our knowledge therefore is Christ, and our wisdom is the same Christ. It is He who plants faith in us about temporal things; he who presents us with the truth about things. Through him we go straight toward him; Through knowledge toward wisdom, without ever turning aside from one and the same Christ, in whom are hidden all the treasures of wisdom and knowledge (Col. 2:3).[34]
>
> (*Trin.* 13.24)

Madec goes on to say: "Telle est la structure de la théologie augustinienne: au rapport ontologique: *éternité-temps*, correspond le rapport épistémologique: *sagesse-science*; et le tout s'unifie dans la personne du Christ."[35] If, as Madec suggests, this passage

---

[31] Ayers, "The Christological Context of Augustine's *De Trinitate* XIII," 134 n. 20: "Book [8] ... emphasizes that we may understand how *scientia* leads to *sapientia*, and thus how faith may grow from and be shaped by the *scientia* of Christ's life."

[32] Hill, *The Trinity*, 366: "But all these things that the Word made flesh did and suffered for us in time and space belong, according to the distinction we have undertaken to illustrate, to knowledge and not to wisdom. Insofar as he is Word, he is without time and without space, coeternal with the Father and wholly present everywhere; and if anyone can utter a true word about this, as far as he is able, it will be a word of wisdom. So it is that the Word made flesh, which is Christ Jesus, has treasures both of wisdom and of knowledge."

[33] Madec, "Christus scientia et sapientia nostra," 78 n. 2. "Augustine considered the doctrine that he developed as thoroughly Christian, fully Christological."

[34] Hill, *The Trinity*, 367. "Scientia ergo nostra christus est, sapientia quoque nostra idem christus est. ipse nobis fidem de rebus temporalibus inserit; ipse de sempiternis exhibet ueritatem. per ipsum pergimus ad ipsum, tendimus per scientiam ad sapientiam; ab uno tamen eodem que christo non recedimus in quo sunt omnes thesauri sapientiae et scientiae absconditi" (CCSL 50A: 416.50-417.55).

[35] Madec, "Christus scientia et sapientia nostra," 79 n. 2, emphasis original. "Such is the structure of the Augustinian theology: to the ontological relationship: eternity-time, corresponds the epistemological relationship: wisdom-science, and everything comes together in the person of Christ."

from *Trin.* can be considered to be the unifying principle of Augustine's other thinking and writing, we certainly cannot ignore its likely function as the unifying theological principle of *Trin.*

Madec suggests that this passage constructs a doctrinal chiasm. Augustine writes, "We [should not] take these two [*scientia* and *sapientia*] as if we could never call this one that is concerned with human affairs wisdom, or that one that is concerned with divine things knowledge. In a broader manner of speaking each can be called wisdom and each knowledge" (*Trin.* 13.24).[36] Such a functional conflation results from the chiasm that Madec highlights. According to this chiasm Christ is the center in which are found the fruition and mediation of *aeterna* and *temporalia*, *veritas* and *fides*, *sapientia* and *scientia*, and of course *deus* and *homo*.[37] "The union of the two natures enables our progress through *scientia* to *sapientia*."[38]

In Book 14 at last we arrive at the image of God in humanity in the action of remembering, understanding, and loving God. In this section we begin to see how Augustine views God as present in humans while they can yet fail to recognize God (*Trin.* 14.16). It seems, according to this discussion, that the function of the incarnation is to remind humans of God when God has been forgotten by them. This reminder not only begins the process of ascent to God but sustains it as well. For in order to continue in the contemplative life, to ascend to the wisdom of God, even to do so through consideration of the image of God in the human mind, one must always be reminded of God through the incarnation. Augustine reminds us constantly of the incarnation and indwelling, even as we "ascend" to God through the contemplation of the *imago* in Books 9–15. Without the incarnation and the indwelling he suggests humans cannot proceed past their own natural reason.

It is not accidental that, in his attempt to access the image of God through contemplation, Augustine seems to undermine his own efforts intentionally. Every attempt is shown to be flawed. Every formulation proved faulty. Compared with what humans already know by the *scientia* of faith, their natural reason and ability fall short. Augustine again emphasizes that the work of the Holy Spirit is critical for knowing and loving God, through the Spirit's work both in the individual and in inspiring the scriptures (*Trin.* 14.21).[39] In addition, he points the reader back to the necessity of the incarnation and affirms the enduring value of its physicality in reminding of the

---

[36] Hill, *The Trinity*, 367. "Nec ista duo sic accipiamus quasi non liceat dicere uel istam sapientiam quae in rebus humanis est uel illam scientiam quae in diuinis. loquendi enim latiore consuetudine utraque sapientia, utraque scientia dici potest" (CCSL 50A: 417.57-60).

[37] Madec, "Christus scientia et sapientia nostra," 81 n. 2.

[38] Ayers, "The Christological Context of Augustine's *De Trinitate* XIII," 120 n. 20.

[39] Hill, *The Trinity*, 388: "But when the mind truly recalls its Lord after receiving his Spirit, it perceives quite simply—for it learns this by a wholly intimate instruction from within—that it cannot rise except by his gracious doing, and that it could not have fallen except by its own willful undoing. Certainly it does not remember its happiness. That was once, and is no more, and the mind has totally forgotten it and therefore cannot even be reminded of it. But it believes the trustworthy documents of its God about it, written by his prophets, when they tell about the bliss of paradise and make known through a historical tradition man's first good and first evil."

resurrection of the body and the bodily state in which the reader may know God fully (*Trin.* 14.24).[40]

As Augustine begins to conclude his work in Book 15 we should recall that he suggests that the image of God in the human mind, as discerned by natural reason, is inadequate to reveal the nature of the triune God accurately. Let us also remember that he has not given up hope for the success of his work by the assertion that "the God himself we are looking for will help us, I confidently hope, to get some fruit from our labors" (*Trin.* 15.2).[41] In this passage, rather than a person hedging his failure, lies an articulation of faith seeking understanding: that even as new knowledge is mysterious and challenging, perhaps even inadequate, the faith still continues to seek.

In light of the pending revelation of the shortcoming of the *imago* as apprehended by natural reason, Augustine returns to the central thesis, refocusing on the chiastic structure of the work:

> If we try to recall where it was in these books that a trinity first began to appear to our understanding, it will occur to us that it was in the eighth book. There we attempted as best we could to raise the attention of the mind by our discussion to understand that supremely eminent and unchangeable nature which our mind is not. .... But when we came to charity, which is called God in holy scripture, the glimmerings of a trinity began to appear, namely lover and what is loved and love. However, that inexpressible light beat back our gaze, and somehow convinced us that the weakness of our mind could not yet be attuned to it. So to relax our concentration we turned ourselves back in reflection, between the beginning and the completion of our search, to what could be called the more familiar consideration of our own mind insofar as man has been made to the image of God. And from then on we lingered over the creature which we ourselves are from the ninth to the fourteenth book in order to descry if we could the invisible things of God by understanding them through those that have been made. So here we are, after exercising our understanding as much as was necessary, and perhaps more than was necessary in these lower things, wishing and not being able to raise ourselves to a sight of that supreme trinity which is God.[42]
>
> (*Trin.* 15.10)

Is Augustine admitting here that the whole trajectory of Books 9–15 has been largely a red herring? Was what he was looking for all along, namely an accurate revelation of the nature of the triune God, to be found in the material already covered in Book 8?

---

[40] Hill, *The Trinity*, 392: "From this it is clear that the image of God will achieve its full likeness of him when it attains to the full vision of him—though this text from the apostle John might also appear to be referring to the immortality of the body. In this respect too we will be like God, but only like the Son, who alone in the triad took a body in which he died and rose again, carrying it up to the heavenly regions."

[41] Hill, *The Trinity*, 395. "Deus quippe ipse quem quaerimus adiuuabit, ut spero, ne sit infructuosus labor noster" (CCSL 50A: 460.1-2).

[42] Hill, *The Trinity*, 402.

In short, the answer is yes. As Williams states, "The image of God in us (as opposed to the mere *vestigia* of triadic structures in the mind) is realised when the three moments of our mental agency all have God for their object."[43] According to Augustine, all the intellectual musings and machinations of reason are powerless without a return to the love of God as it impinges upon human experience in the incarnation and the indwelling. While this emphasis seems to mislead Hill, as his chapter introductions indicate, Augustine's admission of the failure of the image accurately to reflect the processions in 15.4 (re: the Son) and 15.5 (re: the Holy Spirit) might be, rather than an accidental shortcoming, intended to suggest that while the access to God through this image in the mind is flawed, the access we have through the missions of the Son and Spirit is not. The emphasis in 15.5 seems particularly oriented in this direction. Augustine appears to stray from his purpose (as Hill notes)[44] to discuss the mission at length (the purpose of which Hill does not seem to intuit). It is another instance of Augustine pointing back to the incarnation and the indwelling, but Hill believes Augustine to have become confused.[45]

Is it likely that Augustine really forgot his intention? Isn't it more likely that the discussion of the Holy Spirit that Augustine proceeds with is exactly what he believes will benefit the reader, even as it does not neatly fit the schema that natural reason's pursuit would suggest? This long meditation on the Holy Spirit is the necessary capstone in Augustine's discussion of whence human apprehension of the nature of the triune God is derived. It is entirely appropriate that he return to the Holy Spirit as he concludes his search by natural reason for the Trinity in the human mind. In an attempt to make his purpose clearer to the reader Augustine cites the author of 1 John:

> He now wished to say something a little more plainly about this matter, and so he said, *In this we know that we abide in him and he in us, because he has given us of his Spirit* (1 [John] 4:13). So it is the Holy Spirit of which he has given us that makes us abide in God and him in us. But this is precisely what love does. He then is the gift of God who is love. ... So it is God the Holy Spirit proceeding from God who fires man to the love of God and neighbor when he has been given to him, and he himself is love. Man has no capacity to love God except from God ... Nothing is more excellent than this gift of God ... through him the charity of God is poured out in our hearts, and through it the whole triad dwells in us.[46]
>
> (*Trin.* 15.31-32)

Augustine's focus on the locus of dwelling as crucial does not seem accidental.

---

[43] Williams, "Sapientia and the Trinity," 319 n. 17.
[44] Hill, *The Trinity*, 421 n. 1.
[45] Hill, *The Trinity*, 421 n. 1: "The author goes on to point out the dissimilarity of the mental image with reference to the second eternal procession, that of the Holy Spirit from the Father and the Son; though in fact he seems rather to forget his precise intention, only reverting to it at the very end of this chapter; and with scarcely any reference to the image, or its third element of will or love, he discusses at length the propriety of the names we give to the Holy Spirit."
[46] Hill, *The Trinity*, 424–5.

Pursuant to this discourse on the Holy Spirit, Hill again seems to think that Augustine is bewildered in his writing.[47] Once again, it seems more likely that Hill has misunderstood Augustine's purpose than that Augustine himself is confused. For one who has constructed *Trin.* so carefully it seems strange to think that he would, in the very last chapter of his work, write in a way that countermanded his true goals. Rather, I suspect that he is ensuring the accomplishment of his goals by his concluding emphasis:

> As for the reason why he first gave the Holy Spirit on earth after his resurrection and then sent him from heaven, I think it is because charity is poured out in our hearts through this gift, charity by which we are to love God and neighbor according to those two commandments on which the whole law depends and the prophets. It was to signify this that the Lord Jesus gave the Holy Spirit twice, once on earth for love of neighbor, and again from heaven for love of God.[48]
>
> (*Trin.* 15.46)

Here again he places the utmost value on the revelation of God through the indwelling, through the mission of the Holy Spirit in the material world. He affirms human experience in the material realm and earthly relationships, especially through that mode by which he is convinced humans may know God best: love, and particularly that grittiest of all loves: love of neighbor. Without these intimate, proximal experiences no intellectual contemplation will succeed. Indeed, even as we have seen, these must critique and overrule the fabrications of the mind that confuse humans as to the true nature of the triune God.[49] The purpose of Augustine's emphasis on the Holy Spirit in the concluding sections of Book 15 is this: in the act of contemplation humans must

---

[47] Hill, *The Trinity*, 431 n. 1.

[48] Hill, *The Trinity*, 436. "Quid uero fuerit causae ut post resurrectionem suam et in terra prius daret et de caelo postea mitteret spiritum sanctum, hoc ego existimo quia per ipsum donum diffunditur caritas in cordibus nostris qua diligamus deum et proximum secundum duo illa praecepta in quibus tota lex pendet et prophetae. hoc significans dominus iesus bis dedit spiritum sanctum, semel in terra propter dilectionem proximi et iterum de caelo propter dilectionem dei" (CCSL 50A: 525.19-26).

[49] It would not only be uncharitable but simply inaccurate to claim that Edmund Hill entirely misses the point of these emphases in *Trin.*; he does seem to recognize it temporarily when commenting on Book 10. See Hill, *The Trinity*, 286–7 n. 1: "It is interesting to note that he [Augustine] begins his exploration of the image in Book [9], and his deeper analysis of it in Book [10], each time from the starting point of love. The point, I think, is that though love is more difficult to understand than knowledge, just as the Holy Spirit is more difficult to name and find suitable analogous concepts for than the Word, it is for all that more immediate to our experience; more immediate to experience, though less accessible to reflection. The practical theological implication of this for the Christian life is that although the Holy Spirit is a more shadowy person for us than the Word, who is made objectively accessible to us in the incarnation, still he is more immediate to our religious experience than the Word, that is to say than Christ; it is only in the Spirit that we can recognize Christ, and can say *Jesus is Lord* (1 Cor. 12:3). This is the point that has been all too seriously neglected in the Church's theology, and hence in its piety and its practice of the Christian life." But even as he recognizes this emphasis in *Trin.* and this failing in Christian theology generally, Hill still seems to miss the purpose of Augustine's emphasis on the Holy Spirit in the concluding sections of Book 15 (Edmund Hill, "St. Augustine's *De Trinitate*: The Doctrinal Significance of its Structure," *Revue des Études Augustiniennes* 19 [1973]: 285–6): "The mystery is revealed by the economy—the eternal processions of the divine persons by the temporal missions of the divine persons ... [God] is revealed as a triad by the economy, because in fact the eternal divine triad unfolds the saving economy according to the triadic pattern. So the mystery of the Trinity is of the essence of our redemption."

not stray from the true source of understanding of the triune God, namely the action of the Spirit dwelling in the human experience of quotidian time and material space.

Conclusion

It seems likely that whether or not the success of *Trin.* for which this chapter argues was intentional, Augustine did in fact succeed in influencing the thinking and theology of the church by it, certainly stretching into the medieval period, as previously mentioned,[50] but probably into modernity as well.[51] Madec's observation, that the unifying principle of coherence to Augustine's doctrine is the salience and centrality of the Christological data, affirms this chapter's thesis and explains the presence of Augustine's secular data. Madec's assertion that it is only in the Christological event that the Platonic, Plotinian, and Ciceronian philosophies are completed and brought to their full latent value is in harmony with the other elements of Augustine's argument.[52] Indeed, "in both Books

---

[50] Johnson, *She Who Is*, 117–22.
[51] For instance, in *Fides Quaerens Intellectum: Anselms Beweis für die Existenz Gottes* (Zürich: Theologischer Verlag Zürich, 1981), Karl Barth takes as his subject an analysis of the beginning of Anselm's *Proslogion*, best remembered for what has become known as "the ontological proof" (found, in its most famous formulation—aliquid quo nihil maius cogitari possit—in chapter 2, line 4 of Anselmus Cantuariensis, *Proslogion*, in *Opera Omnia*, Vol. 1, ed. F. S. Schmitt [Edinburgh: Thomas Nelson & Sons, 1946], 101). The "proof," which is simply a name for God, seems most likely to have been derived by Anselm from a similar Augustinian formulation found in *Trin.* (*Trin.* 14.11 [CCSL 50A: 436.5-6]: naturae illius qua natura melior nulla est). The thrust of Barth's argument in *Fides* is that Anselm is not attempting to prove the existence of God based on natural reason, or really at all, but rather simply seeking to know and understand *how* God is (theology) from the belief *that* God is (faith). According to Barth, this "faith seeking understanding" is the only appropriate basis for true and accurate theology. Barth's argument is rather convincing and if correct would point toward the success of the aforementioned purpose of *Trin.* Barth later wrote that in *Fides* lay the key to understanding all his subsequent theology (See "Vorwort zur 2. Auflage," in Barth, *Fides Quaerens Intellectum*, 6–7 n. 53). If so, then the line of influence on Barth can be traced through Anselm all the way back to the Christological key to *Trin.* suggested by Madec. A passage from *Die kirchliche Dogmatik* is helpful in understanding some of this influence: "Wir fragen fernerhin unter der Voraussetzung, daß der Gegenstand jedes allgemeinen, d. h. jedes anderswie als im Blick auf Gottes Offenbarung in Jesus Christus gebildeten Gottesbegriffs notwendig ein anderer ist als der, der der Herr und das Heil und so der Gegenstand des Glaubens der Kirche und als solcher der allein wahre Gott ist" (*Die kirchliche Dogmatik* II.28.3, from Karl Barth, *Die kirchliche Dogmatik, Band II.1* [Zürich: Theologischer Verlag Zürich, 1980], 336). "We make our enquiry on the assumption that the object of this universal idea of God, i.e., of any idea of God formed otherwise than in view of God's revelation in Jesus Christ, is necessarily other than He who is Lord and salvation, and therefore the object of the faith of the Church and the only true God." English translation from Karl Barth, *Church Dogmatics*, eds. G. W. Bromiley and T. F. Torrance, trans. T. H. L. Parker, W. B. Johnston, Harold Knight, and J. L. M. Haire (Edinburgh: T&T Clark, 1957), 298. One might legitimately ask whether this approach necessarily negates the witness of Rom 1:20 and all of Augustine's data from secular philosophers. Upon further examination, however, we see how Barth arrives at his interpretation of Anselm's *Proslogion* 2–4: true theology, and knowledge of God, must derive from faith in the received *scientia* of Christ and cannot be achieved outside of it; according to Barth, natural reason by itself cannot attain to God; and to succeed at theology, at finding an accurate revelation of God, one must not only start with the ground of faith based in the revelation of Christ (incarnation) and the indwelling of the Holy Spirit but continually return to them.
[52] Madec, "Christus scientia et sapientia nostra," 84 n. 2.

[13 and 14] the 'philosopher' fails through not providing an appropriately formed faith which may provide a reliable basis for progress toward the goal."[53] By the affirmation of materiality in the incarnation God endows value to "natural" reason and enables the fulfillment of its potential. This is the great observation of *Trin.*: that the image of the Trinity in the human mind is inadequate to access God without the incarnation and the indwelling. By these missions of the Son and the Spirit into material space, God endues *scientia*, with infinite value. According to Augustine, by becoming flesh, Christ endowed materiality with the highest purpose: the ability to witness to and point to "God who is Spirit." In this way the incarnation and indwelling produce meaning for Augustine in material space and *scientia* that is of eternal value.

We might then say that Augustine would consider the reader a fool who seeks to understand the nature of the triune God by reason alone, based on the material creation alone, while having access to that very same God in the incarnation and indwelling. He might consider said reader equally foolish if while having faith he or she never sought any deeper understanding of God using either reason or the knowledge of what God had created. Augustine clearly thought that all the tools within reach[54] must be used to know God, but that they must be used from faith and in love, not neglecting the revelation of God to which he believed his reader already had access.

Perhaps it is a facile observation, but it must be noted that even for Augustine to examine and reject Trinitarian conceptions based in the operations of created things, which are generated by natural reason, he must constantly call on the witness of scripture. Never in any of his work can he avoid dwelling upon scripture—the *scientia* of the incarnation and indwelling—if he is to avoid fabrication of a false image of God. The inherent repeated emphasis of *Trin.* is that the operation of natural reason cannot accurately approach knowledge of the triune God without the *scientia* of the incarnation. Every proposal of a Trinitarian image is not just examined in light of the existing revelation of scripture but is rejected based on it. This is a necessary element of his spatial practice. And while it is possible that, for Augustine, *scientia* is ultimately of lower priority than *sapientia* (the material realm not being the ultimate, permanent goal but rather the spiritual), still for now *scientia* is crucial. For Augustine the message seems clear: humans cannot escape the necessity of the Christ. In Christ, embodied God, are *scientia* and *sapientia*, and in the Spirit of God the most local access in the human realm. The witness of the material and temporal to God is affirmed. The full human cosmos is not an obstacle to be overcome but the ecology upon which understanding God depends. For him it is the realm of God's grace (*Trin.* 13.24). And as long as temporality endures, according to Augustine's *Trin.*, the incarnation and indwelling, mediated through human material experience, are the root, branch, and blossom of understanding of the triune God. *De Trinitate* is Augustine's final affirmation of human ecology and experience.

---

[53] Ayers, "The Christological Context of Augustine's *De Trinitate* XIII," 119 n. 20.
[54] Ayers, "The Christological Context of Augustine's *De Trinitate* XIII," 135 n. 20: "On the one hand we need such an exercitatio if we are to comprehend the structure of the Incarnation, and, on the other hand, it is the Incarnation which, as the core of the redemptive dispensatio, provides such an exercitatio."

8

Conclusions and Prospect: The Core Function of "Ecology" in Scriptural Production and Interpretation

We began Chapters 1 and 2 with a consideration of the Gospel of John, looking closely at John 4, a biblical text most commonly interpreted to suggest the irrelevancy of space. However, from that text we discovered the importance of attending to spatial practice and textual ecology, often reading obliquely the intention of the writer in order to better understand the text. The subsequent chapters of this book have all proceeded in this vein, involving explorations of questions related to these methods, seeing not only whether the methods prove useful but also whether the ancient texts themselves can confirm the relevance of modern theory.

In this final portion of the book, we will consider the key findings from the analyses performed in the preceding chapters. Chapters 1 and 2 dealt with the Gospel of John, Chapter 3 with the undisputed Pauline Letters, Chapter 4 with the *Parables of Enoch*, Chapter 5 largely with the book of Revelation, Chapter 6 the *History of the Rechabites*, and Chapter 7 Augustine's *De Trinitate*. Attention will be given to each chapter separately, then to synthetic conclusions from comparisons of the various texts analyzed, and finally to conclusions related to the employment of modern spatial-critical methods in analysis and prospect for future scholarship.

The Gospel of John (Chapters 1 and 2)

Conclusions Regarding Domestic/Quotidian Phenomenology in the Fourth Gospel

The analysis of the dwelling language in the Gospel of John (Chapter 1) establishes that imagery of "home" and "dwelling" is central for the author (or redactor). The sheer volume of this imagery deserves deeper attention than has been possible in this single chapter, and I hope to devote further work to analysis of the domestic spatial practice at work in the Gospel. Among the phenomenologies of "dwelling" on display in the Gospel are the association between the imagination of home and the experience of rest,[1] the normative function of temporal and spatial conflation in the imagination of home,[2] and a compensatory responsiveness in the imagination of home to experiences of trauma.[3]

The analysis of the Samaritan Interlude (Chapter 2) suggests importance of consideration of spatial practice and textual ecology. Space is not spiritualized, nor made irrelevant, nor entirely subsumed within the person of Jesus. Rather, attention to the spaces likely important to the Johannine community, especially to a material lived experience, allows for not only accurate interpretation of spatial data (e.g., "temple" language) but also the "mythic" outlines of the narrative.

Implications for Johannine Studies

The identification of phenomenologies of dwelling that are likely operative in the Gospel of John has significant implications for the state of Johannine hermeneutics. Rather than a simple blanket suggestion that the operation of the Paraclete in the life of the community solves many of the difficulties in the Gospel,[4] the observations made in Chapter 1 suggest that behind the many anachronisms and spatial "conundrums"[5] in John may be the result of the normative operation of the conflationary psychology of dwelling. According to this psychology, prior experiences of home and rest are conflated in memory with current experiences of home and rest so that any imagination of dwelling, past or present, produces a vision of it that is an amalgam of previous experiences of habitation.[6] This has the potential to solve both spatial difficulties regarding Jesus' location and believers' ultimate expectation, and temporal discrepancies between *einmalig* events and events in the experience of the Johannine community. Further, the spatial-critical solution, based as it is in attention to phenomenologies of domestic space, does not require the unsatisfactory insistence upon a choice according to the artificial bifurcation of history and theology.

Another normative phenomenon of the imagination of home is the process by which a compensatory vision of home may be developed in order to deal with the experience of being "cast out" of a previous home.[7] It is likely that much of the dwelling language of the Gospel, especially that of the indwelling, is a compensatory response based in this phenomenon. Finally, the psychology of home is deeply tied to the experience of rest,[8] and this observation indicates the value of Martyn's emphasis on the catastrophe of synagogue excommunication for the Johannine community and its formative role

---

[1] As detailed in Gaston Bachelard, *The Poetics of Space*, trans. Maria Jolas (Boston: Beacon Press, 1994), 7, 15, 137, 201, 226.
[2] Spatial conflation: Bachelard, *The Poetics of Space*, 5, 6, 17, 51, 207, 226. Temporal conflation: Bachelard, *The Poetics of Space*, 5, 6, 9, 33, 120.
[3] Bachelard, *The Poetics of Space*, 6, 7, 33, 46, 56, 100, 136, 137, 142, 210.
[4] Including the reason for the "two-level drama" and the spatial "conundrums." J. Louis Martyn, *History and Theology in the Fourth Gospel*, 2nd ed. (Nashville, TN: Abingdon, 1979), 143–51.
[5] The term employed in Martyn, *History and Theology*.
[6] Bachelard, *The Poetics of Space*, 6, 226.
[7] Bachelard, *The Poetics of Space*, 33, 56, 100, 142.
[8] Bachelard, *The Poetics of Space*, 7, 15, 137, 201, 226.

in shaping reactively oppositional[9] and compensatory visions of home in response. Essentially, the various aspects of domestic phenomenology examined here affirm the basic observations made by Martyn but furnish a more robust explanatory framework for the various interpretive difficulties that have long vexed students of the Fourth Gospel.

The analysis of Chapter 2 has shown that attention to the "spatial practice" of the Samaritan Interlude indicates that the text is likely based on Judean traditions pertinent to the Johannine community rather than a Samaritan social location or *einmalig* event. Further, interpretation of spatial themes according to this later sectarian-Jewish social location suggests that the valences of the destroyed Temple were not transferred primarily to Jesus (as many interpreters suppose) but rather to the body of believer(s) as temple(s) of the Holy Spirit. Similarly, the well-meeting scene is likely indicative of the influence of the Johannine community social location rather than exclusively an *einmalig* event in the life of Jesus.

The Undisputed Pauline Letters (Chapter 3)

Conclusions Regarding Domestic/Quotidian Phenomenology in the Undisputed Pauline Letters

A significant element of considering a Pauline theological ecology requires attention to how a diaspora Pharisee would attempt to think and advocate on behalf of gentiles. The key idea that flows from this premise is related to access to God: without access somehow mediated outside the Jerusalem Temple, gentiles would not have adequate access. However, Pauline pneumatology points to direct access for gentile Jesus-followers through the Holy Spirit dwelling in their bodies. Such dwelling requires the purification of that space for the dwelling of God. A Levitical sacrificial model that effects the purification of space for the dwelling of God as the interpretive frame for the death of Jesus would fit the need of this particular ecology.

Implications for Study of the Undisputed Pauline Letters

Though the findings of this chapter are highly provisional, they certainly suggest that consideration of a Levitical space-sanctifying sacrificial model for a Pauline understanding of the death of Jesus should not be foreclosed. Such an approach, based on the observations of Jacob Milgrom, makes possible a Pauline soteriology not necessarily dependent on a personal substitutionary atonement model, allowing decolonizing of interpretation. What this chapter does not address at all is the entire suite of possibilities for Paul's own ecology and perhaps most tantalizingly, the carceral ecology of his letters. Further work in this direction is certainly necessary.

---

[9] As indicated by the "world-negating" and polemical language throughout the Gospel. See Bachelard, *The Poetics of Space*, 136, 143.

The *Parables of Enoch* (Chapter 4)

Conclusions Regarding Domestic/Quotidian Phenomenology in *Parables of Enoch*

The analysis of *Parables of Enoch* found a likely identification between those farmers and landowners who had been expelled from their ancestral "dry" lands in Galilee under Herod the Great and the marginal "wet" lands to which they had been unwillingly consigned. Even as these poorer lands would not have been viewed favorably at first by their new inhabitants, the act of dwelling appears to have had an auto-valorizing effect, enabling positive identification with the "waters." The established identification between the powerful and the "dry land" is buttressed by the parallel identification between those currently powerless and the "waters." This spatial identification, or metonym, according to which the powerful who rule the "dry land" are judged when the "waters" rise up in a "flood" appears as an integral part of what can only be described as a veiled "proto-marxist" understanding of class relations in the region. There are certainly also elements of utopic thinking and idealized imagination of the "heavenly habitations," which appear in a compensatory role in response to the experience of being "cast out"[10] from ancestral lands. However, this "ideal" vision is augmented by the comparatively more realistic vision of overthrow of the oppressive landowners.

Implications for Studies of *Parables of Enoch*

The proposed identification of the oppressed disinherited with the "waters" of judgment in parallel to the established identification between the oppressors and the "dry land" contributes to the burgeoning consensus regarding provenance. This association affirms a late redactional stage either at the time of disinheritance under Herod the Great, as described in Josephus,[11] or in the near aftermath of that experience. This conclusion continues to support the possibility of a location of composition in Galilee, with a possible specific locale in the Huleh Valley, or at the Sea of Galilee, with the Migdal synagogue a likely candidate. This possibility is buttressed by the fact that seasonal laborers, lacking work on farms, congregated at the Sea of Galilee in the off-season and in Migdal specifically to help in the fishing and fish-processing industries.[12] The association between marginal dwelling, marginal employment, and "waters" or "watery lands" could not be greater. This provenance helps establish a possible precedent for the Galilean revolt of 6 CE and the subsequent ministry of Jesus of Nazareth among the dispossessed and marginalized in the region in the ensuing years.

---

[10] Bachelard, *The Poetics of Space*, 7.
[11] Josephus, *Ant.* 17.304-314.
[12] James H. Charlesworth, *Jesus as Mirrored in John: The Genius in the New Testament* (London: T&T Clark, 2018), 176, 206–7, 468–9, 538.

The Book of Revelation (Chapter 5)

Conclusions Regarding Domestic/Quotidian Phenomenology of Revelation

Our study of Revelation has revealed that the quotidian phenomenology of doorways may be significant for understanding not only the author's context but the author's production and its reception. When compared with an apocalypse such as *Parables of Enoch*, Revelation appears to display an orientation comparatively less engaged with the material world and its difficulties. Recent research in cognitive psychology[13] suggests that passing through a doorway has a measurable cognitive effect, inducing forgetfulness of prior thoughts. Revelation employs doorway and gateway language repeatedly, while *Parables of Enoch* does not. Revelation combines generic polemic against all the "inhabitants of the earth," an emphasis on the replacement or "wipe" of the old order, and the use of compensatory cultic language to orient the reader away from the existing material world. The narrative employment of doorway language suggests an operative governing psychology of separation and forgetfulness in Revelation. These observations make sense in light of the carceral geography of the Apocalypse. The language of imprisonment is frequent in Revelation, likely the result of the author's own experience of marginal dwelling as one of the incarcerated on Patmos. This experience seems to have affected the author's production of both ideal and cursed spaces in the Apocalypse, transferring negative aspects of his (or her) experience to spaces of judgment and extrapolating the opposite, that is freedom and joy, to the ideal spaces. The narrative deployment of the doorway theme seems to function to separate these spaces, and the people associated with them, through forgetfulness (for the author and readers) of the experiences that transpired outside the doorways and gates.

Implications for Studies of the Book of Revelation

There have been no serious treatments of the door and gate theme in Revelation, and this chapter establishes the phenomenology of doorways as an important consideration for the proper interpretation of the Apocalypse. Further work is also required to explore the carceral geography of the Apocalypse, as begun in this chapter. Recent trends in scholarship have tended to emphasize postcolonial readings of Revelation, suggesting that it represents a meaningful response to political concerns. The findings of this chapter suggest the contrary, that Revelation displays a variety of escapist tendencies and does not really display meaningful political engagement. The narrative function of the doorways in the Apocalypse is one of inducing forgetfulness of what has come before, for example, suffering and incarceration, to prepare the reader to focus on the new Jerusalem. The operation of this phenomenon seems to explain the function of Revelation in its modern popular reception, which is to say, its readers often appear

---

[13] Gabriel A. Radvansky, Sabine A. Krawietz, and Andrea K. Tamplin, "Walking through Doorways Causes Forgetting: Further Explorations," *The Quarterly Journal of Experimental Psychology* 64 (2011): 1632–45.

forgetful of and disengaged from the material world, their responsibilities in it, and those who they believe will be judged.

The *History of the Rechabites* (Chapter 6)

Conclusions Regarding Domestic/Quotidian Phenomenology of *History of the Rechabites*

The main contention of our study of *History of the Rechabites* is that a naturally occurring optical phenomenon, a version of a "Novaya Zemlya Effect," allowing unusual, literal visions of Cyprus from the summit region of Mt. Zaphon/Mt. Kasios/Jebel Aqra, may lie behind the vision of the Isle of the Blessed Ones described in the text. The ascetic provenance of the text is indicated by the text itself and signifies a marginal experience of dwelling (as a hermit in a cave) as a further generative background. This latter context could certainly have been a fecund enough environment on its own for the imagination of ideal dwelling on display in *History of the Rechabites*. However, the various descriptions of the vision present in the text suggest a scenario with characteristics too similar to that produced in a Novaya Zemlya Effect to ignore the possibility of that additional background. But whether or not that phenomenon provided the creative spark to literary appropriation of the Greco-Roman legend of the Isle of the Blessed Ones, the phenomenology of marginal dwelling as productive of ideal images of dwelling is certainly operative. The author has translated the positive aspects of lived experience (holiness, prayer) into an ideal sphere while mitigating the negative ones (suffering, isolation) in that ideal sphere. Particularly suggestive is the frequent "world-negating," reactive language, which is a typical feature of the operation of the imagination in situations of marginal dwelling.[14] The author assuredly dwelt long in isolated hardship, and his (or her) handiwork in *History of the Rechabites* shows the marks of it.

Implications for Studies of *History of the Rechabites*

The proposal set forward for a likely phenomenological background to *History of the Rechabites* both builds on scholarly consensus regarding provenance and contributes a strikingly specific and plausible possibility. It affirms the ascetic background that is largely agreed upon but places the likely location for reception of the vision in a cave on the upper slopes of then Mt. Kasios[15] on the eastern Mediterranean coast just southwest of Antioch. The likely period of provenance would be during the time in the Late Ancient period when Christianity was growing steadily, but the traditional cults were still considered a threat. Sometime in the fourth or fifth century CE seems most likely, which would match with increasing ascetic activity on the high slopes of Kasios. This would also allow for reception of the text in a monastic community (possibly St. Barlaam's) and popularization in an environment with a significant literary culture (Antioch).

---

[14] Bachelard, *The Poetics of Space*, 136, 143.
[15] Now Jebel Aqra in Turkey.

Augustine's *De Trinitate* (Chapter 7)

Conclusions Regarding Domestic/Quotidian Phenomenology in *Trin.*

In *De Trinitate* Augustine affirms that *scientia*, in a host of manifestations, including the material sphere of human experience, or human ecology, is a necessary part of gaining a deeper understanding of God (*sapientia*). The other key elements of this *scientia* that enable access to *sapientia* are the incarnation (God's dwelling in a body, with humans, as and how they dwell), the scriptures (the material record of God's historic dealings with humans in the human sphere), and the indwelling (the ongoing abiding of the Holy Spirit in the body of the believer). For Augustine this suite of elements all co-inform and co-affirm, mediating God to humans. This is an Augustinian affirmation of human ecology and, in general terms, an ecologically based hermeneutics. Of course, any spatial practice is inherently based in a material human ecology, but more than just operating according to this paradigm unwittingly, Augustine appears to acknowledge this and affirm it.[16]

Implications for Study of *Trin.*

Our exegetical analysis of *Trin.* represents at most a mild extension of the insights already made in the field of Augustinian studies (following Madec, Ayers, and Williams). The structure of *Trin.* suggests an affirmation of *scientia* and supports the contention that *Trin.* would not have been viewed as a failure by Augustine. He acknowledged the basis of human ecology, represented in part by the *scientia* of the incarnation, the indwelling, and the scriptures, as necessary for attainment of *sapientia*. In this sense, the chapter simply emphasizes the indirect Augustinian valuation of "spatial practice" and "textual ecology" for hermeneutics. Augustine here sets the stage for medieval analogical theology.

Synthetic Conclusions across All Texts

In retrospect it is shocking how frequently evidence of marginal or marginalized experiences of dwelling appear in the background to the texts considered. Such background is relevant to the primary biblical and para-biblical texts under consideration in every chapter of this project.[17] In the early stages of work on this project only for the Gospel of John was there an expectation that this kind of background had contributed a significant shaping influence. The bulk of the analyses for the undisputed Pauline Letters, the *Parables of Enoch*, Revelation, and *History of the Rechabites* had already been completed before the realization struck that phenomenologies of marginal experiences of dwelling likely contributed significantly to the shaping of the texts. That such a finding was unexpected militates in favor of its legitimacy, as the

---

[16] Much more could be said in terms of the details of Augustine's own personal σχολή and home life as productive literary environs, but the purpose of this chapter is to examine Augustine's intended communication.

[17] Perhaps with the exception of *De Trinitate*.

analysis was not biased toward such a conclusion. The experiences of being cast out in the Gospel of John and *Parables of Enoch*, and those of dwelling in harsh circumstances in Revelation[18] and *History of the Rechabites*,[19] have produced effects of similar kinds.

In each text we find displays of imagined, ideal dwellings which are compensatory hybrid projections combining the positive aspects of lived experience with the absence of negative aspects. Often times the authors have preserved evidence of their difficulties in the cursed spaces they reserve for their judged enemies. This reactively oppositional phenomenon also, across all these texts, preserves elements of "world-negating" language that is the natural result of rejection and marginalization in experiences of home. The degree of disengagement from the world varies between texts, but there is at least a struggle with the issue in the Fourth Gospel and *Parables of Enoch*, while in Revelation the escapism is embraced more fully and in *History of the Rechabites* it reaches an extreme. But even in the extreme portrayal of disengagement on display in *History of the Rechabites* there is fellowship and care for others, even if they are only those who ostensibly share the author's beliefs. In no texts is the separation so complete that everyone is consigned to judgment. The work of the author is, after all, meant to be read, and probably read aloud. Interestingly, the Pauline corpus and *Trin.* exhibit the least influence of this kind, possibly indicating less significant authorial experiences of marginal dwelling.[20]

Conclusions for Employment of Spatial-Critical Analysis to Texts from Antiquity

At the most basic level, the findings of these studies should establish the fact that many of the phenomenologies of dwelling observed and documented in modernity were operative in antiquity as well. The application of Bachelard's work for spatial-critical analysis is only just beginning but should continue apace. As indicated in the introduction to this work, consideration of domestic and quotidian phenomenologies of space is indispensable for responsible analysis of spatial practice in antique texts. Further application of innovative work in the field of cognitive science will pay dividends for this hermeneutical endeavor. And if the work of reversing the traditional avoidance of spatial analysis in favor of historical considerations is to be continued,[21] it must include the most ancient of texts within its purview.

---

[18] In prison.

[19] In a cave not unlike a prison. See Chapter 5 on the equation in Revelation between cave, pit, and prison.

[20] Or at least more pressing or influential priorities.

[21] In line with Michel Foucault's ("Of Other Spaces," trans. Jay Miskowiec, *Diacritics* 16 [1986]: 22) contentions: "The great obsession of the nineteenth century was, as we know, history: with its themes of development and of suspension, of crisis and cycle, themes of the ever-accumulating past, with its great preponderance of dead men and the menacing glaciations of the world ... The present epoch will perhaps be above all the epoch of space. We are in the epoch of simultaneity: we are in the epoch of juxtaposition, the epoch of near and far, of the side-by-side, of the dispersed. We are at a moment, I believe, when our experience of the world is less that of a long life developing through time than that of a network that connects points and intersects with its own skein. One could perhaps say that certain ideological conflicts animating present-day polemics oppose the pious descendants of time and the determined inhabitants of space."

Social Prospect

A review of findings and prospect for further research is not complete for a book interested in space without consideration of that book's social prospect. The religious texts we have discussed continue to shape our societies, as does our analysis and use of them. And as we have seen, literary reproductions of space are not without real-world consequences.

Georges Tchalenko's *Villages Antiques de la Syrie du Nord*,[22] a three-volume French-language catalogue of archaeological, architectural, and inscriptional remains from northern Syria, published between 1953 and 1958, provides an instructive modern example of the dynamics at play in literary reproductions of space. Anyone who has seen this text can really only stand in awe. The documentation is not merely robust, it is aesthetically gorgeous. The maps and figures display the height of modernist artistic sensibility. The photographs are immaculate. The sheer cost that was needed to produce such a documentary marvel is staggering. And that itself allows the reader an avenue into the issues at stake in the spatial practice of this text. The only way that such a text could be produced is with enormous financial backing. Of course, during the period of its production, the French Empire governed Syria.[23] Government support for this work of scholarship was part of the program to establish the legitimacy of its rule. The funding of such research and documentary work was the way the French showed that they were the ones who truly understood the land, who truly appreciated it, who deserved it. It is the staking of a claim. The reproduction of northern Syria in a—ostensibly beautiful—modernist French scholarly idiom in *Villages Antiques* was fully colonial. And this phenomenon, of beauty concealing dynamics of power, should serve as a warning to any who read literary reproductions of space and of particular warning to those who produce texts themselves.

Among the many difficulties that arise regarding biblical scholarship (as was also the case for writers of scripture) is the danger of the misuse of your work. We have seen how many of the biblical authors produced beautiful visions of an ideal or compensatory home in response to experiences of homelessness or trauma, particularly marginal dwelling. While the just might be loath to deprive oppressed peoples of any resource that might ease their plight, including psychological or literary coping strategies for dealing with traumatized experiences of home (and fantasies of just punishment of enemies), the redeployment of these texts is not always to benign effect. It is possible that the veiled revolutionary language described in the *Parables of Enoch* contributed to the disastrous Galilee revolt of 6 CE in which thousands of dispossessed rebels were put to death.[24] We see the way, once Christianity became Constantinian, that church leaders like Athanasius put the condemnatory language of Revelation, originally

---

[22] Georges Tchalenko, *Villages Antiques de la Syrie du Nord: Le massif du Bélus à l'époque romaine*, 3 Vols. Bibliothèque archéologique et historique 50 (Paris: P. Geuthner, 1953–8).

[23] Though of course direct French governance ended before the final publication of the text, much of the background work was already completed.

[24] Led by Judas of Galilee, as mentioned in Josephus' *Ant.* 18.1.

intended for the empire and imperial collaborators, to work against the enemies of the, now imperially backed, church.[25]

The biblical texts of the oppressed have often become tools reemployed by the powerful through hegemonic means toward hegemonic ends. It does not matter to the oppressor that their use is an anachronistic misappropriation. As Jacques Lacan famously wrote, "truth is not in desire's nature."[26] White supremacists have nursed grievance, revenge, and desires for establishment of biblical paradigms derived from the writings of oppressed and marginalized peoples. Such neo-confederates, who fear to relinquish their power, tacitly acknowledge this reality, that oppressed peoples who dreamed ideal dreams of home and of punishment of their enemies (as in the book of Revelation), when no longer oppressed themselves, may redeploy dreams from the time of their oppression for revenge. Israeli settlers, in the twentieth-century Huleh Valley, played out elements of the drama proposed in our interpretation of the *Parables of Enoch* but with colonial success. They took the marginal lands and transformed them, valorizing them by dwelling in them, but at the expense of Palestinians. These are biblical paradigms, but they need not be considered exemplary.

We have seen now how several biblical authors responded to their experiences of dwelling, often reproducing beautiful and, at the time, *needed*, compensatory spaces. The impulse of many biblical readers will be to look to these texts as examples. It is then necessary to say, with respect to the prospective effect of this book, that the Bible itself holds more warnings than its readers are often wont to admit. In 1 Cor 10 Paul describes biblical precedents that have come before as τύποι or τυπικῶς for the community of believers.[27] But these words do not necessarily mean "positive example to be followed" as is often taught as the meaning of "type." Indeed, in 1 Corinthians these words are more clearly intended to suggest "warning" or "negative example." The Bible can be viewed as valuable and authoritative without requiring that its stories, characters, and dynamics be copied uncritically. For those who look to the Bible for guidance, there are good reasons to be cautious of over-replication: warnings are more common than examples.

And so, it is my hope that the analytical work which has preceded will enable further responsible thinking about space in early Jewish and Christian religious texts. But beyond this, I hope that this work will contribute to the confrontation of dynamics of oppression, which ideal imaginations of space have too often been used to conceal. And further, I hope that this book will foster a reimagining of our humble, beautiful world, our "shelter for dreams," that it might host a common future of solidarity with, healing of, and life for the hitherto marginalized among us. BLACK LIVES MATTER.

---

[25] Elaine Pagels, *Revelations: Visions, Prophecy, and Politics in the Book of Revelation* (New York: Viking, 2012), 135, 141–2, 143, 144–5, 165–6, 173.

[26] As translated by Tad DeLay in *Against: What Does the White Evangelical Want?* (Eugene: Cascade, 2019). In a sense, Bachelard's observations regarding the psychologies of dwelling can be understood as a subset of this general dictum.

[27] In 1 Cor 10:6 and 10:11 respectively.

Acknowledgments

This project would never have come to fruition without the efforts and kindness of so many lovely people. Regrettably my indebtedness to you all can hardly be repaid with elegant words and certainly less by my fumbling attempts at eloquence and forgetfulness of my indebtedness. I hope you will forgive this paltry return on your goodwill. Yet among the many who have shaped this work by their good deeds are these:

To George L. Parsenios, for excellent guidance in steering a major stage of this project to completion, for granting me a good deal of leeway in producing it, and for coming through in a pinch on numerous occasions. You "did me [many] a solid." Thank you. To James H. Charlesworth, who never failed to encourage me in my rather atypical academic interests, and who has so willingly offered ideas and dialogue on the subject of space and scripture: thank you. To Dale C. Allison, who has so routinely and gently offered wisdom, kindness, and supportive direction: thank you. To Esther da Costa Meyer, for introducing me to the work of Gaston Bachelard and for your effusive kindness in supporting my work: thank you. And to M. J. P. O'Connor, the only person besides my saintly wife who read this manuscript in its entirety before submission and probably shared more pizza with me than was good for him, who has been a constant friend and brother through graduate school and beyond: thank you.

To my student and faculty colleagues at Princeton Theological Seminary (PTS) and Princeton University, especially Nate Johnson, Jim Neumann, Steve Bohannon, Devlin McGuire, Heelee Joo, Jon Henry, Elena Dugan, Matthew Westermayer, Matthew D. C. Larsen, Stephen C. Russell, Dennis Olson, Ellen Charry, Lisa Bowens, Heath Dewrell, Clifton Black, Lindsey Scott Jodrey, Paul Rorem, Eric Barreto, Martha Himmelfarb, and Mark Smith, who read drafts and who offered critiques and suggestions over the years as this project came together: Thank you.

To the dedicated library and administrative staff of PTS who helped make it a more humane place and who worked so hard to support the students in their care, especially: Kate Skrebutanas, Jeremy Wallace, Rose Ellen Dunn, Betty Angelucci, Marie Grasso, Jan Ammon, Shawn Oliver, and Matt Spina: Thank you. To the members of the department of Biblical Studies at PTS who worked to welcome me and to create an environment of mutual support and respect, including, Jaq Lapsley, Ross Wagner, F. W. Dobbs-Allsopp, Elaine James, Mary Schmitt, Melly Howard, Hannah An, Chris Hooker, Joel Estes, Thomas Dixon, Justin Reed, Leslie Virnelson, Chauncey Handy, John Lewis, Ryan Armstrong, James Klotz, Kristin Wendland, and Ransom Portis: thank you. And especial thanks to Brian Rainey, who has so resolutely and publicly stood for justice in the face of the ongoing challenges of our time and place. Thank you for your inspiration and example.

To Jack Tannous and Elaine Pagels of Princeton University, who supported me in their collegiality, kindness, and invitation to share in their work: thank you. To the faculty of

Dartmouth College who shaped the early trajectory of my studies, including Dick Birnie, James Tatum, Susan Ackerman, Dale Turner, and Charles H. Stinson, but especially Frank Magilligan, who has been an excellent mentor in geographic thinking even as he may yet avow that he doesn't "do" living things: thank you. And to my earliest academic mentors in ancient history Jim Dubois and Merrill Dussault: Thank you both for stoking my interest at a young age. I know you've done the same for many others as well.

Early versions of research ideas that later became part of this book were presented at a number of Society of Biblical Literature Annual Meeting program sessions including the "Space, Place, and Lived Experience in Antiquity" group (2017, 2019, 2020), the "Islands, Islanders, and Scripture" group (2017), the "Mind, Society, and Religion: Cognitive Science Approaches to the Biblical World" group (2018), the "Social History of Formative Christianity and Judaism" group (2019), and the "Pauline Epistles" group (2020). Many thanks to the conveners, respondents, and participants for their helpful feedback, especially: Jaime L. Waters, Eric C. Smith, H.-G. Camilla Belfon, Jutta Jokiranta, Olivia Rahmsdorf, Mika Ahuvia, Erin Runions, Devorah Schoenfeld, Arminta Fox, Laura Dingeldein, Christian A. Eberhart, Paula Fredriksen, and Matthew Novenson. Additional material that also became part of this project was presented at the PTS Graduate Student Conference on "Christianity and the Body" in February 2018 and "The Bible and Cyprus" Conference in Larnaca, Cyprus, in June 2018. To the members of the Foundation on Judaism and Christian Origins for funding my participation in the Cyprus conference, for their generous hospitality, and particularly to Lamar Barden: thank you. Thanks also to the participants and respondents from those conferences (not otherwise mentioned here) and for their helpful feedback including: Rona Avissar Lewis, William S. Campbell, Kathy Ehrensperger, Avraham Faust, Kamil Sari, Anders K. Petersen, and Yii-Jan Lin.

To the Trustees of Princeton Theological Seminary and the Federal Government of the United States of America for directly funding this research and to the Mercer County Board of Social Services for indirectly funding this research. Thank you.

Many thanks to Kyra N. Pruszinski for her beautiful renderings of the figures for the book, and to Steve Bohannon for his production assistance, particularly amid the heightened difficulties of working during a pandemic. And to Dominic Mattos, Sarah Blake, Jessica Anderson, Suriya Rajasekar, Karthiga Sithanandam, and their team at T&T Clark: Thank you for all your work to bring this book to publication.

To all those who have offered friendship and kindness along the way including (but not limited to) Dana Shulman, Julia Ames, Kristen McHenry, Marla Abramson, Emily Meek, David Halbert, Greg Dixon, Peter Hyde, Curtis Ames, Sara Lipka, Colin Peden, Mike Jasick, Dirkje Legerstee, Brett Golden, Chris and Lara Fowler, Carter Wray, Jamie Shandro, Margot Knight, Kate Knight, Joseph Brown, Andy and Emily Schmidt, Katie McCarthy, Dan Becker, Matt and Erin Hood, Mike and Cheryl Pirozzi, Melissa Wise, Aliette Frank, Melanie Watts, Adam Chavez, Sarah and Dan Taylor Black, Dan Stulac, Stevie Clifton, Katie Young Evans, Vera Chokalingham, Clarissa Werre, Nick Koshnick, Erin Horbach, Eli Burakian, Rich Dickinson, Ben Guaraldi, John Brett, Joel Vikre, P. Joshua Griffin, Jesse and Liz Tichenor, Tyler Stahl, Stella Baer, Tim Neuschwander, Rusty Cheney, Ben Zabar, Brian and Marissa Feldman, Nils Ericson, Adin Kawate, Erica Wygonik and Brian Porter, Justin Neuman and Walker Holmes,

James and Tiffany Gregory, Drew and Milly-Ellen Strayer, Truxton Meadows, Geoff and Elizabeth Bennett, Sarah Messner, Riley Lochridge, Sean and Michelle Kersey, Ben and Libby Hunt, Blake Miller, Maura Pritchard, Jackie Chamberlain, Kari Limmer, Laura Curtis, Khoa Ha, Jocelyn Leavitt, Steve Sockol, Evelyn Mervine, Christena Cleveland, Cullen Roberts, Christina Churchill, Essien Ukanna, Hallie Treadway, Adam Holt, Peter and Betsy Rice, David Quaid, Bente Shoen, Allegra Love, Jean Hamlin, Alex Steinberg, Jeff Beardsley, John Beardsley, Nick Gottlieb, Laura Jorgensen, Susan Ferraro, Laura Andreae, Chris Martin, Dana Daugherty, Tim and Christa Loetscher, Allison Forbes, Kurt Nelson, Nicole and George Cannizzaro, Nathan Empsall, Karen and Andy Hill, Lindsey Holzberger, Isaiah Berg, Haley and John Shellito, Ariel and Nathanial Slater, Sarah Gaventa, Jenny Replogle, Peter French, Austin and Mark Shelley, Clare and John Rose, Katherine Rohrer and John Sully, Lauren Larsen, Jeannette Tannous, Patricia McGaughey and Jacob Dlamini, Linda Noel and Scott McGoldrick, Tara Sikma, Nathan and Celeste Arrington, Kristin and Cory Isaacs, Mark and Janine Edwards, Stephanie Merryfield, Caitlin Johnson, Nathalie Portis, Kevin Ireland, Adam and Kendall Wert, Brandon Allen, Felipe Ocampo, Aron Tillema, Aaron Neff, Allie Graham and Ben Hicks, Luke Zerra and Laura DiPanfilo, Tom Seat, Kate and Kyle Unruh, Sara and Adam DeVries, Kevin Vandiver, Phil and Jen Forness, Sarah and Marc Hong, Jamey and Naomi Walters, Jess Rigel, Ry and Marcia Siggelkow, Francisco Palaez and Brandy Alexander, Lawrence Anglin, Rory Chambers, Nick and Mary Hopman, Miles and Kayla Hopgood, Yedea Walker, Nate and Janel Stucky, Catherine Williams, Connor Fluharty, Kermit and Antoinette Moss, Mark and Mollie Dixon, Nicola Whyte, Ari Lamm, Bonnie Lin, Jean and Andrea Chaumont, Nikki Zimmerman, Nayamka and Harlan Redmond, Karin Mitchell, Marie and Hector Herrera, Jason and Martha Myers, Chris McNabb, Melissa Florer-Bixler, Carson and Courtney Washington, J. J. and Ebony Flag, Charles Gilmer, Anthony Bateza, Kara Slade, Danny Velez, Vinod and Kavita Gnanaraj, Lesley and Anibal Pella-Woo, Jon and Valerie Brewer, Alex Kato, John Allison, Jarad Legard, Cambria and Jared Kaltwasser, Alyssa Evans, Ryan and Amelia Irmer, Joanne and Paul Epply-Schmidt, Christina Jeanes, Kellie Silva, Sonia Waters, Paul and Heather Olson, Tara and Derek Woodard-Lehman, Isak de Vries, Brady Beard, Erin and Steve Jacobson, Calli Micale, Rashad and Brandi Grove, Daniel Pedersen, Mark Taylor, Lukata Mjumbe, Samuel Marquez and Merari Candelario, Rachel Stuart, Andrew Peterson, Stephanie Mota Thurston, Dan and Betsy Mazzucco, Michael Toy, Erich and Ashley Kussman, Kris and Rachel Ryan, Sylvia Temmer, Steve Isham, Hannah Johnson, Kelsey Lambright, Sarah Stewart Kroeker, Briana Wong, Emily Dumler, Jordan Loewen, Jeremiah Barker, Emily Chesley, Jenna Reed, Rachel Douglass, Alisa Unell, Mary Hayes, Mackenzie Dull, Craig Rubano, Kevin Wolfe, Maggie Elwell, Kevin Vollrath, Len Scales, Emily Wilton, Chelsea Williams, and especially to Rabbi Ed Boraz, Richard Crocker, Dale and Laurie Edwards, and Paul Jeanes: thank you. And to Andrew Scales, my dear brother, "*vox clamantis in deserto*," who has also eaten more pizza[1] with me than was good for him. Thank you.

To my Mom and Dad, Ellen Rivoir and Glenn Pruszinski. Thank you mom, for raising me with a concern for justice. Dad, thank you for influencing me with your

---

[1] Thanks to Ramunto's Pizza of Hanover, New Hampshire, and to Iano's Pizza (RIP) and Princeton Pi (RIP) of Princeton, New Jersey.

patience and for the study of religion and geography. Thank you both for loving me and making a home that could shape me for good. To Tom and Jill Cullen, Anna and David Reed, Cory and Caitlin Brown, Diane and Debbie Nixon, thank you for all your kindness over the years and your love for our family. To Kyra, Teddy, Joseph, and Balian Pruszinski, my beloved children. Thank you for putting up with a good deal more dinnertime conversation about space, history, scripture, and justice than any of your peers likely have had to do. I love you always! Don't forget!

> If the study to which you apply yourself has a tendency to weaken your affections, and to destroy your taste for those simple pleasures in which no alloy can possibly mix, then that study is certainly unlawful, that is to say, not befitting the human mind. If this rule were always observed; if no man allowed any pursuit whatsoever to interfere with the tranquility of his [healthy] domestic affections, Greece had not been enslaved; Caesar would have spared his country; America would have been discovered more gradually; and the empires of Mexico and Peru had not been destroyed. But I forget that I am moralizing … and your looks remind me to proceed.[2]

It is a privilege to me to know that our home together will always be a part of you and a part of your shelter for dreams.

And, above all, to my beloved wife Emily Sarah Pruszinski, my dearest friend and longest-suffering editor, the best reader and writer in the family. Thank you for the great blessing it is to share in the labor of love of making our home and life together. And thank you, for the comparatively smaller thing which is having made this book possible. It would never have happened without you.

Cohaereamus, amici.
Jolyon G. R. Pruszinski

---

[2] Mary Shelley, *Frankenstein or The Modern Prometheus: The 1818 Text* (Oxford: Oxford University Press, 1993), 37–38.

Bibliography

Aalen, Sverre. "'Reign' and 'House' in the Kingdom of God in the Gospels." *NTS* 8 (1962): 215–40.
Ahuvia, Mika, and Alexander Kocar, eds. *Placing Ancient Texts: The Ritual and Rhetorical Use of Space*. Texts and Studies in Ancient Judaism 174. Tübingen: Mohr Siebeck, 2018.
Ajer, Peter C. *The Death of Jesus and the Politics of Place in the Gospel of John*. Eugene, OR: Pickwick, 2016.
Algra, K. *Concepts of Space in Greek Thought*. New York: Brill, 1995.
Allen, Jon G. *Coping with Trauma: Hope through Understanding*. 2nd ed. Washington, DC: American Psychiatric Publishing, Inc., 2004.
Allison, Dale C., Jr. *Constructing Jesus: Memory, Imagination, and History*. Grand Rapids, MI: Baker Academic, 2010.
Anderson, Gary A. "Sacrifice and Sacrificial Offerings (Old Testament)." Pages 870–86 in *The Anchor Bible Dictionary*, Vol. 5. Edited by David N. Freedman. New York: Doubleday, 1992.
Anderson, Robert T. "The Elusive Samaritan Temple." *The Biblical Archaeologist* 54.2 (1991): 104–7.
Anselmus Cantuariensis Archiepiscopi Opera Omnia, Vol. 1. Edited by F. S. Schmitt. Edinburgh: Thomas Nelson & Sons, 1946.
Ashton, John. *Understanding the Fourth Gospel*. 2nd ed. Oxford: Oxford University Press, 2007.
Attridge, Harold. "Reflections on Research into Q." *Semeia* 55 (1992): 225–34.
Augustine of Hippo. *The Trinity*. 2nd ed. Translated by Edmund Hill. Brooklyn, NY: New City Press, 2012.
Aune, David E. *Revelation*. Vols. 52a–c of *Word Biblical Commentary*. Dallas, TX: Thomas Nelson, 1997.
Aune, David E. "The Apocalypse of John and Palestinian Jewish Apocalyptic." Pages 169–92 in *The Pseudepigrapha and Christian Origins*. Edited by Gerbern S. Oegema and James H. Charlesworth. New York: T&T Clark, 2008.
Aviam, Mordechai. "Two Roman Roads in the Galilee." Pages 133–8 in *Jews, Pagans, and Christians in the Galilee: 25 Years of Archaeological Excavations and Surveys. Hellenistic to Byzantine Periods*. Edited by Mordechai Aviam. Land of Galilee 1. Rochester, NY: University of Rochester Press, 2004.
Aviam, Mordechai. "The Decorated Stone from the Synagogue at Migdal, A Holistic Interpretation and a Glimpse into the Life of Galilean Jews at the Time of Jesus." *Novum Testamentum* 55 (2013): 205–20.
Ayers, Lewis. "The Christological Context of Augustine's De Trinitate XIII: Toward Relocating Books VIII–XV." *Augustinian Studies* 29.1 (1998): 111–39.
Bachelard, Gaston. *The Poetics of Space*. Translated by Maria Jolas. Boston, MA: Beacon Press, 1994.
Bassler, Jouette. "The Galileans: A Neglected Factor in Johannine Community Research." *CBQ* 43 (1981): 243–57.

Bauer, Walter. *A Greek-English Lexicon of the New Testament and Other Early Christian Literature, 3rd Edition (BDAG)*. Revised and edited by Frederick William Danker et al. Chicago, IL and London: University of Chicago Press, 2000.

Baumgarten, Joseph M., and Daniel R. Schwartz. "Damascus Document (CD)." Pages 4–58 in *The Dead Sea Scrolls: Hebrew, Aramaic, and Greek Texts with English Translations, Volume 2; Damascus Document, War Scroll and Related Documents*. Edited by James H. Charlesworth. Tübingen and Louisville: Mohr Siebeck and Westminster John Knox, 1995.

Baur, Ferdinand C. *Kritische Untersuchungen über die kanonische Evangelien*. Tübingen: F. L. Fues, 1847.

Bell, Richard H. "Sacrifice and Christology in Paul." *Journal of Theological Studies* 53.1 (2002): 1–27.

Bernier, Jonathan. *Aposynagōgos and the Historical Jesus in John: Rethinking the Historicity of the Johannine Expulsion Passages*. Biblical Interpretation Series 122. Leiden: Brill, 2013.

Berquist, Jon L. "Critical Spatiality and the Construction of the Ancient World." Pages 14–29 in *"Imagining" Biblical Worlds: Studies in Spatial, Social and Historical Constructs in Honor of James W. Flanagan*. Edited by David M. Gunn, and Paula M. McNutt. JSOTSS 359. Sheffield, UK: Sheffield Academic Press, 2002.

Berquist, Jon L., and Claudia V. Camp, eds. *Constructions of Space I: Theory, Geography, and Narrative*. LHBOTS 481. New York: T&T Clark, 2007.

Berquist, Jon L., and Claudia V. Camp, eds. *Constructions of Space II: The Biblical City and Other Imagined Spaces*. LHBOTS 490. New York: T&T Clark, 2008.

Black, Michael. *The Book of Enoch or 1 Enoch: A New English Translation*. Leiden: Brill, 1985.

Boismard, M.-É. *Moses or Jesus: An Essay in Johannine Christology*. Translated by B. T. Viviano. Minneapolis, MN: Fortress, 1993.

Bowens, Lisa M. *An Apostle in Battle: Paul and Spiritual Warfare in 2 Corinthians 12: 1-10*. WUNT 2/433. Tübingen: Mohr Siebeck, 2017.

Brock, Rita Nakashima. *Journeys by Heart: A Christology of Erotic Power*. New York: Crossroad, 1988.

Brown, Peter. "The Rise and Function of the Holy Man in Late Antiquity." *The Journal of Roman Studies* 61 (1971): 80–101.

Brown, Peter. *The Cult of the Saints: Its Rise and Function in Latin Christianity*. Chicago, IL and London: University of Chicago Press, 1981.

Brown, Raymond E. *The Gospel According to John*, Vols. 1 & 2. Garden City, NY: Doubleday, 1966 & 1970.

Brown, Raymond E. *The Community of the Beloved Disciple: The Life, Loves, and Hates of an Individual in New Testament Times*. New York and Mahwah: Paulist Press, 1979.

Bull, Robert J. "The Excavation of Tell er-Ras on Mt. Gerizim." *Biblical Archaeologist* 31 (1968): 58–72.

Bultmann, Rudolph. *The Gospel of John: A Commentary*. Translated by G. Beasley-Murray, R. W. N. Hoare, and J. K. Riches. Philadelphia, PA: Westminster, 1971. Translation of *Das Evangelium des Johannes*. KEK 2. Göttingen: Vandenhoeck & Ruprecht, 1941. With the supplement of 1966.

Burge, Gary M. *Jesus and the Land: The New Testament Challenge to "Holy Land" Theology*. Grand Rapids, MI: Baker Academic, 2010.

Butcher, Kevin. *Coinage in Roman Syria: Northern Syria 64BC-AD253*. Royal Numismatic Society 34. Ann Arbor, MI: University of Michigan Press, 2004.

Charles, Robert Henry. *The Book of Enoch the Prophet*. London: Oxford University Press, 1912.
Charlesworth, James H. *The History of the Rechabites, Volume 1: The Greek Recension*. Chico, CA: Scholars Press, 1982.
Charlesworth, James H. "The Parables of Enoch and the Apocalypse of John." Pages 193–242 in *The Pseudepigrapha and Christian Origins*. Edited by Gerbern S. Oegema and James H. Charlesworth. New York: T&T Clark, 2008.
Charlesworth, James H. "The Date and Provenience of the Parables of Enoch." Pages 37–57 in *Parables of Enoch: A Paradigm Shift*. Edited by Darrell L. Bock and James H. Charlesworth. New York: T&T Clark, 2013.
Charlesworth, James H. "Did Jesus Know the Traditions in the Parables of Enoch." Pages 173–217 in *Parables of Enoch: A Paradigm Shift*. Edited by Darrell L. Bock and James H. Charlesworth. New York: T&T Clark, 2013.
Charlesworth, James H. *Jesus as Mirrored in John: The Genius in the New Testament*. London: T&T Clark, 2018.
Charlesworth, James H. "Can Archaeology Help Us See Jesus' Shadows in the Gospel of John?" Pages 168–86 in *Jesus Research: The Gospel of John in Historical Inquiry*. Edited by James H. Charlesworth with Jolyon G. R. Pruszinski. London: T&T Clark, 2019.
Charlesworth, James H., with Jolyon G. R. Pruszinski, eds. *Jesus Research: The Gospel of John in Historical Inquiry*. Jewish and Christian Texts 26. London: T&T Clark, 2019.
Charlesworth, James H., and Jolyon G. R. Pruszinski, eds. *Cyprus within the Biblical World: Are Borders Barriers?* Jewish and Christian Texts 32. London: T&T Clark, 2021.
Charlesworth, James H., and Mordechai Aviam. "Reconstructing First Century Galilee: Reflections on Ten Major Problems." Pages 103–37 in *Jesus Research: New Methodologies and Perceptions, The Second Princeton-Prague Symposium on Jesus Research, Princeton 2007*. Edited by James H. Charlesworth with Brian Rhea and Petr Pokorný. Grand Rapids, MI and London: Eerdmans, 2014.
Clark, M., and M. Sleeman. "Writing the Earth, Righting the Earth: Committed Presuppositions and the Geographical Imagination." Pages 49–59 in *New Words, New Worlds: Reconceptualising Social and Cultural Geography*. Edited by C. Philo. Aberystwyth, Wales: Cambrian, 1991.
Cohen Stuart, G. H. *The Struggle in Man between Good and Evil: An Inquiry into the Origin of the Rabbinic Concept of Yeser Hara*. Kampen: J. H. Kok, 1984.
Collins, John J. *The Apocalyptic Imagination: An Introduction to the Jewish Matrix of Christianity*. New York: Crossroad, 1987.
Coloe, Mary L. *God Dwells with Us: Temple Symbolism in the Fourth Gospel*. Collegeville, MN: The Liturgical Press, 2001.
Coloe, Mary L. *Dwelling in the Household of God: Johannine Ecclesiology and Spirituality*. Collegeville, MN: The Liturgical Press, 2007.
Corliss, William R. *Rare Halos, Mirages, Anomalous Rainbows and Related Electromagnetic Phenomena: A Catalog of Geophysical Anomalies*. Glen Arm, MD: The Sourcebook Project, 1984.
Cross, Frank Moore. *Canaanite Myth and Hebrew Epic*. Cambridge, MA: Harvard University Press, 1973.
Culpepper, R. Alan. *Anatomy of the Fourth Gospel: A Study in Literary Design*. Philadelphia, PA: Fortress, 1983.
Culpepper, R. Alan. *The Gospel and Letters of John*. Nashville, TN: Abingdon, 1998.
Dahl, Nils A. "Anamnesis: Memory and Commemoration in Early Christianity." Pages 11–29 in *Jesus in the Memory of the Early Church*. Edited by Nils Dahl. Minneapolis, MN: Augsburg, 1976.

Daise, Michael. "Ritual Transference and Johannine Identity." *Annali di storia dell'esegesi* 27 (2010): 45–51.
Davies, W. D. *The Gospel and the Land: Early Christianity and Jewish Territorial Doctrine.* Berkeley, CA: University of California Press, 1974.
Davila, James R. "Is the Story of Zosimus Really a Jewish Composition?" Paper presented in the Pseudepigrapha Group at the Annual Meeting of the SBL, Atlanta, GA, November 24, 2003. https://www.st-andrews.ac.uk/divinity/rt/otp/abstracts/zosimus/
de Boer, M. C. "Paul and Apocalyptic Theology." Pages 345–83 in *Origins of Apocalypticism in Judaism and Christianity*. Edited by John J. Collins. New York: Continuum, 1998.
de Jong, Irene F., ed. *Space in Ancient Greek Literature: Studies in Ancient Greek Narrative*, Vol. 3. Mnemosyne Supplements 339. Leiden: Brill, 2012.
de Veer, Gerrit. *The Three Voyages of William Barents to the Arctic Regions: 1594, 1595, and 1596.* Translated by Charles T. Beke. London: The Hakylut Society, 1876.
DeLay, Tad. *Against: What Does the White Evangelical Want?* Eugene, OR: Cascade, 2019.
Dillman, August. *Liber Henoch Aethiopice, ad quinque codicum fidem editus, cum variis lectionibus.* Leipzig: Vogel, 1851. Reprinted as Dillman, August. *The Ethiopic Text of 1 Enoch.* Ancient Texts and Translations. Eugene, OR: Wipf & Stock, 2005.
Dillman, August. *Lexicon linguae aethiopicae cum indice latino.* Lipsiae: T. O. Weigel, 1865. Reprinted, New York: Ungar, 1955.
Dodd, C. H. *The Interpretation of the Fourth Gospel.* Cambridge: Cambridge University Press, 1968.
Donner, Herbert, and Wolfgang Röllig. *Kanaanäische und aramäische Inschriften.* 2nd ed. Wiesbaden: Harrassowitz, 1966–9.
Duff, Paul B. *Who Rides the Beast? Prophetic Rivalry and the Rhetoric of Crisis in the Churches of the Apocalypse.* Oxford: Oxford University Press, 2001.
Dunn, James D. G. "Paul's Understanding of the Death of Jesus." Pages 125–41 in *Reconciliation and Hope. New Testament Essays on Atonement and Eschatology Presented to L.L. Morris on His 60th Birthday*. Edited by Robert Banks. Carlisle: The Paternoster Press, 1974.
Du Roy, Oliver. *L'Intelligence de la Foi en la Trinité selon saint Augustin, genèse de sa théologie trinitaire jusqu'en 391.* Paris: Études augustiniennes, 1966.
Eberhart, Christian A. "To Atone or Not to Atone: Remarks on the Day of Atonement Rituals According to Leviticus 16 and the Meaning of Atonement." Pages 197–231 in *Sacrifice, Cult, and Atonement in Early Judaism and Christianity: Constituents and Critique.* Edited by Henrietta L. Wiley and Christian A. Eberhart. Resources for Biblical Study 85. Atlanta: SBL Press, 2017.
Engberg-Pedersen, Troels. *Cosmology and Self in the Apostle Paul: The Material Spirit.* Oxford: Oxford University Press, 2010.
Elliot, John H. *A Home for the Homeless: A Sociological Exegesis of 1 Peter, Its Situation and Strategy.* Philadelphia, PA: Fortress, 1981.
Evans, Rhianon. M. "Forma Orbis: Geography, Ethnography and Shaping the Roman Empire." PhD diss., University of Southern California, 1999.
Fauconnier, Gilles, and Mark Turner. *The Way We Think: Conceptual Blending and the Mind's Hidden Complexities.* New York: Basic Books, 2002.
Flanagan, James W. "Ancient Perceptions of Space/Perceptions of Space/Perceptions of Ancient Space." Pages 15–43 in *The Social World of the Hebrew Bible: Twenty-Five Years of the Social Sciences in the Academy*. Edited by R. A. Simkins and S. L. Cook. *Semeia* 87. Atlanta, GA: Society of Biblical Literature, 1999.
Flanagan, James W. "Mapping the Biblical World: Perceptions of Space in Ancient Southwestern Asia." Pages 1–18 in *Mappa Mundi: Mapping Culture/Mapping the World.* Edited by J. Murray. Ontario: Humanities Research Group, 2001.

Flemming, Johannes. *Das Buch Henoch: Äthiopischer Text*. Leipzig: Hinrichs, 1902.
Flusser, David. *Jesus*. Translated by R. Walls. New York: Herder and Herder, 1969.
Flusser, David. "The Four Empires in the Fourth Sibyl and in the Book of Daniel." *Israel Oriental Studies* 2 (1978): 148–75.
Ford, J. Massyngberde. *Revelation: A New Translation with Introduction and Commentary*. Anchor Bible 38. Garden City, NY: Doubleday, 1975.
Fortna, Robert. "Theological Use of Locale in the Fourth Gospel." *ATRSup* 3 (1974): 95–112.
Foucault, Michel. "Of Other Spaces." Translated by Jay Miskowiec. *Diacritics* 16 (1986): 22–7.
Fox, Robin Lane. *Travelling Heroes: In the Epic Age of Homer*. New York: Vintage Books, 2008.
Frey, Jörg. *Theology and History in the Fourth Gospel: Tradition and Narration*. Waco, TX: Baylor University Press, 2018.
Gager, John. *Reinventing Paul*. Oxford: Oxford University Press, 2000.
Gathercole, Simon. *Defending Substitution: An Essay on Atonement in Paul*. Grand Rapids, MI: Baker Academic, 2015.
George, M. *Israel's Tabernacle as Social Space*. Atlanta, GA: Society of Biblical Literature, 2009.
George, M., ed. *Constructions of Space IV: Further Developments in Examining Ancient Israel's Social Space*. LHBOTS 569. New York: T&T Clark, 2013.
Gibson, Shimon. *The Final Days of Jesus: The Archaeological Evidence*. New York: HarperCollins, 2010.
Gormley, Joan F. "The Cursed Christ: Mediterranean Expulsion Rituals and Pauline Soteriology." *CBQ* 59.4 (1997): 780–2.
Grey, Eleanor. "Beyond the Temple: Blurring the Boundaries of 'Sacred Space.'" Pages 109–18 in *Proceedings of the Fourteenth Annual Theoretical Roman Archaeology Conference, Durham 2004*. Edited by J. Bruhn, B. Croxford, and D. Grigoropoulos. Oxford: Oxbow Books, 2005.
Hays, Richard B. *Reading Backwards: Figural Christology and the Fourfold Gospel Witness*. Waco, TX: Baylor University Press, 2014.
Hill, Edmund. "St. Augustine's *De Trinitate*: The Doctrinal Significance of Its Structure." *Revue des Études Augustiniennes* 19 (1973): 277–86.
Himmelfarb, Martha. *Ascent to Heaven in Jewish and Christian Apocalypses*. New York: Oxford University Press, 1993.
Himmelfarb, Martha. *A Kingdom of Priests: Ancestry and Merit in Ancient Judaism*. Philadelphia, PA: University of Pennsylvania Press, 2006.
Himmelfarb, Martha. *The Apocalypse: A Brief History*. Malden, MA: Wiley-Blackwell, 2010.
Hoffman, Andreas G. *Das Buch Henoch: In vollständiger Übersetzung mit fortlaufendem Commentar, ausführlicher Einleitung und erläuternden Excursen*. Jena: Croeker, 1833–1838.
Hogue, Timothy. "An Image on the Stele or a Ghost in the Shell? A Cognitive Scientific Approach to Katumuwa's *nbš*." Paper presented at the Annual Meeting of the SBL, Denver, CO, November 17, 2018.
Holloway, Paul A. "Left Behind: Jesus' Consolation of His Disciples in John 13,31-17,26." *ZNW* 96 (2005): 1–34.
Horsley, Richard A. *Revolt of the Scribes: Resistance and Apocalyptic Origins*. Minneapolis, MN: Fortress, 2010.

Hurtado, Larry. "Two Case Studies in Earliest Christological Readings of Biblical Texts." Pages 3–23 in *All That the Prophets Have Declared: The Appropriation of Scripture in the Emergence of Christianity*. Edited by Matthew R. Malcom. Milton Keynes, UK: Paternoster, 2015.

Isaac, Ephraim. "1 (Ethiopic Apocalypse of) Enoch: A New Translation and Introduction." Pages 5–89 in *The Old Testament Pseudepigrapha: Volume I, Apocalyptic Literature and Testaments*. Edited by James H. Charlesworth. Peabody, MA: Hendrickson Publishers, 1983.

Janowski, Bernd. *Sühne als Heilsgeschehen: Studien zur Sühnetheologie der Priesterschrift und zur Wurzel KPR im Alten Orient und im Alten Testament*. WMANT 55. Neukirchen-Vluyn: Neukirchener Verlag, 1982.

Johnson, Elizabeth A. *She Who Is: The Mystery of God in Feminist Theological Discourse*. New York: Crossroad Publishing, 2018.

Käsemann, Ernst. *Perspectives on Paul*. Translated by Margaret Kohl. Philadelphia, PA: Fortress, 1971.

Keck, Leander E. "Derivation as Destiny: 'Of-ness' in Johannine Christology, Anthropology, and Soteriology." Pages 274–88 in *Exploring the Gospel of John: In Honor of D. Moody Smith*. Edited by R. Alan Culpepper and Carl Clifton Black. Louisville, KY: Westminster John Knox, 1996.

Keener, Craig S. "The Function of Johannine Pneumatology in the Context of Late First-Century Judaism." PhD diss., Duke University, 1991.

Klauck, Hans-Josef. "Kultische Symbolsprache bei Paulus." Pages 348–58 in *Gemeinde Amt Sakrament: Neutestamentliche Perspektiven*. Edited by Hans-Josef Klauck. Würzburg: Echter, 1989.

Klauck, Hans-Josef. "Sacrifice and Sacrificial Offerings (New Testament)." Translated by Reginald H. Fuller. Pages 886–91 in *The Anchor Bible Dictionary*, Vol. 5. Edited by David N. Freedman et al. New York: Doubleday, 1992.

Klausner, Joseph. *Jesus of Nazareth: His Life, Times, and Teaching*. Translated by H. Danby. New York: Macmillan, 1944.

Klijn, A. F. J. "2 (Syriac Apocalypse of) Baruch: A New Translation and Introduction." Pages 615–52 in *The Old Testament Pseudepigrapha: Volume I, Apocalyptic Literature and Testaments*. Edited by James H. Charlesworth. Peabody, MA: Hendrickson Publishers, 1983.

Knibb, Michael. *The Ethiopic Book of Enoch: A New Edition in the Light of the Aramaic Dead Sea Fragments. Vol. 2: Introduction, Translation and Commentary*. Oxford: Clarendon Press, 1978.

Koestler, Arthur. *The Act of Creation*. London: Hutchinson & Co. Ltd, 1964.

Kovacs, Judith, and Christopher Rowland. *Revelation: The Apocalypse of Jesus Christ*. Oxford: Blackwell, 2004.

Kundsin, Karl. *Topologische Überlieferungsstoffe in Johannes-Evangelium*. Göttingen: Dandenhoek and Ruprecht, 1925.

Kurby, Christopher A., and Jeffrey M. Zacks. "Segmentation in the Perception and Memory of Events." *Trends in Cognitive Sciences* 12 (2008): 72–9.

Kysar, Robert. *Augsburg Commentary on the New Testament: John*. Minneapolis, MN: Augsburg, 1986.

Lambdin, Thomas O. *Introduction to Classical Ethiopic (Ge'ez)*. Harvard Semitic Studies 24. Missoula, MT: Scholars Press, 1978.

Landau, Brent. "'One Drop of Salvation from the House of Majesty': Universal Revelation, Human Mission and Mythical Geography in the Syriac Revelation of the Magi." Pages

83–104 in *The Levant: Crossroads of Late Antiquity. History, Religion and Archaeology*. Edited by Ellen Bradshaw Aitken and John M. Fossey. Leiden and Boston, MA: Brill, 2013.

Larsen, Matthew D. C. *Early Christians and Incarceration: A Cultural History*. New Haven, CT: Yale University Press, forthcoming.

Laurence, Richard. *The Book of Enoch the Prophet: Translated from an Ethiopic Manuscript in the Bodleian Library*. London: Kegan, Paul, Trench & Co., 1883.

Lefebvre, Henri. *The Production of Space*. Translated by Donald Nicholson-Smith. Malden, MA: Blackwell, 1991.

Lehn, Waldemar H. "The Novaya Zemlya Effect: An Arctic Mirage." *Journal of the Optical Society of America* 69 (1979): 776–81.

Liddell, Henry G., and Robert Scott. *A Greek-English Lexicon: A New Edition*. Revised by Henry S. Jones with Roderick McKenzie et al. Oxford: Clarendon, 1925–40.

Lightfoot, Robert H. *Locality and Doctrine in the Gospels*. London: Hodder & Stoughton, 1938.

Lightfoot, Robert H. *St. John's Gospel: A Commentary*. Oxford: Clarendon Press, 1956.

Lightfoot, John. *A Commentary on the New Testament from the Talmud and Hebraica, Vol. 1: Place Names in the Gospels*. Translated by John Strype. Peabody, MA: Hendrickson Publishers, 1997.

Madec, Goulven. "Christus, scientia et sapientia nostra: le principe de cohérence de la doctrine augustinienne." *Recherches Augustiniennes* 10 (1975): 77–85.

Magdalino, Paul. "The History of the Future and Its Uses: Prophecy, Policy and Propaganda." Pages 3–34 in *The Making of Byzantine History, Studies Dedicated to Donald M. Nicol*. Edited by Roderick Beaton and Charlotte Roueché. London: Variorun, 1993.

Malbon, Elisabeth S. *Narrative Space and Mythic Meaning in Mark*. Biblical Seminar 13. Sheffield: JSOT Press, 1986.

Malina, Bruce J., and Richard L. Rohrbaugh. *Social-Science Commentary on the Gospel of John*. Minneapolis, MN: Fortress, 1998.

Maly, Kenneth. "*A Sand County Almanac*: Through Anthropogenic to Ecogenic Thinking." Pages 289–301 in *Rethinking Nature: Essays in Environmental Philosophy*. Edited by Bruce V. Foltz and Robert Frodeman. Bloomington and Indianapolis, IN: Indiana University Press, 2004.

Marcus, Joel. "*Birkat Ha-Minim* Revisited." *NTS* 55 (2009): 523–51.

Margalit, Baruch. "The Geographical Setting of the AQHT Story and Its Ramifications." Pages 131–58 in *Ugarit in Retrospect: Fifty Years of Ugarit and Ugaritic*. Edited by D. G. Young. Winona Lake, IN: Eisenbrauns, 1981.

Martin, Dale. *The Corinthian Body*. New Haven, CT: Yale University Press, 1995.

Martyn, J. Louis. *History and Theology in the Fourth Gospel*. 2nd ed. Nashville, TN: Abingdon, 1979.

Martyn, J. Louis. "Apocalyptic Antinomies in Paul's Letter to the Galatians." *NTS* 31 (1985): 410–24.

Matthews, Victor H. "Physical Space, Imagined Space, and 'Lived Space' in Ancient Israel." *Biblical Theology Bulletin* 33.1 (2003): 12–23.

McLean, Bradley H. "The Absence of an Atoning Sacrifice in Paul's Soteriology." *New Testament Studies* 38 (1992): 531–53.

McLean, Bradley H. *The Cursed Christ: Mediterranean Expulsion Rituals and Pauline Soteriology*. JSNTSup 126. Sheffield: Sheffield Academic Press, 1996.

McWhirter, Jocelyn. *The Bridegroom Messiah and the People of God: Marriage in the Fourth Gospel*. SNTS Monograph 138. Cambridge: Cambridge University Press, 2006.
Meeks, Wayne A. "Galilee and Judea in the Fourth Gospel." *JBL* 85.2 (1966): 159–69.
Meeks, Wayne A. "The Man from Heaven in Johannine Sectarianism." *JBL* 91.1 (1972): 44–72.
Meeks, Wayne A. *The First Urban Christians: The Social World of the Apostle Paul*. 2nd ed. New Haven, CT: Yale University Press, 2003.
Merleau-Ponty, Maurice. *Phenomenology of Perception*. Translated by Colin Smith. London: Routledge, 1962.
Metzger, Bruce. "The Fourth Book of Ezra with the Four Additional Chapters: A New Translation and Introduction." Pages 516–60 in *The Old Testament Pseudepigrapha: Volume I, Apocalyptic Literature and Testaments*. Edited by James H. Charlesworth. Peabody, MA: Hendrickson Publishers, 1983.
Milgrom, Jacob. "The Function of Ḥaṭṭāʾt Sacrifice." *Tarbiz* 40 (1970): 1–8.
Milgrom, Jacob. "Sin-Offering, or Purification-Offering?" *Vetus Testamentum* 21 (1971): 237–9.
Milgrom, Jacob. *Cult and Conscience: The Asham and the Priestly Doctrine of Repentance*. Leiden: Brill, 1976.
Milgrom, Jacob. "Israel's Sanctuary: The Priestly 'Picture of Dorian Gray.'" *Revue Biblique* 83 (1976): 390–9.
Milgrom, Jacob. "Sacrifices and Offerings, OT." Pages 766–7 in *The Interpreter's Dictionary of the Bible, Supplementary Volume*. Edited by K. Crim et al. Nashville: Abingdon, 1976.
Milgrom, Jacob. *Studies in Priestly Theology and Terminology*. Leiden: Brill, 1982.
Milgrom, Jacob. "The Day of Atonement." Pages 1375–87 in *The Encyclopedia of Judaism*, Vol. 5. Edited by Geoffrey Wigoder. New York and London: Macmillan, 1989.
Montgomery, James A. *The Samaritans, The Earliest Jewish Sect: Their History, Theology and Literature*. Philadelphia, PA: Winston, 1907.
Moxnes, Halvor. "Placing Jesus of Nazareth: Toward a Theory of Place in the Study of the Historical Jesus." Pages 158–75 in *Text and Artifact in the Religions of Mediterranean Antiquity: Essays in Honour of Peter Richardson*. Edited by S. G. Wilson and M. Desjardins. Waterloo, ON: Wilfred Laurier, 2000.
Moxnes, Halvor. "The Construction of Galilee as a Place for the Historical Jesus—Part 1." *BTB* 31 (2001): 26–37.
Moxnes, Halvor. "The Construction of Galilee as a Place for the Historical Jesus—Part 2." *BTB* 31 (2001): 66–77.
Moxnes, Halvor. "Kingdom Takes Places: Transformations of Place and Power in the Kingdom of God in the Gospel of Luke." Pages 176–209 in *Social Scientific Models for Interpreting the Bible: Essays by the Context Group in Honor of Bruce J. Malina*. Edited by J. J. Pilch. Leiden: Brill, 2001.
Moxnes, Halvor. *Putting Jesus in His Place: A Radical Vision of Household and Kingdom*. Louisville, KY: Westminster John Knox, 2003.
Moxnes, Halvor. "Body, Gender and Social Space: Dilemmas in Constructing Early Christian Identities." Pages 163–81 in *Identity Formation in the New Testament*. Edited by B. Holmberg and M. Winninge. Tübingen: Mohr Siebeck, 2008.
Moxnes, Halvor. "Identity in Jesus' Galilee: From Ethnicity to Locative Intersectionality." *BibInt* 18 (2010): 390–416.
Moxnes, Halvor. "Landscape and Spatiality: Placing Jesus." Pages 90–106 in *Understanding the Social World of the New Testament*. Edited by D. Neufeld and R. DeMaris. New York: Routledge, 2010.

Moxnes, Halvor. "A Man's Place in Matthew 19:3-15: Creation and Kingdom as Transformative Space of Identity." Pages 103–23 in *Finding a Woman's Place: Essays in Honor of Carolyn Osiek*. Edited by D. L. Balch and J. T. Lamoreaux. Eugene, OR: Pickwick Publications, 2010.

Myres, John L. "Aphrodite Anadyomene." *Annual of the British School at Athens* 41 (1940–5): 99.

Newsom, Carol. "The Rhetoric of Jewish Apocalyptic Literature." Pages 201–17 in *The Oxford Handbook of Apocalyptic Literature*. Edited by John J. Collins. Oxford and New York: Oxford University Press, 2014.

Neyrey, Jerome. "Teaching You in Public and From House to House (Acts 20:20): Unpacking a Cultural Stereotype." *JSNT* 26.1 (2003): 69–102.

Neyrey, Jerome. "Spaces and Places, Whence and Whither, Homes and Rooms." Pages 58–84 in *The Gospel of John in Cultural and Rhetorical Perspective*. Grand Rapids, MI: Eerdmans, 2009.

Neyrey, Jerome. "What's Wrong with This Picture? John 4, Cultural Stereotypes of Women, and Public and Private Space." Pages 143–71 in *The Gospel of John in Cultural and Rhetorical Perspective*. Grand Rapids, MI: Eerdmans, 2009.

Nickelsburg, George W. E., and James C. VanderKam. *1 Enoch 2: A Commentary on the Book of 1 Enoch, Chapters 37–82*. Edited by Klaus Baltzer. Hermeneia. Minneapolis, MN: Fortress Press, 2011.

Nihan, Christophe. "The Templization of Israel in Leviticus: Some Remarks on Blood Disposal and *Kipper* in Leviticus 4." Pages 96–120 in *Text, Time, and Temple: Literary, Historical and Ritual Studies in Leviticus*. Edited by Francis Landy, Leigh M. Trevaskis, and Bryan D. Bibb. HBM 64. Sheffield: Sheffield Phoenix, 2015.

Økland, Jorunn, J. Cornelis de Vos, and Karen J. Wenell, eds. *Constructions of Space III: Biblical Spatiality and the Sacred*. LHBOTS 540. New York: T&T Clark, 2016.

Okure, Teresa. *The Johannine Approach to Mission: A Contextual Study of John 4.1-42*. WUNT 2/31. Tübingen: Mohr Siebeck, 1988.

Olson, Daniel. *Enoch: A New Translation: The Ethiopic Book of Enoch, or 1 Enoch, Translated with Annotations and Cross-References*. North Richland Hills, TX: Bibal Press, 2004.

Origen of Alexandria. *Homilies on Genesis and Exodus*. Translated by Ronald E. Heine. FC 71. Washington, DC: The Catholic University of America Press, 1982.

Origen of Alexandria. *Commentary on the Gospel According to John: Books 13–32*. Translated by Ronald E. Heine. FC 89. Washington, DC: The Catholic University of America Press, 1993.

Osiek, Carolyn, and David L. Balch. *Families in the New Testament World: Households and House Churches*. Louisville, KY: Westminster John Knox, 1997.

Osiek, Carolyn, Margaret Y. MacDonald, with Janet H. Tulloch. *A Woman's Place: House Churches in Earliest Christianity*. Minneapolis, MN: Fortress, 2006.

Pagels, Elaine. *The Johannine Gospel in Gnostic Exegesis: Herecleon's Commentary on John*. SBLMS. Nashville: Abingdon, 1973.

Pagels, Elaine. *Revelations: Visions, Prophecy, and Politics in the Book of Revelation*. New York: Viking, 2012.

Parker, Simon. *The Pre-Biblical Narrative Tradition*. SBL Resources for Biblical Study 24. Atlanta, GA: Scholars Press, 1989.

Parsenios, George. "Jesus and Divine Adaptability in Chrysostom's Interpretation of John 4." Pages 863–73 in *Jesus Research: New Methodologies and Perceptions, The Second Princeton-Prague Symposium on Jesus Research, Princeton 2007*. Edited by James H. Charlesworth with Brian Rhea and Petr Pokorný. Grand Rapids, MI and London: Eerdmans, 2014.

Parsenios, George L. *Departure and Consolation: The Johannine Farewell Discourses in Light of Greco-Roman Literature*. In Supplements to Novum Testamentum 117. Boston, MA: Brill, 2005.
Phillips, Peter. M. *The Prologue of The Fourth Gospel*. New York: T&T Clark, 2006.
Pixner, Bargil. *With Jesus through Galilee According to the Fifth Gospel*. Collegeville, MN: Liturgical Press, 1996.
Portier-Young, Anathea. *Apocalypse against Empire: Theologies of Resistance in Early Judaism*. Grand Rapids, MI: Eerdmans, 2011.
Portier-Young, Anathea. "Jewish Apocalyptic Literature as Resistance Literature." Pages 145–62 in *The Oxford Handbook of Apocalyptic Literature*. Edited by John J. Collins. Oxford and New York: Oxford University Press, 2014.
Prinsloo, Gert T. M., and Christl M. Maier, eds. *Constructions of Space V: Place, Space and Identity in the Ancient Mediterranean World*. LHBOTS 576. New York: T&T Clark, 2013.
Pruszinski, Jolyon G. R. "The Cognitive Phenomenology of Doors in the Book of Revelation: A Spatial Analysis." *Religions* 10.194 (2019): 1–14. doi:10.3390/rel10030194.
Pruszinski, Jolyon G. R. "Roskovec, Daise, and a Developing Consensus: Discussion of Papers IV." Pages 251–60 in *Jesus Research: The Gospel of John in Historical Inquiry*. Edited by James H. Charlesworth and Jolyon G. R. Pruszinski. Jewish and Christian Texts 26. London: T&T Clark, 2019.
Pruszinski, Jolyon G. R. "Visions of Cyprus: A Phenomenological Background to Jewish and Christian Scripture." In *Cyprus within the Biblical World: Are Borders Barriers?* Edited by James H. Charlesworth and Jolyon G. R. Pruszinski. Jewish and Christian Texts 32. London: T&T Clark, 2021.
Qimron, Elisha, and James H. Charlesworth. "Rule of the Community (1QS; cf. 4QS MSS A-J, 5Q11)." Pages 1–52 in *The Dead Sea Scrolls: Hebrew, Aramaic, and Greek Texts with English Translations, Volume 1; Rule of the Community and Related Documents*. Edited by James H. Charlesworth. Tübingen and Louisville: Mohr Siebeck and Westminster John Knox, 1994.
Radvansky, Gabriel A., Sabine A. Krawietz, and Andrea K. Tamplin. "Walking through Doorways Causes Forgetting: Further Explorations." *The Quarterly Journal of Experimental Psychology* 64 (2011): 1632–45.
Rehm, Rush. *The Play of Space: Spatial Transformation in Greek Tragedy*. Princeton, NJ: Princeton University Press, 2002.
Reilly, William J. *The Law of Retail Gravitation*. New York: Knickerbocker Press, 1931.
Rowland, Christopher. *The Open Heaven: A Study of Apocalyptic in Judaism and Early Christianity*. London: SPCK, 1982.
Schmitz, Otto. *Die Opferanshauung des späteren Judentums und die Opferaussagen des Neuen Testaments*. Tübingen: Mohr, 1910.
Schreiner, Patrick. *The Body of Jesus: A Spatial Analysis of the Kingdom in Matthew*. LNTS 555. London: T&T Clark, 2016.
Schreiner, Patrick. "Space, Place and Biblical Studies: A Survey of Recent Research in Light of Developing Trends." *CBR* 14.3 (2016): 340–71.
Schüssler-Fiorenza, Elisabeth. *The Book of Revelation: Justice and Judgment*. Philadelphia, PA: Fortress, 1985.
Shelley, Mary. *Frankenstein, or The Modern Prometheus: The 1818 Text*. Oxford: Oxford University Press, 1993.
Sleeman, M. *Geography and the Ascension Narrative in Acts*. Cambridge: Cambridge University Press, 2009.

Smith, Jonathan Z. *To Take Place: Toward Theory in Ritual*. Chicago: University of Chicago Press, 1987.
Smith, Mark. *Where the Gods Are: Spatial Dimensions of Anthropomorphism in the Biblical World*. Anchor Yale Bible Reference Library. New Haven, CT: Yale University Press, 2016.
Soja, Edward W. *Postmodern Geographies: The Reassertion of Space in Critical Social Theory*. New York: Verso, 1989.
Strauss, David Friedrich. *The Life of Jesus Critically Examined*. Edited by Peter C. Hodgson. Translated by George Eliot. Philadelphia, PA: Fortress, 1972.
Stewart, E. "The City in Mark." Pages 202–20 in *In Other Words: Essays on Social Science Methods and the New Testament in Honor of Jerome H. Neyrey*. Edited by A. C. Hagedorn, Z. A. Crook, and E. Stewart. Sheffield: Sheffield Phoenix, 2007.
Stewart, E. *Gathered around Jesus: An Alternative Spatial Practice in the Gospel of Mark*. Eugene, OR: Cascade, 2009.
Stewart, E. "New Testament Space/Spatiality." *BTB* 29.3 (2012): 139–49.
Swallow, Khena M., Jeffrey M. Zacks, and Richard A. Abrams. "Event Boundaries in Perception Affect Memory Encoding and Updating." *Journal of Experimental Psychology: General* 138 (2009): 236–57.
Swanson, Tod D. "To Prepare a Place: Johannine Christianity and the Collapse of Ethnic Territory." *JAAR* 62.2 (1994): 241–63.
Tchalenko, Georges. *Villages Antiques de la Syrie du Nord: Le massif du Bélus à l'époque romaine*, 3 Vols. Bibliothèque archéologique et historique 50. Paris: P. Geuthner, 1953–58.
Telford, Nicole L. *Sensing World, Sensing Wisdom: The Cognitive Foundation of Biblical Metaphors*. Ancient Israel and Its Literature 31. Atlanta, GA: SBL Press, 2017.
Thompson, Leonard L. *The Book of Revelation: Apocalypse and Empire*. New York: Oxford University Press, 1990.
Trainor, Michael F. *The Quest for Home: The Household in Mark's Community*. Collegeville, MN: The Liturgical Press, 2001.
Tuan, Yi-Fu. *Space and Place: The Perspective of Experience*. Minneapolis, MN: University of Minnesota Press: 1977.
Turner, Victor. *Dramas, Fields, and Metaphors: Symbolic Action in Human Society*. Ithaca, NY: Cornell University Press, 1974.
Uhlig, Siegbert. *Das Äthiopische Henochbuch*. JSHRZ 5/6. Gütersloh: Gütersloher Verlagshaus, 1984.
Valéry, Paul. *Oeuvres*, Vol. II. Edited by J. Hytier. Paris: Gallimard, 1960.
VanderKam, J. C. "Putting Them in Their Place: Geography as an Evaluative Tool." Pages 46–69 in *Pursuing the Text: Studies in Honor of Ben Zion Wachholder on the Occasion of His 70th Birthday*. Edited by J. C. Reeves and J. Kampen. Sheffield: Sheffield Academic, 1994.
Vannier, Marie-Anne. "Saint Augustin et la creation." *Augustiniana* 40 (1990): 349–71.
Vermes, Geza. *The Passion: The True Story of an Event That Changed Human History*. New York: Penguin, 2006.
Vonder Bruegge, John M. *Mapping Galilee in Josephus, Luke, and John: Critical Geography and the Construction of an Ancient Space*. Ancient Judaism and Early Christianity 93. Leiden and Boston, MA: Brill, 2017.
von Wahlde, Urban C. *The Gospel and Letters of John*, 3 Vols. Grand Rapids, MI: Eerdmans, 2010.
Wenell, K. "Contested Claims: Roman Imperial Theology and Matthew's Gospel." *BTB* 29.2 (1999): 56–67.

Wenell, K. "Contested Temple Space and Visionary Kingdom Space in Mark 11–12." *BibInt* 15.3 (2007): 323–37.
Wenell, K. *Jesus and Land: Sacred and Social Space in Second Temple Judaism*. LNTS 334. London: T&T Clark, 2007.
Wenell, K. "A Markan 'Context' Kingdom?: Examining Biblical and Social Models in Spatial Interpretation." *BTB* 44.3 (2014): 123–32.
Whitaker, Robin J. "The Poetics of Ekphrasis: Vivid Description and Rhetoric in the Apocalypse." Pages 227–40 in *Poetik und Intertextualität in der Apocalypse*. Edited by Stefan Alkier, Thomas Hieke, and Tobias Nicklas. WUNT 1. Tübingen: Mohr Siebeck, 2015.
Williams, Rowan. "Sapientia and the Trinity: Reflections on the *De Trinitate*." *Augustiniana* 40 (1990): 317–32.
Witherington, Ben, III. *John's Wisdom: A Commentary on the Fourth Gospel*. Louisville, KY: Westminster John Knox Press, 1995.
Wynn, Mark. *Faith and Place: An Essay in Embodied Religious Epistemology*. Oxford: Oxford University Press, 2009.
Yarbro Collins, Adela. *Crisis and Catharsis: The Power of the Apocalypse*. Philadelphia, PA: Westminster, 1984.
Zacks, Jeffrey M., Nicole K. Speer, and Jeremy R. Reynolds. "Segmentation in Reading and Film Comprehension." *Journal of Experimental Psychology: General* 138 (2009): 307–27.

Ancient Sources Index

Old Testament

Genesis
1:7	88
3:8	32n.113
9:11	94
16	46n.42, 53
21	46n.42
24	46n.42, 53
25:27	32n113
28:17	108, 109
29	46n.42
40:23	113n.85

Exodus
1:21	32n.113
2	46n.42
22:28	81
24	136n.52
24:9-18	136
25	50n.68
25–40	15n.28

Leviticus
4:1-12	70n.66
4:1–5:13	62n.17
4:5-7	63
4:13	70n.66
4:16-18	63n.19
4:20	68n.50, 70n.66
4:22	70n.66
4:25	63n.19
4:26	68n.50, 70n.66
4:27	70n.66
4:30	62n.17, 63n.19
4:31	68n.50, 70n.66
4:34	63n.19
5:9	63n.19
5:10	63n.19
5:10-13	64n.25
5:13	63n.19
8:15	63
15:31	60n.8
16	62n.17
16:14	62n.17
16:16	62n.17
26:11	72

Numbers
3–4	15n.28
9	15n.29
15:22-31	70n.66
19:13	60n.8

Deuteronomy
6:12	112n.84
8:14	112n.84

1 Samuel
5:1-5	109

2 Samuel
7:5	14, 134n.45

1 Kings
5:14	43n.29
10:23	82n.17
14:17	82n.17
	109, 109n.75
19	39
21:10	81
21:13	81

2 Kings
22:4	43n.29
23:4	109
25:18	109
	109

1 Chronicles
9:19	109

2 Chronicles
9:22-23	43n.29
34:9	82n.17
	109

Ezra
  9:7   82

Nehemiah
  9:34   82

Esther
  5:10   16n.36
  6:12   16n.36
  10:6 (gk.)   94
  11:10-11 (gk.)   93

Job
  3:14   81, 83
  26:5-14   136–7
  28:5-6   137
  28:12-13   137
  28:20-24   137
  28:28   146

Psalms
  2:2   82n.16
  2:10   83
  18   134n.45
  29   134n.45
  29:10   91
  48:2   137n.54
  68   137n.54
  68:10
    (LXX)   14
  76:13   82n.16
  77   92
  77:16   91
  78:23   108, 109
  79:2-3   91
  89   137n.54
  89:28   82n.16
  102:16   82n.17
  107   137n.55
  138:4   82n.16
  148:11   82n.16, 83

Proverbs
  5:15   46n.42
  23:26   46n.42

Ecclesiastes
  10:20   81

Song of Songs
  4:13-15   46n.42

Isaiah
  6   109
  6:4   109n.74
  7–10   43n.29
  8:21   81
  8:78   93
  12:3 (LXX)   54
  17:12   91
  24:21   82, 86, 87
  28   43n.27
  28:2   93
  36   43n.29
  40:23   82
  54:12   108, 109
  56   72, 73
  56:6-8   73
  58:11   91
  60:11   108, 109

Jeremiah
  2:26   82
  10:10-13   137n.54
  10:13   91
  23:13   43n.29
  32:32   82
  35   124
  35:4   109
  35:12-19   124n.8
  46   91
  46:7-8   92
  47:2   93
  51:16   91
  52:24   109

Lamentations
  4:12   82n.16

Ezekiel
  1   137n.54
  10:19   108, 109
  16   43n.29
  16:29   105n.38
  26:19   92
  27:33   82n.16
  27:34   92

32:6	91	9:52-54	44n.29
40:6–43:12	108, 109	10:25-37	44n.29
43	50n.68	14:5	54
43:2	91	16:9	13n.22
44:15	69	18:28	16n.36
		21:12	81, 82
Daniel	57n.110, 78, 85n.28	21:34-46	36n.130
9:8	82	22	113n.87
Hosea		*John*	xv, 7, 9–37, 39–57,
5:10	92		161–3
6:3	92	1:4	20n.51
10:7	92	1:10	18
		1:11	16, 16n.34
Joel		1:12	17
2:28	72n.80	1:12-13	34
2:32	72	1:14	9, 15, 15n.29, 19,
			21n.52, 32, 33
Amos		1:16	21n.52
5:24	92	1:17	18n.43
		1:18	16
Habbakuk		1:29	70n.67
3:9-10	92	1:32	14n.24, 48
3:12	92	1:51	48
Zephaniah		2:6	21n.52
1:9	109, 109n.75	2:13-22	15
		2:14-21	48
New Testament		2:16	14
		2:17	14
Matthew		2:21	47, 48n.55
16:27	36n.130	3	33n.116
17:1-8	13n.22	3:3	17
17:25	82n.18	3:4	51
19:3-15	2n.4	3:6	17
19:28	36n.130	3:9	51
25:31-46	36n.130	3:13	31, 48
26	113n.87	3:19-21	20n.51
		3:22	47
Mark		3:23	42
5:29	53n.89	4	39–57, 161
8:38	36n.130	4:1	41n.14
9:2-8	13n.22	4:1-3	41n.14
11–12	2n.4	4:1-42	41n.14
14	113n.87	4:2	41n.14, 42n.20
		4:4	41, 43n.24
Luke		4:4-9	41n.14
8:25	91	4:5	42n.22
9:26	36n.130	4:6	53, 53n.87, 54
9:28-36	13n.22	4:9	43

4:10	33n.116	8:2	48
4:10-15	41n.14	8:12	33n.116
4:11	53, 53n.87	8:35	15
4:11-12	53, 53n.87	8:37	21n.52
4:12	53, 53n.87	8:48	44n.29
4:14	18, 49, 53, 53n.87, 54	9	27n.93, 28, 29, 35n.124
4:15	54		
4:16-18	41n.14, 53n.86	9:20-23	10n.5
4:17-18	45	9:21-22	28n.99
4:19-24	41n.14	9:22	11, 19n.44, 29, 48, 53n.85
4:20	45		
4:21	39, 49n.60, 51	10:7	33n.116
4:23	49nn.59–60	10:11	33n.116
4:23-24	11n.9, 50	10:23	48
4:24	39	11:10	20n.51
4:25	45, 49n.60	11:25	33n.116
4:25-30	41n.14	11:50	33n.116
4:26	33n.116, 49nn.59–60	12:42	19n.44, 29, 48
4:30	45	13:19	33n.116
4:31-34	41n.14	13:31–17:26	115n.96
4:35	49nn.59–60, 56	13:33	34n.120
4:35-38	41n.14	13:36	34n.120
4:39	41n.14	14–17	29
4:39-42	45	14:2	10, 13, 17, 31
4:40-42	41n.14	14:5	34n.120
4:42	56	14:6	33n.116
4:46	42, 42n.22	14:10	14, 14n.27, 17
4:53	15	14:11	17
5	29	14:17	14n.27, 17, 19
5:14	48	14:18	34n.120
5:27	36n.130	14:23	13, 31, 47
5:35	20n.51	15:1	33n.116
5:38	21n.52	15:4	14n.27
6:20	33n.116	15:5	14n.27
6:22-59	48	15:6	14n.27
6:35	33n.116, 36n.129	15:7	21n.52
6:38	36n.129	15:10	14n.27
6:41-59	35	15:16	14n.25
6:56	14	15:18	34n.120
6:60-71	35	16:2	19n.44, 48
6:63	56n.104	16:10	34n.120
7	29	16:32	16, 34
7:2	15	17:1	48
7:28	48	18:5	33n.116
7:39	18	18:20	48
7:40-44	17, 17n.40	19:27	16
7:42	17	19:38-40	47
8	11	21:25	21n.52

Acts

2:17-21	72n.81
2:46–3:1	51n.73
4:26	82n.18
5:20	51n.73
5:42	51n.73
7:44	50n.68
10:45	73n.85
19:2	68n.49
19:9	12n.14
21:26	51n.73

Romans

1:20	148, 159n.51
3:25	64, 66, 69, 71, 72n.79
4:25	72
5:5	67n.47
5:5-6	68
5:5-11	64
5:8	66
5:8-9	71
5:8-10	71
5:15-17	72n.79
6:23	72n.79
8:3-4	68
8:9	68
8:9-11	67n.47
8:13-14	68, 68n.53
8:16	68n.53
8:23	67n.48
8:30-33	64
8:32	66
10:13	72
12:1	67, 75n.90
15:8-9	72n.79
15:16	67
15:16-21	64

1 Corinthians

2:4	68n.52
2:12-16	68n.53
3:9-17	67n.47
5:7	64, 65, 71
6:11	72n.79
6:13-19	67n.47
6:19	48n.55
9:13-15	64, 65
9:13	67n.47
9:21	59
10	170
10:6	170n.27
10:11	170n.27
10:14-33	64
10:16-18	66n.36, 66
11:23-31	64
11:23	66n.38
11:24	66
11:26	66n.37
12:3	71n.69, 158n.49
12:13	67n.48
13:4	151
13:12	150n.21
14:25	67n.47, 72n.78
15:3	64, 66

2 Corinthians

1:21-22	68n.53
1:22	67n.48
3:16-18	68n.53
4:7	67n.47
5	13n.22
5:1-4	15n.30
5:1-5	67n.47
5:7	150n.21
6:16	67n.47, 72, 73n.84
7:10	68n.51
12:1-10	61n.12

Galatians

2:19	68
3:2-5	72n.78
3:3	67, 67n.48
3:13	64, 65n.28
3:14	68
4:6	68n.53
4:29	67n.48
5:24	68
5:24-25	68n.53
6:8	68n.53

Ephesians

1:7	74n.88
2:16	74n.88
5:1-2	74n.88
5:2	76n.93
5:25	67n.45, 74n.88

Philippians
  2:6-11   75

1 Thessalonians
  1:5-6   67n.48, 72n.78
  4:8   68n.53
  4:11   16n.35

Colossians
  1:20   74n.88
  1:24   74n.88
  2:12-13   74n.88
  3:16   32n.115

Hebrews
  8:2   50n.68
  8:5   50n.68
  11:16   13n.22
  12:22   13n.22

James
  1:24   113n.86

1 Peter
  1:18   70n.67

2 Peter
  3:7-13   13n.22

1 John
  2:15   35
  2:18-19   10n.5, 35
  3:1-2   34
  3:10-11   36
  3:10-16   35
  3:14   36
  3:16   36
  4:6   35, 36
  4:8   151
  4:13   157
  5:1   34

2 John
  7-8   53n.85
  10   35, 36

3 John
  5   35, 36
  9-10   10n.5

Revelation   xv–xvi, 7, 85n.28,
                97–119, 165–6
  1:5   82n.18, 104, 104n.33
  1:7   103
  1:9   98, 115
  1:12-18   36n.130
  1:18   100, 100n.17, 101n.21,
                103n.25, 115, 115n.99
  2:1-3:22   114, 114n.89
  2:10   100, 100n.16, 102,
                115, 115n.98
  3:7   100, 100n.17, 101n.21,
                115, 115n.99
  3:8   101n.21, 108
  3:10   104n.32
  3:12   107n.58
  3:20   101n.21
  3:20-21   108
  4:1   101n.21, 108
  5:8   107n.61
  5:13   102n.23
  6:8   103n.25
  6:9   107n.59
  6:10   103, 104n.32
  6:12-14   114n.92
  6:15   82, 82n.18, 83, 103,
                105n.43
  6:15-16   100, 100n.18, 101,
                101n.20, 115, 116,
                116n.100
  7:15   107n.58
  7:17   54, 114n.94
  8:3   107n.59, 107n.61
  8:4   107n.61
  8:5   107n.59
  8:9   107n.59
  8:10   54
  8:13   103, 107n.59
  9:1   54, 101n.21
  9:1-2   100, 100n.17, 101,
                103n.26, 115, 115n.99,
                116
  9:11   103n.26
  9:13   107n.59
  11:1   107n.58, 107n.59
  11:2   107n.58
  11:7   100, 100n.18, 103n.26,
                115
  11:10   103, 104n.32

11:19	107n.58, 107n.60, 108	19:19	82n.18
12:6	103n.27	20:1	101n.21
12:14	103n.27	20:1-2	103n.26
12:26	103n.24	20:1-3	100, 100n.17, 115, 115n.99
13:3	103		
13:4	103	20:1-8	101
13:7	102	20:3	101n.21
13:8	103, 104n.32	20:4	102
13:12	103, 104n.32	20:7-8	100, 100n.16, 115, 115n.98
13:14	104n.32		
14:2	91	20:10	100, 100n.17, 115, 115n.99
14:6	104n.32		
14:7	54	20:11	114n.92
14:8	103	20:13	103n.25
14:15	107n.58	20:14	103n.25
14:17	107n.58	21:1	13n.22, 114n.92
14:18	107n.59	21:1-2	114n.93
15:5	107n.58, 108	21:1-4	138n.58
15:6	107n.58	21:3-4	102
15:8	107n.58	21:4	101, 114
16	92	21:6	54
16:1	107n.58	21:6-8	138n.58
16:4	54, 82	21:8	115
16:7	107n.59	21:10	102, 116, 138n.56
16:10	100, 100n.17, 115, 115n.99	21:10-11	138n.58
		21:12-13	101n.21, 108n.71
16:17	107n.58, 107n.59	21:15	101n.21, 108n.71
17:1	94	21:16	101
17:1-2	104n.35	21:18-20	138n.58
17:2	82n.18, 102, 104n.32	21:21	101n.21, 108n.71
17:3	103n.27	21:22	50n.64, 107n.58
17:5	94	21:23-25	102, 138, 138n.58
17:6	102	21:24	82n.18, 102n.23, 104
17:8	100, 100n.18, 103n.26, 115	21:25	101n.21, 108n.71
		22:1-2	102
17:9	102	22:14	101n.21
17:18	82n.18, 102, 104	22:14-15	108n.71
18:2-3	104n.35	22:15	109
18:3	82n.18, 102, 104	22:17	108n.69
18:9	82n.18		
18:9-11	104n.35	Deuterocanon and Old Testament Pseudepigrapha	
18:11	105		
18:23	105		
19:2	103	*1 Enoch*	20n.49, 50n.67
19:5	103	6:2-6	139
19:6	91	6:3	90n.60
19:11	108	7:6	90n.60
19:17-19	83	9:2	90n.60
19:18-21	103	13:7-8	95

14:8	90n.60	55:1	86n.29, 105, 105n.41
18:15	90n.60	55:2	86n.29, 88, 105, 105n.41
21:6	90n.60		
25:3-5	139	55:3-4	105
25:5	139n.59	55:4	81, 86, 86n.29, 88, 105, 105n.41
32:1	139n.59		
37–71		56:3	103n.26
(Parables)	xv, 7, 13, 13n.21, 31, 36n.130, 56, 75, 77–96, 97, 97n.2, 103–107, 108n.68, 112n.83, 114–15, 115n.95, 116–18, 118n.108, 119n.111, 121, 141, 142, 161, 164–5, 167–70	56:8	103n.25
		58:5	88
		60:5	86n.29, 105, 105n.41
		60:8-9	103n.27
		60:9	88
		60:11	88
		60:22	86n.29, 105, 105n.41
		61:5	103n.27
37:2	86n.29, 105, 105n.41	61:10	88
37:3	85, 87, 94	62:1	81, 88, 105n.45
37:5	86n.29, 105, 105n.41	62:3	81, 88, 105n.45
38:1	87	62:6	81, 88, 105n.45
38:2	86n.29, 105, 105n.41	62:9	81, 87n.38, 88, 105n.47
38:3	87		
38:4	88, 105n.46	62:11	87n.37
38:5	87	63:1	81, 88, 105n.48
39:7	106n.54	63:10	103n.25
40:6	105n.41	63:12	81, 88, 105n.45
40:6-7	86n.29, 105	65:5	90n.56
40:7	105n.41	65:6	86n.29, 87n.32, 105, 105n.41, 106n.55
42:1	21n.52		
42:3	103n.27	65:10	86n.29, 105, 105n.41
43:4	86n.29, 105n.41	65:12	86n.29, 90, 105, 105n.41
45:4-5	88, 114n.91		
45:5	106n.53	66:1	86n.29, 105, 105n.41
46:3	87n.38	67:4	103n.26
46:4	106n.53	67:5-8	86
48:5	86n.29, 105n.41	67:7	86n.29, 105, 105n.41
48:8	81, 88, 105n.44, 106n.50, 106n.53	67:8	81, 86, 86n.29, 88, 105, 105n.41
48:9	88n.41	67:12	81, 88
51:1	103n.25	69:1	86n.29, 105, 105n.41
53:1	86n.29, 88, 103n.26, 105n.41	69:4	88
		69:7	86n.29, 105n.41
53:1-2	105	69:16	89
53:5	81, 88	69:21	80, 90
54:5-6	103n.26	69:21-25	89
54:6	86n.29, 105, 105n.41	69:22	79, 79n.12, 89, 89nn.51–53, 90
54:7-10	86		
54:8	90	69:22-24	89, 90
54:9	86n.29, 105, 105n.41	69:25	89, 90

70:1	86n.29, 105n.41	*4 Ezra*	57n.110, 78, 85n.28
71:5-8	106–7	3:19	108, 109
72:3	90n.60	6:17	91
75:1-2	90n.60	6:48	91
77:3	139n.59	15:20	82
77:4	139n.59	15:39-43	94
81:7	90n.60		
85–90	90n.60	*Baruch*	
95:3	88n.41	1:16	82
98:12	88n.41		
100:11	90n.60	*History of the*	
101:7	90n.60	*Rechabites*	xv, 7, 7n.21, 96,
108:5-6	90n.60		121–44, 166–8
		1–7	140n.62
1 Esdras		1:1	141
8:74	82n.18	1:2	122, 125
		1:3	125, 141
1 Maccabees		2:1	125, 141
1:12	82n.18	2:6	122, 125, 130
3	43n.29	2:6-7	125
		2:8	122, 125, 132
3 Maccabees		3:1-4	125
6:18	108, 109	4:2 (gk.)	125
6:27	16n.36	4:8-9 (gk.)	125
6:37	16n.36	7:2	141
7:8	16n.36	7:3	141
		8–12	140n.62
2 Baruch	78, 85n.28	8:3	141
8:7-8	93	8:5	141
28:2	93	9:2	141
36	92	9:8	141
36:4	92	9:9	141
39:5	92	10:7	122, 125, 130, 141
53	92	10:8	122, 125 (gk.), 132
54–74	92	11:2	141
56:15-16	92	11:5	122, 125 (syr.), 126,
61	93n.64		130 (syr.)
62	93n.64	11:7	141
64	93n.64	13	140n.62
66	93n.64	13:2	141
67	93n.64	14–16:7	140n.62
68	93n.64	16:8	141
70	93n.64	16:8-18	140n.62
72	93n.64	17:3a (syr.)	125
		17:4b (syr.)	125
3 Baruch	50n.64, 50n.67, 78	17:5b (syr.)	125
		18:4	141
4 Baruch		19:4-8 (gk.)	141
8	43n.29	21:2 (gk.)	141

21:8 (gk.) 141
22:1 (gk.) 141
22:4 (gk.) 141
23:1 (gk.) 141

Odes of Solomon
12:12 32n.115

Prayer of Azariah
1:38 91

Sirach
16:37 16n.37
24 16n.37, 17
24:7 19n.46
24:8 32n.115
24:30 92
26:9-12 45n.30, 46n.42
43:20 91
50:25-26 43n.27

Testament of Abraham
11:1-4 109

Testament of Levi
7:2 43n.27

Tobit
13:16-17 108, 109

Wisdom of Solomon
1:1 82
3:9 151
5:22 91
9:8 50n.68
9:15 15n.30
13:2 92
19:20 91

Dead Sea Scrolls

1QS
3:18-19 21n.51
8:4-7 69

CD
4.2 69n.62
4.3-4 69

Rabbinic Texts

b. Sabb.
6a 109n.76
8b 109n.76
9a 109n.76
91b 109n.76

b. Soṭ.
17a:24 136n.53

b. Yoma
69a 45n.34

Masechtot Qetanot
Kutim 45n.36, 51n.77

Greek and Latin Works

Aeschylus
Ag.
888 53n.89

Agathias
Historiae 117n.105

Ambrose
Spir.
3.11.82 39n.1

Anselm of Canterbury
Monologion
20 39n.2
Proslogion
2–4 159n.51

Antoninus Liberalis
Metam.
33 126n.21

Apollodorus
Library
3.10.1 126n.21

Athenaeus
Deipn.
15.695 126n.21

Ancient Sources Index

Augustine		Cicero	
Trin.	7, 7n.21, 56, 145–60, 167	*Off.*	
1	149	1.150	105n.39
1.1	149	Clement	
2	149	*1 Clement*	
2.1	149	20:8	123n.7
3–4	149		
4	149	Euripides	
5–7	149	*Hel.*	
8	150, 153, 156	1676	126n.21
8–15	149n.19		
8.3	148	Herodotus	
8.4	150	*Hist.*	
8.6	150	3.26.1	126n.21
8.7–8.8	150–1		
8.11	151	Hesiod	
8.12	151–2	*Op.*	
8.13	152	155–173	126n.21
9–15	148, 151, 153, 155, 156	168–173	122n.2
		286	105n.39
10	158n.49		
11.2.10	153	Hilary of Poitiers	
12.12	145	*Trin.*	
12.22	146	2.31	39n.1
12.23	146, 153		
12.3.20	153	Hippolytus	
13	147, 149n.19, 154, 154n.31, 155n.38, 160n.53, 160n.54	*Haer.*	
		9.22	123n.7
13–14	146, 160	Homer	
13.24	154, 155, 160	*Il.*	
14	155	20.9	53n.89
14.11	159n.51	23.205	126n.19
14.16	155		
14.21	155	Jerome	
14.24	156	*Epist.*	
15	153, 156, 158, 158n.49	108.16	43n.26
15.1	148	*Vigil.*	
15.2	148, 149, 156	6	123n.7
15.4	157		
15.5	157	Josephus	
15.10	148, 156	*Ant.*	
15.31-32	157	13.3.4	45n.34
15.45	148	17	79
15.46	158	17.304-314	79n.11, 83, 106n.52, 164n.11
Tract. Ev. Jo.			
15.16	54n.94	17.305	83n.22

17.307	83n.21	*Legat.*	
18.1	169n.24	36.278	48n.55
18.2.2	45n.35	36.290	48n.55
20.6.1	45n.35	*Mos.*	
Jewish War		2.36.194	48n.55
2.8.154-58	121	*Opif.*	
Vita		18.55	48n.55
52	43, 43n.24	47.137	48n.55
		Plant.	
Justin Martyr		12.5	48n.55
2 Apol.		30.126	48n.55
8	18n.42	*Post.*	
		2.5	48n.55
Libanius		*Praem.*	
Or.		3.17	48n.55
18.172	140n.65	*Sacr.*	
		5.32	48n.55
Origen		20.72	48n.55
Comm. Jo.		*Somn.*	
13.175-178	46n.42	1.8.45-46	48n.55
Hom. Gen.		1.20.122	48n.55
10.5	46n.42	1.23.149	48n.55
Hom. Exod.	46n.42	1.32.185	48n.55
Princ.		1.37.215	48n.55
1.1.4-5	39n.1	2.34.230-232	113
		2.41.272	48n.55
Philo		*Spec.*	
Abr.		1.12.66	48n.55
16.72-74	48n.55	1.29.146	48n.55
18.85-86	48n.55	2.27.148	48n.55
Aet.		3.23.130	48n.55
26	123n.7	*Virt.*	
Agr.		11.73	48n.55
14.65	48n.55		
Cher.		Philostratus	
29.100	48n.55	*Vita. Apoll.*	
Conf.		4.32	105n.39
17.82	48n.55	5.3	125n.12, 126n.21
Ebr.			
34.136-138	113	Pindar	
Flacc.		*Ol.* 123	
14.123	48n.55	2.55-75	126nn.21–22
Fug.		2.61-78	123n.3
14.76	48n.55		
Gig.		Plato	
15.67	48n.55	*Criti.* 142n.73	
Her.		113d-e	126n.20
22.110	48n.55	116c	126n.20
58:287	48n.55	*Gorg.* 123	
Leg.		523a	123n.4, 126n.21
3:1	21n.52, 32n.113	526c	126n.21

Menex.
   235c   126n.21
   237e   53n.89
Resp.
   370b   12n.14
Symp.
   179e   126n.21
Timaeus   18
   29c-d   18n.42
   49a   18n.42
   50d   18n.42
   52b   18n.42

Pliny
  Natural History
   12.4-13   98
   12.23   98

Plutarch
  Sert.
   8   125n.12

Ptolemy
  Geogr.
   7.5.14   125n.12

Seneca
  Med.
   361   105n.39

Strabo
  Geogr.
   3.2.13   125n.12, 126n.21

Tacitus
  Annals
   3.68   98
   4.30   98
   15.71   98

Tertullian
  Val.
   7   123n.7

Theodore of Mopsuestia
  Comm. Jo.
   2 4.23-24   39n.1

Thomas Aquinas
  Summa Theologiae
   1a.8.3   39n.2

Modern Author Index

Aalen, Sverre 16n.32
Abrams, Richard A. 110n.80
Ahuvia, Mika 3n.5
Ajer, Peter Claver 2n.4
Allen, Jon G. 117n.106, 118n.108
Allison, Dale C. 31n.108, 72n.82
Anderson, Gary 60n.8, 62n.17, 63, 64, 64n.24, 67n.50, 70n.66, 71
Anderson, Robert T. 45n.37
Ashton, John 27n.93, 43n.27, 47n.45
Attridge, Harold 60n.4, 61n.12
Aune, David E. 98n.6, 104n.29, 105n.39, 105n.43, 108n.68
Aviam, Mordechai 19n.48, 42n.19
Ayers, Lewis 149n.19, 154n.31, 155n.38, 160nn.53–54, 167

Bachelard, Gaston xv–xvi, 6–7, 6n.19, 9–10, 10n.4, 12–13, 13nn.16–20, 16n.32, 17n.41, 19, 19n.45, 21, 21nn.51–52, 22, 22nn.53–63, 23, 23nn.64–69, 24, 24n.70, 24nn.72–74, 25, 25nn.75–80, 26, 26nn.81–89, 27, 27nn.90–91, 28, 30, 32n.112, 35, 35n.122, 36, 36nn.134–135, 37, 37nn.136–137, 37n.139, 78n.8, 79, 79n.9, 96, 96nn.70–72, 98, 99, 99nn.7–14, 100, 101, 102, 103, 110, 110nn.77–78, 115, 142n.71, 144, 147n.10, 162nn.1–3, 162nn.6–8, 163n.9, 164n.10, 166n.14, 168, 170n.26
Balch, David L. 2n.4
Barth, Karl 159n.51
Bassler, Jouette 39n.3
Baur, Ferdinand C. 37n.138
Bell, Richard H. 60n.5, 62n.15, 64n.25, 70n.64
Bernier, Jonathan 11n.10, 30n.105
Berquist, Jon L. 1n.4, 2n.4
de Boer, M. C. 61n.12
Boismard, M.-É. 41n.16
Black, Matthew 89nn.52–53
Bowens, Lisa M. 61n.12

Brock, Rita Nakashima 75n.92
Brown, Peter 141n.69
Brown, Raymond 19n.47, 40n.5, 43n.26, 48n.56, 52n.83
Bull, Robert J. 51n.78
Bultmann, Rudolph 16n.34, 39n.4, 41n.13, 45, 45n.32, 52n.82
Butcher, Kevin 140n.66
Burge, Gary 40n.5

Camp, Claudia V. 1n.4
Charlesworth, James H. xiii, xv, 11n.10, 14n.26, 30n.105, 32n.115, 40n.8, 42n.19, 45n.36, 46n.42, 48n.55, 60n.4, 69n.61, 69n.63, 79n.10, 81, 81nn.14–15, 83, 83n.20, 84, 84nn.23–24, 85n.25, 85n.27, 88, 88n.48, 97n.2, 104n.29, 106, 106n.49, 106nn.52–53, 121n.1, 125nn.13–14, 140nn.63–64, 164n.13
Clark, Martin 2n.4
Cohen Stuart, G. H. 18n.42
Collins, John J. 61n.12, 61n.14, 77n.1, 77n.3, 78n.6, 117n.103
Coloe, Mary L. 10n.6, 46n.43, 48n.56, 50n.71
Corliss, William R. 127n.29, 129n.32
Culpepper, R. Alan 17n.39, 19n.47, 27n.93, 39n.4, 46n.42

Dahl, Nils 49n.61
Daise, Michael 10n.6, 15n.31
Davies, W. D. xv, 40n.5
Davila, James R. 140nn.61–62
DeLay, Tad 170n.26
Dillman, August 89n.54, 90n.56
Diolé, Philippe 24n.70
Dodd, C. H. 40n.5, 48n.56
Dunn, James D. G. 65, 65n.33, 70n.67

Eberhart, Christian A. 63n.21, 70n.67
Elliot, John H. 10n.6
Engberg-Pedersen, Troels 49n.62, 74n.89

Fauconnier, Gilles 24n.71
Flanagan, James W. 2n.4
Flemming, Johannes 90n.58, 107n.62
Flusser, David 37n.138, 78n.6
Ford, J. Massyngberde 98n.5
Fortna, Robert 39n.3
Foucault, Michel 61, 61n.9, 77n.4, 97n.1, 115n.97, 168n.21
Fox, Robin Lane. 134n.47, 139–40, 140n.67, 143, 143n.77
Frey, Jörg 9n.2, 11n.10, 27n.93, 30n.105, 31n.108, 34n.120, 43n.26, 45n.39, 50n.64, 55n.99

Gager, John 59n.1, 73n.83
Gathercole, Simon 60n.5
George, Mark K. 1n.4, 2n.4
Gibson, Shimon 40n.8
Gormley, Joan F. 64n.26
Grey, Eleanor 143, 143n.76
Gunn, David M. 2n.4

Hanson, K. C. 85n.26
Hays, Richard 40n.5, 48n.56
Hill, Edmund 145n.2, 152, 152nn.26–29, 153, 157, 157nn.44–45, 158, 158n.47, 158n.49
Himmelfarb, Martha 78n.6, 107n.57, 107n.64
Hogue, Timothy 24n.71
Holloway, Paul A. 115n.96
Horsley, Richard A. 78n.6
Hurtado, Larry 50n.72, 73–4, 74n.87

Isaac, Ephraim 79n.12, 81, 86nn.30–31, 87n.32, 87nn.34–36, 89, 89n.50, 90, 90n.57, 90n.59, 95n.66, 105, 105n.41, 106n.51, 106nn.54–55, 107n.56, 114n.91

Janowski, Bernd 66n.39
Johnson, Elizabeth A. 147n.9, 159n.50
Johnson, Nathan C. 54n.93
de Jong, Irene F. 7n.21

Käsemann, Ernst 60n.6
Keck, Leander 17, 17n.39, 39n.4, 40n.12
Keener, Craig 10n.6
Klauck, Hans-Josef 60n.3, 66n.39
Klausner, Joseph 37n.138
Klijn, A. F. J. 92n.63, 93n.64

Knibb, Michael 89n.53, 106n.50
Knights, Christopher 140n.61
Kocar, Alex 3n.5
Koestler, Arthur 24n.71
Kovacs, Judith 117n.107
Krawietz, Sabine A. 97n.4, 165n.13
Kundsin, Karl 40, 40n.10
Kurby, Christopher A. 110n.80
Kysar, Robert 52n.83

Lacan, Jacques 170
Lambdin, Thomas 88n.43, 88n.45
Landau, Brent 126n.19, 126n.24
Larsen, Matthew D. C. 100n.19
Laurence, Richard 89n.53
Lefebvre, Henri xv, 4, 4n.12, 5, 5n.15, 12, 12n.13, 47n.48, 55n.100, 56
Lehn, Waldemar H. 129n.34
Lightfoot, John 43n.26
Lightfoot, R. H. xv, 39n.3, 43n.23

Madec, Goulven 146, 146nn.6–7, 147, 147n.11, 154, 154n.33, 154n.35, 155, 155n.37, 159, 159nn.51–52, 167
Magdalino, Paul 117n.105
Maier, Christl M. 2n.4
Malbon, Elisabeth S. 2n.4
Maly, Kenneth 41n.17
Marcus, Joel 11n.10, 47n.46
Martin, Dale 49n.62, 74n.89
Martyn, J. Louis 9, 9n.1, 10–11, 11nn.7–8, 11n.10, 12, 12nn.11–12, 19, 27, 27nn.92–93, 28, 28n.97, 29, 29nn.101–104, 30, 30nn.105–107, 31, 31n.108, 31nn.110–11, 32, 32n.114, 33, 35, 35nn.125–127, 36, 36n.129, 36nn.131–133, 37, 40, 40n.6, 41n.15, 47, 47n.46, 47n.48, 52n.81, 61n.12, 162, 162nn.4–5, 163
Matthews, Victor H. 2n.4
McLean, Bradley H. 60n.7, 62, 62nn.15–16, 63, 63n.22, 64, 64nn.26–27, 65, 65n.29, 70, 70nn.64–65, 70n.68, 71, 71n.70, 71n.74
McNeil, Brian 140n.61
McNutt, Paula M. 2n.4
McWhirter, Jocelyn 46n.42
Meeks, Wayne A. 3, 3n.6, 4, 4nn.7–8, 4nn.10–11, 5–6, 6nn.16–17, 12, 12n.12, 28n.100, 39n.3, 47, 47nn.47–48

Merleau-Ponty, M. xv, 49n.62, 95n.67, 111, 111n.82, 112n.83, 118, 118n.109
Metzger, Bruce 91n.62, 94n.65
Milgrom, Jacob 60n.8, 62, 62nn.16–18, 63, 63nn.19–21, 64, 64n.24, 66, 66n.44, 67n.50, 68, 70, 70n.66, 71–2, 74–5, 75n.91, 163
Montgomery, James A. 51n.77
Moxnes, Halvor xv, 2n.4
Myres, John L. 139n.60

Newsom, Carol 117nn.103–104
Neyrey, Jerome 2n.4, 16n.32, 39n.3, 48n.56, 50n.64, 50n.70, 52n.80, 53n.86, 57n.112
Nickelsburg, George W. E. 87, 87n.33, 88, 88n.42, 88n.44, 88nn.46–47, 88n.49, 89n.53, 90n.55, 105nn.41–42, 105nn.44–48, 106nn.54–55, 139n.59
Nihan, Christophe 63n.21

Økland, Jorunn 1n.4, 2n.4
Okure, Teresa 41n.14, 46n.41
Olson, Daniel 89n.51, 90
Osiek, Carolyn 2n.4

Pagels, Elaine 39n.2, 98n.6, 114n.90, 170n.25
Parsenios, George L. 33n.119, 34n.121, 46n.42, 115n.96
Phillips, Peter M. 112n.83
Pixner, B. 1n.2
Portier-Young, Anathea 78n.6
Prinsloo, Gert T. M. 2n.4
Pruszinski, Jolyon G. R. 40n.8, 60n.4, 97n.3, 121n.1
Pruszinski, Kyra N. 44, 80, 111, 127, 128, 130, 131
Pushkin, Alexander 37

Radvansky, Gabriel A. 97n.4, 110n.79, 111, 111n.81, 112n.83, 118, 118n.110, 165n.13
Rehm, Rush 7n.21, 47, 47n.49, 48n.53
Reilly, William J. 6n.18, 47n.50
Reynolds, Jeremy R. 110n.80
Rowland, Christopher 61, 61nn.13–14, 77, 77nn.2–3, 97n.1, 108n.70, 117n.107

Said, Edward 45, 45n.40
Schmitz, Otto 65n.30

Schreiner, Patrick 2n.4, 3n.5
Schussler-Fiorenza, E. 114n.90
Sleeman, Matthew 2n.4
Smith, Jonathan Z. xv, xvi
Smith, Mark 4n.9, 48n.55, 134n.45, 134n.48, 135n.49, 138n.57
Soja, Edward W. xv, 1, 1n.1, 1n.3, 4, 5n.14, 12, 61, 61n.10, 77n.4
Speer, Nicole K. 110n.80
Stewart, Eric 2n.4
Strauss, David F. 40, 40n.9, 125n.11
Swanson, Tod 54n.96

Tamplin, Andrea K. 97n.4, 165n.13
Tchalenko, Georges 169, 169n.22
Telford, Nicole L. 7n.21
Thompson, Leonard L. 98n.6
Tuan, Yi Fu 5n.13, 53n.84, 61, 61n.11, 77–8, 78n.5
Turner, Mark 24n.71
Turner, Victor 4, 4n.8

Uhlig, Siegbert 90n.57

Valéry, Paul 7, 7n.20
VanderKam, James C. 87, 87n.33, 88, 88n.42, 88n.44, 88nn.46–47, 88n.49, 89n.53, 90n.55, 105nn.41–42, 105nn.44–48, 106nn.54–55, 139n.59
Vannier, Marie-Anne 146n.5
de Veer, Gerrit 127n.27
Vermes, Geza 37n.138
von Wahlde, Urban C. 40n.8, 41, 41n.14, 42n.21, 43n.26, 45, 46n.41, 52n.83
Vonder Bruegge, John M. 3n.5, 40n.8
de Vos, J. Cornelis 1n.4

Wenell, Karen 1n.4, 2n.4
Whitaker, Robin J. 108n.69
Williams, Rowan 146, 146n.8, 157, 157n.43, 167
Witherington III, Ben 46n.44, 53n.86
Wynn, Mark 53n.88

Yarbro Collins, Adela 98n.6

Zacks, Jeffrey M. 110n.80

Topical Index

apocalypses 77–96, 97–119, 121–44
   and eschatology 61, 77, 97
   definitions 77nn.1–2
   phenomenology of 116–17
   spatial dimensions of 77, 103–104
Atlantis xv, 123n.5, 123n.7, 126, 126n.20, 126n.23
atonement. *See also* "*ḥaṭṭa't*"
   and "sacrifice"
   and Christ's death 64–7, 68, 70, 70n.66, 73
   and the Temple 64
   for the Earth 69
   in Levitical tradition 60, 60n.8, 62, 71, 74, 75n.90
   in Paul 60–1, 71–3, 74–5
   removal of Sin 63
Augustine 145–60, 167–8
   Holy Spirit 155, 157–9
   image of God 155–6
   on Incarnation 147–8, 151, 152

baal cycle/traditions 43n.29, 134–7, 134n.46, 143, 144
Bernie Sanders 95n.68
Birkat Ha-minim 11, 11n.10, 47n.46
Black Lives Matter 170

Canigou Effect 121–2, 126n.20, 127–29, 133–9, 142–3, 142n.73
carceral geography/ecology xv, 7, 15, 59n.2, 97–103, 113, 115–16, 116n.101, 118–19, 163–5
colonial/postcolonial/decolonizing concerns 114, 119, 165, 169, 170. *See also* "Marxist Dynamics"

door, doorway 7, 51, 97–8, 101, 103, 107–14, 116, 118–19
dwelling 14, 17
   and "becoming" 18
   and derivation 17, 39
   and light 20–1, 20n.51

and "rest" xv, xvi, 10, 12, 16n.32, 19, 22–3, 25–9, 35, 79, 99, 100n.15, 106n.53, 147, 162
and *scholē* (σχολή) 12, 12n.14, 147, 167n.16
and spatial conflation 10, 19n.48, 23–4, 31–3, 37, 48, 48n.55, 50, 100n.15, 162
and temporal conflation 10–11, 24–5, 29–31, 37, 47, 100n.15, 162
and the "corner" 22, 26, 27, 35, 36, 99, 100, 102n.23, 142
and the synagogue 19 (*see also* "synagogue")
and trauma xvii, 25–7, 33–6, 54, 56, 57, 78, 97–100, 114, 115, 117n.106, 118, 162, 169
and "world negation" 20, 27, 33, 35, 99, 103, 142, 163n.9, 165–6, 168
as image xvii, 10–17, 19–26, 28–37, 96n.71, 99–100, 161, 166
auto-valorization 7, 25n.78, 34, 78, 78n.8, 79, 96, 164, 170
complexity of image 21–2, 31, 32, 100n.15, 116
heavenly 13–14, 31, 78, 96, 101, 104, 106–7, 164
imagination of xvi, 12–13, 22, 24–28, 30, 35–37, 75, 78, 96n.71, 99, 117n.106, 121, 161–162, 164, 166, 170
in the current American experience xvi, 118–119, 165–166, 169–170
in the Farewell Discourse (Gospel of John) 13–14, 16, 17, 31–32, 34, 49
marginal 7, 26, 56–7, 75, 77–96, 97, 98, 99–100, 103, 118, 121, 141–2, 144, 164–70
phenomenology of 10, 12–13, 21–7, 28, 32, 57, 79, 95n.67, 118, 161–7
translation in Gospel of John 15–17

ecology xv, 10, 37, 59, 62, 73, 74, 146, 147, 163, 167. *See also* "carceral ecology," "dwelling," "textual ecology"
  and literary productions of space 6–7
einmalig event 9, 11, 29–33, 36n.129, 57, 162–3
  and memory 31n.108
  definition 9, 29
  Samaritan Interlude 40, 40n.6, 41–6, 48n.56, 50n.64, 51

Festival of Booths 15

Galilean Revolt (6 CE) 164, 169, 169n.24
Galilee 1n.2, 2n.4, 3n.5, 17n.40, 39n.3, 40n.8, 41, 42, 42n.19, 43, 43n.42, 79, 80, 81, 85, 95, 164, 169, 169n.24
gates 97, 101–3, 107–9, 112, 114, 118–19, 165
Gerizim 42, 42n.22, 45, 51, 51n.78, 56, 56n.102
gravity model 6n.18, 47n.50
  definition 6

ḥaṭṭa't 60, 60n.4, 62–4, 62nn.16–17, 72, 75. *See also* "sacrifice"
Holy Spirit
  at Qumran (spirit of holiness) 69
  in Augustine 146, 151, 153, 155, 157–9, 167
  in Revelation 102, 138n.58
  in the Gospel of John 9, 18, 27, 28n.94, 33n.119, 35, 47–50, 51n.72, 56, 163
  in the undisputed Pauline Letters xv, 59–61, 67–8, 72–4, 163
home. *See* "dwelling"
homelessness 10n.6, 169
  American xvi
  in the Gospel of John 16, 28
household 2n.4, 10n.6, 15–16, 16n.32, 17, 34, 46n.42
Huleh Valley 79–80, 84–5, 95, 106, 164, 170

imprisonment. *See* "carceral geography"
incarceration. *See* "carceral geography"
indwelling xv–xvi, 10, 12–14, 18–21, 31–4, 36, 47, 49n.63, 55–6, 59, 67–8, 72,

74, 148, 153, 155, 157–60, 162, 167. *See also* "Holy Spirit"
interdisciplinary methods. *See* "phenomenology"
cognitive psychology 7n.21, 24, 24n.71, 97, 109–13, 118, 165, 168
critical geography (*see* "spatial practice", "gravity model", "textual ecology")
NT scholars' hesitance toward 3
Wayne Meeks on 5–6
Isle(s) of the Blessed Ones xv, 7, 121–44, 166
  as physical place 122, 125
  in Greco-Roman sources 121–4, 126, 126n.23
  in *History of the Rechabites* 121–2, 124–7, 130, 143–4

Jamnia 11n.10, 30n.105, 47n.46
Jesus 13–14, 16, 21n.51, 30, 159n.51, 162
  as sacrifice xv, 60n.4, 64–7, 70, 71, 73–5, 163
  as scapegoat 65, 70–1, 74–5
  and the paraclete 18, 20, 31, 34, 36, 47, 50, 158, 163
  and Temple 15, 39–41, 49–52, 162–3
  conflict with "the Jews" 11, 29, 52
  historical xv, 1, 2n.4, 9–11, 29, 31n.108, 33, 37n.138, 40–6, 57, 163, 164
Jerusalem 14, 20n.51, 39, 43, 43n.24, 45n.35, 48n.55, 50n.67, 51, 51n.78, 56, 56n.102, 56n.105, 69, 93n.64, 101, 102, 104, 107–109, 112, 114–116, 124n.8, 125n.10, 138n.58, 140n.62, 163, 165
Johannine community xv, 9–12, 18, 20, 27, 32–3, 36, 39n.3, 57, 162
  and Samaritan woman 40–1, 43, 46–52, 53n.85, 54–7, 163
  and the synagogue 19, 28n.97, 29–31, 34, 52, 54–5, 162–3
  missional aspects 35
  Qumran's influence on 21n.51, 35n.128
Judea 39n.3, 41–43, 43n.25, 43n.28, 45n.32, 47, 48, 48n.55, 52n.79, 57, 163
judgment 36–7, 69, 77–9, 83, 85–8, 90–6, 102–3, 105, 108–9, 119, 139, 164–5, 168

landowners
 of the *Parables of Enoch* 79, 81, 83–8, 90, 95–6, 97, 103, 105–6, 118, 164

Marxist Dynamics 119n.111, 164. *See also* "colonial/postcolonial/decolonizing concerns"
merkabah mysticism
 connection to Rechabites 124n.9
Migdal 19n.48, 85, 164

neo-confederate plague xvi
Novaya Zemlya effect xv, 127, 127n.29, 129n.32, 129n.34, 130, 142n.73, 166

Patmos 98, 100, 115, 165
Paul xv, 7, 13n.22, 49n.62, 59–75, 141–2, 161, 163, 167–8, 170. *See also* "atonement," "holy spirit," "sacrifice," "scapegoat traditions," "spatial theory," "temple"
phenomenology 7, 10, 12–13, 21–8, 32, 37, 49n.62, 57, 79, 95n.67, 96n.70, 97n.3, 99n.7, 109–10, 111n.82, 112n.83, 116–19, 121n.1, 136n.50, 136n.52, 141, 143, 161–168
Philo 21n.52, 32n.113, 48n.55, 113, 123n.7
Plato 12n.14, 53n.89, 123, 123n.4, 123n.7, 126nn.20–21, 142, 145–146, 152, 159
 cosmological structure 18n.42
 writings' impact on John 18, 18n.42
prison. *See* imprisonment

sacrifice xv, 60, 62–7, 68, 70–5. *See also* "Jesus as sacrifice," "atonement," "*ḥaṭṭa't*"
 and gentiles 60, 67–9, 72–5
 Qumran 69
Samaritans (and Samaria) 39–57
 Jewish views of 41–8, 51–2, 55–7
 trope in John 51, 55–6
scapegoat traditions 65, 70–1, 74–5
scripture as warning, not example 170
Sea of Galilee (Kinnereth) 80, 85, 95, 164
space. *See also* "thirdspace," "gravity model," "spatial practice," "textual ecology"
 and social life, as co-informing 5, 48
 as a key to interpreting ancient texts 1–3, 167–70
 theory and Gaston Bachelard (*see* Modern Author Index)
 theory and Henri Lefebvre (*see* Modern Author Index)
 theory and Jonathan Z. Smith xv–xvi
 theory and Michel Foucault (*see* Modern Author Index)
 theory in biblical and religious studies xv–xvi, 1–7, 161–70
spatial practice xv, 2n.4, 7, 161, 168–9
 and the Johannine community 12, 40–1, 47–9, 47n.48, 51–2, 55–7, 162–3
 definition 4–6
 in Augustine 145, 147, 160, 167
 in Revelation 118
synagogue 48, 50n.64, 164
 and Home 19, 28, 35–6
 excommunication from 10n.5, 11, 19n.44, 27n.93, 28–30, 34, 35n.124, 52, 55, 162

tabernacle 2n.4, 50n.68, 60n.8, 113
 dwelling of God 14–15
 human body as tent 15
Temple 2n.4, 10n.6, 14–15, 19n.48, 28n.98, 45n.35, 48, 56, 57, 64–5, 69, 72–3, 108–9, 112–13, 115, 125n.10, 163
 at Qumran 69
 Atlantean 126n.20
 body as 48–52, 56, 57, 61, 67, 67n.47, 74–5, 163
 heavenly 103, 106–8, 112, 115
 Ezekiel 50n.68, 69, 108–9, 112
 in Gospel of John 10n.6, 14–15, 19n.48, 28n.98, 41, 46n.43, 48–52, 56–7, 162–3
 in *Parables of Enoch* 103, 106–7, 107n.57
 in Philo 48n.55, 113
 in Revelation 103, 106–7, 108–9, 112, 115
 in Undisputed Pauline letters 61, 64, 65, 67, 72–5, 163
 Jesus as (not) supplanting 41, 48–52, 162–3
 siting 143

to Baal 134n.46, 135n.49
to Zeus 140
textual ecology xv, 4, 47, 57, 97, 103, 118, 145, 161–2, 167. *See also* "ecology"
definition 6–7
thirdspace xv
two-level drama 9–37
and Son of Man traditions 36
and the spirit 27–8, 34
in the Gospel of John 9, 11, 27, 29, 30n.105, 32–3, 36

water 24, 45nn.30–31, 52, 102, 103, 122, 123n.3, 125, 126, 129, 130, 132, 136–8, 142
and Judgment 77–9, 86, 90–4, 164
and Samaritan woman 18, 45, 45n.31, 52, 52n.83
and Spirit 49
and Wetlands 79, 85, 88, 95–6, 164
anthropomorphic usage 79, 89–91, 93–5, 164

biblical connotations of drawing 46n.42, 53–4
symbol of new creation 18, 33n.116, 37, 102
well xv, 41, 52–7, 56n.102, 163
meeting at, sexual connotation 46n.42
meeting at, time of 45, 52–3, 53nn.85–86
wisdom traditions
in Prologue of *John* 16–37

Zaphon traditions 122, 133–8, 137n.54, 140, 144
in Exodus 136
in Hist. Rech. 122–44
in job 136–7
in Libanius 140
in the Baal cycle 134–136, 144n.78
in the Psalms 137nn.54–55
in Revelation 138, 138n.58
Zosimus 121, 124–5, 140–2

www.ingramcontent.com/pod-product-compliance
Lightning Source LLC
Chambersburg PA
CBHW062223300426
44115CB00012BA/2196